THE COMMON LAW IN TWO VOICES

To Professor Silbey

Best Wishes,
Kwai
Aug 20, 2009

THE COMMON LAW IN TWO VOICES

Language, Law, and the Postcolonial Dilemma in Hong Kong

Kwai Hang Ng

Stanford University Press
Stanford, California

Stanford University Press
Stanford, California

Printed in the United States of America on acid-free, archival-quality paper

Library of Congress Cataloging-in-Publication Data
Ng, Kwai Hang.
The common law in two voices : language, law, and the postcolonial
dilemma in Hong Kong / Kwai Hang Ng.
p. cm.
Includes bibliographical references and index.
ISBN 978-0-8047-6164-2 (cloth : alk. paper) —
ISBN 978-0-8047-6165-9 (pbk. : alk. paper)
1. Conduct of court proceedings—China—Hong Kong—Language.
2. Law—China—Hong Kong—Language. 3. English language—Social
aspects—China—Hong Kong. 4. Cantonese dialects—Social aspects—
China—Hong Kong. I. Title.
KNQ9335.N46 2009
347.5125'05—dc22
2008055821

Typeset by Bruce Lundquist in 10/15 Sabon

To the memory of my parents,
Ng Woo Tsung and Chan Pik Shan

Contents

Preface

THE TERMS *colonialism* and *postcolonialism* mean many things in the academic literature. But as scholars of colonialism attest, there is no one, single, homogeneous colonialism. To make sense of the practices in different colonial societies, we need grounded theories and historically specific accounts. In this book I attempt to reflect on what colonialism was and what postcoloniality means in the specific context of Hong Kong through the grounded study of legal bilingualism. To begin with, I was motivated by a curiosity to crack a theoretical nut: How and why does language not just reflect social structure (a point well rehearsed and well taken already among sociolinguists) but in fact *constitute* social structure? In the specific case of Hong Kong common law, the question is translated into a question of how English and Cantonese reinforce and undermine the practice of legal formalism. My goal is to show how different language practices embedded in English and Cantonese at times constitute and reproduce what we see as the dominance of institutions but at other times challenge and disrupt their fundamental mode of operation.

At the same time, this book is very much a story about Hong Kong in its current postcolonial moment. Through the presented legal dramas, I try to weave together an ethnographic account of a place known as a former British colony and a current "special administrative region" of China. Why is the implementation of legal bilingualism riddled with unresolved tensions? Why does English continue to dominate the legal arena when it is deafeningly obvious that most people in Hong Kong in fact find it easier to express themselves in Cantonese? Amid the receding landscape of colonialism, the common law today stands as the most unmistakably identifiable cultural landmark and social institution of British legacy in Hong Kong. The common law is one of the most trusted institutions for the people of Hong Kong. The notion of the rule of law is also entrusted to become the banner ideal that defines post-1997 Hong Kong. Trapped between the conflicting needs of integrating itself with China and retaining its uniqueness from the rest of China is a flickering notion of Hong Kong–style postcoloniality. The most significant trend in the postcolonial public discourse is the ever expanding role of the rule of law. I argue that the problems created by legal bilingualism itself show how the merging of the new ideal with the old formalist system of the common law is riddled with tensions.

In a way, this book is also autobiographical. The initial inspiration for this project goes back to some of the rather mundane assignments I received as a young reporter in Hong Kong. I was amazed by the order that English imposed on the courtrooms of Hong Kong that was just not there when Cantonese was used. More important is the fact that I belong to the generation of Hong Kong people who came of age in the twilight years of the colonial era. The choice between English and Cantonese, or, more specifically, the underlying power dynamics that make the choice difficult, is something that most people who grew up in the colonial period have experienced firsthand. Cantonese is the vernacular, but it is parochial and crude, by our own admission. Meanwhile, English is, then as now, the language of knowledge, education, and law, among other things. English is the voice through which a more modern, progressive society is articulated and envisioned. Yet it is the same elite language in Hong Kong that most people do not speak in their everyday lives. This book is a reflection of this dilemma, through the grounded study of bilingual common law in Hong Kong, which so characterizes the historical conditions of colonial Hong Kong and continues to shape the outlook of postcolonial Hong Kong today.

In the long course of writing this book, I wavered more than once on my answers to the questions that I raised. On the one hand, I have increasingly come to realize the limitations of English-language institutions like the common law in a society such as Hong Kong. For someone who sees himself as a Western-influenced progressive (but not a cultural anglophile), I find it hard to embrace an institution that is by design inaccessible because of its medium of language. On the other hand, in the course of my fieldwork, I got a chance to take a good long look at the predilections and prejudices of a common law voiced in Cantonese, so much so that I have reached a point where I can no longer arrogantly assume that a common law in my mother tongue would be likely to prosper and thrive. If there is a sense of ambivalence about my account of legal bilingualism, it is perhaps in part because I have tried my best to capture the complexity that people of my generation experienced with the dilemmatic choice between English and Cantonese that was at once personal and political. My goal is to try to let the people I studied speak in their own voices, not to reduce them to the silent enigma of Western imagination or for that matter to the generic subaltern figure of resistance in some of the postcolonial literature.

A book that concerns itself with language should talk about its own language. After all, I made the choice to write it in English. There are, in fact, two "Englishes" appearing in this book. The first is the English in Hong Kong, the English that is juxtaposed to Cantonese in the bilingual common law in Hong Kong. This English in the first sense is part of the object of my study. The second is English as the third language, an academic English that stands above the English and Cantonese in Hong Kong in my analyses. But as I hope my readers will recognize, the analytical English I use also bears traces of the Hong Kong English I knew and analyzed, mixed in with the academic English I learned during my years in the United States. In this sense, this book is as much a critique as a product of the English-Cantonese diglossia with which I grew up. I would frankly admit that, however inadequate my command of English is, it is perhaps the best medium I have at my disposal. English allows me to step back and paint in broad strokes and to present my thoughts in a reflective voice appropriate for a book of this kind. This is so not because English is a more accurate language, as many people would say; instead, consistent with the argument made in the following pages, it is because of the ways I came to learn and use the language.

Acknowledgments

I AM INDEBTED to the litigants, lawyers, and judges whom I write about in this book. Many of them agreed to spare their precious time to be interviewed. This project would not have been completed without their generosity and help. I thank former chief justice Ti Liang Yang and the chairman of the Hong Kong Bar Association at the time of my research, Alan Leong, SC, for agreeing to be interviewed. I am most thankful to then registrar Christopher Chan of the Hong Kong Judiciary, who graciously allowed me access to official tapes of some of the trial sessions that I attended.

Through his exemplary scholarship and always inquisitive questioning, Andrew Abbott advised the framing of my ideas with characteristic insight and creativity. His writings on the sociology of professions have been an important influence on my framing of the problem. He kept asking me what one big puzzle I could find in the mass of empirical data and pushed me not to settle for handy instant answers. Susan Gal welcomed me into the study of language practice. I am most grateful for her patience and willingness to guide me through the massive literature. She has been a perceptive and constructive interlocutor throughout this undertaking. Her thoughtful comments on earlier drafts of this work pushed me to rethink my argument in fundamental ways. I also benefited greatly from the example of Leslie Salzinger, who taught me what ethnography could be and whose critical approach to sociology was vital in shaping my own vision of sociology. Leslie challenged and pushed me to situate the narrative of this book more firmly in the social context of Hong Kong. Elizabeth Mertz, of the University of Wisconsin, Madison, an expert in the field of legal language, also graciously advised me on the research on which this book is based. I am most grateful for her insightful comments.

Many kind colleagues at the University of California, San Diego, have helped to bring this book into being. Foremost among these are

Isaac Martin and Richard Madsen. I am indebted to Isaac not just for the help he offered in the publication of the book but also for his detailed comments on various chapters of the manuscript. I owe a special debt of gratitude to Dick, who has been a patient mentor and a generous supporter of my scholarly efforts. The manuscript was much improved by thoughtful comments by Steve Epstein, Jeff Haydu, Martha Lampland, and John Skrentny, all of whom read and or commented on chapters of the book. I also extend special thanks to Kit Woolard and John Haviland, two linguistic anthropologists at UCSD who reached across the chasm to enlighten me with their helpful comments. Richard Biernacki introduced me to the historical studies of Barbara Epstein. Andy Scull offered valuable help during the publication process. Both John Evans and Harvey Goldman gave me useful advice. Jenny Tran provided editorial help during the manuscript's final stages. At Stanford University Press, I thank Kate Wahl, my editor, who was most helpful and efficient at every stage of the project. I also thank Gregory Matoesian and another anonymous reader provided by the Press, whose detailed and insightful comments helped me to make substantial improvements to the manuscript.

In Hong Kong, Dr. Sin King-kui, Mr. Sin Wai Man, and Dr. Alan Tse of City University of Hong Kong and Dr. Anne Cheung and Mr. Wilson Chow of Hong Kong University generously shared with me their research and ideas. I want to express my gratitude here. Sy Li Yee, Lam Oi-shun, Ernest Chi, and Ben Kwok all offered their help in different ways. I would also like to thank Wing Kay Po for frankly sharing her experience as a barrister with me. Of course, I do not expect her to agree with all the things I have written. I also thank Derry Wong, a practicing barrister who has written a lot on the subject, for sharing his knowledge with me.

The research on which this manuscript is based was made possible through funding from a number of institutions. Fieldwork in Hong Kong was financially supported by the Social Science Research Council. I also received funding from the Charlotte W. Newcombe Foundation and the University of Chicago. I am grateful to these institutions for their confidence in my project. Further work on the manuscript benefited from the support of the University of California's Faculty Career Development

Program. The Hellman Fellowship Program also provided support for research, and I am grateful to its donors for their generous help. A lot of the writing and rewriting of the book was done in the library of the California Western School of Law. I wish to thank the very helpful staff there for allowing me to use their facilities. In Chapter 4, Table 3 ("Mode of Address of Judicial Officers") is reproduced with the permission of LexisNexis, for which I express my gratitude.

My wife, Ngai Ling, as always, contributed to the writing of the book by offering her honest criticisms. I wish to thank her for her gracious acceptance of my academic preoccupation and, not least, for her refusal to be easily impressed. Her help and support also took the form of actually typing out all the Chinese characters appearing in the book. My sister, Chui, has always supported my academic pursuits in different ways and has always believed that my pursuits would bear fruit. My brother, Sheung Yi, and his family have also sent their regards throughout the years. My daughter, Kate Yiu, has been a lovely distraction.

A Note on Orthography and Transcription

THERE ARE TWO MAJOR PROBLEMS with transcribing Cantonese speech on paper. The first is the lack of a fully standardized Cantonese script. In this book, I have done my best to produce the transcripts in ways that I think reflect common existing practices. In 1999, the Hong Kong Special Administrative Region government published a Chinese character set known as the Hong Kong Supplementary Character Set (HKSCS). The latest version of the HKSCS (2001) contains 4,818 Chinese characters that are specific to the Hong Kong environment (Hong Kong Special Administrative Region Government, Information Technology Services Department 2004). This character set can be seen as a first step toward a standardized Cantonese script. As a rule, all the characters used in my transcriptions are taken from the HKSCS.

The second is the problem of romanization. Several romanization schemes for Cantonese are in circulation. The Yale and Meyer-Wempe systems appear to be the most commonly adopted in the English-language literature. In this book, I follow the new Cantonese Romanization Scheme, or Jyutping system, promoted by the Linguistic Society of Hong Kong. Jyutping is intuitive to Cantonese speakers. It is also convenient, because it is based solely on alphanumeric characters (unlike the Yale system, for example, which uses diacritics). But Jyutping is a relatively new system; readers who are familiar with the Yale system may find the new system difficult to follow in the beginning. The key features of the Jyutping system are the following.

1. *Consonants.* In Cantonese, consonants (shown in Table 1), are divided into initial consonants, or onsets (those that occupy the initial position of a syllable), and final consonants, or codas (those that occupy the final position of a syllable). The semivowels *w-* and *j-* also occur in the position of a consonant; *w* is pronounced much as it is

TABLE I *Initial consonants*

	Unaspirated	Aspirated	Fricative	Nasal
Bilabial	b	p	f	m
Alveolar	d	t	s	n/l
Velar/glottal	g	k	h	ng
Labiovelar	gw	kw		
Alveolar affricates	z	c		

SOURCE: Based on Yip and Matthews (2000: 1). Courtesy of Taylor and Francis Books, UK.

in English. *j* is pronounced as a *y* in English. On the other hand, final consonants are further divided into two groups: (1) unreleased stops (*-p, -t, -k*) or (2) nasals (*-m, -n, -ng*).

2. *Vowels and Diphthongs.* There are nine vowels, or what some linguists call nuclei, in the Cantonese system. These are *a, aa, i, u, e, o, yu, eo* (short), and *oe* (long). The first six are comparable to English vowels, whereas the last three are closer to French (cf. Yip and Matthews 2000).

Diphthongs are produced by shifting from one vowel to another over the course of one syllable. In Cantonese, they include *ai, aai, au, aau, iu, oi, ou, ei, ui,* and *eoi.*

3. *Tone.* Like other Chinese languages, Cantonese is tonal. According to the Cantonese Romanization Scheme, there are six common tones in the language. Each tone is represented by a numerical tone mark put at the end of a syllable: high level (1), high rising (2), midlevel (3), low falling (4), low rising (5), low level (6).

For readers who speak Cantonese, I provide transcripts in original Cantonese to encourage alternative analyses. And to make this work more accessible to non-Cantonese speakers, I provide roman transliterations of the key phrases and terms in my discussions. (In the interest of space, I do not provide word-by-word romanization of my Cantonese transcripts.) I also choose not to provide transcripts that make use of technical symbols and features, hoping that the simpler form will make the book more readable.

Transcription aside, Putonghua pinyin is used in the text for standard Chinese terms. Jyutping is used for local terms in Hong Kong and names of people and places. Because many of these names and terms are used mainly in the context of Hong Kong, they would be incomprehensible if romanized as Putonghua.

Finally, all English translations from the Cantonese were done by me.

A Note on Terminology

A FEW TERMS HAVE MEANINGS that are complicated by the unique context of Hong Kong. Also, the legal terminologies between Hong Kong (which usually follows the English terminology) and the United States are noticeably different. I have prepared this note on terminology, which draws in part on Atiyah and Summer's (1987) note in their book *Form and Substance in Anglo-American Law*, to minimize confusion for readers who are less familiar with the English-style terminologies in law.

Cantonese is often referred to, even by Cantonese speakers in Hong Kong, as a colloquial dialect with no standardized written form. In this book I follow the way most people in Hong Kong understand the term *Cantonese*, by confining its reference to an oral form of Chinese practiced in Hong Kong and parts of Guangdong (I offer an explanation of such understanding in Chapter 3). Hence, when I discuss how Cantonese is used in various parts of the book, I am, unless otherwise stated, discussing the use of Cantonese in oral settings.

Chinese is, on analysis, a complicated term because it means different things in oral and written contexts in Hong Kong. Invariably, when I use the term *Chinese*, I am referring to the way Chinese is predominantly practiced in Hong Kong—that is, Cantonese in oral settings and Standard Modern Chinese in written contexts. *Standard Modern Chinese* (SMC), a written form that is more or less based on vernacular Putonghua (Mandarin), or *baihua* in Chinese, is taught in the schools of Hong Kong as the proper written form of Chinese.

Costs in Hong Kong, following the English practice, include legal expenses and fees payable to a lawyer. In the United States, costs refer only to court costs and do not include legal fees.

The *Court of First Instance* is part of the High Court in Hong Kong (the other part is the Court of Appeal). Many of the cases that I analyze here are cases heard in the Court of First Instance. In the United States the term *High Court* is sometimes used to refer to the United States Supreme Court.

District Court is a lower court in Hong Kong. Unlike the district courts in the federal system of the United States, the District Court of Hong Kong has both limited criminal and civil jurisdiction. At the time of this writing, the District Court has civil jurisdiction to hear monetary claims up to HK$1 million (about US$128,200). In its criminal jurisdiction, the District Court may try the more serious cases (rather than the magistrates' courts), with the main exceptions of murder, manslaughter, and rape. The maximum term of imprisonment it may impose is seven years.

English law appears in various places in the book. The term *English*, not *British*, is used because England and Wales together constitute a jurisdiction; Scotland is a different jurisdiction with its own court structure (although the House of Lords is the court of final adjudication for Scotland in civil cases). Historically, the common law in Hong Kong is modeled after English common law.

Expatriate is a contested and confusing term. I reluctantly use it because it is used by many non-Chinese lawyers and judges (from England and other Western Commonwealth countries) when they describe themselves. Expatriate legal professionals are citizens of Western nation-states who stay and work in Hong Kong indefinitely or temporarily because of their legal expertise. Most professionally monolingual counsel and judges are expatriates (because they do not speak Cantonese). By this definition, there could arguably be ethnic Chinese lawyers or judges who are expatriates. (An example of this would be an ethnic Chinese lawyer born and educated in England who now works in Hong Kong.) Furthermore, some judges and lawyers in Hong Kong are professionally monolingual but should not be defined as expatriates. There are judges and counsel who grew up in the local English communities of Hong Kong (mainly South Asian minorities). They speak Cantonese casually but do not write, read, and speak to the degree considered professionally bilingual.

Senior counsel, or *SC*, is the postcolonial equivalent of *Queen's Counsel*, or *QC* (also known as *King's Counsel* (KC) when the British monarch is a king). It is used in Hong Kong and some other former British colonies. Senior counsel in Hong Kong continue to fashion themselves as silks (they wear silk gowns, just like the Queen's Counsel in England; see Chapter 4). Senior counsel are appointed by the chief justice in Hong Kong, in consultation with the two local professional associations for practicing lawyers. The award of the title is taken by both lawyers and the public in Hong Kong as a definitive recognition of the professional standing of a particular lawyer.

Judgment and *opinion* appear to be used interchangeably by lawyers and judges in Hong Kong. Opinion in relation to legal cases is the term used in the United States for what would be referred to in England as the judgment of a court. Also, the word *opinion* in Hong Kong does not carry the meaning of superior judgment, as in the case of the English legal system. Unlike the judges in the House of Lords, who give "opinions" at the end of a hearing, the judges in Hong Kong's Court of Final Appeal give judgments.

There are other terms, such as *examination-in-chief*, *reexamination*, *barristers* and *solicitors*, or *chambers* (the office of barristers), that might be unfamiliar to readers who have come to know the common law through the system of the United States. But I believe the meaning of these terms will be clear from the context of use.

PART ONE

Understanding Law and Language in Hong Kong

CHAPTER 1

The Challenge of Legal Bilingualism in Hong Kong

T HE ENGLISHNESS of the legal system in Hong Kong holds many things for outsiders to marvel at: the seventeenth-century English wigs and gowns worn by judges and lawyers, the elaborate decorum of lordship and learned friendship, and the stentorian tone of some of the judges. All give the impression that one might well be in an English court.

Excerpt from an English Trial in the Court of First Instance

COUNSEL: If the estate was worth that amount of money, did you know then what your entitlement was worth at the time?

WITNESS: No, I don't know.

COUNSEL: Did you ever find out?

WITNESS: Is it worthwhile to find out?

COUNSEL: Are you saying that if the amount is of that . . . if the estate is of that amount, it is not worthwhile to find out how much your entitlement was?

WITNESS: I didn't say that. No, it's just that whether it is worthwhile for me is not because of the financial term, you see, see what I mean. . . .

COUNSEL: Do you understand why you are here? You want a share of your father's estate. Is that correct?

WITNESS: I'm entitled to a share of my father's estate.

COUNSEL: Correct. And are you telling us . . .

WITNESS: OK. And also I am seeking for justice

JUDGE: Oh, please. Let's just stick to the facts, all right? This isn't Canada, or Australia, or America. Let's sort of leave aside that kind of, that kind of thing.

WITNESS: OK.

JUDGE: And please try and confine yourself to the facts.

WITNESS: OK.

JUDGE: If he asks you what somebody said, never mind, fair enough. Just tell us if you can remember what the person said, and say what it was. Or if you can't remember what the person said, please just tell us that you can't remember. All right?

WITNESS: Yeah.

JUDGE: Thank you.

COUNSEL: I'm grateful my Lord.

In his popular *Rumpole* novels, John Mortimer was offering a semirealistic portrayal when he described how the highly successful Phyllida (Trant) Erskine-Brown, whom Rumpole, Mortimer's alter ego, admiringly names the "Portia of our chambers," would occasionally disappear from her chambers for a few weeks to take on a case in Hong Kong.[1] In fact, a barrister from London would feel right at home in a courtroom in Hong Kong. At least, that is, until he stepped into a Cantonese-language one.

Excerpt from a Cantonese Trial in the District Court

WITNESS: Altogether, I gave them altogether. They needed money to spend for the New Year. So I advanced the money.

COUNSEL: Yes.

WITNESS: They needed money to spend for the New Year, they said to me.

COUNSEL: That means you at that time . . .

WITNESS: Sometimes there weren't many jobs for people to do. Their lives were very miserable. [*sigh*] That's so true. Workers didn't have money to spend for the New Year. They needed money to buy their food. Mr. Barrister, do you know?

COUNSEL: I think I do know.

WITNESS: [*laugh*] What?

COUNSEL: I think I'm more miserable. [*laughter from the workers*]

WITNESS: So, so [*laugh*] . . .

JUDGE: You two shouldn't keep doing this here . . .

COUNSEL: I'm sorry.

WITNESS: [*simultaneously*] Is that right?

The difference between the English and Cantonese courtrooms lies not simply in the switch of language. There is something more fundamental, something at once more elusive and yet gripping that accompanies the switch. In the English trial example, we see that a judge spells out a certain hidden vision of law for the witness, who tells the court that he is looking for justice. The judge's cold, almost Benthamite response to the witness's appeal to justice ("Oh, please") suggests a formalistic vision prevalent among legal professionals in Hong Kong—that law should be taken more as a rules-based adjudicatory machinery than as a freewheeling expression of the society's morality and values.[2] English courtrooms are governed by rules, extensively so in Hong Kong. A typical courtroom exchange between a barrister and a witness is orderly, detached, and impersonal (I discuss this in more detail in Chapter 4). Witnesses are boxed in, both literally and figuratively; their narratives are on a leash; and their replies are strictly confined to direct answers to the questions raised by counsel. Hong Kong, we are told, is not Canada or Australia or America, where law more openly values and incorporates social norms of equity, fairness, and justice in its articulation. As the judge in the example pronounced, a witness should stay with the facts. Of course, as we will see, there is a lot to be said about what counts as the facts in the court of law. On the other hand, in the second example, we are given a brief glimpse of the lively exchanges that are not uncommon in Cantonese courtrooms. The exchange is fluid, jaunty, and, above all, carnivalesque, in the subversive Bakhtinian sense of the term. Witnesses are let loose; they talk more and are often more pugnacious. Freestyle storytelling, intense sparring matches, peppery sarcasm, and slaphappy remarks prevail in this environment, and the trials are louder, noisier, and often edgier. They are also less predictable. Sometimes cross-examination turns into the telling of a life story through the details of one's distant past, and sometimes cross-examination proceeds disarmingly on the surface yet is loaded with piercing insinuations and mischievous smirks; at still other times cross-examination even breaks down into emotional shouting matches, resembling scenes from Cantonese soap operas.

Since the political changeover, as it is called, in 1997, Hong Kong has had a bilingual common law system; Chinese (which often means Cantonese in the oral context and Standard Modern Chinese in the written context) and English share equal status within the system.[3] In other words, the law stipulates that English and Chinese are to be used, received, understood, and treated as the same.[4]

What happens on the ground, that is, in the courts, however, suggests a different picture. Such differences obviously do not go unnoticed by the legal professionals involved in the everyday workings of the law. Barristers who use both languages describe English and Cantonese trials as trials that take place in two different worlds. English trials are, in their words, solemn, respectful, and dignified. Cantonese trials, again in their words, are noisy, mundane, and belittling. One judge I interviewed insisted on playing for me an official tape of a Cantonese trial. Other lawyers and judges advised me to listen to the trials in person, which I did for one year.

But if it is surprising to see litigants *act* differently when they *speak* in the different languages of English and Cantonese, it is even more surprising to find out how easy it is for bilingual counsel and even judges to engage in some of the demeaning and trivial Cantonese speech acts that they disdain. This puzzle suggests that language cannot be taken as some sort of tool or medium that is entirely at the actor's disposal. People do not always consciously use language to *do* what they *want*, or at least to do it exactly *how* they want it to be done. This is because the way we use language, or in this case, languages, is thoroughly a social practice—embodied, intuitive, and habitual—and is not entirely transparently accessible for conscious inspection. The metaphor of language as purely a tool assumes a fantastical degree of separation between a people and their language that is simply empirically unwarranted. It is in this sense that one can say that language is constitutive, a theme that I will come back to again and again in this book. Cantonese sets up a different background environment (compared to the English environment) that makes it easier for someone to act in some ways but more difficult to act in other ways. When put this way, it seems that it is all about language and that I am making an argument of linguistic relativism of sorts. What I hope to show, in fact, is that it is not about language per se (its syntax and other structural traits) but about the social practices that language embodies. The contrasting ways that people perform in the English and Cantonese courtrooms demonstrate that language is a socially enduring form. Language remembers; it is something, as Bakhtin puts it, that "has lived its socially charged life" (1981: 193). It is thus made up of a set of living practices that reach back to the past and stretch into the future—practices that are predicated on social sensibilities that define what works and what does not work within an environment. Language is enduring because it is something that cannot be easily changed (even today, language remains one of the most obvious legacies of colonialism for most places that were once colonized); it is also enduring because as a form it transcends individual idiosyncrasies. Its recognizable social character exists sometimes despite the absence of intentions and sometimes in spite of the intentions of the actors. Language gives social performances of different kinds their appropriate voices that people tacitly recognize.

If to start a revolution is to let things get out of control, then the use of Cantonese in the courtrooms of Hong Kong is revolutionary, in more ways than one.[5] In the magistracies of Hong Kong, where Cantonese has become the dominant language, it is not uncommon to find litigants displaying a jutting sense of defiance to the magistrates on the bench, even at the cost of a stiff penalty. Magistrates are called the lackeys of the court;[6] shoes, apparently the only "hard" objects available to a defendant on the dock, are sometimes even thrown at the magistrates.[7] One magistrate working at the busiest magistracy in Hong Kong told me that this had happened to him not once but twice. "Luckily, they both missed," he quipped.

THE SOCIAL CHARACTER OF INSTITUTIONS

What happens in Cantonese and English courtrooms has implications far beyond the scope of a case study of legal bilingualism in a Chinese society. In its broadest formulation, the everyday practice of legal bilingualism presents a puzzle about why a particular institutional form, that is, formalism, in virtually the same external environment in which it has dominated for more than a century, must now struggle for control in that same environment even though only one thing has changed—language. At its root, this anomaly challenges the received wisdom about the nature of institutions among sociologists and questions whether institutions, of which the modern legal system is in many ways the institution par excellence, operate as autonomously as many of us believe. Sociologists are trained to believe in the power of institutions, so much so that many of us often visualize modern society as a constellation of autonomous institutional regimes. We are too enamored of the power of an institution to induce behavioral stability by stipulating that the institution must follow its own rules within its own environment.[8] If an institution could speak, its motto would have to be "This is my house!"

But if the modus operandi of an institution is making and implementing its own rules to run its own house, then how could two languages, English and Cantonese, which are stipulated to be of the same status and to perform the same function within the same system, differ so palpably in situ? How is it that the legal system of Hong Kong, arguably the most formalized legal system in Asia, fails to seal its own rules in its own house?

In this book I try to offer a different picture of the relation between institution and society. The crux of my argument can be stated in a simple form: that the success or failure of formalism as a prevalent institutional form turns on the existing power structure in the wider society. To my mind, the question is not why institutions are autonomous; the question is why some institutions achieve the *appearance* of autonomy, despite the many facts to the contrary. No institution operates in a social vacuum without recourse to and uninfluenced by the wider society of which it is a part. The situation is doubly tricky for the common law system in Hong Kong, which was established by British colonial officials who were socially remote from the local contexts where the law would be applied and its sanctions imposed.

The difficulty with studying the social foundations of an institutional form is precisely that sociologists are also members of the society they study. We stand inside history. Institutions, successful institutions in particular, acquire an appearance of autonomy. They are social fixtures; they seem to exist forever; and their practices become a given, achieving a status that Pierre Bourdieu (1977: 164) calls doxic. In such cases, it is difficult to find a visible point of reference from which to track the social processes that legitimized the arbitrariness of the institution in the first place. This explains why our sociological common sense is not very good at grasping the deep-rooted connection between institutions and society. We are often blind to it because we have long taken it for granted.

Hong Kong's bilingual common law interests me as a case (as much as, admittedly, I am making a case out of it) because of its liminality, that revelatory moment it offers to befuddled observers to step out of their interpretative rut (Turner 1974). First, in the most obvious sense, it is liminal for its unique bricolage of English and Chinese elements. It is the Anglo-American common law by way of postcolonialism—Cantonese vernacular mixing with English decorum. It is transitional, open, and pregnant with ambiguities. But second, in a more profound sense, liminality refers to a kind of epistemological reflexivity; the case of bilingual common law itself offers an *external* standpoint from *within* that allows sociologists to stop going in circles. Its in-between, transitional character allows us to see, yet again, the strange in the familiar. What is crucial about the bilingual common law in Hong Kong is that it is not the result of any coherent ideological campaign or singular political movement. As in so many other things Hong Kong, it is the result of a compromise negotiated by Britain and China, which at different times have owned Hong Kong's sovereignty. It would be hard to dream up from scratch an institutional design that features a common law system with English and Chinese as its languages. Here, in the unique context of Hong Kong, the *political* necessity of using Chinese is bound up with the *legal* concern to maintain institutional continuity.

For reasons I will further elaborate in this book, Cantonese was the most unprepared of all languages (or for some, of all dialects)[9] to be thrust on a common law system. For almost 150 years, English monopolized the legal realm in Hong Kong.[10] It was the exclusive legal language of any general court above the level of magistracy.[11] In 1997, as part of the changes adopted in light of the transfer of sovereignty, Chinese (which usually means Cantonese in oral settings) was made an official language of the law alongside English.[12] This was done at a time when the linguistic diglossia between English and Cantonese that defined colonial governance was still very much intact. Each of the two distinct linguistic habituses, or habitual structures, one in English and the other in Cantonese, maintains its own standards and limits of pragmatic effectiveness, outliving the colonialism that created them in the first place.[13] English, besides being the traditional language of the law, is the language of business, politics, and other serious public activities; Cantonese is the language of the family, the mass media, and the street. I will say more about the two habituses in Chapter 3. Here I simply want to point out that the presence of two languages—two languages so different in their historical functions and social positions—provides us with an opportunity to identify through comparison the otherwise naturalized and therefore hidden social dynamics involved in the implementation of formalism. I will discuss the meaning of formalism in more detail in Chapter 2; here I just want to refer to formalism as a mode of doing law characterized by strict compliance with preset rules rather than appeal to substantive values or norms. The serendipitous, even ironic, nature of the introduction of legal Cantonese means that it is contrapuntal to any legal formalism built from the ground up. Its raw, direct encounter with a formalistic system provides a liminal moment of rupture in which one can identify, through its contrast with English, the hitherto invisible social configurations on which the institutional culture of formalism relies.

SITUATING LEGAL BILINGUALISM IN CONTEXT

I started off this chapter by saying that the introduction of Cantonese as a legal language is, *in more ways than one*, revolutionary. I did not choose the phrase lightly. In a most obvious sense, the use of Cantonese often results in a more, for want of a better word, casual and sometimes rowdy atmosphere; events in the courtroom become harder to control. But just looking at it in this way trivializes the problem, because the challenge of Cantonese pushes further into the fabric of the common law system in Hong Kong. The introduction of Cantonese is revolutionary in a deeper, more classical sense—the beginning of something new (Arendt 1963), much to the chagrin of the officials and judges who oversaw the move. As a story about Hong Kong, the discrepancy between Cantonese and English courtrooms means far more than a problem of institutional efficacy, or judicial policy. My goal in this book is to show how the unresolved tensions that riddle the implementation of legal bilingualism should be taken as an *emblem* of the postcolonial dilemma facing Hong Kong today.

To appreciate the postcolonial significance of the presence of legal bilingualism, one has to first understand the colonial mode of legal operation. Historically, Hong Kong's colonial legal system was, in Weberian terms, formalistic and yet *noncomprehensive*. A legal order is considered comprehensive if no social actions are beyond its reach, if "every social action of human beings" can be "visualized as either an 'application' or 'execution' of legal propositions, or as an 'infringement' thereof" (Weber 1978: 657–658).[14] Yet the common law in Hong Kong operated and, in a significant way, continues to operate through a minimally integrated social-legal system that makes little connection between law and society. When the British arrived in Hong Kong, they brought with them their standard legal start-up package (Hong Kong was the last British colony in Asia): the common law, the doctrines of equity, and the statutes of general application that were in force in England in 1843.[15] For a whole century after the establishment of the crown colony, the civil side of the legal system of Hong Kong maintained minimal interaction with the local population. As one legal scholar writing about the period points out, "Beyond the criminal law and other necessary adjuncts of public control, such as registration of the population, the government hoped that it could leave the Chinese to look after their own affairs" (D. M. E. Evans 1971: 13). In the early years of the colony, knowing that the common law might differ greatly from the sense of popular justice of the residents of Hong Kong, the British implemented a policy of legal segregation through a truncated form of a dual legal system often seen in larger settler colonies (the truncated dual system in Hong Kong was implemented within a single court system). The colonial courts in Hong Kong operated as an eclectic combination of direct and indirect rule that the British Colonial Office often emphasized in the heyday of colonialism. Direct rule manifested itself as a mode of urban governance bound by a thin notion of the rule of law and a limited regime of rights. Indirect rule was the colonial reenactment of so-called tribal order, which in the context of Hong Kong referred to the application of Chinese customary law to the local population under appropriate circumstances. Together, direct and indirect rule were complementary methods of legal control seen in British colonies, particularly nonsettler colonies, all over the world (Mamdani 1996: 18–19). As mentioned, unlike in some larger colonies, the British did not establish a dual court system in Hong Kong to handle customary law and common law separately; instead, the colonial court system implemented a so-called fused common law system (Hsu 1992: 13), applying two sets of civil law, according to the ethnicity of the litigants involved (for the Chinese majority, customary law; for the European minority, the common law). Thus, before the end of World War II, two de facto sets of civil law were in force in the courts of the colony: English law and Chinese customary law. While holding a firm grip over the crucial area of criminal law, the colonial government adopted a policy of leaving the Chinese to look after their own private affairs.

For the entire nineteenth century, the civil cases that came before the then Supreme Court of Hong Kong (renamed the High Court after 1997) almost exclusively had European litigants. Although ethnic Chinese might occasionally be involved in these contacts, they usually appeared before the court as parties in commercial disputes; the judges were therefore able to apply predominantly English law (D. M. E. Evans 1971). In fact, the court professed to be ignorant of Chinese custom and law. Sir Francis Piggott, a chief justice (1905–1912), acknowledged this with disarming candor in a judgment in 1911.

It is an extraordinary fact that the Court of this Colony, in which the Chinese live and trade as freely as Englishmen and citizens of other countries, should do with regard to the Chinese what it would never dream of doing with regard to Frenchmen or Germans or Americans; and not only that, but that it should be entirely in ignorance of Chinese law on any subject which concerns the family life and family law of those who form the bulk of its inhabitants, which is so often before the courts—its marriage laws, and the rights of property it gives; its law applicable to children. . . . The attitude of the Court has been to let the troublesome question wait until it is definitely raised by the parties.[16]

This kind of legal laissez-fairism in the civil domain is most manifest in the area of family law. Much of Chinese customary law in the areas of family constitution (including the system of concubinage) and succession was retained, albeit indifferently and with diminishing significance, until the 1970s (cf. Cheung 1996; D. M. E. Evans 1973; Hsu 1992; Lewis 1983; Pegg 1975). For example, the limited dual system also recognized customary marriage (i.e., marriage conducted in accordance with traditional customs and rites) as one of the two legal forms of marriage, so long as the participants themselves were ethnic Chinese.[17] It was not until 1971 that the English legal concept of monogamy was introduced to both the "Chinese" and the "Western" populations of Hong Kong. In reality, the colonial courts wanted family disputes among Chinese residents to be settled outside the legal system. For one, judges in Hong Kong during the early days of colonialism were mostly recruited directly from England and had little knowledge of the customs governing the complex Chinese kinship system. Furthermore, the implementation of Chinese customary law within the formal procedural framework of the common law was loaded with problems (cf. Cheung 1996; D. M. E. Evans 1971: 23–24). It changed the outlook of Chinese customs and ossified a living tradition by freezing it at a certain cutoff date (in Hong Kong the cut-off date was precise: April 5, 1843; see Haydon 1962). This was, of course, a recurrent story in the legal histories of many British colonies that at one point made up as much as a quarter of the earth (cf. Chanock 1985; Cohn 1989, 1996; Furnivall 1948; Merry 1991, 1992). For example, Bernard Cohn (1989), in his wonderful study of legal dualism in colonial India, describes how the formalization and scrutiny to which the English evidential rules subjected Hindu customs fossilized the very nature of the customs themselves.

With the massive influx of refugees in the 1950s immediately after World War II, the texture of Hong Kong society underwent fundamental changes. Hong Kong quickly developed from an entrepôt into an industrialized colony. Although political governance remained colonial in style and substance, the civil domain of law developed in the image of the English legal system, a legal infrastructure whose predictability and certainty were conducive to the development of a market economy. In the area of family law, previous laissez-fairism was replaced by legislative intervention. By the beginning of the 1970s, the colonial legislature decided to scrap Chinese customary law from the colonial legal system.[18] Facing rapid change, the government finally realized that it was futile to insist on the validity of nineteenth-century Chinese customs or even to presuppose the existence of a defined set of Chinese customs.[19]

In other areas of civil law, institutional arrangements explained why the Hong Kong common law system resembled to a significant extent the English system. First, certain Hong Kong statutes, technically known as reception statutes, stipulated the application of the English common law in Hong Kong. Despite variations over different reception statutes during the colonial period, the general principle was that the common law and the rules of equity applied in Hong Kong insofar as they might be applicable to the circumstances of Hong Kong and subject to modifications as local circumstances might require.[20] In practice, historically, the applicability of the common law in Hong Kong was generously interpreted.[21] A strict test was adopted that stipulated that courts in Hong Kong could deviate from English common law only if the law's application would lead to "injustice or oppression"; however, the test was seldom explicitly mentioned.[22] Peter Wesley-Smith, a scholar who specializes in Hong Kong common law, points out that in cases in which the applicability of the common law of England was contested (in most cases it was a nonissue), the courts of Hong Kong decided to follow the common law, despite contentions, on such topics as champerty and maintenance, the law of ancient lights, the rule against perpetuities, the freedom from liability of a highway authority for nonfeasance, and the consequence in relation to contributory negligence of failure to wear a seat belt (Wesley-Smith 1994: 136–137). When the common law was regarded as inapplicable, it was mainly because the courts deferred to Chinese customs (before 1971) or to the customs (on matters such as succession) of the indigenous population in the then rural area (known as the New Territories) of Hong Kong.

Second, with regard to the hierarchy of legal authority, the Judicial Committee of Her Majesty's Privy Council in London was the court of final adjudication of the colony.[23] W. S. Clarke, another scholar writing on Hong Kong law, suggests that the Privy Council held a tight rein on Hong Kong, in stark contrast to the liberal attitude it displayed toward other Commonwealth jurisdictions such as Australia and Malaysia. The Privy Council instructed its courts not only to follow its rulings but also to "treat House of Lords decisions on questions of common law as having such great persuasive authority as, in effect, normally to be binding" (Clarke 1990: 747).[24] This was all the more remarkable because in terms of their social fabrics, a country such as Australia was more similar to England than Hong Kong ever was. Clarke (1990) speculates that the tight rein was partly due to the lack of any local judicial campaign (as in Australia and Malaysia) that resisted the authority of the Privy Council. In reality, there was no need for the colonial courts of Hong Kong, ever loyal followers of English common law, to be reined in. Hong Kong courts closely followed decisions of the Privy Council whether on appeal from Hong Kong or not, and to a greater extent, the same can be said regarding decisions of the House of Lords.[25] In important areas of civil law, such as torts and contracts, Hong Kong closely followed precedents from England and Wales with only occasional exceptions on issues where the local situation was markedly different from that of England.[26] By and large, the similarities between the case laws of the two jurisdictions by far outweighed their differences. Consider, for example, tort law. The one area in torts where a unique body of local cases has developed is the area of defamation. Ironically, it is because many libel and slander cases involved the uses of colloquial Cantonese insults, mockery, and innuendos that English precedents were rendered irrelevant. In other torts, however, Hong Kong tort law has been criticized as being blindly faithful to English precedents, greatly at the expense of paying due consideration to the local situations in Hong Kong. Abstract principles formulated in the highest English courts—for example, the scope of duty of care in the tort of negligence—have been uncritically applied. This is especially problematic because tort concepts such as duty of care are often policy driven, if not subject to the influence of morality and culture, and there is no reason to assume that policies originating in Britain apply to Hong Kong (Glofcheski 2002). As Robyn Martin, a legal scholar who taught torts in Hong Kong for a decade, comments, "The large number of English cases which still have authority in Hong Kong indicates that the Hong Kong courts have not yet taken up the challenge of developing a uniquely Hong Kong vision of legal obligations. There is much in English tort law which could do with rethinking and revising, and other common law jurisdictions (Australia and Canada for example) have, over time, become sufficiently confident in the integrity of their own societal values to reject the wisdom of the English House of Lords in favor of law which is more appropriate to home ground" (2002: 728; see also Cottrell 1996).

In some areas, differences between Hong Kong and England were due to the rapid statutory development of English law (especially in areas where changes were made to harmonize English law with European Union law) with which Hong Kong law did not keep pace. If one takes a bird's-eye view of the civil side of Hong Kong's common law during the colonial period, one thing that jumps out is the exceptionally strong degree of "authoritative formality" (Atiyah and Summers 1987: 12) that Hong Kong's common law accorded (and still accords to a great extent) to the case law of England and Wales. English precedents were considered authoritative not because of specific substantive reasons they put forward but simply because they were English precedents and were formally considered legally valid. Peter Wesley-Smith attributes the close adherence of local judicial interpretation to English precedents to "narrowness of outlook and minimal creativity" (Wesley-Smith 1999: 1). A study published in 1984 showed that in the preceding 10-year period as much as three-quarters of the cases cited in the *Hong Kong Law Reports*, the officially authorized law report of Hong Kong, were from England and Wales, a ratio much higher than for other English-style common law jurisdictions such as Australia and New Zealand, and that local cases made up only 20 percent of the total (Cooke 1983, cited in Clarke 1990: 755; Wesley-Smith 1984: 140). An updated version of the study reveals that the same level of dependence on English decisions persisted until the final days of British colonialism (Wesley-Smith 1999: 1). Even when judges saw a clear need to deviate from English case law, they would seek *alternative* authoritative formality from decisions of the American, Australian, Canadian, New Zealand, and to a lesser extent Singaporean and Malaysian courts. The tendency for lawyers and judges in the superior courts of Hong Kong to window-shop at other common law jurisdictions rather than to argue by reference to substantive reasons shows the inherent outward-looking nature of Hong Kong common law in the past and to a significant extent even today. In practice, the common law was made more amenable to litigants in Hong Kong when some culturally sensitive judges took "judicial notice" of the facts of local life, as Kemal Bokhary, now a permanent judge of Hong Kong's Court of Final Appeal, wrote when he was a young barrister practicing in Hong Kong (cf. Bokhary 1975). But the discretionary use of judicial notice was a way to introduce legal flexibility on the ground without disrupting the formal resemblance between the shared principles and rules of the common laws of Hong Kong and England on the books.

Thus, in terms of substantive content, colonial law mostly derived its legal contents by closely following English law. Driving the transplantation of English law into Hong Kong were the colonial legal institutions that were minimally involved with the local society of Hong Kong. The courts were a highly concentrated, bounded form of technical institutionalism that gave the common law in Hong Kong its style and character. As a form of power from without, colonialism saw little need and made little effort to root its law in the moral or cultural foundations of the society to which it was transplanted.

During the last decade of the colonial period, with the change of political sovereignty quickly approaching, the then Hong Kong government finally began to "localize" the legal system. But localization involved minimal institutional adaptation. It by no means altered the formalistic style and character of the common law. In fact, under China's policy of "50 years unchanged," Chinese leader Deng Xiaoping promised that the common law system could continue beyond 1997.[27] Hence localization is understood in the minimalist sense—legislation would be amended to reflect the change of political sovereignty, the power of final adjudication of the system would be vested in a new local Court of Final Appeal, and finally, almost as a footnote to the whole exercise, Chinese would become, alongside English, an official language of the courts. So, the common law system made its transition to the postcolonial era without much fanfare. It was a stark contrast to the fierce political rows between Britain and China on the transition of the legislature and the executive.

However, the political changes that began in the last decade of British colonialism and continued in the first decade of the postcolonial era put the legal system of Hong Kong in uncommon limelight. Electoral democracy of the legislature and the executive remain, at best, a partial exercise.[28] As their frustration deepened regarding democratic reform, or the lack thereof, in the political system, liberals and progressives of Hong Kong more actively deployed the notion of the rule of law. In 2003, a massive protest officially crowned the ascendancy of the rule of law to become a charter for Hong Kong values. On the sixth anniversary of the city's return to China, half a million people, about 7 percent of the population, bore the cruel, pounding heat of a typical midsummer afternoon and took to the streets.

They demonstrated in the name of the rule of law, in light of the imminent passage of a proposed antisubversion law. Endless rows of demonstrators literally filled every corner of the central business and commercial district. Protestors uttered litany upon litany of sententious slogans calling for the integrity of the rule of law and sang songs in praise of human rights. Western media immediately saw the political implications of the protest—it was dubbed the rebellion or the Long March. The consequences of that day are impressive for anyone who is casually familiar with modern Chinese history. The then unpopular chief executive, Tung Chee-hwa, with the implicit agreement of the Chinese government in Beijing, made an official retreat to table the proposed legislation. Western media described the protest as "one of the most effective statements of popular will ever in the history of the People's Republic."[29] It is the only peaceful popular protest in the 54-year history of the People's Republic that achieved an official backdown.[30]

In hindsight, the 500,000 people who took to the streets did so for many reasons—the unfulfilled promise of democracy, the slumping economy at that time, the earlier outbreak of SARS, and above all the inept governance of Tung Chee-hwa. But it was the rule of law that became the slogan around which the demonstrators rallied. Why? Beyond the proximate threat of the proposed antisubversion law, the appeal of the rule of law has much to do with what has happened in the course of Hong Kong's unfulfilled quest for democracy.[31] In a place where liberal democracy is a near universal aspiration for politicians of all stripes (publicly at least), the perpetual delay of its implementation is frustrating, to say the least. It is under such circumstances that the rule of law has been rendered the raison d'être of postcolonial Hong Kong—the banner concept that the Hong Kong people, particularly the educated, use to deliberate about the essence of the city, about how it is different from the rest of China.[32] Like it or not, law and its discourse in Hong Kong have officially waded into the domain of politics (cf. Jones 1999).

THE RULE OF LAW IN COLONIAL HONG KONG

But the rule of law rehearsed in the public discourse is a different species from the rule of law practiced by the previous colonial government. What was the rule of law in colonial Hong Kong? The use of the term by the colonial government bordered on a euphemism for the practice of governance through law (regardless of legal content), just as the government in Hong Kong had for years described itself as "executive-led" (C. K. Lau 1997). Beneath the veneer of this businesslike description was a formidable armory of tools of legal coercion at the colonial governor's disposal, including the power to introduce laws relatively unchecked by his subjects (S. K. Lau and Kuan 1988). This belief in the centralization of power reflected the philosophy of English colonialism, particularly in its Utilitarian formulation. In the writings of the British Utilitarians, which very much shaped British colonial policies (the most famous example of which is of course John Stuart Mill; see Fitzpatrick 1992: 107–111), despotism is considered a legitimate mode of government in colonial settings. During the colonial period, Hong Kong was subject to the Colonial Laws Validity Act of 1865 and other legal mechanisms whereby Westminster and Whitehall, as the ultimate colonial authority, could, if they so wished, intervene in the everyday affairs of Hong Kong's governance (Clarke 1990: 750). Also, the local legislature had in its history enacted laws that significantly infringed civil liberties—for example, the draconian Emergency Regulations Ordinance of 1964, which empowered the colonial governor alone to legislate restrictions on the freedom of movement in an emergency.[33] In general, however, any tendency toward the actual exercise of legal authoritarianism was restrained by complicated political considerations that involved Hong Kong's delicate geographic position (its proximity to China) and its overwhelmingly ethnic Chinese population. But it would be wrong to conflate exercised restraints based on political calculation with the liberal practice of the rule of law.[34] Restraints came in the form of prosecutorial discretion and the colonial governor's executive prerogative of mercy. There were no institutional checks and balances to prevent the colonial governor from practicing local despotism if he so wished. On paper, the power of the colonial governor was comparable in range and scope to a dictator's.[35] The separation of powers, which so often features as an institutional safeguard to the rule of law, was not in place at any time during the colonial period. For most of the colonial period, the colonial legislature, known as the Legislative Council, had been dominated by so-called ex officio and official appointees—bureaucrats at the top positions of the government hierarchy and members appointed by the governor himself, respectively. It was not until 1985 that some forms of indirect election were introduced to the legislature; and direct elections through geographic constituencies did not appear until 1991, a mere six years before the changeover, and only for a limited number of seats (18 out of a then total of 61 seats).[36] Power was centralized in the hands of the colonial governor, who in turn delegated it to his bureaucratic machinery, the civil servants of Hong Kong. Colonial Hong Kong also had an unusually large police force in relation to its population (Miners 1975); during most of the colonial era, the police were empowered by law to ban or impose limits on public meetings if necessary.

As for judicial checks on the executive, hardly any significant cases of judicial review of administrative action came up during most of the colonial period. Even though the courts of Hong Kong were theoretically empowered to review the constitutionality of legislation (unlike English courts, which have no written constitution to rule on and are formally subordinate to Parliament), the colonial courts maintained an extremely narrow notion of justiciability (the suitability of a matter for judicial review) and a restrictive doctrine of ultra vires (e.g., the principle of Wednesbury unreasonableness was not successfully invoked in the courts of Hong Kong until 1992).[37] In short, before the 1990s, judicial reviews of any substantive nature were basically nonexistent.[38] The judiciary in the colonial period was by and large a "civil service judiciary" (Downey 1976). Even as recently as 1978, the then new chief justice of Hong Kong, Sir Denys Roberts, had served as attorney general, chief secretary (head of the civil servants), and occasionally acting governor! Institutionally, judges were employees of the colonial government. As such, the appointment and dismissal of colonial judges were devoid of constitutional safeguards (Cottrell and Ghai 2001: 209–210; Harris 1978: 84).[39]

It was only in its twilight hours that the colonial government began to engage in a project of constitutionalism and human rights that approximated the standards of contemporary Western liberal legalism, evidently in response to the crackdown in China on the fateful day of June 4, 1989. Before then, human rights were seldom a topic on the colony's agenda. The Letters Patent, the main constitutional document during colonial rule, contained few normative provisions that could form the basis for legal challenge to legislation or policy (Cottrell and Ghai 2001). And although the United Kingdom ratified the International Covenant on Civil and Political Rights (ICCPR) and extended it to Hong Kong in 1976, the covenant would not enjoy any direct legal status in Hong Kong for another 15 years.[40]

Thus, for most of the colonial period, the cherished idea of the rule of law was a rather thin concept—even by the standard of A. V. Dicey (1898), whose famous definition of the term is frequently criticized as merely a fancy version of "legality" (conformity with lawyers' law).[41] The rule of law was detached and not engaged, technical and inaccessible, stripped-down and not expansive. In other words, the rule of law that the colonial government practiced was a narrow adherence to the established rules of a legal institution that was not intrinsically oriented toward and was in fact quite indifferent to social sensibilities. What the rule of law in colonial Hong Kong amounted to was a by-the-book certainty—often regardless of what was actually written in the book—within a strict framework of procedural justice. This was formal in the sense that it allowed judges and lawyers to focus exclusively on the proper implementation of existing law rather than to raise questions about the reasons justifying the contents of law (the contents of law would be the job of the legislature). Historically, the rule of law in Hong Kong did not entail any metacritique that questioned the possible gap between law-as-it-is and law-as-it-ought-to-be. The idea served perfectly well as the ideological linchpin for the kind of juridical formalism in the English courtrooms in Hong Kong that I will describe in later chapters. What I want to emphasize here is that the notion of the rule of law in colonial Hong Kong was a highly formalistic one. It bordered on its less glamorous sibling concept of rule by law, often associated with authoritarian political regimes. What distinguished the rule of law from rule by law was a set of residual rights inherent in the framework of procedural justice. These rights are better perceived as a body of inherent values and practices developed from the tradition of the common law: the presumption of innocence in criminal trials, the presumption against retroactive legislation, jury trials for serious criminal cases, and the requirement that court proceedings be open to the public (Wade and Philips 2001).

Yet the colonial Hong Kong version of the rule of law, however insubstantial, was cherished by many of the people there.[42] The exigencies of political unrest were all too familiar to the older generations, many of whom had directly suffered under Maoist China, when law was often mobilized to serve political purposes through numerous campaigns and movements. Still, going to court in the colonial period had its Kafkaesque aspects; the law was constructed as a remote institution whose authority was derived from a site entirely beyond everyday life in Hong Kong. Throughout the colonial period, locals tended to avoid courts as much as possible by conducting their individual affairs through extralegal means. It was in part for this reason that Hong Kong Chinese were known to be antilitigious.

But since the 1990s, this notion of the rule of law, historically highly formalistic, detached, and technical, has been thrust into the center of public discourse. As mentioned, with full political democracy beyond reach, the only way that a viable political grand narrative could be developed was to yoke the postcolonial identity of Hong Kong to the notion of the rule of law. The passing of a bill of rights in the last decade of British colonialism could be conveniently identified as a watershed that marked the gestalt shift on the conception of the rule of law. In 1991, the colonial government, in a clear response to the 1989 crackdown, introduced the local Hong Kong Bill of Rights Ordinance. Despite its dubious status as a superior legislation (it was not a constitutional document and was subject to the constraints of the Basic Law, Hong Kong's constitution), the bill aimed to incorporate the ICCPR into the law of Hong Kong. Framed in a vocabulary of natural, universal rights, the bill introduced a new moral dimension to the concept of legality that went beyond the authoritative formality attached to English precedents. Furthermore, the Basic Law, despite its controversial Article 23 (the reason that the antisubversion law was proposed in the first place), which requires Hong Kong to impose restrictions on rights and freedoms of its residents, also offers its own eclectic mix of rights. Although the Basic Law is a document short on political rights (democracy and political freedom), it incorporates its own list of traditional liberal rights in the ICCPR (such as freedom of association, expression, privacy) and rights fundamental to the efficient operation of a market economy, such as land rights, private property rights (as Ghai, a constitutional scholar, comments, the Basic Law is a "charter for capitalism" (1993: 345)), and the right to confidential legal advice, access to courts, and choice of lawyers for timely protection of lawful rights. At a minimum, the rights provisions in the Basic Law, however restricted, legitimized a new form of rule of law discourse that had been dominating the political landscape of postcolonial Hong Kong.

During the process, the colonialist minimal idea of the rule of law was replaced by a new public discourse that shifted from a formal to a substantive conception of it. This new discourse arguably goes beyond the scope of rights promised by the Basic Law and ambitiously incorporates in its vision democratic aspirations, liberal ideals of freedom, and moralistic notions of justice. It imagines a system of law embedded in an engaged and vibrant civil society. This, of course, is a common strategy among the weak (Scott 1990). By taking a concept more seriously than its original writers did, progressive members in Hong Kong managed to occupy not just the rhetoric but also the moral high ground. That said, this expansive notion of the rule of law is clearly a newfangled one. Unlike the previous (formalistic) version promoted by colonial officials, the new discourse entails an expansive rights-based notion of the rule of law that is derived from an expansive account of justice. It is this new rule of law that allows different social groups to articulate a coherent political voice. The new rule of law embodies definite political and moral aspirations; it establishes the ideals of constitutionalism, in which the basic values of human dignity are taken to be intrinsic features of the law. For liberal progressives in Hong Kong, the rule of law has become an icon of postcoloniality and a measure of how far Hong Kong has advanced from its humble beginnings. And it has become a sign that distinguishes Hong Kong, the global city, from the rest of China. Any political act said to violate the rule of law is also interpreted as an act that forces Hong Kong a few steps backward—and closer to the rest of China. Thus, despite its traditionally thin content, the concept of the rule of law harbors thick imaginative potential for political progressives in postcolonial Hong Kong.[43] Lawyers, in particular barristers, have been at the forefront of defending the rule of law and articulating its role in defining the identity of postcolonial Hong Kong.[44]

In 2003, the demonstrators claimed that the proposed antisubversion law legislation was a threat to, among other things, the rule of law in Hong Kong. The protest itself constituted probably the clearest public statement of a departure from the previous orthodox view of the colonial concept of the rule of law, where the content of a proposed piece of law, despite its apparent authority (the Basic Law stipulates legislation in the area), was subject to the critique of a rights-based discourse. What is clear is that since 1997 public discourse has transformed the notion of the rule of law from a narrow juristic concept of certainty to a political ideal with substantive content; local politicians, some of them lawyers, have been most vocal in this shift from a narrow formalist definition to a rights-based definition. In fact, the transformation has been so complete that the colonialist conception of the rule of law, which the new Special Administrative Region (SAR) government and China have invoked several times to justify their policies, is now considered an idea that belongs to the other side. This was vividly captured in a speech made by Alan Leong (then chairman of the Hong Kong Bar Association, who later became the first candidate to force a contested election for the chief executive of Hong Kong) at the annual ceremony marking the opening of the legal year in 2003.

I want to state once again for the record that the Rule of Law is a fundamental attribute that the Special Administrative Region possesses which stands it apart from any other city on the Mainland. The Rule of Law as an institution in which men and women present in this auditorium have learnt to believe and trust is based on *its staunch respect for rights of individuals, whether it be rights we are born with or rights created by consensual legal documents.*

The Rule of Law is never a means to an end. It insists on due process being observed and demands a justification fully grounded in the law for every act of the Government. The Rule of Law does not and should never yield in the name of alleged expediency and efficiency of government. Regrettably, however, what Hong Kong has witnessed since July 1997 is quite to the contrary. The political will of the Government has prevailed over due process. The law is here to serve political objectives; *the law has been relegated to a means to achieving political ends.* Examples are numerous. The more obvious ones were the hasty introduction of the ministerial accountability system, legislating for civil servants pay cut and the repeated assertion of July 2003 to be the Government's target date for passage of laws implementing Article 23. The Rule of Law is uncompromising: any government that is not just paying lip service to the institution must insist on observing the due process. Fundamental principles of and core values pertaining to the Rule of Law must be strictly adhered to at all times without exception. Short of a state of emergency being declared, such principles and values must prevail over any other consideration whenever there are conflicts between them.[45] (emphasis added)

THE CHALLENGE OF CANTONESE

It was during this historic transition that legal bilingualism was quietly introduced into the legal system of Hong Kong. It came at a moment when the rule of law was elevated to the political ideal of the city, the very ideal around which the public in Hong Kong had been rallying. However, the unintentional consequences of the introduction of Chinese, an act seen by many legal professionals as a merely symbolic gesture to honor the change of political sovereignty, opened up the legal system in ways it had not been throughout the entire colonial period. Above all, the introduction of Chinese meant that for the first time since the inception of colonialism, the common law of Hong Kong, always formalistic and ever so English, could be directly heard and used by the locals in Hong Kong, most of them Cantonese speakers.

The official policy of bilingualism, however halfheartedly, allows litigants who would find it too intimidating to speak before English-speaking judges and counsel to argue in their own vernacular. In the voice of Cantonese, they bring along a different vision of law. By that I mean loose, inchoate beliefs and ideals about what the law is and what the law does that challenge the thin concept of the colonial rule of law— its rules, its hierarchy, and its control. But this vision does not neatly conform to the grand vision embedded in the rights-based rhetoric deployed by the local elites. Instead, the new voice of Cantonese embodies the beliefs and prejudices of the local society. This voice often brings with it visceral encounters between litigants and the court, where disorderly shouts and volcanic emotions often blur the line that separates talk of legal rights from talk of cultural entitlements. Some litigants choose to flagrantly and defiantly talk back to judges and counsel and, in so doing, challenge the established interaction order of the courts. These hot exchanges of an emerging talking crowd, voiced in the "new" language of Cantonese, had been sealed off from the high-walled courtrooms of the English-style common law system in the colonial days. As an indication of the emergence of the new voice, the judiciary of Hong Kong, for the first time in its history, now has to seriously deal with the problem of so-called vexatious litigants, a problem usually faced only by the judiciaries of more litigious societies, in which some court users are said to abuse the legal process. Since 1997, a new type of frequent court users have become a nuisance to many Chinese-speaking judges. They are usually too financially strapped to afford a lawyer. Their cases are mostly considered lacking in legal merit, but the litigants zealously use the court as a forum to voice their moral outcry, often with complete disregard for the court's rules and procedures. Judges for a while attempted to impose the procedural rules of the court on them but often found it difficult to do so, of course, in Cantonese. One of the best-known litigants who launched numerous lawsuits against the rich and powerful in Hong Kong is Ma Kwai Chun. Between 2000 and 2005, Ma was involved in no less than 32 sets of legal proceedings (sometimes with numerous interlocutory applications and appeals in the same set of proceedings) in the High Court. She was eventually ruled a vexatious litigant in 2005, which means that since then she has been forbidden to issue civil proceedings in any court in Hong Kong without permission of a designated judge.

In that judgment, Judge Johnson Lam of the Court of First Instance said that Ma "repeatedly behaved improperly in the course of hearings," "hurled abuses at lawyers acting for the opposite party," and "had no qualm in making wild allegations against judges without proper basis."[46] What Ma said and wrote to the courts was described by the judge as mostly irrelevant to the legal disputes of which she was a party. The judge wrote, "Instead, insofar as they were intelligible, they contained a lot of scandalous remarks and vitriolic attacks on her adversaries, the lawyers acting for them and the judges who had previously decided against her. Lately, she included the Chief Justice as the target of her scurrilous attacks."[47]

For some of the legal professionals I talked to during my fieldwork, the tempest caused by these vexatious litigants who do not know their place is proof enough of the disruptive nature of legal bilingualism. But as a group, these "garbage cases" (Merry 1990) expose the structural gap between formalistic common law and local society after the English veil is lifted. From a different standpoint, litigants can be said to become more vexatious only because their melioristic hopes, fueled by but different from the elite's discourse of rights-based civil society, are dashed by the formalistic legal system of Hong Kong. Their cases have to be treated as vexatious because the existing limited causes of action made available by the formalist system fall short in addressing the situations for which these litigants seek legal redress. Behind the catchy headlines of vexatious litigants and their seemingly frivolous lawsuits lies a more circumspect yet widespread systemic phenomenon: a sharp rise in the percentage of unrepresented litigants since 1997. Since Chinese was accepted as an official language by the courts in Hong Kong, litigants, unaccompanied by lawyers, arrive at the doorstep of the court buildings in profusion. Legal bilingualism in its present form does not close the gap between the common law and the local society; it only exposes it in the most blunt and uncompromising form.

PLAN FOR THE BOOK

This is a book about why legal bilingualism in Hong Kong means far more than the introduction of another language into the legal system. I describe how formalism in the common law of Hong Kong, historically facilitated by the use of English, is not only complicated but also undermined by the arrival of Chinese (Cantonese in oral context and Standard Modern Chinese in written context). My approach is sociological. The empirical focus of my study is not the hard rules and dry concepts that legal formalism is famous for but the *doing* of rules and the *making* of concepts in the everyday institutional practices that give formalism its character, or practices that make formalism formalistic. I work from the ground up by comparing English and Cantonese courtroom interactions, two types of courtrooms that purportedly follow the same rules and deploy the same concepts. So understood, this is also a book about the recalcitrance of the social in the face of the institutional and the role of language in the liminal process of a social coup within what appears to be a rather tenacious institution. In later chapters I describe how Cantonese has become a language of resistance in courtroom interactions. I explain how its appearance has caused upsets and clashes throughout a legal system tooled to operate in Hong Kong–style English. It is my argument that despite its apparently unruly nature, the use of Cantonese opens up a space, albeit highly contested, that allows litigants to articulate, debate, and even manipulate local senses of justice in a formalist legal institution in ways unseen during the colonial era. Legal bilingualism does not simply cause less order and more arguments in the courts of Hong Kong. It has also begun to change the social character of the legal system in Hong Kong. When the formalistic interaction order is challenged, it triggers a change in the moral temperament of the law that such order embodies. I hope that, as the story unfolds, readers can see how the two sets of rules—institutional rules and social rules—are in competition. For obvious reasons, it is easy for social scientists to fall for the dominance of institutional rules. They are often clearly articulated and backed by sanction, and they appear in the official transcripts and public records. But when I look at the working out of legal bilingualism on the ground, the empirical reality challenges theories that assert or take for granted the dominance of institutions. Elaborating the thesis in full detail requires a careful comparison of how the two languages steer the flow of courtroom interactions in different directions, a comparison I make in Chapters 4, 5, and 6. In Chapter 2, I develop the theoretical framework of the book, in particular, the meaning of the term *juridical formalism* and why language plays a pivotal role in its implementation.

In Chapter 3, I present a historical overview of the roles of English and Cantonese in Hong Kong society in general and in the Hong Kong legal system in particular. My purpose is to present, in broad terms, the historical landscape of societal bilingualism, where English and Cantonese occupy different linguistic domains in the society. For a long time English has been regarded as the language of power and prestige, whereas Cantonese, despite its role as the vernacular of the overwhelming majority of the population, has been curiously absent in the colonial legal space. In Chapter 3 I set out the wider sociolinguistic context in which my story of legal bilingualism takes place.

Chapters 4 through 6 are the central part of the book. Together they offer an account of what litigants and professionals do in the languages of Cantonese and English, as circumscribed within an institutionalized locale of bilingual courtrooms. In Chapter 4, I provide a detailed ethnographic account of what I mean by juridical formalism in the English-language courtrooms of Hong Kong. My goal is to lay out the spectrum of linguistic possibilities in English and Cantonese courtrooms by analyzing how different interactional structures are enacted there. My argument is that English and Cantonese courtrooms invoke two visibly different interaction structures for legal processes. In contrast to the highly structured and semantically focused interactions characteristic of English trials, courtroom interactions in Cantonese trials exhibit a more opaque, playful style that borrows features from everyday conversation. I devote Chapter 5 to a sustained discussion of the mechanism of court interpretation through a detailed look at one revealing example. Court interpreters in Hong Kong perform the important role of a linguistic court marshal. Precisely because of the differing pragmatic dynamics between the two languages, the process of interpretation is as much a translation of denotational codes as a repragmatization of raw Cantonese utterances into well-processed English evidence. In Chapter 6, I demonstrate that the interactional order in Cantonese courtrooms is inchoate and flexible; at times it allows litigants to bring the constitutive dispositions of everyday life into the courtroom or to deploy storytelling practices that situate their personal experiences within local contexts.

After that, in Part 3 of the book, I describe how the desire of legal professionals to maintain the formality of Hong Kong common law and their distrust of the Chinese language have fueled a series of institutional adaptations that redefine the practice of legal bilingualism on the ground. The legal institution comes up with its own way of coping with the Cantonese challenge. In Chapter 7 I draw from my in-depth interviews with judges and barristers to explain how the legal professionals' understandings of legal bilingualism are constructed through a stereotypic characterization of what English and Chinese are good at, and in fact, bad at. I describe how linguistic ideologies of English and Cantonese—those complex systems of ideas and interests through which people interpret linguistic practices—rationalize and affect the use of the two languages in the legal realm.

In Chapter 8 the focus is on the institutional responses that the Hong Kong Judiciary derived in the face of the challenges posed by legal bilingualism. Legal professionals justify new practices to delimit the scope of Cantonese by arguing how a linguistic division of labor can bring out the best in English and avoid the worst in Cantonese. Together with Chapter 7, the process underlines the close interactions between language ideology and institutional behaviors.

In the last chapter (Chapter 9), I reprise the core arguments of the book and locate my story of legal bilingualism within the context of the social transition of Hong Kong from colonialism to postcolonialism. I discuss what I see as the dilemma facing postcolonial Hong Kong, emblematized by the challenge of legal bilingualism. English, historically the language of the colonizers, is now also a language of outreach and shelter for Hong Kong, provisionally foreclosing the merging of Hong Kong law into the murky waters of Chinese law. Yet there is a price to be paid for a legal system that continues to use a language that most people in Hong Kong are less familiar with.

TYPES OF CASES OBSERVED

The cases I study are general civil cases, cases that in legal parlance would fall within the loose categories of torts, claims in equity, probate, and trust, and employment and labor claims. Like the English legal system (and unlike the U.S. legal system), Hong Kong has effectively abolished the civil jury, so all the trials I observed were tried by judges. The selection of cases is motivated by the hypothesis that the introduction of Cantonese triggers an alteration in the relation between the common law and Hong Kong society. I therefore focus on cases in which local culture can be potentially on display and normative standards of conduct, such as duty and reasonableness, can be raised in the process. Parties to a civil dispute often come to court with their own ideas of what is right, normal, and fair (Merry 1987: 2063). The research setup is explained in closer detail in the Appendix.

Also, I wish to explain the way I use the term *common law*. The definition of the term is much debated among legal scholars. The simple and common definition of viewing the common law as nonstatutory, that is, law whose authority lies not in any statute but in case precedents, ignores how often the common law is modified by statutes and how statute law is often encrusted with case-law interpretation. In fact, scholars have questioned whether a firm demarcation between the common law and statute law is nowadays empirically warranted (e.g., Atiyah 1985; Edlin 2007; Schauer 1989). I make no attempt to come up with an analytical definition of what the common law is. I use the term instead to refer loosely to the making and interpretation of law in the courts of Hong Kong. In other words, I identify my subject matter of the common law as the process by which ideas, practices, and decisions with institutionally stipulated legal consequences are derived and modified. If anything, the common law is marked by its distinctive adversarial trial process and its prominent day-in-court justice (see Chapter 2). Thus my usage of the term covers areas that legal scholars may exclude from their definition of the common law, such as statutory interpretation or equity.

BEFORE WE CONTINUE

Finally, a couple of disclaimers. There is a venerable tradition in the sociology of law and in the legal realist tradition of uncovering a list of salient outside factors that affect and in some cases even determine the outcome of a legal trial. This book is not a study within that tradition. Works assessing how institutional features of a legal system affect outcomes have their own goals and benefits. My main concern is the social processes by which negotiations proceed, not the outcomes. Of course, what happens to the dynamics of the processes in question has important implications for the institution as a whole. I return to this question in Chapter 9. Second, this book is not a study that pursues an argument of linguistic relativism. The comparative study of Cantonese and English courtrooms does not ask the question of whether English or Cantonese is adequate as *a medium of representation*, an interesting but different question. My concern and my approach to address that concern are sociological. The focus of my study is not language per se but, to borrow a phrase from Jürgen Habermas (1996: 4), "the very facticity of linguistically structured forms of life" in the institution of Hong Kong's bilingual common law. Other studies in the vein of the so-called linguistic relativistic thesis have been conducted, some even in the context of Hong Kong, most notably the controversial study of Alfred Bloom (1981).[48] I do not consider myself qualified to judge the merits or demerits of this version of semantic determinism. Suffice it to say that in light of the linguistic turn in contemporary philosophy and the social sciences (in some quarters at least), it is more interesting, to me at least, to take the two languages in question as two different social tools whose utility can be understood only in the context of performing certain activities, or, to invoke the famous Wittgensteinian metaphor, in the playing of games, language games to be exact.

CHAPTER 2

Juridical Formalism and the
Mechanism of Legal Rearticulation

S O F A R, I have talked glibly of formalism. I now want to come up with a more precise definition of the term. Among legal philosophers, the term *formalism* is one of those sticky labels, such as *liberal* in American politics, or *functionalist* nowadays in sociology—terms that are used only by people who are critics of them (cf. Sebok 1998: 57; Stone 2002). Historically, in American jurisprudence at least, formalism is frequently associated with a traditional black letter approach to the study of law; representative here is the work of Christopher Langdell, who became the first dean of Harvard Law School in 1870. The purpose of law, according to Langdell, is to develop a formal scheme within which every conceivable social act can be placed. It is for this reason that critics of formalism— legal realists, for example—describe Langdell as promoting a version of conceptual formalism that is determinate, systematic, and autonomous (cf. Grey 1983, 1999; Llewellyn 1960a). More recently, jurists of different philosophical inclinations have defined formalism in other ways, including "anti-consequential morality in law," "immanent moral rationality," "apurposive rule-following," "meaning-based gaplessness," "deductivism," and "socially unresponsive decision-making"—in short, a jumbled collection of near synonyms with subtle but obscure distinctions, much of which stems from whether one understands formalism as a product of the traditions of natural law or as positive law (cf. Kennedy 2001; Pildes 1999; Stone 2002; Weinrib 1988).[1]

I am going to gloss over these differences here. For our purposes, I want to try another tack to define formalism, one pioneered by Max Weber in his monumental *Economy and Society*. Weber's account remains one of the most daring and influential attempts to ground the phenomenon of modern law as a social enterprise. How does Weber understand formalism? Put simply, formalism is taken as an institutional form in which its character, its raison d'être, is intrinsic to its form rather than its content.

Weber's concept of formalism has two related but analytically distinct dimensions. First, much akin to the ways in which legal philosophers approach formalism, Weber uses the term to refer to the rule-based nature of legal order. The most rational legal system is characterized by the "integration of all analytically derived legal propositions in such a way as to constitute a logically clear, internally consistent, and, at least in theory, gapless system of rules, under which, it is implied, all conceivable fact situations must be capable of being logically subsumed" (Weber 1978: 656). Law is most predictable when it is made up of highly abstract rules that are the "logical generalization of abstract interpretations of meaning" (Weber 1978: 657). Second, and this is an aspect that shows Weber's leaning toward the so-called neo-Kantian tradition, Weber holds that our perception of the external world is structured by certain cognitive categories internal to the mind of an observer. Weber believes that a formal system must have the ability to create a world of its own, or what some scholars call a sense of self-referentiality. A legal order is said to be formal-rational only when its rules can be internally interpreted with reference to other rules of the system (i.e., the criteria for decisions are intrinsic to the legal system itself) and when the rules are logically related to each other. Formality in this sense goes beyond a reference to the systematic and generalizable character of a legal system. It points to the tendency to closure that formal law often exhibits. According to Weber, it is only when formality in this sense is achieved that the law can shield itself from the influences of "a featureless conglomeration of ethical and legal duties" (Weber 1978: 810). Weber's vision of modern law is thoroughly *positivistic*, a term in modern jurisprudence that suggests that morality and legality are independent of each other (cf. Kronman 1983; Mommsen 1984).

Modern legal rationality, according to Weber, is a peculiar kind of rationality, one not based on its substantive content but instead on its *process* and *form*. This *formal* rationality, or legal rationalization, as Weber sometimes called it, is at once naked and introspective. It is the most naked form of rationalization because modern law makes no pretense about being merely a set of rules with relatively arbitrary historical origins (Weber 1978: 217). A formalism built on a system of rules is—in contrast to the "magically conditioned formalism" that Weber calls primitive law—a thoroughly secular phenomenon. Legal formalism, with its rejection of a substantive rationality that might still refer to external values or ideals, lays bare its own artificiality. For this reason, Weber himself acknowledged that legal legitimation in the form of positive law is hardly as compelling as the historically earlier system of natural law.[2] Yet legal rationalization is introspective as well. It is an inward-turning rationality; it is rationalization for the sake of rationalization, the ultimate triumph of form over content, means over ends. Thus legitimacy is not to be grounded in the substantive content of law, which can be entirely determined by historical contingencies, but instead in the form of law, which guarantees its systematicity and predictability. Weber would go so far as to say that virtually "any law" can be passed so long as it is formal-rational (Weber 1978: 217).[3] As part of his pessimistic prognosis for modernity, Weber's view on legal rationalization is akin to an existentialist response to the disappearance of the transcendental, a coming to terms with the disenchantment of the world. In such a disenchanted world, the modern rule of law has drifted further and further from the Enlightenment's belief in universal natural law. For Weber, legal legitimacy has become nothing more than a self-referential proclamation: "Law is law."

Weber's approach presages what sociologists today would call an institutionalist approach to the problem. Weber suggests that any legal system that relies on its procedures to determine its outcome is formal. One can find formality in a system of trials by force or by combat or even by luck, so long as there are formal procedures (usually in the form of conventionalized rituals) to incorporate the element of luck into the trial. Numerous historical forms of trial by ordeal—ordeal by fire, ordeal by water, ordeal by poison—manifested formality in their own ways, albeit an irrational formality (cf. Tewksbury 1967). Hence ancient oracular adjudication, according to Weber, was a form of "magically conditioned" formalism (Weber 1978: 882). In magical formalism the procedures are formal only in a superficial way, and much of the outcome is still left to chance. Consider the colorful example of the Azande provided by anthropologists (e.g., Evans-Pritchard 1976). The oracle is carried out by feeding chickens a controlled dose of a special poison by an expert at the so-called *benge* ritual, in which two chickens must die to prove that the suspect is guilty as charged. Such a ritualized form of casting the dice twice is to-tally arbitrary (of course, casting dice itself can be a highly ritualized act, as is the case with some high rollers playing craps in Las Vegas. They go through elaborate rituals of "prepping the dice"—one starts with blow-ing on the dice, then a religious standing of the dice with the six facing up, or down, then a deliberate, measured shake before rolling it off one's fingertips, all in psychological slow motion), but the practice serves to justify an arbitrary outcome by ritualizing the procedure against the back-drop of a world of deities and spirits. Elaborate ritual aside, however, the outcome remains arbitrary, at least according to Weber.

What is unique about the process of legal rationalization is its con-joining of *form* and *content*. Legal rationalization can thus be interpreted as a process in which the form *becomes* the embodiment of content. It is only as legal procedure becomes more formal that the foundations of law become more abstract and universal (Schluchter 1981: 82–138). Legal formalism is achieved when the content of law is legitimated through its procedures alone (without the intervention of extralegal entities such as spirits or demons or without a consideration of extralegal values such as good and evil).

Thus it is not difficult to understand the apparently counterintuitive elective affinity between formalism and colonialism and to see why for-malism provided such a fitting institutional form, in normal times at least, for governance during the heyday of British colonialism. To wit, formalism is a form of reasoning or justification in which, as critical legal scholar Roberto Unger puts it, "the opened disputes about the basic terms of so-cial life, disputes that people call ideological, philosophical, or visionary," are already ruled out of the question (Unger 1983: 564). Given the reality of colonialism as a form of domination (the British were quite open that the so-called cession of Hong Kong was for the commercial interests of Britain), it would be hard to appeal to theories of natural law, theories that assert morality as the ground of law, for ultimate legitimacy. Formalism in the colonial context offers a consolatory form of legitimacy to the ruled; although the colonized could not decide for themselves their own rules of governance, they at least could be assured that rules, once declared, would be followed. In return, the colonized had a duty to obey the law.

In the seventeenth and eighteenth centuries, British colonialism was not considered an illegitimate form of conquest in Europe; instead, colonialism was marketed as a form of civilizing mission, pitted against the repression and disorderliness of Oriental despotism. Formalism, with its adherence to rules and procedures, distinguishes enlightened British governance from the barbaric varieties it replaced. Nasser Hussain examined the concept of law in the context of colonial India and had this to say:

Legal procedure was to be the ultimate answer to the question of what it meant to bring law to India. It was to be the form of a civilized despotism, for it would both declare to subjects that their identity, their offenses, their grievances, all began and ended in the authority of the law, and would reflect the morality of publicity and process lacking in the authority of a native despotism. Procedure was not substance but spirit, and in its exactitude it covered all law, English and Indian, statutory or customary, insisting that no authority preceded law, or more specifically, the workings of law, and that these workings created and reflected their own authority. (Hussain 2003: 65).

The historical obsession with procedural rules in colonial common law systems reveals a glaring problem in Weber's treatment of the English common law. Admittedly, the common law system has undergone a lot of changes since Weber wrote *Economy and Society*, and what Weber once chided as irrational has been subsequently criticized by legal realists for being exactly the opposite—too abstract, too formal, too rigid, too lifeless. But the biggest reason that Weber underestimated the rational element of the common law is that he overlooked the elements of procedural formality in the common law.[4] In his own substantive sociohistorical works, Weber approached legal formalism by examining the coherence of legal concepts and rules at the systemic level rather than by looking into *institutional procedures and operations* at the level of practice.[5] This explained why Weber failed to detect the formal-rational elements in the common law. As Arthur Stinchcombe (2001: 184) rightly observes, one cannot read even a few pages of *Wigmore on Evidence* and believe that Anglo-American law is unrationalized in this aspect. The rise of complex formality in the rules of evidence and other pretrial procedures has much to do with the centrality of the jury trial (one of the key features in the common law that Weber identified as irrational!) in Anglo-American common law. This is what comparative lawyers call the phenomenon of the concentration of trials in the common law system—that is, a host of procedures are institutionalized in preparation for the singular, irreversible event known as the trial. This form of day-in-court justice differs from proceedings in the civil law system, which are more episodic and less concentrated. Thus a precise formulation of the relevant issues is seen as a necessary preparation to pleading; discovery (advance information about the opponent's witnesses and evidence) and other pretrial procedures are given the closest attention (cf. Damaska 1997; Merryman 1985; Zweigert and Kötz 1998). In a jury trial, evidence must be filtered through the use of careful rules to prevent the lay jury from being misled. Hence the rules of evidence, as pointed out by some legal scholars, are motivated by a distrust of juries as reliable triers of facts (R. J. Allen and Pardo 2003a). In the civil law system, on the other hand, there is no elaborate law of evidence because professional judges are believed to be sophisticated enough to remain untainted by anything they hear (Zweigert and Kötz 1998: 274–275).

Contrary to Weber's prognosis, one can find formal-rational elements in the analogical reasoning of the common law. Despite its suspicion toward grand principles, the common law in practice achieves a formal-rational legitimacy through a process of linguistic formalization—that is, the cumulative historical development of legal argots and terms of art that eventually allowed the case law method to develop a self-referential system of formal rationality. It is for this reason that the meaning of common law terms has to be specially stipulated, particularly those terms of art that troped homonymically on everyday terms. An obvious example here would be the concept of legal person, which does not coincide with our common understanding of a natural person but refers to the status of personhood in law. Other examples would be the legal concepts of consideration, trespass, or recklessness. These terms have specialized meanings in law that are not captured in common usage. Anthropologist Lawrence Rosen suggests that one only has to try to draw up one's own will and then give it to a lawyer for correction to have a taste of the "wonders of legal language"—you can "transform 'children' into 'the issue of my body' or watch our highest courts comparing generations of cases in order to decide if the legislature meant to include a capon as a chicken or a biplane as a vehicle" (Rosen 1989: 39).

Such linguistic transfiguration enforced by various legal terms of art must be seen as part and parcel of the process of transforming an everyday problem into a legal problem in the process of adjudication. Law adjudicates by first converting everyday disputes into its own terms (Felstiner et al. 1980). This mechanism of creating a text analyzable by the expertise of a particular profession is what Andrew Abbott (1988) termed "the cultural machinery of jurisdiction." It is through this machinery that an everyday task is construed as a known "professional problem" through which claims to classify a problem (diagnosis), to reason about it (inference), and to take action on it (treatment) are legitimized.

My favorite example here is a well-known English trust case known as *Paul v. Constance.*[6] It started out as a simple probate case. Mr. Constance died without a will. He was not a wealthy man. His estate consisted mainly of a bank account with a balance of about £1,000 (this was in the 1970s). His surviving wife, Mrs. Constance, from whom he separated in the last nine years of his life, took out letters of administration of his estate. She also closed the bank account. Until his death, the man had been living with another woman, Mrs. Paul. Mrs. Paul wanted a share of her lover's estate. The deposit account that later became the core of the man's estate was opened under Mr. Constance's sole name. But Mr. Constance and Mrs. Paul played bingo together and deposited some of the money they won from the game into that account. On more than one occasion, Mr. Constance told Mrs. Paul, "This money is as much yours as mine." When taken to court, this dispute between the man's separated wife and his lover was transformed into a question at the core of trust law—the question of the formality requirement of an express trust. The English Appeal Court judge found for Mrs. Paul. He ruled that the statement "This money is as much yours as mine" is sufficient to constitute a declaration of trust. This example illustrates nicely the transformative power of the common law process. Who would have thought the meaning of an everyday utterance—"This money is as much yours as mine"—would become the subject of the formality requirement of an express trust?

DEFINING JURIDICAL FORMALISM

For the reasons stated, I am not investigating the thick encrustations of concepts and principles that concerned Weber's discussion of legal formalism. The subject matter here is the practices of juridical formalism, that is, the courtroom practices that transform everyday disputes into legal problems. I should point out that the term *juridical formalism* also appears in *Economy and Society*, where Weber famously said that "[juridical] formalism enables the legal system to operate like a technically rational machine" (1978: 811). My appropriation of the term here, however, is to signify an examination of formalism from the ground up. When Weber wrote that formal rationality within the law requires that "in both substantive and procedural matters, only unambiguous general characteristics of the *facts of the case* are taken into account" (1978: 656–657; emphasis added), he overlooked the construed nature of the facts of the case in the first place. The so-called facts of the case are made unambiguous in the practice of formalism. The present study takes what was presupposed by Weber as problematic. My empirical focus is a comparison of how facts resistant or amenable to legal analysis are produced through the differing courtroom interactions in the English and Cantonese courtrooms in Hong Kong. This point is picked up by Pierre Bourdieu when he describes the force of law as the power to *retranslate* a social controversy "as the Romans said, to *ponere causam* (to 'put' the case), that is to institute the controversy as a lawsuit, as a juridical problem that can become the object of juridically regulated debate" (Bourdieu 1987: 831–832).

Therefore, to see how legal rationality is worked out in a common law system, we must look at the ways that disputes are adjudicated through the making and remaking of facts in the courtroom. Fact, a concept as familiar as it is vaguely defined, first acquired its character as the secular, institutional approximation of truth in the English courts (B. J. Shapiro 1983, 2000). In the postcolonial context of Hong Kong, the fundamental difference between the English and Cantonese courtrooms within the bilingual common law in Hong Kong is best investigated by looking at *what* kind of facts are generated and at *how* these facts are generated in the process. If one simply sees the contrast between the English and the Cantonese courtrooms as a mere difference in atmosphere, then the problem is trivialized. Instead, I approach the common law trial as a highly institutionalized process of textualization or entextualization (cf. Ewick and Silbey 1998; Scheppele 1991; see also Chapter 3). What juridical formalism aims to create is a specific juridical or legal text, a text that sees the world from a thoroughly legal point of view. Of course, in the most straightforward sense, the legal process physically produces a high volume of texts. An inordinate amount of human and financial resources have been deployed to produce texts of different tangible forms: in the drafting of writs and affidavits, in the production of trial transcripts, and in the delivery of judgments, not to mention the production of a virtual infinity of case reports that become the rubric of the common law. But there is a more abstract notion of text that is central to the legal process. Here, I use the term *legal text* to refer to the rearticulation of reality through an interlocking grid of facts and law in the adversarial trial context. As we saw in the example of *Paul v. Constance*, this is a process in which the peculiarities of any instance of a unique human conflict are gradually broken down and subsumed into an identifiable fact-law nexus in such a way that law and facts constantly refer back to each other. This ongoing process of textualization becomes most evident when it gets to appellate courts; as Kim Scheppele points out, appellate judges rarely see the parties to the lawsuit and have only a written record, that is, the legal text, to consult (1991: 44). So understood, the legal process is a process that sets out to do two things at once: It abstracts a dispute away from its immediate context, and it relocates it within the institutional setting of law.

I question the common but misleading distinction between fact and law—that is, witnesses testify about facts and lawyers and judges debate and apply the law after the fact. Such a dichotomy is presupposed, for example, in the popular phrase "thinking like a lawyer"—itself a formulaic expression that refers to a methodical way of thinking. The method of a thinking lawyer is first to clarify what the evidence is and then to apply the relevant legal principles. But as legal historians and comparative legal scholars point out, the fact-law distinction, easy to state but hard to apply, is a "relatively novel concern" in Western legal systems (Damaska 1997: 26; Langbein 2003: 30). Scholars of evidence generally agree that the distinction is fragile at best (e.g., see Twining 1997). That the distinction is elusive is admitted by, of all institutions, the Supreme Court of the United States.[7] What this dichotomy fails to acknowledge is how the actual reasoning process of the common law intertwines law and fact. One cannot really break down a trial sensibly into terms such as "Trial A is 40 percent law and 60 percent facts."

In practice, there is always that back-and-forth mutual referencing between law and fact in the analogical reasoning process of the common law (hence I used the term *fact-law nexus*), a process such that, in the vivid and famous description of Edward Levi, "the classification changes as the classification is made" (Levi 1949: 3). Facts give law an anchorage that is essential for them to be rendered thinkable. This is particularly so in common law systems, a legal tradition known for its aversion to abstract conceptual reasoning. In the common law, it is only through the selection and stringing together of what lawyers call material facts that law is made flesh in a case. In the practical terms of trial advocacy, lawyers must always come up with their own fact theory in the course of addressing, or better yet, constituting, a legal issue (cf. Murray 1995). The legal and the factual are inextricably interpenetrated. As Justice Oliver Wendell Holmes put it, "General propositions do not decide concrete cases."[8] Jurist H. L. A. Hart famously suggested that definitions of law are open-textured, allowing "at the point of actual application, a fresh choice between open alternatives" (1961: 123).

Legal facts are not facts "out there" in any objectivist sense of the term. Legal facts do not present to us a realm of material objects or discernible events. I am not suggesting that one cannot find any referent in a reality outside law. That the concept of fact in law is complex and multifarious is commonplace among legal scholars of evidence and proof. American legal philosopher Wesley Newcombe Hohfeld, known for his famous typology of rights, also made the influential distinction between "evidential" and "constitutive" facts. According to Hohfeld (1923), facts can be distinguished into at least two types in the legal context: evidential and constitutive. An evidential fact is one that, on being ascertained, affords some logical, albeit nonconclusive, basis for inferring some other facts. *Other* facts that judges and lawyers are interested in are labeled by

Hohfeld as constitutive facts, or what lawyers simply call facts in issue. It is the determination of constitutive facts that clearly shows that facts can never be simply equated to what happened in a strictly positivistic sense. As legal scholars Paul Roberts and Adrian Zuckerman point out in their book on evidence (2004), practical procedures of the finding of constitutive fact often involve the entanglement of factual inference *and* juridical classification (p. 140)—for example, when a judge or jury has to decide whether the accused has inflicted grievous bodily harm[9] or has committed an act that is sufficiently proximate to the commission of an offense for it to constitute a criminal attempt. Whether grievous bodily harm was inflicted or not is a factual finding, but what qualifies as grievous, bodily, and harm is certainly legally constructed. Other examples of constitutive facts in noncriminal settings involve the meanings of offer, acceptance, and trespass; the definition of activities such as trade, insulting behavior; and the identification of immoral purposes and so on (Abimbola 2002; R. J. Allen and Pardo 2003a, 2003b; Roberts and Zuckerman 2004). The implication of these examples is clear. Legal facts are not something that can be defined ostensively by pointing to some empirical object. Instead, they are events, actions, or states of affairs or minds that are not just interpreted through but also construed by categories created in law. Legal facts are found through a process of triangulated referencing, as summarized by a formula put forward by Bruno Latour: "A is an instance of B *as it is defined by* article C" (Latour 2004: 104; emphasis in the original).

Although Hohfeld's distinction between constitutive and evidential facts tends to overlook the intimate linkage between the two (it still, in its own way, reproduces the old dichotomy of law and fact) and also the inferred and construed quality found even in evidential facts, it does suggest that what lawyers and courts commonly refer to as the questions of fact are far from the meaning of self-evident truth in ordinary talk. Constitutive facts are a cocktail made up of fact, value judgment, and law. For example, in English criminal law, a specific test (the Andrews/Adomako test) is used to determine the scope of gross negligence in gross negligence manslaughter. Similarly there is the Feely/Ghosh test for dishonesty to determine dishonesty in theft and related offenses. In the Andrews/Adomako test the jury is invited to determine whether the accused's conduct fell so far below the standard of reasonable care to be expected of a person in the accused's situation that criminal punishment is warranted. In the Feely/Ghosh test the jury must determine whether the accused realized that his conduct was dishonest according to the standards of ordinary decent people (Roberts and Zuckerman 2004). Similar tests also exist in the U.S. legal system. It is clear from these examples that questions of this type, although conventionally labeled factual questions by lawyers, are not factual questions as such. They involve the exercise of legally stipulated normative evaluations in a regulated manner. To ask a jury or a judge to determine whether or not a person is grossly negligent or whether or not a person is dishonest is hence quite different from, say, asking them to decide whether a defendant accused of murder was present at the scene of the crime at the material time. The factual questions that count in the common law are not merely factual questions in the sense that they are only concerned with the truth of past events; they are also questions that adjudicate the consequences of the facts deemed relevant by law. And there are many factual questions that do not count before the law. For example, the fact that I was in a bad mood the other day may well be the reason that I drove over the speed limit on the freeway; by my own common sense, my bad mood *caused* me to drive over the speed limit. But bad mood is irrelevant to the factual question of whether I was negligent or not, and it definitely has no relevancy at all in addressing the issue of *legal causation* in negligence, which is a totally different matter.

Despite their obvious construed character, it is not uncommon for lawyers and courts to treat legal facts as plain, pristine, and self-evident, as vividly captured by the common phrase "Just the facts!" The discursive conflation of legal facts with conventional facts has the effect of naturalizing legal reasoning; it wipes out the institutional footprints of the common law system by equating legal reasoning with commonsensical and logical thinking. Such equation is most obvious in the classic writings of Thayer (1898). But Thayer's commonsense approach was countered by another famous jurist in evidence: John Henry Wigmore (1923). Wigmore argued that the concept of relevance in law is a quality determined not simply by logic and common sense but also by law. All lawyers would agree that not everything said or done qualifies as evidence and that not every piece of evidence presented can be considered relevant for the purpose of putting together the facts of a case. But it is Wigmore who suggests that relevance in law is determined not simply by common sense and logic but also by the reflexive rules of law themselves. The so-called common law maxim *res ipsa loquitur* (the thing speaks for itself) is never as straightforward as the literal meaning of the doctrine suggests.[10] A kitchen-sink defense is thus as useless for lawyers as a kitchen-sink regression is to sociologists.

HOW WE DO LAW WITH LANGUAGES

To get a fresh look at how legal facts are construed, to see how a fact-law nexus amenable to legal analysis is readily produced, we need to look into how juridical formalism actually works. We need to study the institutionalized linguistic practices that guide and discipline interactions in the courtroom. Sociologists, anthropologists, and others studying legal language have developed a growing literature on the constitutive role of language in courtrooms. The pioneering works by John Conley and William O'Barr (1990, 2005) and Susan Philips (1992, 1998) as well as the more recent works by Gregory Matoesian (2001), Elizabeth Mertz (2007), and Susan Hirsch (1998) have demonstrated in different ways that legal language is no mere conduit. Instead, language itself is pivotal in shaping how conflicts are framed and resolved, how equality and justice are interpreted and delivered, and how social identities are constituted and negotiated in modern legal institutions. It is a central theme in the works of these scholars that how language is used, and how some people are able to use language in some ways, is one of the most subtle but enduring ways through which social inequalities persist. As Elizabeth Mertz points out, legal language and discourse together constitute a contested terrain where individual strategic actions are played on an unleveled field.

Such a framework posits linguistic practices in court as the main vehicle through which the law is imagined, negotiated, and deployed. Other anthropologists and sociologists have also studied the challenges facing litigants in the linguistically alienating courtroom (Atkinson and Drew 1979; Bennett and Feldman 1981; Berk-Seligson 1990; Conley and O'Barr 1990, 2005; Matoesian 2001; Richland 2005; Trinch 2003).

Sometimes the language is alienating even though litigants are familiar with it. As Conley and O'Barr (1990) demonstrate in their work, English speakers who do not couch their narratives in terms of rules and principles are judged negatively as narrators by officials in small claims courts in the United States. Shonna Trinch, for example, in her recent work about Latinas' narratives of domestic abuse, demonstrates how the nonstandard narrative forms used by Latinas in protective order interviews become a cause for prejudice in the U.S. legal system.

The present study of Hong Kong's bilingual courtrooms offers an interesting site for parochializing the contrast between legal talk and everyday talk that sometimes came prepackaged in earlier sociolegal works. The unique bilingual setting allows us to see how carefully orchestrated institutional practices negotiate the boundary that separates legal talk from everyday talk; and the efficacy of these practices is in turn enabled or undermined by the languages through which the speeches are uttered. The bilingual setting shows why language is a socially enduring form. At root, this study is about how the contrasting discursive possibilities made available by the two languages can leave their marks even on the most restrictive institutional environment. It refers to the socially creative capabilities of language practices, how the shift from one language to another in a bi- or multilingual setting points to, brings about, or indexes new social context hitherto rendered invisible inside an institution (Mertz 1992, 1994a; Silverstein 1993, 1998).

The emphasis on linguistic practices is also meant to distinguish my approach from different variants of linguistic determinism, theories that argue in one way or another for a direct correlation between language structure and human cognition, theories that suggest implicitly or explicitly that not all languages are equal and that the peculiar features of our native tongue determine the way we speak and think. I point this out because linguistic relativism is a surprisingly popular explanation subscribed to by legal professionals in Hong Kong. My way of approaching linguistic relativism is to turn it around into an object of study; I want to study how discourses on the nature of languages, or expressions of linguistic ideology, justify the ways that people use languages (Duranti 1994; Gal 1998; Silverstein 1998; Woolard 1998). As we will see, it is indeed quite common for bilingual legal professionals in Hong Kong to view Cantonese as a deficient language, an alternative that is inferior to English. Many lawyers and judges in Hong Kong say they have difficulties articulating legal concepts in Cantonese because Cantonese is not a precise language to begin with. They say that it is much easier to express legal argots, technical terms, and established words and phrases in English (despite the fact that most of these expressions are in Latin or French) than to translate them into Cantonese. It is alluringly easy for counsel to fixate on individual words or expressions, particularly so in the case of legal language, given its exotic splendors and mellifluous pomposity. Whatever the convenience of using English in law is, it has nothing to do with the alleged inferiority of Cantonese. After all, government officials before and after 1997 derived as many neologisms as necessary to accommodate the common law, to root the common law in the Chinese language (Hong Kong Special Administrative Region Government, Department of Justice 1999: 41). The use of neologisms is the linguistic equivalent of a chartered flight. By using newly coined terms in Chinese to denote common law terms such as equity or tort, not to mention more technical legal terms such as hereditament, fee simple, or encumbrance (D. Tse 1996), it was believed that the Englishness of the common law could be preserved in the linguistic territory of Chinese. As I show, the problem facing legal bilingualism is not that one can only say "equity" or "encumbrance" (more precisely, to convey the concept denoted by the token words of "equity" and "encumbrance") in English or only *mens rea* or *de bene esse* in Latin but that no equivalent terms can be found in Chinese. The problem, at once more practical and more social, is that most counsel and judges, for reasons to be explained, do not talk law in Chinese.

An adequate account of juridical formalism from a sociolinguistic perspective must resist any direct and simple correlation between language and society or accounts that prefer an immediate initiation into sociological theorizing to the grounded study of the mechanics of juridical formalism through a study of the language practices endorsed. What is required here is a wholesale reorientation of our understanding of language. In the words of pragmatist philosopher Richard Rorty, it is important to take language not so much as a medium for representation but as tools with which we do things in the world (Rorty 1989). In a typical common law trial, participants engage in a host of distinct language activities from gavel to gavel. They *do* many things with language. Each step in the trial is made up of palpably distinct forms of linguistic activities. Language is used to recount and describe, to probe and examine, to deliberate and analyze, to persuade and mitigate, and, above all, to pronounce and declare. The addition of Cantonese adds a new wrinkle. The focus here is not so much to identify a certain style or way of speaking in Cantonese and to contrast it with English. Instead, of central concern to my comparative analysis is the efficacy of the speech act of statement making in the linguistic environments of English and Cantonese, an act integral to the making of legal facts in common law trials. As noted, the carving out of facts amenable to legal analysis is an integral part of juridical formalism. It is one of its most crucial "practical accomplishments," to borrow a description used by ethnomethodologists (cf. Zimmerman 1974). The finding of facts is in many ways the end point of a long and complex process in which evidence is first adduced and admitted (or sometimes excluded) and then examined and reexamined. A fact is something that a judge or jury finds to be true, which in principle may or may not be consistent with the evidence presented (Vandevelde 1996: 57–63).

But if the generation of legal facts is the consequence of prescribed speech acts in court, then the nature of the facts constituted is bound to be transformed by the copresence of other speech acts in Cantonese. The use of Cantonese brings about new practices that have not been considered in the standard repertoire of a trial but that have their roots in the everyday life of Hong Kong. To invoke Wittgenstein's famous notion of language game, there are different games with different rules when one switches from one language to another within the same system. My goal is to show how the emerging linguistic acts performed by litigants in Cantonese, on top of and sometimes even as a replacement for the official prescribed act of statement making, confound the nature of the facts generated in the same institution.

At this point, I want to anticipate my argument about the consequences of doing different things in the two courtrooms. In later chapters I show that, although facts established in English courtrooms are predominantly legal, facts emerging in Cantonese courtrooms are more noticeably moral. In the English courtroom facts are construed in such a way that they become able to be processed by the machinery of juridical formalism. In the Cantonese courtroom, however, one can find chunks of undigested facts, not so much in the sense that they are truer but more in the sense that they remain alien to the machinery of rearticulation that is central to the generation of legal facts. These are facts that have been rendered significant in terms of the mundane logic of everyday life, which is allowed to slip into the institutional arena through the back door of Cantonese.[11] The two types of facts are ideal-typically defined. The English courtrooms in Hong Kong are not altogether legal fact courtrooms; and the Cantonese courtrooms in Hong Kong are not altogether moral fact courtrooms. But surely evidence in Cantonese courtrooms carries more of the features of moral fact than its English counterpart does. These concepts are therefore derived to make visible and salient the features of the two types of courtrooms that distinguish their social characters.

CHAPTER 3

The Practices of English and Cantonese in Colonial Hong Kong

T HE SOCIAL USE of English and Cantonese in Hong Kong has historically been bifurcated to such an extent that the two languages
constitute two distinct linguistic habituses (Bourdieu 1977, 1991). In this
chapter I present a historical outline of this social usage, thus setting the
stage for my later discussion of legal language from a social and historical perspective in subsequent chapters of the book. The prior histories of
English and Cantonese form the backdrop to the tension of legal bilingualism that I return to in the next few chapters.

Pierre Bourdieu defines a habitus as "a universalizing mediation which
causes an individual agent's practices, without either explicit reason or
signifying intent, to be nonetheless 'sensible' and 'reasonable'" (1977: 79).
A habitus is a learned yet not entirely reflexive system of dispositions.
For the present purpose, linguistic habitus can be understood as an interrelated group of speech domains. The linguistic concept of speech domain attempts to designate "major clusters of interaction situations that
occur in particular multilingual settings," and such domains are deeply
related to "widespread socio-cultural norms and expectations" (Fishman
1965 [2000]: 93). The colonial governance of Hong Kong depended on a
linguistic distinction marked by the English-Cantonese code boundary;
the consequence was a social diglossia that compartmentalized the use
of these languages into different domains, which coalesced into English
and Cantonese habituses. Each habitus displays its own structure of relations among the actors involved in the interactions (e.g., trash talking
between two players during a soccer game, a government official taking
questions from politicians in a public forum, an academic offering an
analysis at a conference panel). It promotes different types of encounters, in Goffman's sense of the word, that exhibit a different "sanctioned
orderliness arising from obligations fulfilled and expectations realized"
(Goffman 1961: 19).[1]

This difference between the sensibilities in the uses of English and Cantonese in Hong Kong is the result of an enduring institutional-*cum*-social segregation of language uses that began in the colonial period and continues to the present day. A linguistic habitus is the result of the dialectical interactions between a language and its specific contexts of use. Each habitus lays out its own principles for the generation and structuring of linguistic practices. Each defines commonsense rules that come to be taken for granted.

ENGLISH AND CHINESE IN COLONIAL HONG KONG

Despite its history as a British colony for more than 150 years, Hong Kong was for much of this time a predominantly monolingual society, or more precisely, a bi-monolingual society. The emergence of English-Cantonese bilingualism is a relatively recent phenomenon (Lord 1987). For much of the colonial era, the linguistic situation in Hong Kong can be described as a "diglossia without bilingualism" (Ferguson 1959; Fishman 1972). In the context of colonial Hong Kong, this description refers, first, to the fact that the high variety (English) was primarily used in writing and formal speech events and that the low variety (Cantonese) was used in casual conversation; and second, to the parallel existence of two monolingual communities (a large local Cantonese community that used the low variety most of the time and a small but powerful English community that used only the high variety), with in between the two groups, a small group of bilingual "linguistic middlemen" who functioned as mediators (Luke and Richards 1982; cf. Fishman 1980). It has been only recently, when English began to assume a role that went beyond the notion of elite language among the Cantonese-speaking population, that patterns of bilingualism emerged.

How, then, can one characterize the current situation of bilingualism in Hong Kong? To begin with, bilingualism in Hong Kong might be described as a case of what linguists call social bilingualism. Cantonese and English each perform different and compartmentalized functions in the society. As with other cases of social bilingualism, the functions and roles of English and Cantonese in Hong Kong are asymmetric. Cantonese clearly assumes the role of the vernacular language for the overwhelming majority of the population. The proportion of Cantonese native speakers by far outweighs the proportion of English native speakers (90.8 percent versus 2.8 percent according to the 2006 by-census [Hong Kong Special Administrative Region Government, Census and Statistics Department 2007: 38]). English, on the other hand, has long been perceived by the public as the language of power and success (Y. S. Cheung 1984; Pierson 1998), bringing tremendous social and instrumental advantages to its users (Axler et al. 1998; Pennington and Yue 1994).

Furthermore, bilingualism in Hong Kong is asymmetric with respect to the pattern of language acquisition among those who speak both languages; that is, people who are bilingual in Hong Kong predominantly acquire Chinese as their primary language first before learning English at school. Historically, the British population in Hong Kong, with the exception of some civil servants whose jobs required interaction with the locals, had little need or motivation to pick up Cantonese. They self-consciously identified themselves as upper class, in the English sense of the term (Lethbridge 1978). Because the population of Cantonese-speaking locals clearly outnumbers the English-speaking population in Hong Kong, bilingualism is predominantly practiced among those for whom Cantonese is the first language and English the second acquired language.[2]

In what follows, I attempt to offer a preliminary picture of Hong Kong's social bilingualism by looking at the following four areas: (1) the social groups of Cantonese and English speakers, (2) the linguistic domains of the two languages, (3) common speech styles, and (4) local metalinguistic beliefs about the two languages. Altogether they form a picture that should allow us to see the contrast between the two linguistic habituses.

The Social Demography of English-Language Speakers in Hong Kong

It is often said that Hong Kong has never been a settler colony. The longtime absence of a sizable local population of native English speakers meant that it was never the priority of the colonial government to make English a mass language, let alone the lingua franca of the colony. As recently as the 1960s, Hong Kong was still operating within a system of elite bilingualism, in which only the socially privileged could afford to have their children learn English. It was only in the 1970s that the colonial government began to shift to a policy of mass bilingualism with the introduction of compulsory secondary school education (Bolton 2002b; Bolton and Kwok 1990; Lin 1997). Thus, according to a 1970 survey, "only a small proportion of the total sample read unabridged fictions, magazines and newspapers in English, with an ability to understand most of everything they read. . . . Not more than 10 percent of the (3,784) respondents derive much pleasure from reading in English" (Wescott 1977; cited by Luke and Richards 1982: 53). And despite today's frequent complaints by the business elite and educators in Hong Kong about the so-called decline in English standards, empirical surveys suggest a different picture: During the late colonial period (from the late 1960s to 1997) and well into the present day, knowledge of English among the general population of Hong Kong has steadily expanded. Only a modest 9.7 percent claimed knowledge of English in 1961 (Bolton 2002c: 34), compared to 44.7 percent who gave a positive response to the same question in 2006.

The proportion of English-language speakers in Hong Kong can be roughly measured by the "official language question." As mentioned, the latest 2006 by-census reported that 44.7 percent of the population claimed a knowledge of English. This figure is of course a rough estimate, because the census question relies on self-assessment and also leaves the ability of a person who makes such a claim unspecified. A corroborating indicator, however, can be found in the proportion of the population that completed at least eleven years (six years primary and five years secondary) of education in Hong Kong. The same census (Hong Kong Special Administrative Region Government, Census and Statistics Department 2007: 44) suggests that 50 percent of the population received at least eleven years of education.

Fluency in English is often used in Hong Kong as an index of the amount and the quality of local or overseas education that a person has received. People who speak English well are generally considered better educated and socially privileged. Earlier studies on language attitudes in Hong Kong have shown that when bilinguals in Hong Kong use English among themselves, they give others an impression of status and Westernization. When they use Cantonese, they give others an impression of Chinese humility and solidarity (Lyczak et al. 1976).

During the colonial era, the linguistic situation in Hong Kong showed a pattern that reflected a typical colonial irony in which public issues were deliberately discussed in a language that most of the public could not understand. Government officials, politicians, academics, and professionals used English on formal public occasions. Besides the dominance of English in the legal domain, English was the working language of the executive and legislative branches of the colonial government.[3] Only in the late 1980s and early 1990s, when the process of decolonization began with, first, the introduction of indirect elections and then partial direct elections, were Cantonese speeches made in the colonial legislature, most of them by directly elected members. But English remained the predominant language of the legislature as recently as the early 1990s (Yau 1997). The dominance of English was even stronger in the executive, where there was no political appointment or election to speak of. Until the end of colonial rule in 1997, the governor's highest consultative body, the Executive Council, had been made up of an elite group for which the ability to speak English well was a prerequisite. They were the colonial bureaucrats, taipans of traditional British-related trading firms, representatives of local old money, professional technocrats, and local elites from the old co-optation system.[4] It was by no means a coincidence that in the early days of colonialism in the nineteenth century, the few Chinese who eventually made it to the rank of local elites often began their careers as interpreters; the fact that they were interpreters indicates that their English was probably much better than that of other Chinese (Smith 1975). This was the case with Ng Choy (also known to historians who study China as Wu Tingfang), the first Chinese appointed to the colonial Legislative Council in 1880. Ng started out as a court interpreter in Hong Kong and later studied law (becoming the first Chinese called to the bar in England) (Cameron 1991; Carroll 2005; Smith 1975).

Historically, the screening function of English fluency was institutionalized in a number of ways. Lin (1996) identifies four key mechanisms. First, there was the role of English in education. For example, the University of Hong Kong, Hong Kong's oldest university, has to this day maintained a policy of using English as the sole medium of instruction in most disciplines. Second, there was the British-based accreditation system of professional qualifications (e.g., accountancy, medicine, engineering, and, of course, law). Under this system, individuals had to earn their credentials through English-language instruction. Lin argues that learning English was and continues to be a prerequisite for anyone aspiring to become a professional in Hong Kong. Third were the policies upholding English as the official language (see the section on English domains). And fourth, as a consequence of this policy, English was required for individuals who aspired to join the civil service. Traditionally, high-ranking colonial officials were either British expatriates who moved to Hong Kong or local elites with an excellent command of English. The first Chinese chief secretary of Hong Kong, Anson Chan, for example, was adored by the local press for her ability to speak English with a native (RP [Received Pronunciation]) accent.[5]

Cantonese Domains

Cantonese is the vernacular of the overwhelming majority of the Hong Kong population.[6] As mentioned, according to the 2006 by-census, 90.8 percent of the population identified Cantonese as their usual language. In short, the general Cantonese speech community includes nearly all ethnic Chinese in Hong Kong. And precisely because of the status of Cantonese as a default vernacular, Cantonese is less salient as a status marker compared to English, even though people who speak Cantonese with regional dialectal accents (especially northern Mandarin varieties) are sometimes branded by locals as new immigrants and are often assumed to have lower socioeconomic status.

This book is not the place to offer a comprehensive survey of the use of Cantonese in Hong Kong. Instead, I briefly mention the more important linguistic domains in which Cantonese resides. Hong Kong has been described by some as "the greatest Cantonese city that the world has ever seen" (Harrison and So 1997: 12). Broadly, Cantonese is widely used in the informal spheres of everyday life in Hong Kong. Perhaps the most important domain of Cantonese is the family. Few ethnic Chinese use English in their family conversations, even those who are educated and regularly use English in their workplaces. Another Cantonese domain is interpersonal communications with friends and acquaintances; it would be considered awkward for a local in Hong Kong to insist on using English when communicating with another local (although a kind of Hong Kong–style code switching, i.e., throwing in English words and phrases within Cantonese dialogue, is common; see Gibbons 1987; Li 2002). Cantonese can also be found in local schools, but its use as an official medium of instruction is limited to so-called Chinese schools. In reality, many teachers in English schools do switch to Cantonese to explain things to students when English instruction fails. Cantonese is the language used by students during recess and in between classes. Cantonese is also clearly the language of popular culture, and it is the dominant radio and television language of Hong Kong. Famous for their extravagant, high-flying, nonstop action sequences, Cantonese action movies now command global appeal. Finally, Cantonese is used in religious activities, for example, in traditional ancestor worship, in Buddhist and Taoist temples, and in the local Christian (both Catholic and Protestant) churches.

English Domains

The ubiquity of Cantonese as the everyday vernacular makes it easy to overlook its absence in the more formal spheres of everyday life, especially those that were traditionally the domains of English. How can one describe the English domains in Hong Kong? The question has long been an issue of debate among linguists studying Hong Kong (cf. Bolton 2002c; Luke and Richards 1982). Again, it is not my intent to offer a comprehensive treatment on the topic. It is safe to say, however, that virtually any linguists studying English in Hong Kong would agree on two things. First, one cannot treat "Hong Kong English" as a vernacular in the same sense that Cantonese is; English is not a language shared by all strata of the society. Second, English in Hong Kong has never been and is not a language that covers all aspects of everyday life. Its linguistic habitus is made up of a number of narrow, well-demarcated, and functionally specific domains.

Hong Kong English is best conceived as an ancillary and yet prestigious language whose linguistic habitus is made up of a number of distinct but partially overlapping domains. These domains are, to a noticeable extent, distinguishable by their own lexis, yet they share a formal speech style common to all message-oriented communications. The most identifiable domains include school English, workplace English, political English, bureaucratic English, and a number of professional argots.

Precisely because English is not an everyday language in Hong Kong, most people there acquire the language through the formal means of education. The bilinguals of Hong Kong are what some linguists would call compound bilinguals; they follow a definite sequence of language acquisition (Stockwell 2002); an overwhelming majority of them learn Cantonese as their first language and learn English when they begin primary school education at age 6 or later.[7] This mechanism of formal acquisition explains why there has been a wide gap between the percentage of the local population who claim a knowledge of English (44.7 percent in the 2006 by-census) and the percentage of the population who identify English as their usual language, which is defined as the language a person uses in daily communication at home (2.8 percent in the same census) (Hong Kong Special Administrative Region Government, Census and Statistics Department, 2007: 38, 44). The difference between the two figures suggests that English is not an everyday language for most people who know and use English in Hong Kong; rather, English is a functional language whose linguistic habitus is composed of a number of specific domains. The most important domain, and the one that ensures the continued existence of English in Hong Kong, is the official medium of instruction in secondary schools.

Traditionally, English has been the language of instruction in the more prestigious public and private schools. The University of Hong Kong, established in 1911 and until 1963 the only local university recognized by the government, uses English as its medium of instruction. During the colonial years, the use of English in a predominantly Chinese colony was not without debate, even among the British officials themselves. In 1935, a British education inspector, R. Burney, visited Hong Kong and completed a report in which he criticized the Hong Kong government for neglecting vernacular education. He recommended that the teaching of English be reformed on a utilitarian basis and that more time be devoted to the study of Chinese. Subsequent studies commissioned by the colonial government arrived at similar conclusions.[8] However, English remained the medium of instruction for most grammar schools in Hong Kong throughout the colonial period (Lin 1997; Pennycook 1998). As recently as 1994, research has shown that more than 90 percent of Hong Kong secondary schools use English as their official teaching medium (Johnson 1994: 186–187).[9]

Hong Kong school English constitutes a register of its own. Historically, Hong Kong school English was and, to a large extent, still is taught by local school teachers who learned the language from the same system. Thus school English reproduces itself within a rather closed circuit. School English in Hong Kong is used almost exclusively for either one-way pedagogical purposes (class lectures) or two-way vertical communications (communications between teachers and students in class). With the exception of a few private international schools in Hong Kong, English is seldom used as a medium for horizontal communications (i.e., interactions among students and interactions among teachers). The classroom setting dictates that school English in Hong Kong carries a formal tone and style. Indeed, this tone is carried over into other linguistic registers of English and becomes part of Hong Kong's English. Also, the lexis of school English is closely related to the technical, formal lexis of academic and scientific discourse.

The second domain of Hong Kong English originated in the colonial government and continues in a truncated form today in the Special Administrative Region (SAR) government. Like any sizable bureaucracy, the colonial government developed its own argots and styles. For the first century of the colonial period, English was the sole working language of the then Hong Kong administration. It was not until the late 1960s, after witnessing some serious signs of social crisis, that the colonial government gradually began to grant Chinese status as an official language. The colony had been rocked by waves of social unrest that from 1966 to 1967 erupted into civil disturbances and violence in the streets. Although colonial officials at the time viewed much of the rioting as a spillover effect of the Cultural Revolution in China, the colonial government's post hoc inquiries suggested that a key cause of the riots was the language gap between the rulers and the ruled. In 1969 and 1970, the colonial government faced increasing pressure from university students who were campaigning for the use of Chinese as an official language (cf. A. H. Y. Chen 1985). It decided to defuse the movement through the standard bureaucratic procedure of establishing a committee to review the matter (Faure 2003). A Chinese language committee was set up in October 1970 to examine the use of Chinese in the colonial administration; the committee came up with a list of comprehensive recommendations for the increased use of Chinese in governmental affairs. Some of the committee's more radical recommendations were rejected by the colonial administration, but what remained of them was implemented in a local statute known as the Official Languages Ordinance of 1974. The ordinance declared that both English and Chinese were to be the official languages of Hong Kong and that the two languages were to possess equal status for most official purposes (with law being an important exception, as I discuss later in this chapter). Yet despite its supposed official status, Cantonese was seldom used in important government meetings or formal communications, even when expatriates were not involved. Senior colonial government officials, local and expatriate, were far more accustomed to giving formal addresses in English rather than Cantonese. Cantonese was used mainly for external communication by frontline government workers who dealt with members of the public on an everyday basis. For example, Cantonese was used in post offices, police stations, government hospitals, and clinics; it did not become a medium for internal communications among higher ranking government officials until the early 1990s, when the transfer of sovereignty to China became an impending reality.

Today, English is still used internally for oral communications inside the SAR government on some occasions, although Chinese (here I mean not just Cantonese but also Putonghua) is clearly on the rise. Upon inquiries by the press, a government spokeswoman said in 2001 that "formal [government] meetings had been held in English even when there were no expatriate officials present" and that Cantonese was used "at smaller, informal meetings" (Hon 2001). The historical association with power and status means that English is still seen by some Chinese officials as an effective means to impose authority (S. Evans and Green 2001: 261). As a written medium, English remains the main working language for today's SAR government (S. Evans and Green 2001: 253). Letters, faxes, notices, and reports released to the public continue to be issued mainly in English (not to mention meeting agendas, minutes, records, memos, and other internal paperwork). The adoption of written Chinese by many of the colony's administrative departments has been a recent phenomenon. Indeed, Chinese government documents were so uncommon in 1996, just one year before the political changeover, that the then colonial government decided to set up an official languages agency to promote the wider use of Chinese in the civil service.

Another domain of English can be found in the corporate and business world of Hong Kong. English is still the standard language for written business communication, especially in larger foreign-owned corporations (S. Evans and Green 2001). Like today's government English, workplace English in Hong Kong is more dominant as a written medium than as an oral medium (Du-Babcock 1998, cited by D. C. S. Li 1999; S. Evans and Green 2001). This is true in both the government sector and the private business sector. Sometimes, English, or a form of code-mixed speech (Cantonese laden with English terms), is used when people discuss topics that involve technical expertise or trade terms. Stephen Evans and Christopher Green have described the prevailing bilingualism of job interviews in Hong Kong, where English and Cantonese are assigned clear roles. Employers use English to discuss technical issues with interviewees or to test their professional expertise; Cantonese, the language of solidarity and intimacy, is used more often to discuss personal matters, such as career ambitions, personal qualities, interests, or contractual issues (S. Evans and Green 2001: 258–259).

Linguists have come up with different terms to describe the kind of functional bilingualism we see in Hong Kong. Brown and Yule (1983) distinguish between interactional language, which is listener oriented, and transactional language, which is message oriented. Following the distinction, we can stereotypically describe the English domains in Hong Kong as mostly transactional, whereas the Cantonese domains are primarily interactional. Similarly, Bonnie Urciuoli (1998: 77), in her study of the Puerto Rican community in New York, distinguishes between outer and inner spheres of interaction. Again, the English domains fall squarely in the outer spheres, which include work and business settings, government activities, and political debates. The rarity of English in the inner spheres (e.g., personal conversations among family, friends, and neighbors) confirms the thesis that English is a functionally specific language in Hong Kong. English there is a prestigious but culturally sterile language and is used mainly in technical and professional contexts. This combination of power and aloofness, iconic of the very character of British colonialism itself, has also been found in other former colonies. In discussing the uses of English in India, Probal Dasgupta amusingly suggests that English is an auntie rather than a mother. It is not "one of us but is an important presence that one must be polite to" (Dasgupta 1993: 201).

Describing English Speech Styles

Having considered the nature of English and Cantonese speech domains in Hong Kong, I now turn to the speech styles of English and Cantonese utterances in Hong Kong. This is a difficult yet understudied area; few empirical studies have been conducted on the linguistic characteristics of Hong Kong Cantonese and English speech styles. For this reason, my discussion here is, to a certain extent, explorative and impressionistic.

The analysis of speech styles is connected to the notion of communicative competence introduced by linguistic anthropologist Dell Hymes (1972). Hymes argues that speakers' ability to use the right style of language is one of the key constituents of their communicative competence. The totality of styles (both spoken and written) available to a speech community is known as its *linguistic repertoire*. According to Hymes, the best way to understand speech styles in a speech community is to identify the most commonly recurrent *speech events* in that community.

Because of the vernacular status of Cantonese, speech events most commonly involved with the language are listener oriented, following Brown and Yule's (1983) distinction. These speech events cover a much wider emotional repertoire than English in Hong Kong. Cantonese is the language used in all major types of interpersonal speech events, especially linguistic practices that incorporate the expressive aspects of language. It is in Cantonese that locals chat, tease, joke, curse, argue, and mourn, among other speech acts. The short, discrete, tonally colorful sound (Cantonese has six basic tones) of Cantonese is often seen by the locals themselves as capturing the temperament of a typical Hong Kong person—energetic and vibrant, if not a bit brash. But an important aspect that cannot be overlooked is how often educated Hong Kong people see Cantonese as a dialect. This has important implications for how Cantonese is received as a legal language. I come back to this point in Chapter 7. Suffice it to say here that Cantonese is considered a language that is better spoken than written down. Many Republican intellectuals of the earlier generations who escaped to Hong Kong after World War II did not bother to learn Cantonese for the simple reason that Cantonese was considered unliterary and provincial.[10] Standard Modern Chinese (SMC)—more or less based on vernacular Putonghua, or *baihua* in Chinese—is taught in the schools of Hong Kong as the common written form of Chinese. Most people do not write in Cantonese. Written Cantonese is used in informal or subcultural genres such as newspaper gossip columns, diary-style novels, comics, or satirical writings. Because Chinese characters, unlike the English alphabet, are not orthographic in any systematic manner, local authors who write in Cantonese sometimes have to make up their own characters, which are often totally incomprehensible to non–Hong Kong Chinese. The nonstandardization of written Cantonese is crucial to our understanding of the styles of Cantonese conversations. Unlike English, which in the context of Hong Kong often shows the intertextual influences of formal writing on its spoken form, Cantonese conversations are particularly lively and free-flowing because the colloquial status of Cantonese means that it receives little textual standardization. For some, this lively quality represents authenticity; for others (e.g., the educated and the professionals; see also Chapter 7), Cantonese means baseness in action. Without a literary canon or tradition, Cantonese has been highly fluid, almost mercurial, in its lexical development. As two Hong Kong–based linguists have pointed out, "the vigor of Cantonese in Hong Kong is apparent in the uses to which its speakers put it, the rate at which its slang and idioms change and the confusion this causes for Cantonese speakers from elsewhere" (Harrison and So 1997: 13).

By contrast, speech events that most commonly involve the use of English are message oriented. People in Hong Kong use English to teach, to lecture, to interview for jobs, to hold meetings, to announce and to notify, among other things. The language style that is adopted in these message-oriented speech events, as sociolinguists point out, is "usually instrumental and goal-oriented, with the whole point of a message-oriented utterance being the communication of a propositional or cognitive message to the listener" (Brown 1982: 77; cited by Milroy and Milroy 1999: 101). The most extreme form of message-oriented speech event is one-way communication in the traditional sender-receiver model, where the receiver is not expected to interact with the sender. Despite the contention of some linguists that Hong Kong English exhibits creativity (cf. Bolton 2002b), it is clear that as a genre, Hong Kong English is characterized by its relative lack of performativity, precisely because its uses are often so functionally specific. It is not surprising that most educated locals in Hong Kong find it much easier to give a professional presentation in a workplace setting than to engage in casual small talk in English.

The lack of performativity in Hong Kong English can be traced to two key factors. First is scripted orthodoxy of schooled literacy. I am well aware of the danger of overstating the dichotomy between orality and literacy (cf. Collins 1995; I attempt to contextualize the distinction in Chapter 4), but it is noteworthy to point out that the English language is acquired mainly through the highly restricted contexts of structured learning. The emphasis on grammar and rules means that English is projected as a system of syntax rather than as a medium of lively communications. Second, as we have seen for the government and business sectors, English dominates more as a written language than as a spoken one (S. Evans and Green 2001). As Luke and Richards (1982: 53) pointed out, a junior clerk might have to type letters or reports in English or a technician might have to read an instruction manual in English, but neither of them might actually have occasion to frequently speak and thereby interact in English. Even when they do, they model their speech on the English of government reports and instruction manuals. The formal quality of spoken English in Hong Kong is thus likely, in part, a consequence of the intertextual influences of writing on the spoken form.

The liveliest form of English heard in Hong Kong is a variety far removed from the dominant domain of educational English. In fact, this colloquial form is much despised both by local teachers and English promoters. It is a form of street English in so-called old Hong Kong, a form that was learned by people who lived on the peripheries of society and outside the formal educational system. The character of this English can be traced back to Cantonese Pidgin English, which first emerged in Canton sometime between the eighteenth and nineteenth centuries (Bolton 2002a; Holm 2000: 95). Cantonese Pidgin English was developed as British trading ships began to establish regular trade ties within the Canton region. A knowledge of some 700 to 750 Chinese Pidgin English words was sufficient for most trading purposes, the pidgin's only real domain (Holm 2000: 107). This is the Pidgin English one still hears spoken by old Chinese laundrymen in Hollywood movies, with "Long time no see" its best-known phrase. But the depidginization and standardization of English would soon enough take place through the scholastic literacy promoted by the missionary schools that spread across China in the late nineteenth and early twentieth centuries. Nowadays, people who speak Cantonese Pidgin English in Hong Kong are dwindling. These speakers usually acquire their English outside the formal education system and belong to small inconspicuous speech communities that for various reasons allow the use of this colloquial form of ungrammatical English. For example, one can hear Pidgin English spoken among older merchants who run little jewelry or camera shops in the smaller alleys of the tourist districts of Hong Kong or among the relatively uneducated people who work in the seedier neighborhoods of the city. One group that has often captured the imagination of local writers and filmmakers is the middle-aged *mama-san*s working in the red-light zones of Hong Kong. The Japanese term *mama-san*, when used in a Cantonese context, refers to the madams, or "guardians," of young women who work in girlie bars and nightclubs. Many of them have spent much of their adult lives chatting up British and American sailors. It is precisely because of their inattention to prescriptive rules of grammatical correctness that speakers of this colloquial English often display moments of lively fluency, uninhibited delight, and an underground coolness seldom found among the more educated locals, albeit in their own grammatically "mistaken" way.[11]

The Linguistic Ideology of Cantonese and English
in Hong Kong

As indicated, Cantonese is often devalued, even among its more educated users, as a dialect that cannot and should not be written out. Nothing illustrates this lack of standardization better than the absence of grammar books on Cantonese (in either English or Chinese). This is especially striking when one considers that Cantonese is a "big" language even on a global scale; it is spoken by more than 70 million people around the world. Most books on Cantonese are quick guides to everyday Cantonese phrases and expressions and are usually targeted for Westerners who love Hong Kong movies, from Jackie Chan's to Wong Kar-wai's.[12] Literature written in colloquial Cantonese had become trendy in Hong Kong in the early 1990s, including popular novels such as the "Diary of a Yuppie" series (小男人周記 [siu2 naam4 jan4 zau1 gei3]), which attempts to capture the wit of the language in writing. A few popular columnists have also written in the vernacular style for decades. Precisely because of the unorthodox status of Cantonese, writers find it easier to create their own voice through crafting their own phrases and expressions. That said, the use of newly coined Cantonese characters and inclusion of English words to do code mixing in writing is frowned on in traditional Chinese literary circles. For the educated, writing Cantonese is considered both a parochial and a vulgar practice (see also Chapter 7). It is considered unthinkable, for example, to write a front-page news story or a serious editorial in Cantonese in the so-called quality press (Lo and Wong 1990).

Some scholars have claimed that during the 1970s and 1980s, before the political issue of sovereignty transfer began to loom large on the public agenda, the use of Cantonese was seen as an identity marker that promoted the distinct identity of "Hongkonger."[13] However, since the market reforms of China began to take effect in the early 1990s, Hong Kong and Guangdong province in China have become more closely integrated economically and socially, and that trend has been stronger since 1997. It is clear that the ethnolinguistic identity of Hongkonger is now becoming less salient than it was during the 1980s and even during the last decade of colonialism (the 1990s).

As for English, it remains a prestigious language acquired by the educated public of Hong Kong. But what exactly do people think of the English language itself? What are their metalinguistic beliefs about the English language? For most people in Hong Kong, English is considered a prestigious yet essentially foreign language. It is identified as an icon of Western modernity that most people aspire to learn but do not consider a language with which they live, even though Hong Kong is often portrayed as a Westernized hypercapitalist city. Despite its elevated status, English is implicitly recognized as a "foreign" language both by members of the public and by the elite who are themselves committed to promoting English in Hong Kong. Public discourses used to justify the continued use of English in Hong Kong invariably offer pragmatic arguments for doing so: Like the Cantonese merchants who learned Pidgin English in order to trade with the British in the eighteenth and nineteenth centuries, the primary reasons driving many Hong Kong people to learn English today are instrumental. As noted by a local journalist, proficiency "in English has remained a universal requirement for most white-collar jobs and for those in the service industries. The higher the position, the greater is the need for a good command of English" (C. K. Lau 1995: 102; cf. Pennycook 1998).

Such pragmatic arguments are made by the local elites, who enthusiastically promote the importance of English: Hong Kong people must know English because it is the passport to global capitalism. "Hong Kong's world-class economic success is due in no small measure to . . . the use of English, and the ability of the civil service to operate with a high degree of English proficiency is integral to that success," noted a 1995 government report.[14] This instrumental mentality was again vividly articulated when Hong Kong lawmakers passed a motion in 1999 that called for more extensive use of English.[15] James Tien Pei-chun, then chairman of the pro-business Liberal Party, said at the debate that Hong Kong was losing its competitive edge because of its falling standards of English. Many global companies had moved their regional bases from Hong Kong to Shanghai because the standard of English there was better, he suggested. Tien explained the benefits of English.

Madam President, we are living in an international city. Being international is that which pays our rents, buys our food, and puts our children through school.

This is the reality that we must not ever forget. Our lifeblood is trade and finance. Our outlook is global. Our culture is rooted in both the East and the West. English is the universal language of art, commerce, science and technology. We were able to transform our economy from manufacturing to servicing because we could communicate with the world in English. (Hong Kong Legislative Council 1999)

Despite the zeal and enthusiasm elites displayed for promoting the use of English, English has always been taken as a foreign language in Hong Kong.[16] In using the term *foreign language*, I am referring to the metalinguistic belief that English is taken to be a language inappropriate for communication internally among locals in Hong Kong. Most people use English only when they communicate not inwardly but outwardly, either when interacting with English-speaking foreigners (presumably Britons and increasingly Americans) who may or may not have lived in Hong Kong or in so-called outer spheres when the linguistic transactions are formal and instrumental. Using English to talk to other bilingual locals in casual settings is viewed as a sign of snobbery, as reflected in the common Cantonese phrase 扮晒鬼佬 [baan3 saai3 gwai2 lou2], meaning "acting like a foreigner" (cf. C. K. Lau 1997: 101–150).[17]

In the same paradoxical way, the foreignness of English is obliquely reflected in the refusal to acknowledge the existence of a "Hong Kong accent" in mainstream pedagogical discourse. For many educated people in Hong Kong, the term *Hong Kong English accent* is taken as a euphemism for wrong pronunciation. But to call an accent wrong is to ideologically erase its presence, or more precisely, its intrinsic worth to have a presence. From a linguistic standpoint, it is impossible not to notice that the English spoken by Hong Kong people evidences interlinguistic influences from Cantonese. Linguists working in this area have identified a modified phonology of English that exhibits traces of the vowel and consonant features, as well as nonrelease and deletion patterns, that are characteristic of spoken Cantonese. Such a Hong Kong accent does not represent idiosyncratic or sporadic individual mistakes but rather cumulative variations that are the consequence of bilingual speakers' use of more than one language (cf. Romaine 1995: 51–55). For example, in the vowel system, because of the monosyllabic nature of Cantonese words, the Hong Kong accent is often syllable-timed and not stress-timed, as one would usually detect in speakers of RP English. This means that each syllable occurs at regular intervals, rather than each stressed syllable occurring at regular intervals (Trudgill and Hannah 2002). The RP English schwa /ə/ is usually stressed and pronounced with the same force as other vowels by Hong Kong English speakers. In the consonant system, /v/ is often replaced by /w/, apparently because of the absence of /v/ in Cantonese (e.g., divide is pronounced as [diwaɪ]; for a more systematic description, see Bolton and Kwok [1990] and Hung [2002]). Such systematic local variations, however, have not been recognized, let alone encouraged, by local educators and English promoters in the mass media, notwithstanding the fact that these features of the Hong Kong accent are found in varying degrees across the entire spectrum of locally educated Hong Kong English speakers. Promotion of a local accent is self-defeating, the argument goes, because English is for communication with foreigners (presumably Britons and Americans), and one tries to get rid of an accent that foreigners find difficult to comprehend. Thus the model for standard English has long been RP English; its orthodox status has been challenged only recently by GA (General American), also known as "network American" English (cf. Bolton and Kwok 1990; C. K. Lau 1995). In either case the criteria for determining the correctness of English in Hong Kong are mainly exonormative (i.e., with reference to British or American English) rather than endonormative (i.e., locally developed) (Kachru 1990; Luke and Richards 1982). The result of such a metalinguistic belief that English is a foreign language is that local variations of English are systematically branded as mistakes. The whole pedagogical narrative categorizes local variations of Hong Kong English as learner's mistakes, despite the fact that many of these so-called learners have used English extensively for decades.

A cursory look at many of the English-language textbooks and reference books written by Hong Kong writers reveals a predominantly prescriptive approach to the language's pronunciation and usage. A 1988 survey of 131 first-year students at the University of Hong Kong, the territory's most prestigious university, showed that the majority of them (65.1 percent) indicated that they wished to speak English like a "British native-speaker," compared to 25.6 percent who wanted to speak English like a "Hong Kong bilingual" (Bolton and Kwok 1990).[18] If one thinks about it, this is an almost masochistic belief to hold. For many of the people who have a local Hong Kong English accent (e.g., me), this means having to acknowledge that one's English is fundamentally "wrong." It would be much easier to acknowledge the existence of a Hong Kong accent and to consider these "mistakes" a part of the local flavor of the language. But apparently too much symbolic capital is at stake when it comes to native accents, by which I mean British or American English accents, in Hong Kong. Thus the psychologically more comforting alternative has not been taken seriously by the local elite. Instead, the Hong Kong accent is some-thing that is empirically visible yet ideologically invisible. It is like the weeds found in an English garden; they must be uprooted not because they are intrinsically harmful but because they have come uninvited into a space that commands admiration by virtue of its constructed neatness and purity. Locals who are subjectively confident about their English do not believe they speak with a Hong Kong accent; in a 1999 motion debate in the legislature, Martin Lee, arguably one of the best-known barristers and politicians in Hong Kong, recalled his experience learning English in London decades earlier.

Madam President, perhaps I should share with members, and perhaps through the mass media with the community, my experience when as a young man I went to study law in London. I went to the marketplace and I was surprised that the people there called me "love," but of course they pronounced it as "Louvre"! Then, I understood that there was such a thing as Cockney. Then to my horror, after a few days, I discovered that I was speaking English with a heavy and pronounced Cantonese accent. I never realized that I had that accent when I was in Hong Kong. So I said to myself, "How on earth do I go back and represent clients in English and speak in English in the courts if I speak English with such a heavy Cantonese accent!" (Hong Kong Legislative Council 1999)

Studies of bilingualism often identify a trend in which a more pres-tigious language taking over the linguistic territory of a less prestigious language eventually pushes a speech community toward monolingualism.

In Susan Gal's (1979) study of the use of German and Hungarian in the Austrian village of Oberwart, she found that younger people were giving up Hungarian and switching to the more prestigious German. German was more than a functional language; it was an identity marker that symbolized urbanity and the rejection of peasant life. It is quite unlikely that the same thing will happen in Hong Kong; or, more precisely, I would argue that if the role of Cantonese as the vernacular is ever challenged, it will not come from English. The improbability of a complete English takeover has much to do with the local perception of its foreignness. Largely because of the colonial presence over the past 150 years, English remains a distinctly foreign, albeit highly prestigious, functional language in Hong Kong. Surely English is a marker, but it is much more a status marker than an identity marker. In the context of Hong Kong, a proper dose of English is often sprinkled over Cantonese conversation by bilingual Chinese to show that they are educated, not to show that they are non-Chinese. In other words, the social mechanism underlying the linguistic practices of English in Hong Kong is a mechanism of distinction, not identification. In 2000, the government launched a HK$50 million (US$6.4 million) campaign to encourage junior employees to improve their language skills by offering tuition subsidies. The chairman of this Workplace English Campaign, Michael Tien, said in a press interview that a decline in the use of English would lead to the perception that Hong Kong is "just another" city of mainland China (Regan 2000). Tien, of course, would not deny that Hong Kong is a Chinese city, but the operative phrase here is "just another."[19] It is the possibility that Hong Kong is just another Chinese city that Tien and the local elite want to reject. Meanwhile, the SAR government has already made "biliteracy and trilingualism" its language policy—the two written languages are English and Chinese, and the three spoken languages are Cantonese, English, and Putonghua. Today, the linguistic domains of Putonghua are still pretty narrow (cf. D. C. S. Li 1999), but in the long run, Putonghua is likely to become the high-status local language that Hong Kong Chinese can speak and identify with. I return to this point in the context of the common law in Chapter 9. If this becomes the case, Cantonese may face a similar challenge to that which Hungarian did in Gal's study.

ENGLISH AND CHINESE IN THE LEGAL DOMAIN

In this last section, I discuss the traditional roles of English and Chinese in the legal domain of Hong Kong. When it comes to legal language, it is advisable to make a distinction between written legal language and spoken legal language.

English and Chinese as Written Legal Languages

As a written medium, the history of Chinese in the law is exceedingly brief, despite the fact that the overwhelming majority of the population speak and read Chinese. Even today, Chinese plays only a peripheral role in the production of legislation, pretrial documents, legal records, and case reports. As mentioned, Chinese was made an official language in response to the social unrest that took place in the late 1960s. But Chinese would continue to remain unrecognized as an official language for the law throughout the following three decades. The same Chinese language committee that suggested granting official language status to Chinese also recommended that the laws of Hong Kong—at that time written only in English—be translated into Chinese. However, the colonial government rejected the proposal at the time, commenting that the translation of the laws of Hong Kong "cannot be regarded as essential, is not a practical proposition and should not be contemplated" (Hong Kong Government, Attorney General's Chambers 1986: para. 7).

Thus the resulting Official Languages Ordinance of 1974, which established the official status of Chinese, specifically excluded the use of Chinese in the enactment of legislation. "Every Ordinance shall be enacted and published in the English language," the ordinance reads (sec. 4). The idea of translating law into Chinese was shelved until the signing of the Sino-British Joint Declaration in 1984, when June 30, 1997, was set as the definite date for the transfer of Hong Kong sovereignty from Britain to China and the enactment of statutes in Chinese before that date became a looming political necessity.[20] Three years later, in 1987, the Official Languages Ordinance was amended to stipulate that "all ordinances shall be enacted and published in both official languages" (sec. 4(1)). The first bilingual ordinance was enacted in April 1989.[21] For the whole body of already existing statutes in English, the Official Languages Ordinance stipulated that an "authentic version" of Chinese text be provided to these statutes. The first such translation was officially announced in 1992, and more than 500 principal ordinances and roughly 1,000 pieces of subsidiary legislation had been translated into Chinese by 1997 (E. T. M. Cheung 2000). In terms of pages, the translation is even more staggering. Between 1992 and the changeover in 1997, 19,294 pages of English legislation were translated into Chinese (see Table 2).

So, within slightly less than a decade, a project that was once considered by the same colonial government as impractical was swiftly completed without much debate and discussion. Why was that the case? Was the colonial government's previous stance of regarding the project as "not practical" a mere pretext to maintain the dominance of English? And what do the translated statutes in Chinese really look like? Although the earlier colonial government was clearly lackadaisical in giving Chinese the same official role as English, if not downright reluctant to do so, the unexpectedly swift, almost mass-production style in which the statutes were translated had much to do with the nature of the "translation" project conducted in the 1990s. As Kenneth Au, a Hong Kong linguist, describes, the process was not so much the translation of the common law into Chinese as the transplantation of the common law into the soil of the Chinese language (Au 1996: 23). Almost serving as a warning to would-be readers about the obscurity of Chinese translated statutes, a

TABLE 2   *Volume of bilingual legislation prepared since 1992*

Year	Pages of bills	Pages of subsidiary legislation	Total
1992	722	92	814
1993	906	476	1,382
1994	1,738	812	2,550
1995	2,054	1,502	3,556
1996	3,038	1,636	4,674
1997	2,612	3,706	6,318

SOURCE: "Item for Establishment Subcommittee of Finance Committee," February 4, 1998. Retrieved April 25, 2004, from http://www.legco .gov.hk/yr97-98/english/panels/ajls/papers/aj13016c.htm.

government discussion paper on translating the common law into Chinese makes the following remark: "The common law will, in future, under-lie the Chinese text of the laws of Hong Kong in precisely the same way it does the English text. The consequence of this is that the meaning of the Chinese text in the courts of Hong Kong may not be what a reader unfamiliar with our legal background (e.g. a reader in China) may think it to be" (Hong Kong Government, Attorney General's Chambers 1986, para. 6). The prerogative of the exercise was not to make the laws of Hong Kong in Chinese accessible but to preserve the Englishness of the law in Chinese. This was done by coining neologisms, whenever neces-sary, to represent common law terms such as *consideration* (in contract law) or *resulting trust* (in trust law), not to mention more technical legal terms such as *hereditament* or *encumbrance* (cf. D. Tse 1996). This was an exercise of translation in a thin sense, a move that tiptoed between translation and transliteration.

Neologisms aside, English words as simple as *good*, *hire*, or *safe* were elaborately translated into different Chinese expressions to capture their multifaceted meanings in different legal contexts. The deadly combination of neologisms and technical renditions of simple English words means that the resulting Chinese texts are barely, if at all, readable.[22] Even today, when new bilingual legislation without a previous English text is drafted, Hong Kong legislative drafters are still accustomed to preparing an English text first and then a Chinese text by means of translation (Zhao 1999).[23] It is no wonder that Chinese legislation has been described as "totally English" or "anglicized Chinese" in terms of language structure, style, and concepts (Au 1996: 24). The government claimed in its own defense that legal accuracy had to be preserved at the cost of linguistic niceties, but the obvious result is that, to date, the obscure Chinese texts of Hong Kong statutes have seldom been referred to by lawyers and judges (Yen 2001; see Chapter 8).

Its peripheral role as a legislative language aside, Chinese was rarely used before 1997 as a written medium for other legal documents, includ-ing pretrial paperwork (writs of summons, affidavits, pleadings, interlocu-tory applications, etc.), court records, judgments, and case law reports, even though some magistrates' court cases were tried in Chinese before

1997 (see the next section). These cases established a pattern that, to a great extent, continues to the present day—the elicitation of evidence in the hearings of these cases are conducted in Cantonese, but the court documents and judgments are written in English. So, instead of cross-examining his witness through an interpreter, a bilingual counsel can interrogate the witness directly in Cantonese, if he so chooses. Likewise, a bilingual judge can speak directly to a litigant in Chinese, again without the relay of an interpreter. However, the proceedings, even when conducted in Cantonese, are not always recorded in Chinese for the sake of official recordkeeping. It was only in the mid-1990s that amendments were proposed to allow judges to write down their notes of proceedings in either of the two languages (Hong Kong Judiciary 1993). Yet, until 1997, Chinese was rarely used as a language for legal documents and records. Lawyers were, and to an extent still are, accustomed to filing their pleadings or writs in English. Also, although in theory judges can now write their official records of proceedings in either language, they most often choose English as a matter of preference or habit.

But it is in the area of judgments, the most important legal records of all, that Chinese finds it most difficult to gain entry. At the time of this writing, the available corpus of Chinese case law was paltry, to say the least. And that trend is not going to change in the foreseeable future. English remains the dominant written medium of judgment in Hong Kong. The two published case reports in Hong Kong, *Hong Kong Law Reports and Digest* and *Hong Kong Cases*, report judgments delivered primarily in English. Even today, legal reference books on Hong Kong cases and materials are produced mainly in English. For example, when the British legal publisher Butterworths began to embark on a project to publish a 27-volume legal encyclopedia on Hong Kong law (*Halsbury's Laws of Hong Kong*, modeled on the famous *Halsbury's Laws of England*), it made the decision to publish it in English and English only.[24] The first volume was published in 1995, just two years before the change of sovereignty. At the time of this writing, the series has produced 40 independent volumes on all subject areas of the laws of Hong Kong. I return to this point in Chapters 8 and 9 when I discuss the challenges of developing Chinese case law in the postcolonial environment.

English and Chinese as Spoken Legal Languages

The use of English and Cantonese as spoken languages in the legal process can be divided into three historical stages. The first stage, which lasted more than a century (from 1842 to 1974), was one of English monolingualism. During this period, Cantonese was not an official language at any level of the judiciary. Judges—from the law lords in the Privy Council of the House of Lords to local magistrates—all spoke and wrote in English. Counsel who appeared at different levels of the court system, in criminal or in civil trials, prosecuted, defended, cross-examined, deliberated, and mitigated in English. Of course, Cantonese did have some presence in the 132 years before 1974; after all, Cantonese was spoken by many litigants who stepped into the witness box in various capacities—as defendants, as witnesses, as victims, and as plaintiffs. However, during the whole colonial time before 1974, the de facto status of Cantonese as the vernacular had no impact on its legal status. Like any nonofficial language, Cantonese had to be interpreted into English, enunciated in English, and recorded as English, even when all the litigants involved spoke Cantonese. The official dominance was such that a legal historian who set out to study the Cantonese narratives in court before the 1970s would find a cold trail today, with basically no primary documents left to investigate. Nothing was left to record what was said in Cantonese in court during the period. All the historical utterances in Cantonese evaporated into thin air; what remains today are English court records, English judgments, and English case reports.

In the second stage, from 1974 to 1997, legal Chinese was offered a limited and restricted role. As mentioned, the social unrest in the 1960s prompted the colonial government to respond to local demands for the use of Chinese. The enactment of the Official Languages Ordinance in 1974 accorded Chinese the status of an official language for the first time in colonial history. However, such status was semi-official at best—a sandwich status, so to speak—inferior to English but superior to all other languages. Despite the enactment of the ordinance, English remained the only language for legislation. In oral settings, similar restrictions were applied to the use of Cantonese. As a spoken language, Cantonese (and other varieties of Chinese) was allowed to be used only in the proceedings of the lower courts of Hong Kong (mainly the magistrates' courts and other special-purpose courts and tribunals).[25] At the time, Chinese was considered inadequate for handling complicated points of law often raised in the higher courts; these were handled strictly in English (Hong Kong Government 1971; cf. A. H. Y. Chen 1985: 24).

The third stage began in 1997 and continues to the present day. Chinese, in theory, has been given equal status with English in the legal system of Hong Kong. In reality, there continues to be a linguistic division of labor within the official bilingual legal system of Hong Kong. Again, I will come back to this point in detail in Chapter 8 when I analyze how legal bilingualism is in fact practiced in the courts in Hong Kong today.

CONCLUSION

The linguistic habituses of English and Cantonese in the colonial society of Hong Kong have now been identified. It is with this background in mind that we can understand how historical dominance of English over Chinese or Cantonese in the legal domain continues to the present day, even though, institutionally, English and Cantonese putatively enjoy equal status in the bilingual legal system. This history sets the stage for my concrete analysis of the bilingual common law, which is not a study of the abstract syntactical structure or semantic meanings that English and Cantonese share or in which they differ but a look at the actual ways English and Cantonese are contrastingly practiced in Hong Kong. Indeed, as Hong Kong scholars who work on legal language agree (e.g., Sin 1992; A. C. Tse 1996), if it were only about the creation of a common law lexicon in Chinese, this could be relatively easy to accomplish through the means of linguistic reclamation—that is, by creating new words to denote legal concepts and by instilling new meanings in existing words to give them a new legal sense. In any case, such a job of translation has already been completed, in the form of the legal glossary. But the problem facing Hong Kong's legal bilingualism today—the seemingly insurmountable difficulty involved in replacing English with one's own language as the language of the law—is at root a problem of language practice that no study of grammar or lexicon can answer. And it is to these questions that I now turn.

PART TWO

How Cantonese and English
Work in the Courts

CHAPTER 4

English Courtrooms in Hong Kong

The Haven of Formalism

DESPITE THE COMMON PERCEPTION that courtroom interactions in English and Cantonese trials in Hong Kong are governed by the same procedural rules, there are palpable systemic differences between the dominant interaction structures of the two for which idiosyncrasies of individual judges, lawyers, and litigants cannot wholly account. That is, the effectiveness of the same set of institutional rules differs sharply when used in the two language environments. This difference is the empirical focus of Chapters 4–6. Courtroom English and Cantonese in Hong Kong produce two different kinds of social encounter, in the Goffmanian sense of the term (see Chapter 3). It is this discrepancy that animates the inadequacy of analyzing juridical formalism on its own terms, that is, as merely a set of abstract rules. In this chapter, I analyze the English-language courtrooms in Hong Kong today and describe how the institutionally defined interaction structure constitutes the key mechanism that brings juridical formalism into being. I am arguing for a view that understands trial procedures and rules in a common law trial as the institutionalization of a particular interaction structure. The imposition of a specific interaction structure is central to the sustenance of juridical formalism. It is through the institutionalized control of interaction that utterances are turned into legally analyzable facts. Through in-depth descriptions of interaction episodes in court, we will see how the structure of statement and reply limits witnesses to straight facts, simple answers, or just yes and no. The efficacy of this mechanism is tied to the specific character of Hong Kong English.

THE DEMARCATION OF LEGAL SPACE

The physical setting of a typical Court of First Instance courtroom in Hong Kong is loaded with legal symbolism and is indeed part and parcel of the juridical context. As a performative event, an adversarial trial is primarily but not exclusively a linguistic affair. A better way of viewing it is to see it as a special kind of interactive performance that happens in a well-defined institutional context. That institutional context constitutes the performative stage on which legal dramas unfold. The constructed space in which legal proceedings are carried out is not merely a space where legal proceedings take place but is more centrally part and parcel of a legal context. The architecture of an English-style courtroom in Hong Kong aims to create a world of its own by underscoring the distinction between legal space and the social space of everyday life.

The courtroom environment is carefully built to be iconic of the institution of juridical formalism that I described in Chapter 2.[1] Such a space is built not just to facilitate the practical needs of administering an adversarial trial but also to promote the guiding ideals of formalism (Rapoport 1982).[2]

The High Court Building is situated in Admiralty (east of the Central in Hong Kong). The white tower was built in 1985. In style, it is bland, nondescript, and dully efficient. It is a far cry from the conspicuous dome and pillared walkways of its neoclassical-style predecessor, the old Supreme Court Building, which now houses the Legislative Council of Hong Kong. Inside, the courtrooms are clean, functional, and, above all, modern. They all feature an enclosed space carefully designed to separate itself from the outside world. As such, the courtrooms are generically modern, so much so that one could easily mistake them for courtrooms in Liverpool or Manchester, Sydney or Brisbane, or Singapore. That is especially the case given that the English wig and gown worn by judges and barristers are retained in Hong Kong, as in many other Commonwealth countries and former British colonies. The only symbol that reveals the locality is the emblem of the Hong Kong Special Administrative Region. The red emblem is hung on the wall behind the judge's seat, with the words "People's Republic of China Hong Kong Special Administrative Region" (in Chinese) and "Hong Kong" (in English) circling the emblem. At its center is a stylized bauhinia flower, the symbolic flower of Hong Kong. The bauhinia (*Bauhinia blakeana*, also known as the Hong Kong orchid tree) is a flowering tree that grows all over Hong Kong. It was discovered on Hong Kong's coast by a French missionary in the early twentieth century and was cultivated in large numbers on Hong Kong Island from then on. In 1965, it was adopted as the colony's official flower. It was subsequently used, perhaps because of its apolitical nature, as the symbol of postcolonial Hong Kong.[3] But the bauhinia emblem has a short history in the courtrooms of Hong Kong. For more than 150 years before the end of the colonial era in Hong Kong in 1997, courtrooms in Hong Kong had displayed the colonial crown crest (a lion, a unicorn, a crown, and a coat of arms).

The spatial organization of Hong Kong courtrooms remains fundamentally similar to that of contemporary English courtrooms.[4] A courtroom in the High Court Building is typically a large square or rectangle.[5] Through symbolic demarcation of space, the courtroom perspicaciously places different people in their institutionally defined places. The judge's seat is centered along one of the walls perpendicular to the entrance.[6] The judicial bench is elevated (and elevated higher in the higher Court of First Instance than in the lower District Court). From his perched position, the judge can see everyone in the courtroom clearly. This kind of stage management is obviously by design; the setup of the furniture and the locations of different actors in a courtroom physically patent the details of role differentiation in an ideal adversarial trial.[7]

Directly in front of the judge (but a few steps below) sits the court clerk, who is the personal assistant to the judge in and outside the courtroom. During a trial, the clerk is responsible for keeping track of the case documents for the judge, informing technicians when to start and stop recording, signing in witnesses, and ushering witnesses to the witness box. Farther away from the judge, behind the clerk's table, is a long table known as the counsels' row. Litigants (or defendants in criminal trials) do not sit next to their counsel (as in the United States); the counsels' row is reserved only for robed barristers.[8] Litigants, when not testifying, find their seats in the public gallery; sometimes they sit behind their counsel, in the back rows in the center of the room, together with the unrobed instructing solicitors. In criminal trials, the defendant is held in a dock (again different from the practice in the courts of the United States). The difference between the English-style setup in Hong Kong and the setup in the United States in part explains the difference between the interactional dynamics of cross-examination in the two places. Attorneys in the United States are allowed to freely approach the witness box and sometimes menace witnesses with their bodily presence, but counsel in Hong Kong, like their English counterparts, are confined to their own space in the counsels' row. They barely move their feet during cross-examination and remain physically aloof from the witnesses they interrogate. Some of the Hong Kong barristers I observed even avoided making eye contact with witnesses.

In between the counsels' row and the clerk's table is a forbidden zone, where counsel are cautious not to trespass. It is a space that both physically and symbolically separates the judge and the counsel.[9] Barristers, let alone parties and witnesses, cannot physically get too close to a judge. When, for example, a barrister submits a document to a judge, she must do so by handing it first to the court clerk. The judge never steps down to the so-called well of the courtroom occupied by counsel and other parties. Likewise, when a judge enters the courtroom, he always enters through his own door; he does not enter his elevated bench from below, an arrangement that signifies the judge's social distance from and authority over the rest of the room (cf. Rock 1993: 197–262). In the common law, judges who intervene too much in adversarial trials risk undermining their impartiality and superiority. Lawyers say judges are not supposed to "descend into the arena" but should stay "above" the debates between counsel, both literally and figuratively. The spatial quarantine mimics the social quarantine that a judge must not violate by getting involved in the exchanges between counsel and witnesses.

Sitting in the counsels' row and to the left of the judge is the plaintiff's counsel (or the prosecutor in a criminal trial); and to the right of the judge is the defendant's counsel. Behind them are the instructing solicitors on both sides, sometimes accompanied by their own assistants and trainees. In a simple civil case, a legal team usually consists of two to three lawyers (a barrister, a solicitor, and a legal clerk or sometimes a trainee solicitor). In some highly complicated commercial trials in which a large amount of money is at stake, it is not uncommon for a client to fly in a "London silk" (Queen's Counsel from England) along with a local silk and their juniors. In those cases, a legal team can easily add up to eight or nine lawyers.[10]

Further away from but facing the judge, at the far end of the room is the dock, which is where defendants sit in a criminal trial.[11] On the two sides off the main axis of the judge's line of sight are the jury box and the public area. Juries are seldom used in civil trials in Hong Kong; libel and malicious prosecution cases are the only exceptions.[12] The jury box is located on the far side (with reference to where the doors are located) of the court; the jury enters through a separate door from behind the judge's bench.[13] The witness box is on the near side of the courtroom facing the jury box. An interpreter, if needed, usually sits nearby. No shorthand writers or stenographers are present in the courtrooms these days. Instead, microphones are placed in front of all the key actors (judge, counsel, witness), and the proceedings are digitally recorded. Behind the witness box lies the press bench and the public gallery. Trial proceedings are open to the public. Most often, the only people sitting in the public area are parties to the trial and relatives and friends of those parties. At times, reporters may attend cases with a human interest angle, such as trials involving celebrities.

The courtroom is thus not a neutral space within which trials begin and end. Besides the hierarchy of roles created through its spatial demarcation, the courtroom is furthermore a symbolic space carefully laid out to create an iconic resemblance of the vision of juridical formalism. For example, the courtroom is fully enclosed with no view to the outside (the law as a self-referential, bounded entity). From the outside, one can only get a view of the counsels' row through a small window in the double doors. Visually, the courtroom is neither embracingly warm nor harshly cold; it is characterized by a kind of business-as-usual blandness that is maintained by the artificial lighting of halogen bulbs and fluorescent strips within a completely walled space. Auditorily, the courtroom is maximally transparent—strangely enough, suffocatingly so. The acoustics inside the courtroom feature a carefully managed dead background that completely envelops the ear. The deadness is further enhanced by a sound lobby that separates the two entrance doors of the courtroom; the sound lobby is designed to insulate the courtroom from noises made in the public concourse.[14] Sound really carries in the courtrooms. Some counsel say that they have to remind themselves to speak in hushed tones with their instructing solicitor on matters they do not want the opposing counsel to hear. The deadness is not simply some kind of silent background to the human voices. It is as integral to the transparency of the testimonies given by witnesses as the silence in a cloistered monastery is to the majesty expressed in the sound of Gregorian chant. This pin-drop silence, in other words, is *iconic* of the supposedly pristine, accurate, and unambiguous nature of courtroom exchanges in a trial.

Outside the courtroom is the public concourse, where people wait and chat. Each floor of the court building has a few meeting rooms that are built to allow barristers and solicitors to converse in private on matters related to their cases. Even when there are no meetings, the consultation rooms are often used as resting places for barristers and solicitors. They allow lawyers to get away from the direct gaze of clients, both their own and those of the opposing side. It is surprising to see how little interaction there is between counsel and clients; in the course of my fieldwork, it was not uncommon to see, particularly in the lower courts, counsel talk more with their counterparts during breaks than with their own clients, despite the apparent antagonism displayed inside the courtroom. Not just the courtrooms but indeed the whole building is built around an artificial ecology of controlled segregation among judges (who for most of the time remain invisible), counsel (who are offered their own space and privacy), and laypeople. For this reason, there is a lawyer-only canteen (or cafeteria, as it is called in the United States) located inside the public canteen for the High Court.[15] Counsel are also given their own space to put on their wigs and gowns inside the High Court Building.

RITUALISTIC ANACHRONISM
IN THE COURTS OF HONG KONG

Distancing the legal space from everyday life is a crucial step for any formalist system to create a world of its own. This world is decorated and choreographed to make it different from the familiar and the mundane. The mechanism in Hong Kong to create such distinctiveness is unmistakably colonial, achieved by means of a special form of theatricality that I would describe as anachronistic. If the architecture succeeds in sealing off Hong Kong courtrooms from the noisy streets of the city and prepares the actors for their appropriate roles in trials, it is the alien costume that imbues the courtroom dramas with a different tradition. Anachronism effectively symbolizes the gap between interactions that happen in a courtroom and interactions on the street; it is this gap that juridical formalism relies on—one can neglect the obvious only at one's own peril. In fact, courtroom symbolism is doubly anachronistic, a form of theatricality that is borrowed not just from a different place but also from a different time. Together, this combination of distancing and embeddedness builds up an institutional context in which formalistic procedures are carried out.

The Englishness of courtroom practice is literally woven into the fabric of the clothes of judges and counsel. To begin with, there is the famous horsehair wig. Judges are required to wear a short wig (also known as a bob wig) that has no side curls but is frizzled all over and has two tails at the back; counsel, on the other hand, wear a tie wig, which has rows of curls at the side, a frizzled crown, and a tail (cf. Ede and Ravenscroft 2007). And then there is the wardrobe of gowns and robes. Judges sitting at different courts wear different robes. A judge presiding over a civil trial in the Court of First Instance wears a black silk robe. In a criminal trial, the judge wears the famous scarlet robe with a scarlet hood or tippet. The costume also includes a black scarf and girdle (see Figure 1). A District Court judge (similar to a Circuit Court judge in England) wears the same robe in criminal and civil trials. It is a black robe with mauve trimmings in the middle. There is also a red tippet over the left shoulder.

Barristers always wear their gowns when appearing in open court. It is a visual display of privilege, because only a robed counsel has the right to legally represent clients and address a judge in open court. The differences between the black gown worn by a junior barrister and the black gown worn by a senior barrister are indistinguishable to the untrained eye, but they are visible among lawyers. Junior barristers wear an open-fronted black stuff gown with open sleeves and a gathered yoke. Senior barristers, known as Queen's Counsel in the colonial days and, since 1997, by the less glittering title of senior counsel, wear a silk gown with a flap collar and long, closed sleeves. Underneath the gown, a Senior Counsel wears a court coat, like a black morning coat, instead of a suit jacket.

FIGURE 1. *Court of First Instance judges in their famous scarlet robes marching at the ceremonial opening of the legal year.*

It is a running joke among lawyers in Hong Kong that a High Court courtroom is probably the coldest place indoors in all of Hong Kong, apparently because the temperature has to be kept low enough for judges and lawyers to don the seventeenth-century traditional English attire, known to be "itchy, unhygienic, and uncomfortable" (Yablon 1995; cf. Baker 1978), to say nothing of putting them on in subtropical Hong Kong. On ceremonial occasions, such as the opening of the legal year each January, judges and senior counsel must even wear full-bottomed wigs with curls hanging down the front. It is perhaps no coincidence that the opening of the legal year in Hong Kong does not follow the English calendar, which opens in October. Instead, Hong Kong's legal year opens in January, the coldest month in Hong Kong and understandably the least uncomfortable month to don the robe and hood and, above all, that heavy full-bottomed ceremonial wig (see Figure 2).

The way the English-style court system goes about its business would surely seem confusing to someone who has not been exposed to its culture and who looks at it with fresh eyes. Where else can one find an institution where the purported pursuit of a universal ideal of justice is so embedded in the meticulously defined contours of prestige and power? Yet cultural traditionalists, a label one can use to describe many legal professionals in Hong Kong, believe that the practice preserves the dignity of the justice process. Hence the question of preserving the colonial costume is rarely debated in Hong Kong. The practice of wearing wigs and robes has been seriously questioned in other common law jurisdictions where the practice is kept, such as Australia and, of course, England, but in Hong Kong the robing practice is still revered; an overwhelming majority of judges and barristers are still in favor of maintaining the tradition.[16] Many, particularly well-established judges and barristers, argue that the wigs and gowns promote the dignity of the legal system. Some lawyers in Hong Kong would go so far as to say that the practices represent the "best tradition of the rule of law."[17] The argument often made in support of the continued wearing of wigs and robes is how the costume depersonalizes counsel in a trial. Robing is said to be a practice that at once highlights the role and deemphasizes the persona of a judge. In the course of my

FIGURE 2. *Hong Kong's chief justice Andrew Li speaking at the ceremonial opening of the legal year. Courtesy of the Hong Kong Judiciary.*

fieldwork, I was often surprised by how judges looked and spoke differently when I met with them in plain clothes. The arcane costume, the wig in particular, does offer some form of thin disguise. But as a practice originated in colonial Hong Kong, it had, and still has, not only the effect of depersonalizing the role of the judge but also of delocalizing that same role. Donning the ostentatiously English judicial attire obliterates any affinity, ethnic or cultural, between Chinese judges and the litigants being judged. It reminds litigants that whoever the judge is, Chinese or non-Chinese, once he puts on the black robe and silvery wig, he has a role to play and to display, even if in practice he can only approximate the principled image conferred by his dressed persona. It is a role whose considerations are not determined by the local beliefs and customs of a Chinese society but by the English common law.

ANACHRONISTIC ETIQUETTE

Besides the wigs and gowns, anachronistic theatricality is further heightened by an elaborate greeting system. A system in which a judge is still addressed as "My Lord" and counsel address each other as "learned friends" clearly belongs to a different time and space. Its argot and elaborate mannerisms are unknown to most native speakers of English. Table 3 shows an elaborate system of nomenclature that lawyers have to learn during their legal training. This nomenclature is spelled out in a professional guide to advocacy in Hong Kong and covers the proper modes of address for different levels of the courts. These instructions capture the elaborateness of the well-formed "manner."

Courtroom English in Hong Kong, modeled after the English system, is a speech genre of its own. Through the use of abstruse legal jargon and highly stylized mannerisms, courtroom regulars create a ritualistic space of the legally learned distinct not just from the rest of the society but also from the rest of the laypeople in the courtroom. Such an inner space within the four walls of a courtroom is quite literally created by means of language. By deploying a set of elliptical formulaic expressions, lawyers and judges are able to mark out the boundaries of a world of legal expertise. For example, counsel often begin a cross-examination with the formulaic "May it please Your Lordship," an arcane style of exchange

TABLE 3 *Mode of address of judicial officers in Hong Kong*

Mode of address in court

Justice of the Court of Appeal	My Lord, My Lady
Judge of the High Court and Deputy Judge	My Lord, My Lady
Judge of the District Court	Your Honour
Magistrate	Sir, Madam, or less common today, Your Worship
Master in chambers or open court	Master (irrespective of the gender of the bench)—never Your Mastership
Member of tribunal or board	The Tribunal, the Board, as, e.g., "If it please the Tribunal . . ." When addressing one member, use their personal title as "Your Honour" in the Lands Tribunal

Mode of address outside court

Justice of the Court of Appeal	Judge ——
Judge of the High Court and Deputy Judge	Judge ——
Judge of the District Court	Judge ——
Magistrate	Mr. ——, Ms. ——
Master	Mr. ——, Ms. ——
Member of tribunal or board	If a judge, then as above, otherwise Mr. ——, or Ms. ——, Mrs. ——

Mode of address by letter

Justice of the Court of Appeal	The Honourable Chief Justice ——
	Dear Chief Justice ——
	The Honourable Mr. Justice ——
	Madam Justice ——
	Dear Mr. Justice ——
	Dear Madam Justice ——
Judge of the High Court or Deputy Judge	The Honourable Mr. Justice ——
	Dear Mr. Justice ——
Judge of the District Court or Deputy Judge	His or Her Honour ——
	Dear Judge ——
Magistrate	Mr. ——, Ms. ——
	Dear Mr. ——, Ms. ——
Master	The Registrar
	The Deputy Registrar
	Dear Mr. ——, Ms. ——
Member of a tribunal or board	If a judge, then as above, otherwise Mr. ——, Ms. ——

SOURCE: Wilkinson et al. (2007: 151–152). Courtesy of LexisNexis.

reminiscent of the old society of manners and a language of traditional-ism that displays hierarchy by means of its elaborate system of address. In this space, a simple "Thank you" gives way to the more theatrical "I'm much obliged." This kind of verbal mannerism is, as British sociologist Pat Carlen aptly describes, a form of "collusive interprofessional show-manship" (Carlen 1976: 32).

Hence arcane courtroom English bestows on the group a mysteri-ous, almost sacred quality by turning ordinary conversations into a code through which its users recognize and communicate with one another to the exclusion of outsiders. In fact, courtroom English used by barris-ters operates on the explicit, albeit no longer realistic, assumption that the bar is a small exclusive club within which all its members know each other on a personal basis; hence barristers address each other as learned friends. In a trial, if a counsel is opposed by another counsel whom she does not know, she does not say, "I'm sorry, I don't know your name"; instead she says, "I'm sorry, I've *forgotten* your name" (K. Evans 1998: 29–30). A cultured counsel is supposed to know and acknowledge her opponent. Such exclusivity is most manifest when barristers as a practice do not address solicitors as "learned."[18]

Whether the person addressed is indeed learned or not, what is said is less important than the social distinction displayed through the prag-matic performance of the address. Like most systems of social distinc-tion (Bourdieu 1977), this is a speech genre that is never systematically taught, not even in the local law schools, but is acquired only when one submerges oneself in the proper habitus. As a retired judge in Hong Kong suggested, real-life advocacy is best learned by "sitting next to Nelly," that is, by observing how the master does it (Law Society of Hong Kong 2000). A young pupil can learn to talk like counsel only by listening to the way experienced counsel talk. A competent English counsel is ex-pected "to entice, to flatter, to insult" (Pannick 1992: 1). She is even expected to display a degree of sycophancy toward the judge, as shown in the hyperbolic addresses of "My Lord" or "Your Lordship." It is this element of exaggerated theatricality that allows counsel to play the role of orator, very much in the classical sense of the term—that is, one who is good at advocating views she does not necessarily believe. Sincerity is not a necessary ingredient for this speech genre; instead it is wit, eloquence, and an aura of aloofness that make an advocate formidable.[19] There is no mistaking that, alongside the horsehair wig and the flowing gown, it is this style of English language that reminds people of the system's colonial English origins. Many judges and lawyers in Hong Kong are cultural traditionalists, as mentioned earlier. For them, the elaborate manner and dress together create an idealized tableau of the majesty of law in Hong Kong. They defend the elaborate etiquette by arguing that these practices confer dignity upon the legal process. Like the colonial wig and gown, the faithful preservation of little oral rituals shows that this legal system, despite the change of sovereignty, remains an English, or at least an English-style, common law system.

This system, adopted in Hong Kong in its early colonial days, is still alive and well at different levels of courts in Hong Kong today; but as we will see in greater detail in Chapter 6, the degree of meticulousness people expend on observing court etiquette hinges greatly on whether English or Cantonese is used as the language of the trial. Much of this elaborate system of address is lost in trials when Cantonese is used. I asked counsel why they did not re-create the same system in Cantonese. Most of them wondered whether an elaborate system of address could be developed in Cantonese. But simply word for word, or phrase for phrase, this can surely be done in Cantonese. After all, the Chinese have an even longer history of feudalism than the English, if one wants to talk about the source of this honorific system.[20] Hierarchical titles and addresses can be readily borrowed from the feudalistic system of Imperial China. But this is beside the point. The reason that lawyers suggest they cannot do the same thing in Cantonese is not so much that it is semantically impossible but more because it is pragmatically unbearable. The elaborate manner, when done in Cantonese, is no longer theatrical to the ears of people in Hong Kong; instead it is realistically strained, so much so that it becomes unbearably awkward. As a counsel told me, a well-executed "My Lord" in English sounds quaint and dainty, but the same expression in Cantonese is just too odd and ridiculous. Another counsel said he broke out in goosebumps when he heard the phrase "learned friend" uttered in Cantonese (see Chapter 7).

George Steiner, in *After Babel* (1998), remarks how cultural remoteness miraculously creates a sense of poetic exoticism that is not trapped by any conventional sense of "what the thing is or ought to be like" (p. 380). "My Lord" is "untranslatable" in Cantonese precisely because its reverence and good sense originate from an anachronism that can be uttered only in the remote voice of English. The innocence of distance vanishes once "My Lord" is uttered in the familiar and mundane sounds of Cantonese. Whatever the translation, to say "My Lord" in Cantonese is joltingly awkward because the way Cantonese is used is contrary to the elaborate and extravagant tone that such a system aims to convey; Cantonese, as the vernacular language, also lacks the anachronistic distancing that allows the phrase to be heard from afar. In Hong Kong many of the English legal set-piece phrases can be uttered only in the context of a courtroom and pragmatically only in English. As we will see, for related but different reasons, when addressing a judge in Cantonese, litigants and even lawyers often resort to the more colloquial title of address 法官大人 [faat3 gun1 daai6 jan4] (literally, "Judge, Your Big Man" but roughly meaning "Judge, Your Excellency"), despite the fact that officially the Hong Kong Judiciary prefers the more formal address of 法官閣下 [faat3 gun1 gok3 haa6] (which can be roughly translated as "Sir/Madam Judge"). I will come back to this point in Chapter 6.

The untranslatability of this address system is the first important and perhaps the most easily recognizable sign pointing to the difference between Cantonese and English courtrooms. As I said, the address system is untranslatable not so much because semantically one cannot find equivalent or similar Cantonese terms but more because the pragmatic effect of the English address cannot be reproduced in Cantonese, because English and Cantonese constitute two distinct linguistic habituses that do not overlap. English in Hong Kong is particularly suited for the task, because for many locals in Hong Kong, it plays a negligible part in everyday life. Its status as a prestigious language (see Chapter 3) allows it to facilitate the kind of anachronistic theatricality that is exotic by design.

It is important to point out that theatricality in English-language courtrooms is limited to conversations among members of the so-called legal fraternities. Such a style prevails in the interactions among the professionals in a courtroom, that is, among counsel and judges. But when lay litigants are involved, counsel and judges often quickly switch to a different style of English—a supposedly plain, textbook-like style, to which I now turn.

"PLAIN ENGLISH," HONG KONG STYLE

Theatrical courtroom English is confined to interactions among members of the inner space of legal professionals. When interacting with lay witnesses, courtroom regulars, including lawyers (barristers and solicitors), judges, and interpreters, adhere to a form of English that would be described by people in English-speaking societies as more stripped down and bland but at the same time more impersonal and bookish. This type of English is what people would commonly call the English of nonnative speakers (although the term misleads rather than clarifies). The avoidance of metaphors and idioms is often the first thing expatriate counsel and judges mention when they are asked to describe the English they use to communicate with witnesses. It is part of a conscious attempt to manage language in a manner that judges believe to be most conducive to conveying meaning. From the judges' standpoint, idioms, conventional metaphors, or colloquial expressions are all linguistic features that complicate understanding, because meaning conveyed by these devices cannot be easily glossed from the so-called literal meaning of the component words. During my fieldwork in Hong Kong, in an interview Tom Harper (pseudonym),[21] an expatriate District Court judge who started his legal career in England and then worked in Hong Kong for many years, made the following observation: "I don't think idiom is used as much here because there is a fear of misunderstanding." Judge Harper gave an example: "You wouldn't say two defendants are like 'peas in a pod' for instance to a Chinese jury because that's an expression that native speakers would understand but one might fear that non-native speakers might not understand."

The same judge also explained in the interview that it is not just idioms and colloquialisms but also vivid references that are more locally rooted, references that breathe life into a language, that are purged for the simplicity of communication. This explains the dry, textbook-like quality of English in Hong Kong. Harper remarked:

If you go to court in England, people make references to things [that] are perhaps part of the culture, like literature and television programs, all the sort of things that make up the sort of native culture. . . . Because there is an uncertainty here as to whether people do understand that, one would perhaps tend to avoid that sort of things. I think you'll find for instance literary allusions which are sometimes made by judges in their judgments in England wouldn't be made here or in addressing juries because they seem rather out of place.

The lack of reference to local culture is compensated for, so to speak, by the use of bookish words and expressions that would sound pedantic to the ears of many English speakers in other societies. If one looks at the choice of words in oral conversations in English-language trials in Hong Kong, "adjourn" is preferred to the colloquial "put off," "terminate" is more common than "end," "implement" is used rather than "carry out," "aforesaid" rather than "mentioned earlier," "bona fide" rather than "honest" (not exactly English, but my point is not primarily linguistic; on "bona fide" see Chapter 5), and so on. The English language in the courtrooms of Hong Kong thus follows a style that comes closer to writing than conversing. It follows closely the kind of textbook English that is characterized by a distinctly formal lexicon acquired through school learning rather than everyday practice. In his memoir, *Tales from No. 9 Ice House Street*, Patrick Yu Shuk-siu, a pioneering Chinese counsel in postwar Hong Kong, offers another nice example of how the use of bookish English terms can sometimes cause confusion. Yu recounts an interesting case involving a court interpreter who "loved to show off his knowledge of English." Yu was the defense counsel for a man charged with attempted rape. Besides the court interpreter, Yu was the only person in the court who spoke and understood Cantonese. The victim, a young Chinese woman, gave her evidence in Cantonese and told the court that she had met the defendant only briefly. When asked by the prosecuting counsel whether she had seen the accused again thereafter, she replied, "事後我地耐不久都有來往" ("Thereafter we saw each other every now and then") (Yu 2002: 146). Yu remarks, however, that the court interpreter was noted for his tendency to use long, bookish words. His interpretation read, "After that initial encounter, we had intermittent intercourse." The double entendre of the word *intercourse* in speech was completely missed by the interpreter, who interpreted in his bookish, hyperformal style.[22]

It is not difficult to understand why, in the context of Hong Kong, the hard becomes easy and the easy becomes hard. Of course, what is hard and what is easy is always a matter of local pragmatics, particularly for a language as globally varied as English, a language spoken in a multitude of accents, phonologically as well as socially (cf. Kachru 1990; Schneider 2007; Trudgill and Hannah 2002).

For many locals in Hong Kong who learned their English through grammar books and dictionaries and use English mainly in their workplaces, colloquial expressions commonly found in spoken British and American English are the most difficult for them to master. English, in part because of its historical association with colonialism, has been and remains an elite formal language that plays a big role in most things big but a small role in the everyday lives of Hong Kong people. It is not the language one can hear in the sweaty streets, the noisy markets, and the boisterous dim sum restaurants of the city. As I concluded in Chapter 3, there is no such thing as colloquial English in Hong Kong.[23] In other words, there is a conspicuous absence of a full-blown colloquial register in Hong Kong English. The domains where English is used are mostly functionally specified and task oriented. The most typical and also influential genre within these domains was the bureaucratic English used by the colonial civil servants. Theirs was a form of paperwork English, rigid and formal, honed to facilitate a style of oral exchange characterized by its barrenness in playfulness and vitality, a form of stoic exchange where nothing is left to what philosopher H. Paul Grice (1975) calls "conversational implicature"—that is, the you-know-what-I-mean, are-you-thinking-what-I'm-thinking kinds of conventionalized intuition.

JURIDICAL FORMALISM IN PRACTICE

Somewhat paradoxically, it is because of this social history of English that the language is primed for the work of the formalistic courts in Hong Kong. To understand this, we need to look further into the ways language is used in court. As mentioned, the phenomenon of the concentration of trials is a key feature unique to the common law system. Complex rules have been developed for the making of evidence in courts. Underlying all these rules (e.g., the famous evidential rule against hearsay in criminal trials) is an attempt to effectively turn what a witness says in court into part of a legal *text*. The way I use the term *text* here is not restricted narrowly to physical texts (e.g., a textbook); instead, I am referring to some kind of bounded, connected whole that exhibits formal coherence by the very ground rules that stipulate its production. One can view the making of evidence as the most institutionalized form of *en*textualization—that is, a process in which utterances are turned into some recognizable text readily decoupled from its immediate context (Bauman and Briggs 1990; Blommaert 2001). In the context of a common law trial, the entire institutional setup is designed to make what a witness says in court as readily segmentable, transcribable, and quotable as possible for the eventual purpose of adjudication. Counsel and judges routinely quote what witnesses said in court in their deliberations and decisions about critical events, so much so that direct quotes in oral evidence are like x-rays in medical examination; they are considered objective enough to take the guesswork out of diagnosis (cf. Hirsch 1998; Philips 1986).

But the belief that words in quotation are a lossless reproduction of utterances presupposes a particular view of language, a view that privileges abstract semantic meaning over situational pragmatics. Despite its apparent precision, semantic meaning is in essence a gesture of abstraction, a generalization of experience.[24] There are two problems inherent in a purely semantic view of language. First, the semantic view tends to equate the identity of words with the identity of meaning. More precisely, it tends to conflate what linguists and philosophers call the identity of *utterance-inscriptions* with the identity of *utterances* (cf. Lyons 1995). A quick example can easily illustrate the difference between utterances and utterance-inscriptions. Consider the apparently tautological sentence "Snow is white." The meaning of this sentence is as self-evident as actually existing English sentences can possibly get. However, we can easily imagine some situations in which the statement can be taken to mean something totally different. For example, in a seminar on social movement, a young graduate student asks his professor if the African American scholar presenting at the conference is David Snow (a well-known sociologist of social movements); his mentor replies, "Snow is white." In such a case, it would be a mistake to say that the tautological sentence and the mentor's reply mean the same thing despite the fact that they share the same utterance-inscription.

Second, and more important for my analysis, direct quotations alone tend become generic by rendering the context within which an utterance is made invisible. I am not just referring to words such as *now*, *this*, or *there* and pronouns such as *you*, *she*, or *they*, which have been conventionally considered by linguists as *indexical* (i.e., their reference varies from context to context) (Bar-Hillel 1954). I am instead referring to the indexicality, or indexical quality, of everyday utterances that word-by-word re-presentations are not able to make explicit.[25] Again, a couple of examples will help. Let's say someone makes the remark "Ming is so tall!" A listener cannot tell, just by hearing those words, whether the remark is meant to be sincere or sarcastic unless one knows, among other things, the height of Ming. Or consider the well-known example of "supplying a quarter of potatoes" used by Elizabeth Anscombe, a student of Ludwig Wittgenstein. Anscombe explains that there are ways of supplying potatoes that might not satisfy our everyday meaning of supplying a quarter of potatoes, for example, if the grocer who was supposed to supply the potatoes to Anscombe, after delivering them, asked someone else to come and take the potatoes away from her again. But it would be absurd to conclude that whenever one asks a grocer to supply potatoes, one must add that the grocer should not take them away again. Anscombe's point is that we seldom find our everyday descriptions ambiguous because "every description presupposes a context of normal procedure, but that context is not even implicitly described by the description" (Anscombe 1958: 71). Through her potatoes example, Anscombe suggests to us that our day-to-day understanding of so-called brute facts already entails our knowledge of the contextual background in which these facts normally operate.

How does juridical formalism address the problem of the ambiguity of situated meanings? Its solution, drastic as usual, is to attempt to minimize, if not totally eliminate, the role of context in the interpretation of meaning. Among the vast and practically infinite repertoire of speech acts, juridical formalism delimits the scope of legitimate speech acts for testifying down to just one: the supposedly universal speech act of *statement making*. In a way, statement making is the speech act equivalent of Kantian pure reason, deriving and deploying nuggets of truth from which all contextual conditions have been removed. Statement making, from the perspective of speech act theory, is an act that negates its own performative element, a null act of doing. Its only "act" is to describe. In contrast, performative utterances are produced when the speaker performs an act of doing. According to the official theory of formalism, the main function of calling a witness is not to ask her to *interact* performatively with counsel before the judge but to *describe* things that happened in the past in unambiguous statements whose truth value (the statement is either true or false) is determinable.

The judges I interviewed in the course of my fieldwork said that ambiguities could be avoided if a witness described all the relevant information to the court. Hence a witness is expected to describe (and counsel is expected to ask) not just the remark "Ming is so tall!" (to return to our example) but also how tall Ming is (our conclusion would be different if Ming were 7 feet rather than 5 feet tall). It is a basic belief underlying such a mode of inquiry that accurate descriptions in statement form can make up for the unfamiliarity that judges and juries have with the immediate context of so-called relevant facts. Pure description, through the use of language, can allow juries and judges to know, or at least know enough, of events that cannot be reenacted in court. It is of course questionable whether a clear line can be drawn between *statement* (or description) on one side and *comment* (or interaction) on the other, a point that I return to in Chapter 6. Suffice it to point out here that complex and highly technical rules are developed in the common law precisely to see to the making of statements in evidence. From the moment a witness steps into the witness box, she is required to swear in or affirm that she is well aware of what she is going to do. An oath or an affirmation is a quintessential speech act, involving the use of performative verbs ("I swear," "I affirm") to underscore the legal obligation of telling "the truth, the whole truth, and nothing but the truth"; it makes explicit that the person who testifies is fully aware of the nature of the speech acts she is about to perform and of the legal consequences of her failure under the law against perjury, so much so that if a person (e.g., a child) fails to appreciate the nature of such a speech act, despite explicit metapragmatic rendering, he is considered, in the technical jargon of evidence law, *incompetent*. A person is required to understand "the solemnity of the occasion" and "the special duty to tell the truth" before he or she is deemed competent to give sworn evidence in court.[26]

In the course of testifying, witnesses are further reminded by the presiding judge that they should testify about facts and only facts (with the exception of expert witnesses). The way the term *fact* is used in law can be confusing, in part because it is often used as a slogan term for judges and counsel to censor unruly witnesses from making irrelevant comments; but more important, it is also because the law holds a surprisingly constructivist view of the idea of fact. Facts often mean facts *asserted* in law talks, that is, the retelling of events that, subject to the examination of appropriate evidence, might be accepted as part of the legal retelling of what happened.[27] As historian Barbara Shapiro points out, the English courtroom is perhaps the single most important arena for facilitating a modern reconception of fact "from something that had to be sufficiently proved by appropriate evidence to be considered worthy of belief to something for which appropriate verification had already taken place" (2000: 31). Of course, what counts as appropriate verification is the one key question that the law of evidence tries to resolve. The singular purpose of a most elaborate system of evidentiary rules in the common law is to ensure that only the right information is heard and used to establish the facts of the case.[28]

But my focus here is not so much on the evidential rules that govern the contents of evidence as how linguistic practices used in trials constitute evidence that is deemed appropriate (although understandably the two aspects are correlated). In actual practice, eliciting oral testimony from a witness involves first and foremost breaking down the witness's story into what Matoesian calls "tightly segmented episodes of verbal action" (2001: 71). These segments then become the building blocks for the legal retelling of what happened, or simply put, legal facts. And this breakdown and recomposition is facilitated by a highly structured series of questions and answers.

It is for this reason that witnesses testifying in court are designedly restricted to only answering counsel's questions; they are discouraged from, for example, offering comments or asking questions in return. A witness in an English courtroom in Hong Kong veering away from the activity of statement making is liable to be sanctioned by counsel and judge. Consider the following example. In a case that I will discuss in further detail later in this chapter, a witness, Chi Keung, tried to playfully dodge a question from the defense counsel. When asked what the defendant had told him, the witness replied, "What do you think?" His act of answering a question with another question, rhetorical no less, was greeted icily by the judge, who reminded him, with a poker face, of his duty as a witness.[29]

Cross-Examination in English of Chi Keung (W) by Defense Counsel (C)

C: Why did you never think of asking Chi Lok earlier before 1994?

W: Of course there's numerous request.

C: Numerous request?

W: Of course. I just asked verbal [*inaudible*].

C: And what did Chi Lok say?

W: What do you think?

JUDGE: We are not here to think. You tell us.

W: OK, most of the time he just dragged us around. You know, he didn't say no. You know, he tells other stories. You know, how hardworking he is. All the old stuff. You have to sit down and listen, and then in the end we were talking about other topics. He jumped from A to B. We never get a straight answer.

In the English trials in Hong Kong, any nonreply, or more precisely, any reply that does not directly address the question in statement form, is readily sanctioned by judges and lawyers—or sometimes by court interpreters who translate the evidence from Chinese into English.

The guiding belief is that by restricting witnesses to answering only questions raised by counsel, the court can elicit from them utterances of a purely *constative* nature. In developing his well-known speech act theory, English philosopher J. L. Austin made the distinction between constative and performative utterances (Austin 1962). An utterance is constative, or descriptive, when it makes statements whose meaning can be reduced to a matter of either truth or falsity. When judges and counsel ask witnesses to tell them just the facts, they mean witnesses should confine themselves to making only constative utterances. Sometimes, this "drive for reference" (Mertz 1985) is made known explicitly to witnesses. One only needs to take a cursory look at the most common formulaic expressions used by counsel. Expressions such as "Is it *true* that . . . ?" "Are you *saying* that . . . ?" "I *put* it to you that . . ." all use explicit markers to force the answerer to confirm or refute the assertion in question. The witness is expected to reply with a simple yes or no, in correspondence with the binary value of truth or falsity in a propositional statement. In fact, counsel and judges at times explicitly instruct witnesses to do just that: "Please just answer yes or no."

I will spend the rest of the chapter explaining how the interaction structure of cross-examination is set up to facilitate the elicitation of constative utterances in English-language courtrooms of Hong Kong. To wit, cross-examination follows a basic structure that distinguishes it from commonplace conversation, a structure that I describe as statement and reply, to borrow from Erving Goffman. This structure reifies a vision of formalism that is emblematic of the reflexive understanding of the rule of law by legal professionals in Hong Kong—rule-bound, impersonal, and orderly. The key feature of English-language trials in Hong Kong is the tight structural reciprocity between their institutional form and their interactional form. The tight fit constricts the legal space, precluding any alternative view of the hierarchy of power. My next task is to describe in further detail how one can approach the process of cross-examination as a specific interaction structure with unique linguistic features.

EXAMINATION-IN-CHIEF
AS GUIDED STORYTELLING

In a typical common law trial, the whole process of testifying is made up of three separate stages, of which cross-examination is by far the most crucial. The first stage, known as examination-in-chief, or direct examination as it is called in the United States, presents the sequence of events from the perspective of the plaintiff or the defendant. It is, in common parlance, telling your side of the story. It presages the points of contention that are to follow. At this stage, the litigant is guided (but not led, because leading questions are not allowed) by the gentle hand of his own counsel. In giving his oral account of what happened, the witness is said to be giving evidence in support of his version of the facts. The following example is taken from a case that involves a family dispute that is not uncommon among Chinese families. The key defendant, Chi Lok, is the eldest son of the family; the two plaintiffs, Chi Hung and Chi Keung, are the defendant's younger brothers. Their father established one of the oldest undertaking businesses in Hong Kong. The patriarch of the family died in the early 1970s. The dispute can be traced back to a meeting right after the father's death. According to the account offered by the two plaintiffs, at the meeting Chi Lok begged other family members, with tears in his eyes, to let him carry on the family business. The family agreed, on the understanding that Chi Lok would operate the undertaking business as a trustee for other family members. To say that Chi Lok was a trustee means that he did not inherit the business but simply looked after the business in the interest of the whole family. Not surprisingly, Chi Lok's account about what happened in that meeting is different. He told the court that there was no agreement about his being the trustee of his father's estate. He simply inherited the entire family business as the eldest son of the family. It was a case of primogeniture. The nature of the agreement is central to the question of how the family estate should be distributed among the sons, which is the center of the whole lawsuit. According to Chi Hung and Chi Keung, Chi Lok was not entitled to inherit the family estate. They further suggested that it was the wish of their mother to give the four younger sons an equal share of half the family property left by their late father, according to the Chinese tradition. They told the court that their oldest brother was a spendthrift. They accused him of squandering the money without giving the rest of the family their fair shares. In the episode taken from the examination-in-chief of Chi Keung, by his counsel Paul Scott, one can see that, although the testimony follows a basic question-and-answer sequence, the witness is given room to tell his story in the way he wants. Scott, a veteran barrister, simply asks open-ended questions to help his client tell his side of the story. This is very different, as we will see, from the kind of forceful segmentation often found in hostile cross-examinations; the screw has yet to be tightened, so to speak.

Examination-in-Chief (Direct Examination) in English
of Chi Keung (W) by Paul Scott (C)

C: Did your mother make any stipulation regarding her interest in this property of Shau Kei Wan? Not then, but later on, did she tell you about it?

W: Oh yes, because . . . Put it this way, my mother lived with me since I got married in 1979. She had been with me for . . . til she died. OK?

C: Yeah.

W: And she had numerous complaints about events. That's how my mother had arranged something like, like, if you're talking about how to split the estate in the event of her death, she said that half would go to brother, I mean brother Chi Lok, and half would go to the four brothers.

C: That was her intention. She expressed to you. Did she?

W: That was mother's wish and order.

C: Her share would in fact go to the four brothers, including yourself.

W: Ah yes. Yes.

C: Did you at that time, say, either before or after you left Hong Kong, know about the property at 40 Lee Garden Road?

W: Yes, I was there. I spent a little time there.

C: Did you know who in fact was the registered owner of Lee Garden Road?

W: You mean who is the registered . . . , whose name registered for the property?

C: Yeah.

W: Yes, my father and Chi Lok.

C: During his lifetime, did your father express his wishes regarding this property in the event of his death?

W: Yeah, we always have . . . I mean sort of instruction, like an explanation but it's not in writing. So it's exactly identical to mother's wish, half to go to brother Chi Lok, half to go to four brothers. That's sort of a tradition in Chinese culture or something like that. I don't know.

The counsel here plays the role of a facilitator; he tries, within the limit of the rules, to string together a coherent account for his witness. At times, he rephrases and clarifies answers offered by Chi Keung. At times, he even borders on asking his client leading questions (e.g., "She expressed to you. Did she?"). Scott seldom interrupts Chi Keung; he tries not to break his answers down. Within this broad statement-and-reply framework, Chi Keung elaborates on a particular point and at times even offers details of an account that may not be entirely relevant to the question asked. Chi Keung has plenty of room to maneuver within the friendly questions asked by Scott; the witness is in control of the narrative flow, and Scott's gentle questions along the way to bring out his client's story. But despite its amicable tone, there is something that separates direct examination from everyday conversation. Throughout the entire testifying process, the roles of counsel and witnesses are clearly differentiated. Participants are required to stick to their roles assigned for the process (hence Scott asked questions and Chi Keung offered his answers). Also, a witness is expected to describe what happened. He is expected to tell his version of the story in a string of statements whose truth can be validated or, in some cases, invalidated.

Despite its seemingly straightforward format, the counsel I interviewed mostly consider examination-in-chief a tricky exercise. In Hong Kong, which follows the procedural rules of England, counsel are prohibited from rehearsing with a witness actual questions that will be raised during examination-in-chief. Witnesses at times give answers that surprise even their own counsel. When that happens, counsel have to find ways to do repairs, to fit an unexpected answer to the version of the story that their clients already told in earlier statements and interviews.

STATEMENT-AND-REPLY:
CROSS-EXAMINATION IN ENGLISH COURTROOMS

After the examination-in-chief comes the central drama of the trial, the cross-examination. Counsel from the opposing side enters the stage, and the witness has to endure a battery of questions that challenge his character or the reliability of his memory by undermining the coherence and reasonableness of his account. A witness is boxed in and is subjected to the gaze of the judge and, in a jury trial, the jurors. Cross-examination is undoubtedly the central procedure of a common law trial. John Henry Wigmore famously described cross-examination as "beyond any doubt the greatest legal engine ever invented for the discovery of truth" (1923, v. 3: 27, §1367). Cross-examination is frequently compared to games (Blumberg 1967; Danet and Bogoch 1980; Garfinkel 1956) or a contest (Goodpaster 1987; Woodbury 1984); the process is role specific, rule governed, and above all, competitive. It is an intense game, because the stakes are high. Money, honor, reputation, personal freedom, and, in some cases, a person's life may be at stake.

Role specificity is even more strictly enforced in cross-examination, when an uncooperative witness can be explicitly instructed to answer the questions counsel has raised. The adversarial examination process facilitates elicitation of evidence through carefully segmented question-and-answer sequences, and these turns are asymmetrically distributed between a counsel and a witness: The counsel asks questions, and the witness answers them.

It is interesting to note that in an adversarial system, counsel, not the witnesses, are the lead characters in cross-examination. Cross-examination is a highly asymmetric form of interaction. The counsel who asks questions is in the driver's seat, in full control of the flow of interactions. He decides not just what to ask but also when to dwell on something, when to move quickly, and when to interrupt. In terms of structure, cross-examination displays a kind of rigidity seldom seen in casual conversation. In fact, it is the process that gives the common law trial (as opposed to a civil law trial) its adversarial name. It is arguably the best-known form of institutionalized verbal combat, through its constant dramatization in American and British television programs and movies. Counsel take it as their duty to expose the inconsistencies of a witness's account, to tear apart its narrative unity, and hopefully to put a big dent in the credibility of the witness. A skilled counsel can take advantage of the inherited asymmetry of narrative power to undermine the story told by a witness. Studies have pointed out that underneath questioning and answering in a courtroom lies a whole gamut of sophisticated interactional crossfire (Atkinson and Drew 1979; Drew 1990, 1992; Matoesian 1993, 2001). A seasoned counsel, given the right to question, can weave his accusation, rebuttal, or insinuation through a series of seemingly straightforward questions and thus in the process achieve the purposes of undermining a witness's story, exposing or even creating incoherency out of the witness's story, and undermining the witness's credibility. A witness, although not completely passive, undoubtedly has far fewer linguistic apparatuses at her disposal (cf. Matoesian 2001). The role differentiation between the questioner and the answerer puts the witness in a more vulnerable position because, even though a witness has no control over the questions asked, she is expected to answer most if not all of them. In principle, a witness can refuse to answer a question, asserting her right to remain silent, although she has to explicitly indicate her refusal to the judge. Sometimes, a witness may resort to the frailty of human memory, but claiming "I don't remember" too many times will likely leave the judge with a suspicious impression unless the events in question happened a long time ago. Or the witness may offer an alternative description (Drew 1992) of the facts that contradicts and thereby undermines the narrative implied by the counsel's questions. A witness's ability to offer an alternative description is constrained, however, by the structural rule that stipulates that utterances from a witness must be in the form of a reply to counsel's questions. But even though the witness can only offer her descriptions reactively, the structurally privileged position of a counsel as questioner-*cum*-storyteller enables him to approximate narrative closure by selecting, juxtaposing, and sometimes omitting "facts" from a seemingly coherent story.

In his long essay "Replies and Responses," Goffman works out two ideal types in the structure of interaction: statement and reply, and call and response (Goffman 1981). Everyday interaction, according to Goffman, rarely corresponds to the tight, neat structure of statement and reply but more often fits into the loose format of call and response. A statement-and-reply sequence is characterized by a chain of questions and answers that sustain the flow of a dialogue. A statement refers to a move characterized by an orientation to some sort of answering to follow, and a reply refers to a corresponding move characterized by its being seen as an answering of some kind to a preceding matter that has been raised

(Goffman 1981: 24). It is deliberate, focused, and highly structured. In its ideal form, a statement elicits a reply and, in turn, the elicited reply answers the statement. Participants who follow the statement-and-reply structure operate with a one-move attention span in their utterances; the only difference between the nature of the attention given by the questioner and the answerer is in the orientation of their attentions—as the questioner anticipates an answer, the attention of the person giving the statement is prospective; the attention of the answerer is retrospective, as he or she replies in response to the preceding question. Hence a distinct binary differentiation arises between the role of a questioner and that of an answerer in the enactment of the sequence. A questioner is someone who is "oriented to what lies just ahead, and depend[s] on what is to come." An answerer is "oriented to what had just been said; and look[s] backward, not forward" (Goffman 1981: 5).

For Goffman, the structural straitjacket of statement and reply is considered too restrictive to be of practical use in studying everyday conversation. I find it useful, however, as a heuristic device to study highly restrictive talks conducted in institutionalized settings. The ideal type serves to illustrate the kind of distant formalism inherit in statement-and-reply types of interaction, a formalism that, in Goffman's words, is "independent of *what* is being talked about, and whether, for example, the matter is of great moment to those involved in the exchange or of no moment at all" (1981: 6). Statement and reply is used here as a heuristic model to outline an orderly, rule-bound mode of interaction that finds its full execution in English-language cross-examination in Hong Kong.[30]

The witness in the last example, Chi Keung, is cross-examined by his eldest brother's counsel, Jonathan Yeung. Chi Keung, like other witnesses in the hot seat during cross-examination, has become more suspicious and at times uncooperative with the questions from the opposing counsel. According to the two younger brothers, the defendant was a spendthrift and eventually squandered the family fortune. Yeung uses his questions not just to raise doubts about the story told by Chi Hung and Chi Keung but also to paint a different picture of Chi Lok in cross-examination. In the cross-examination, Yeung tries to show that Chi Keung expected

Chi Lok to give money to the family and that it is likely that the younger brother knew his brother had in fact contributed to the family.

Cross-Examination in English of Chi Keung (W) by Jonathan Yeung (C)

1 C: Let's concentrate on the situation in May 1972, all right? May?

2 W: May 1972.

3 C: You were in Hong Kong.

4 W: Yeah.

5 C: Do you know if any of your elder brothers and sisters were making contributions, giving money, meaning, to your father and mother?

6 W: No, I don't. [*pause*]

7 C: But you would not be surprised if they did. Is that correct?

8 W: No comment about that.

9 JUDGE: What did you just say?

10 W: I said no comment. He asked whether I would be surprised.

11 C: Is it not the Chinese tradition or is it in your family tradition that you give money to father and mother whenever you come out and earn money?

12 W: Yes, occasionally, yes. Should be.

13 C: Right.

14 W: But not necessarily the case.

15 C: Right, should be. Therefore you would not be surprised if your elder brothers and sisters did the same.

16 W: I really hope so.

17 C: All right. Thank you.

In cross-examination, counsel can use leading questions. A leading question is a question framed in such a way as to suggest to the witness the desired answer. It communicates what conversation analysts would call a distinct preference organization to the addressee (Atkinson and Drew 1979; Pomerantz 1984). Put differently, leading questions convey a preference structure that communicates to the person asked a response or a set of responses as natural, unmarked. Some leading questions lead by encompassing the preferred response in the question itself. A statement followed by a tag question is an obvious example. The question "You were drunk on that night, weren't you?" favors a yes answer as the preferred or the unmarked response. A witness who answers the dispreferred or marked response of no puts herself in a suspicious position that requires further justification. Less explicit but still leading is a negative question (a form often used by political talk show hosts and commentators in the United States), such as "Don't you think he's an idiot?" The negative question itself presupposes an unmarked response of yes that implicitly puts down a no as problematic. In the cross-examination of Chi Keung, Yeung first tries to see whether Chi Keung will confirm in his reply that Chi Lok gave money to the family back in 1972 (para. 1). He asks Chi Keung if he knew that his elder siblings gave money to the family (para. 5). Chi Keung says he did not know (para. 6). Yeung then uses leading questions to convey to the court the thesis that it should not be surprising at all for Chi Keung to expect Chi Lok to contribute to the family. Yeung does that in a circumspect way, though. Instead of asking whether Chi Keung would be surprised to know that his client gave money to their parents or not, his leading question (notice its negative form) appeals instead to traditional Chinese filial virtue. "Is it not the Chinese tradition or is it in your family tradition that you give money to father and mother whenever you come out and earn money?" (para. 11). This question, coupled with the fact that 30 years had elapsed between the disputed meeting and the time of the trial, implies that Chi Lok had likely given money to the family back in those days or else he would long have been criticized by his younger brothers. It is a leading question that marks no as an unnatural response. Chi Keung is caught in the tension (Chinese virtue versus his dislike of the defendant) created by the preference structure of the leading question. As he tries to wiggle out of the dilemma the question creates, Chi Keung replies with a cautious "occasionally" (which is not so much a direct answer) and then adds "Should be," before finally qualifying his answer with "but not necessarily the case" (para. 12). But that is enough concession from Chi Keung for Yeung to follow that up with another leading question, to show the one thing the defense wants to establish: that no one raised any complaints at the time even though it was expected that Chi Lok, the eldest son, should give money to the family. It implies that the likely explanation of the absence of complaints is of course that Chi Lok *did* give money to the family. By deploying the embedded evaluative structure of a leading question, Yeung successfully coaxed an opposing witness to admit that he would not be surprised to see his client giving money to the family, which in turn undermines the plaintiff's portrayal of the defendant as a selfish spendthrift. Chi Keung manages to add "I really hope so" (para. 16) at the end, indicating he was doubtful of Chi Lok's generosity. But Yeung already had the answer he wanted and decided to quickly move on to another topic. The example demonstrates how leading questions can be a powerful tool for counsel; through the sliding of one leading question into another, the lumping of one layer of implied meaning upon another, an opposing counsel can weave together a contrapuntal narrative in between the lines of the answers offered by the witness without stating that other story himself.

At times, counsel might not resort to leading questions but to questions that prescribe a simple yes/no reply. Yes/no questions present a clear-cut either/or option that no honest witness should find difficult to answer, or so it seems. But although a witness is asked one yes/no question at a time, counsel, especially a skilled one, can plot a yes/no question sequence that stretches across many turns. It is one of the most effective tools for counsel to perfect the cross-examination art of "slowly making mountains out of molehills" (Mauet 1996: 225, quoted by Matoesian 2001: 69).

The next example is taken from the cross-examination of another plaintiff in a different case. The plaintiff is a former ballerina named Ada Chan; she seeks compensation for what turned out to be a career-ending injury sustained during a training session in the early 1990s. She sued her own ballet company and what was then the Urban Council in Hong Kong (similar to city councils in Britain and the United States) for negligence. The Urban Council was involved because it was responsible for managing the venue, known as the Hong Kong Cultural Centre, at which the accident took place. The excerpt is taken from the cross-examination of Chan by the counsel for the Urban Council, Gautam Khilnani. Like many people who testify before the court in Hong Kong, the ballerina chose to speak through an interpreter, although it was clear from her responses in the trial that she understood English well. In the interest of space, I skip the original Cantonese replies made by the ballerina.

In the English trials in Hong Kong, witnesses often have to speak and listen through a court interpreter. The rigidity of taking turns is all the stronger in Hong Kong because the presence of a court interpreter sets practical limits on the length of each turn. (I discuss the important influence of court interpreters on the speech of witnesses in Hong Kong in Chapter 5.) Importantly, though, the presence of an interpreter tips the balance of linguistic power further in favor of opposing counsel during cross-examination. A witness eager to tell the judge her story would have to be held in check because court interpretation is like instant replay in sports—it slows down the tempo of the whole game for both players and spectators. A witness is told before giving testimony that she has to pause after a couple of sentences to wait for the interpreter to translate what she said into English. If the witness fails to do so, the interpreter will interrupt and ask the witness to pause and wait, for example, by telling her in Cantonese 等等先 [dang2 dang2 sin1] (meaning "wait"). This is so even when a witness uses conventional continuation markers in Cantonese, such as 同埋 [tung4 maai4] (meaning "and") and 重有 [zung6 jau5] (meaning "also"), to indicate she hasn't finished what she wants to say.

The example illustrates how counsel can take advantage of his role as a questioner to weave a favorable account for his client out of short, controlling questions directed to the plaintiff.[31]

Cross-Examination in English of Ada Chan (W) by Gautam Khilnani (C)

1   C: Do you agree that people who remain as corps de ballet dancers for up to five years or more may remain at that level of corps de ballet dancer for five years or more?

2   W: Yes.

3   C: And they come to a point when there is no progress to a higher level at coryphée and they just leave the company. Do you agree?

4   W: Yes.

5   C: And do you also agree that people offered solo spots, as you say you were in Pakita, might sometimes not be promoted?

6   W: Yes.

7   C: Now, Ms. Charles [ballet instructor] has also said that although you have a good physique, you have little stage personality. Again, is it

your evidence that she is being dishonest when she expresses that view, or are you prepared to accept that that is a view she expresses in good faith?

8   W: Yes.

9   C: You agreed that view is expressed in good faith.

10 W: Yes, on this point.

11 C: And do you not agree that this aspect of little stage personality is in other words talking about a dancer's charisma, which is that intangible thing beyond technique?

12 W: That would depend on the number of times of performance a dancer has got. A dancer would be able to acquire such stage personality through the performances.

13 C: That's not correct. As a matter of common sense, that's not correct, isn't it?

14 C: In reality, some people have charisma and some don't. Some don't and some acquire it; some don't and some never acquire it. That's the reality, isn't it?

[*The witness tries to say something.*]

15 C: Madam Chan, please wait for the question before you answer.

16 C: Do you agree that's the reality of the situation?

17 W: Yes.

18 C: I'd like to move to another area if I may.

19 C: You . . . What's the first teaching job that you returned to after the accident?

The counsel starts out with three hypothetical questions. The first one is basically tautological—whether or not people who remain as corps de ballet dancers for up to five years or more may remain corps de ballet dancer for five years or more (para. 1). The second one is, if anything, commonsensical—whether or not some corps de ballet dancers might leave the ballet company when there is no prospect of their being promoted to become a coryphée (para. 3). The third one is apparently no less innocuous—whether or not there were people who had been offered solo spots in performance, such as the plaintiff, who did not get promoted afterwards (para. 5). To all three questions, Chan answers with a simple yes. Khilnani follows up by asking Chan if she agrees that her instructor's remark that she lacked stage presence was made "in good faith" (para. 7). She replies yes again. Khilnani then asks if stage presence, or charisma, is something that can be acquired through practice or experience. Chan struggles to explain herself (para. 14) and is then interrupted by Khilnani (para. 15), who asks her to wait for the whole question before starting to answer it (in fact, the counsel has already asked his question in the form of a question tag when Chan tries to say something). Eventually, she replies yes one more time (para. 17). Bit by bit, one step at a time, the counsel brings out the logic of accusation tacitly embedded in the sequencing of the questions. The questions, innocuous when examined separately but accusing as a sequence, imply that many corps de ballet dancers were as well regarded as the plaintiff but did not enjoy successful careers—that the plaintiff would have been a failure because she lacked charisma, a God-given gift that she could not have trained to acquire. Of course, what Chan probably did not know was that by admitting that she lacked the charisma required for more accomplished ballerinas, she helped the defendants by giving them a good reason to limit the amount of damages, if they were proved to be negligent.

Questions of this highly restrictive type, when powerfully deployed, put a lot of pressure on inexperienced witnesses (and most lay witnesses are, in the well-known formulation of Marc Galanter (1974), "one-shotters") to either respond with a yes or no. A vigorous, powerful cross-examination is capable of eliciting an unbroken string of yeses from the witness. From a lawyerly point of view, this episode comes close to an ideal cross-examination. It is deftly structure conforming when the examiner faultlessly constrains the interaction into a sequence of predictable yeses.

Equally significant is the counsel's full control of the agenda through topic introduction, as we saw in this example and also in the cross-examination of Chi Keung by Yeung. This is a form of unilateral departure (Goodwin 1987)—the questioning counsel can choose to depart from a topic without involving the witness in an interactional huddle. Although the lawyer apparently expresses a wish ("I'd like to move on . . .") embedded with a permission ("if I may"), the interpreter, a regular in the courtroom, understands full well these utterances are pure formality and decides not to convey to the witness the intended shift of topic. Once again, the asymmetry of power is manifested by the contrast in ease of access to a turn in cross-examination.

Despite its surface structure as a dialogue, the ballerina example aims to achieve monologic closure whereby a cross-examiner dictates the flow of the narrative embedded in the question-and-answer format. This is achieved through adherence to the statement-and-reply structure, which prescribes an institutionally prespecified turn-taking order. The constraints inherent in the statement-and-reply frame, commonly coupled with the presence of court interpreters (see Chapter 5), inhibit witnesses from elaborating their stories at any length. They are asked to answer specific questions raised by counsel, sometimes confined to the dichotomous yes/no choice. It is not uncommon for a witness to come out of a cross-examination frustrated. The frustration stems from the fact that, despite the apparent choices offered in even the most restrictive questions (e.g., a yes/no question), their answers are placed, sometimes unwittingly but more often unwillingly, in an evaluative narrative (an opposing counsel's fact theory) that reads the implications of these answers in a different light. In other words, the questions put forward in cross-examination are normally driven by a desire to connect the narrative dots backwards. For this reason, young counsel are always reminded of the following cardinal rule of cross-examination: Never ask a question unless you know what the answer is going to be. Ideally, cross-examination is the making of a foregone conclusion, albeit one that is contrary to the intentions of the witness (unless the disputed case involves no factual disputes). This is why cross-examination is an uncommon kind of linguistic transaction that is structurally lopsided. From the official standpoint of formalism, this structural lopsidedness in an adversarial trial is allowed, in fact encouraged, because it is believed that the truth can be tested and uncovered only through adversarial questioning by counsel from both sides (plaintiff and defendant).

Cross-examination is thus a verbal game that is drastically different from most everyday conversations, when participants are allowed to explain themselves. The detached, bookish quality of the English language in Hong Kong is most effective in creating an interaction context to carry out these rule-governed, formalistic talks. Once again, it is not so much that English gives language to things and concepts that do not have a language in Chinese but that English gives a convincing voice (for sociolinguistic reasons) to act out these orderly but asymmetric verbal transactions.

REEXAMINATION AS DAMAGE CONTROL

After cross-examination, the evidence process concludes with a rejoinder by the witness's own counsel, known as reexamination (also known as redirect examination in the United States), a kind of coda to the process. The process provides a witness's own counsel the final opportunity to use questions to help the witness explain or otherwise qualify any damaging testimony brought out in cross-examination. In some cases, if a witness comes out of cross-examination unscathed, a counsel may simply choose to pass on raising any further questions.

The three stages of testifying are all conducted in a question-and-answer format; the difference between cross-examination, and examination-in-chief and reexamination is that although questions are asked by one's own counsel to bring out and demonstrate the coherence of a witness's account in examination-in-chief and reexamination, cross-examination is conducted by opposing counsel and is meant to challenge, undermine, and expose any of the available inconsistencies in a witness's story. The same sequence of examination-in-chief, cross-examination, and reexamination is repeated for each and every witness for the plaintiff and then subsequently for the defendants (if they choose to testify) and their witnesses.[32]

The stricture of the process of evidence elicitation aims to reduce and segment the speech of a witness into a string of statements. In Hong Kong, such stricture is further reinforced by the presence of court interpreters. Chi Keung was one of the few witnesses I saw during my fieldwork in Hong Kong who chose to testify in English. Other witnesses, even highly educated ones, preferred to testify through an interpreter in English trials. The fact that a court interpreter can interpret only one segment of speech at a time under the mode of consecutive interpretation makes it necessary to break up a witness's narrative. The three-way interactional dynamics among counsel, the interpreter, and the witness is the focus of my discussion in Chapter 5.

THE CONSTRUCTION OF LEGAL TEXT

What I have shown is how cross-examination in English-language court-rooms in part enacts and in part reproduces a statement-and-reply structure that gives rise to its rule-abiding character. It is through the enactment of such a rigid interaction structure that a legal text analyzable by the machinery of the common law is produced in the process. Although it has become commonplace among comparative jurists to suggest that a common law adversarial trial is unique in its orality and concentration (Damaska 1997; Merryman 1985; Zweigert and Kötz 1998; see also Chapter 1), the interactions between the two—that is, the question of *what* kind of orality is produced in trials—is empirically understudied. If we look at how orality is sanctioned by the interaction rules governing cross-examination, it becomes clear that the aim is to produce a carefully controlled form of *textual* orality in English-language courtrooms in Hong Kong. It is simply not enough to make a sweeping distinction of orality versus textuality in an asocial manner. Universally asserting that orality is experiential and unpredictable, whereas textuality is abstract and rule governed, ignores, in the current case, how social institutions work to disrupt the boundary separating the two. Here, the overlooked question is how legal text amenable to juridical formalism is orally produced at the site of a courtroom. Although English cross-examination in Hong Kong is an oral practice in form, the statements expected from witnesses are segmentable, transcribable, and quotable texts that stand on their own. What comes out from my fieldwork is how impressive the English language is in molding utterances into legal facts in the juridical context of Hong Kong. To go back to the distinction I made between constative and performative utterances, the institutional process of textualization requires the ferreting out of the performative from the constative, because the concept of evidence in the common law is institutionally linked to the speech act of statement making. So understood, the institutional process of testifying, first introduced by the colonial common law system and still retained in the English-language courtrooms in Hong Kong today, is by design antiperformative—a speech act that negates its own *active* and inter*active* quality, that purports to simply describe something as it is, to tell the way things happened, no more and no less. Judges and counsel emphasize constative coherency (e.g., whether a witness contradicts himself or whether what he said was contradicted by some known facts) above and beyond everything else. This belief in the robustness of plain description is all the more salient in Hong Kong for two additional reasons triggered by the social role of English as an elite second language. First, the overwhelming use of court interpreters in Hong Kong makes the slow process of "making mountains out of molehills" in cross-examination even slower; witnesses are often one extra degree separated from directly interacting with counsel. Furthermore, when court interpretation is used, it is obviously difficult for judges and counsel who do not speak Cantonese to focus on the performative elements of language use (such as irony, sarcasm, or humor) and the other corporeal features of the act of speaking (demeanor, bodily gesture, pause, silence, tone, emphatic stress, etc.).[33] Even when a local witness chooses to testify in English, expatriate judges who have been in Hong Kong long enough know that the ways a local stresses a sentence or raises or lowers his tone could well be different from English speakers in other places. Once again, constative coherency is the one criterion they fall back on.

It is through this institutionally stipulated bifurcation of constative and performative utterances that power is structurally differentiated in the process of cross-examination. However, what is swept under the carpet in the official theory of cross-examination is the double-bind treatment of the role of a witness. On the one hand, a witness is expected to simply describe what she knows; on the other hand, she is expected to *act*, albeit subordinately, in response to the counsel's performance of cross-examination. A skilled advocate is entitled to, in fact expected to, showcase his eloquence, to implicate and to challenge, to intimidate and to attack an opposing witness, but the witness is asked to be cooperative, to answer counsel's questions, to tell the court what she knows, and to say whether something is or is not the case. In other words, according to the official theory, a witness constatively describes and a counsel performatively interrogates. But in actuality, even the most cooperative witness does not simply describe— the person *performs* the role of a witness, so much so that it complements and makes complete the counsel's performance of cross-examination. The witness can thus be taken as a supporting character in a drama in which the counsel is the heroic orator. Indeed, no constative utterances can be so constative that they cease to be performative. In practice, judges and counsel constantly pass judgment on a witness's performance of statement making, through the use of labels such as "reliable" and "trustworthy" or "unreliable" and "elusive." This important point is demonstrated, for example, in the work of Conley and O'Barr (1990), who in their study show how a certain style of constative utterances (rule oriented) *performs* better than another style (relationship dominated) in courtrooms in the United States. Hence it is impossible to draw a line that distinguishes saying something from doing something or to insist that the constative and the performative are two mutually exclusive types of utterances, a point that Austin came to acknowledge in the lectures that became *How to Do Things with Words* (Austin 1962).

Drawing a line between constative and performative utterances also obscures the fact that saying something is never *just* saying something, particularly within the institutional framework of juridical formalism. The common law courtroom is loaded with institutionally stipulated magical words that must be said to complete an action. The reality is that in trials there is no such thing as backing up words with action, because the words are the action. Pat Carlen has the following wonderful example in her book *Magistrate's Justice* (1976: 111):

MAGISTRATE: Do you plead guilty or not guilty?
DEFENDANT: Yes, I did it.
MAGISTRATE: No, I'm asking whether you plead guilty or not guilty. You must use either the words "not guilty" or "guilty."
DEFENDANT: [*Looking toward probation officer*] She said, "Say guilty."
MAGISTRATE: No. You must say what you want to say.
DEFENDANT: Yes. I'll say what you like. I did it.
MAGISTRATE: No. You must use the language of the court.

JURIDICAL FORMALISM
AND ENGLISH IN HONG KONG

The evidence I garnered from English-language courtrooms shows that the everyday operation of juridical formalism relies not only on the explicit institutional rules of the legal system in Hong Kong but also on the particular context that the English language and the constellation of other English cultural paraphernalia work together to create. Discourse practices that would be considered pragmatic violations in ordinary conversation are institutionalized in cross-examination. English in Hong Kong, precisely because of its marginal presence in the daily lives of the local people, becomes a palpable linguistic marker that licenses a set of pragmatic norms and rules that are different from everyday conversation. Legal formalism turns on the social space of power that English in Hong Kong carves out. As we will see, the situation is markedly different when Cantonese creates a wave of performative disruptions that break down the boundaries between law and civil society.

CHAPTER 5

Marshaling the Legal Boundaries

Court Interpreters and Juridical Formalism

THE REALITY OF LANGUAGE USE in Hong Kong courts is far more complex than the neat Chinese-English division deployed in the official statistics. In terms of language, trials in Hong Kong are classified as either English or Chinese. English trials are those in which judgments and other official records of the proceedings are kept in English, and in Chapter 4 we saw how the anachronistic context created by the English language facilitates the working of juridical formalism. It is possible, and often is the case in practice, that witnesses testify in Cantonese in English trials and that their testimony is then interpreted into English with the aid of court interpreters (see Table 4). In this chapter I discuss the role of court interpreters in the common law system of Hong Kong. (Another actually existing category of trials in Hong Kong are mixed-language trials, to which I return in Chapters 7 and 8.)

Many litigants who appear in what would officially be classified as English-language trials do not give their evidence in English. The ubiquity of court interpreters is a distinctive feature of English-language trials in Hong Kong. In the course of my fieldwork, I observed few litigants who did not ask for the service of a court interpreter in an English trial (Chi Keung is one; see Chapter 4). As true today as it was in the colonial period, Hong Kong is one of the most "interpreted" legal systems in the world. The irony is hard to miss—court interpreters, unlike in most other jurisdictions, are hired to serve not the linguistic minorities but the majority of the population. Court interpreters were and to an important extent still are the medium or, as we will see, apparently the conduit through which local ethnic Chinese- and English-speaking judges communicate.

A litigant testifying in Cantonese through an interpreter before an English-speaking judge inhabits a Cantonese space between herself and the interpreter, in contrast to the larger English space of the courtroom. That Cantonese space is rendered invisible from the standpoint of juridical formalism. Court interpreters are not supposed to interact with litigants; an interpreter is someone a witness speaks *through* but not *to*. It is the job of an interpreter to restrict herself to translating questions of counsel and statements made by a witness in the most faithful and accurate way possible. This is known officially as the conduit model of the role of court interpreters. Yet, contrary to the prescribed ideal in juridical formalism, this is not the case in practice. Court interpreters are linguistic marshals who police the boundary separating English evidence from Cantonese utterances. In an important sense, they *perform*—sometimes knowingly, sometimes unwittingly—because in the course of interpreting, they often see the need to level out the pragmatic gap between two language habituses when they move back and forth between Cantonese and English in court. The evidence of their performance questions the textual model of

TABLE 4 *Uses of Cantonese and English in Hong Kong's bilingual system by party and trial language*

Party	Trial language		
	Cantonese	*English*	*Mixed language**
Litigants**	Cantonese	Most speak Cantonese; judges and lawyers listen through court interpreters; only expatriate litigants or locals very comfortable with English use English	Cantonese
Counsel	Cantonese; some barristers code-switch to English when referring to legal jargon	English	Cantonese in examinations of witnesses; English in legal deliberations
Judges	Cantonese	English	Cantonese to interact with witnesses; English to interact with counsel and to deliver judgments

*Officially, the Hong Kong Judiciary acknowledges only Cantonese and English trials. Mixed-language trials are lumped into the category of English-language trials in the official statistics.

**Sometimes, there are litigants whose native language is neither Cantonese nor English (e.g., Putonghua). There are also litigants who speak other Chinese regional dialects or languages other than English and Chinese. In these cases, interpreters are generally provided.

input and output on which the conduit model is based. Instead, court interpretation should be understood as an integral part of the practices of juridical formalism in the English courtrooms in Hong Kong.

The substantive analysis of this chapter focuses on a relatively long episode during cross-examination in an interpreter-mediated English trial that for the most part involved a three-way turn-by-turn interaction among a counsel, a witness, and a court interpreter. Through this example, I illustrate how court interpreters in Hong Kong have to face the inescapable task of translating into English and, in the process, altering social meanings and pragmatic features of Cantonese utterances. What often happens in the process is that two ongoing dialogues occur at the same time: one between the interpreter and the witness and the other between the interpreter and the legal professionals.

The cross-examination episode is selected from the personal injury action already discussed in Chapter 4. A ballerina, who suffered an allegedly career-ending accident in the early 1990s, sued her former employer and the management of the venue where the accident occurred for negligence. The episode, although quite lengthy when transcribed on paper, circled around basically one question. During this episode, the issue of interpretation is also explicitly raised; elaborate disquisitions are made by the counsel and the judge about what it means for something to be an accurate interpretation. The episode thus renders explicit metalinguistic assumptions about differences between languages that prompt legal professionals to question the accuracy of interpretation in a courtroom context. The episode features what standard manuals for court interpreters would label common mistakes, including practices that linguists would describe as cleanup, side conversation, deictic switch, and linguistic coercion (cf. Crooker 1996; de Jongh 1992; Edwards 1995). My purpose, however, is not to question the accuracy of the given interpretation or to list the mistakes that were made and how they can be avoided. For court interpreters, infallibility is an impossible standard. The ideal of perfect accuracy also perpetuates the belief that there is only one right answer to each word, phrase, and sentence that a court interpreter interprets. Quite to the contrary, my argument is that these so-called inaccuracies and mistakes arise in part because of the structural tensions embedded in the contrasting habituses of English and Cantonese in Hong Kong. My purpose therefore is to demonstrate that the differences engendered by judges and counsel speaking in English and litigants speaking in Cantonese cannot simply be resolved by the presence of a two-way interpreter (English to Cantonese and vice versa). Interpretation only refigures these differences into another form. My analysis of actual court interpretation in this chapter is framed by the following questions: What means of semantic and pragmatic clarification do court interpreters use? What specific kind of (textual) coherence are court interpreters aiming at when they consciously or even unconsciously renarrate a witness's testimony as official evidence? In a highly institutionalized setting such as a courtroom, what are the evidential standards that impose forms and rules on the interpretation of a witness's utterances, and what discursive elements are thereby excluded?

For clarity of presentation, I divide the episode into six main segments. The first segment shows how, far from being a mere conduit, court interpretation plays an active role in molding a witness's utterances into the pragmatic and metapragmatic standards of evidence. It is through a dual process of explication and erasure that a witness is made to conform to the evidential standard prescribed by the court. The second segment shows how court interpretation can complicate the social meaning of a question in the process of repragmatization. The third segment shows how the court interpreter intervenes during the witness's emotional outbursts, in order to make sure that she remains in an "interpretable" state. The fourth segment shows how the cross-examination takes a dramatic turn when the defense counsel singles out the interpreter's translation as a possible mistranslation. The query leads to a discussion that reveals how the judge and the counsel understand the notion of translational accuracy. The fifth segment shows how a liminal state is momentarily created when the interpreter distances herself from the counsel who queries her interpretation. It shows how the unified voice of the court breaks down into a triadic interaction between the counsel, the interpreter, and the judge. The sixth and final segment marks the restoration of the interactional order. The witness finally "gets" the question and "offers" her answer, which is then commented on by the defense counsel.

Before I proceed to the substantive analysis of the episode, I want to first discuss how the process of court interpretation is understood in the Anglo-American common law tradition and how this has been adopted by legal professionals in Hong Kong.

THE CONDUIT MODEL

The presence of court interpreters in Hong Kong can be dated to the early days of the British colonial period when Britain began to establish common law courts in the colony—although historical documents suggest that, at least in criminal trials, the earliest interpreter was a policeman who also served as the main witness against the defendant whose testimony he interpreted (Norton-Kyshe 1971: 223). Today in Hong Kong, interpreted trials still make up the majority of all trials in the District Court and the Court of First Instance.[1] One seldom finds an English trial in which interpreters are not required. In the course of my yearlong fieldwork, I encountered only one such case; the plaintiff himself was a seasoned solicitor who once served in public office. Even though many locals in Hong Kong, particular those under the age of 50, learned and studied English in school for years, they feel more comfortable speaking Cantonese (and understandably so), given the stakes involved and the stress endemic to an adversarial trial.[2] Court interpreters also have an important, albeit often inconspicuous, role to play in influencing the outcome of a case. Judges who do not speak Chinese (virtually all non-Chinese judges) rely entirely on court interpreters to understand what a witness says. Even bilingual judges who understand Cantonese are supposed to consider only the interpreted version as the official testimony once English is chosen as the language of a trial. And it is the interpreted evidence produced by a court interpreter, not the original evidence in Cantonese or other languages, that is kept as the official record of the proceedings for the purpose of appeals (E. T. M. Cheung 2000: 247). In the colonial era, when the courts were staffed mostly with expatriate judges, court interpreters were known to have tremendous power, because they were often the only people in the court who could hear and understand everything (i.e., English and Cantonese) that was said. Historically, however, the role of court interpreters has been given scant attention in sociolegal studies of the legal system of Hong Kong (see K. H. Ng 2009).

Court interpretation involves primarily consecutive interpreting, where the interpreter translates a message into the target language after the speaker says it in the original. This requires the source-language speaker to pause at intervals to allow the interpreted message to be relayed. More specifically, the kind of consecutive interpreting practices that takes place in courts is known as short consecutive interpreting, as opposed to long consecutive reporting, which allows more liberal use of paraphrases and summaries. Short consecutive interpreting attempts to reproduce a lossless replica, a verbatim reproduction of the primary speaker's message in the target language (de Jongh 1992). Court interpreters sometimes perform a form of simultaneous interpretation known as dockside interpretation. In principle, a court interpreter has the responsibility of interpreting what happens in the court (e.g., conversations between a judge and counsel) to the key litigants involved. The term *dockside* refers to the circumstance where the court interpreter stands or sits in a chair adjoining the prisoner's dock and interprets conversations for the defendant in a criminal trial, often in a form of whispered interpreting known as chuchotage.[3] In civil trials, at least the ones I observed, it is not always the case that an interpreter performs this kind of interpretation for the litigants. If a litigant shows signs of understanding a fair amount of English, the interpreter on duty will sometimes skip the process.

What is the role of a court interpreter? How are they understood in an orthodox account of the common law? As in many other formal legal systems, the common view in Hong Kong is to equate court interpretation with verbal translation—that is, the conversion of a message from the source language to the target language. When I interviewed judges and barristers and asked what qualifies for good interpretation, the answer I most often heard was that interpretation must be faithful. An interpreter should not add or subtract things from what a witness says. Consistent with what Susan Berk-Seligson found in her study of English-Spanish courtrooms in the United States, legal professionals and court interpreters, who privilege statement making over other speech acts, tend to judge accuracy by means of semantic congruence rather than pragmatic compatibility (Berk-Seligson 1990: 53).

Court interpreters are thus not expected to make any inputs to the trial proceedings; ideally they serve as mere conduits bridging the language gap between parties. The 1958 English case of *R. v. Attard*[4] has been the precedent that Hong Kong judges rely on when it comes to defining the role of court interpreters. In this case, the prosecution proposed to use as evidence an interview that a police officer had conducted with Attard, a Maltese, through an interpreter. The defense argued that because neither the police officer nor Attard could understand what the other said, the evidence of the police officer was hearsay and thus inadmissible and that only the interpreter could give evidence of the questions that he put to the prisoner on behalf of the police officer and of the answers given to him by the prisoner in the prisoner's own language. The trial judge in *Attard*, Justice Gorman, agreed with the defense and held that the evidence ought not to be given through the mouth of the detective superintendent in the witness box. *Attard* has stood the test of time and was first (obliquely) applied in Hong Kong in *R. v. Ip Chiu*.[5] Its principle was accepted in *R. v. Li Kin Wai*[6] and expressly followed in *R. v. Tam Kwok Yeung*,[7] *Attorney-General v. Phung Van Toan*,[8] and *R. v. Thakoen Gwitsa Thaporn Thongjai*.[9]

What *Attard* did was to apply the exclusion rule of hearsay to situations that involve interpreters. Hearsay is anything said by another that the witness heard said, when the purpose of adducing that piece of information is to establish the truth of the facts stated (C. Allen 2004: 148). Oral statements by a person other than the one testifying are usually not admissible in court. Although what has been seen by a witness is considered admissible evidence in a common law court, this is not so with what has been only heard. Implicitly, common law court considers the ear less reliable than the eye.

But if the police officer in *Attard* could not testify because the defendant's interpreted answers were considered hearsay (i.e., if he had testified, he would have given secondhand hearsay evidence), what about cases in which non-Cantonese-speaking counsel conduct cross-examinations based on "hearsay" from the interpreter or cases in which judges rule based on equally "hearsay" evidence given by Cantonese-speaking witnesses? Does translation compromise the authority of these judgments? As usual, the Hong Kong Judiciary follows the principles adopted by the English and Australian courts and subscribes to the conduit model to circumvent the hearsay rule. By declaring court interpretation as a "mere conduit," it legitimizes a double standard that renders interpreters invisible in the hearsay test. In the Australian case of *Gaio v. R.*,[10] J. Menzies said in the judgment:

Let it be supposed that there were a machine that itself translated from one language to another so that one party to a conversation both spoke and heard in his own language; if such were the case the element that is here relied upon as hearsay would be absent and, upon proof of the accuracy of the machine, one party's account of the conversation would be unobjectionable. In my opinion, Arthur [the interpreter] like such a machine, was merely a translator. (*Gaio v. R.*, 104 CLR 419 [1960], at 432–433; cited by Laster and Taylor 1994: 112)

The passage succinctly summarizes the idea that the court interpreter, as a conduit, only plays the role of a direct channel of communication between the witness and the questioning counsel (Laster and Taylor 1994). A court interpreter is present in a courtroom for her ability to bridge the language gap in communication. Hence, by law, she must swear or declare that she knows both languages and that she truly, distinctly, and audibly interprets the contents of the conversation. Among the regulars in everyday courtroom dramas, the court interpreter is, on the official interpretation, the quintessential Goffmanian "non-person," someone who is invisible, someone who is physically present but does not take on the role of either performer or audience (Goffman 1959).

"GRANDE CABRIOLE OUVERTE"

I now turn to the example that anchors my discussion. The episode is drawn from the ballerina case introduced in Chapter 4. It involves a personal injury lawsuit for damages. The plaintiff, Ada Chan, a young woman who was 22 years old at the time of the accident, sued her former employer, Hong Kong Ballet Limited (first defendant), and the Urban Council (second defendant), a now disbanded public body that at the time of the accident owned and managed the premises, Hong Kong Cultural Centre, where the accident took place. One summer day in 1994, Chan partially tore her anterior cruciate ligament while performing a *grande cabriole ouverte* during a practice session. Chan claimed that the practice floor was slippery and that this had been a cause for concern among the dancers before her accident occurred.[11] The defendants claimed alternatively that the plaintiff was aware of the inherent risk of injury in becoming a ballet dancer and that she fell because of her incorrect technique in performing the movement. They denied that the floor was slippery or at least so slippery as to cause a danger to the plaintiff. The *grande cabriole ouverte* is a basic jump in ballet dancing: the dancer leaps into the air, brings her feet together, and then lands on one foot, briefly extending the other leg horizontally. In her testimony, Chan said she slipped while landing the *cabrioles*, twisted her knee, and thus damaged her anterior cruciate ligament. For reasons that were disputed, the injury turned out to be career-ending. Chan remained with the company for roughly two more years before it finally decided not to renew her contract in 1996.

What lies at the heart of most claims for damages is money. Tort actions under common law epitomize the transformation of disputes over injuries into disputes over money (Mather and Yngvesson 1980: 784). Should the court find the defendants liable, the next question is, of course, how much the plaintiff should be compensated for the wrong done to her. In the first excerpt from this trial, the one question implicitly guiding the whole cross-examination is how good a dancer Chan would have been if the accident had not occurred (which is key to the calculation of "loss of future earnings"). If the judge sustained Chan's claim for personal injuries, future loss of earnings would be calculated based on the difference between the money she could have made had her career progressed and the money she now earns. If the judge believed, for example, that Chan would have become a prima ballerina, this would be reflected in the calculation of the money Chan would have made had it not been for the accident. Furthermore, if the judge believed that Chan was immensely talented, he would be more likely to award her compensation for "pain and suffering and loss of amenities," reflecting the fact that the accident did not merely cost her a job but a career that could have been glittering fame. The goal of one of the opposing counsel, Gautam Khilnani, is to detract from whatever good impression Chan has made on the judge. It is his task to convince the judge that Chan was *not* a once promising dancer who had been unjustly punished by the hand of fate but merely an average dancer who still would have had to struggle to reach the top had the accident not taken place.

The trial features three experienced junior counsel—those who have yet to or have chosen not to take silk (i.e., become senior counsel) but have practiced long enough to be considered old hands. Chan is represented by Peter Smith, a Briton who began his practice in Hong Kong in the mid-1980s. The ballet company is represented by Eddie So, a local Chinese barrister who started his practice in the late 1980s. The Urban Council is represented by Khilnani. At the time of the trial, Khilnani had approximately 15 years of practice under his belt. The presiding judge of the case is Judge Pitt. Again, at the time of the trial, Pitt had been on the bench in Hong Kong for about 15 years. English is the native language of Smith, Khilnani, and Pitt.

IN SEARCH OF COHESION

The episode selected took place on the third day of what would turn out to be a 13-day trial. On the first day, Smith opened Chan's case by presenting Chan as a promising young ballerina who would have at least progressed to the rank of coryphée, finished her dancing career in her early 30s, and then easily secured a career as a professional ballet teacher. On the second day, So began his cross-examination; he challenged Chan's allegation that the floor was slippery and suggested instead that the whole explanation of the slippery floor was a recent invention to sustain her case. On the afternoon of the second day, So finished his cross-examination and Khilnani began his. He raised challenges along similar lines and questioned whether the accident was the result of a simple mistake by Chan herself. In Khilnani's account, Chan did not *slip*, but *fell*, perhaps because of her own lapse of concentration. The atmosphere in the courtroom was intense. Chan broke down and cried twice on the second day. On the third day, Khilnani continued with his cross-examination. His focus shifted to Chan's ability as a dancer. The episode features Khilnani trying to portray Chan as a mediocre dancer, based on her former ballet instructor's comments. When I observed the trial in person, I was impressed by Khilnani's rhetorical skills. Unfortunately, his quick wit, his demeanor, and his gestures may not survive the process of textualization that renders the episode a readable transcript. The interpreter had been present since the first day of the trial; I will refer to her as Rebecca Ma from now on.

Cross-Examination of Ada Chan (W) by Defense Counsel
Gautam Khilnani (C1) Through Interpreter Rebecca Ma (I)

		Gloss	Original
1	C1:	Now, Mercy Charles is your ballet mistress, right?	Now, Mercy Charles is your ballet mistress, right?
2	I:	Your ballet mistress is called "Mercy Charles," right?	你嘅芭蕾舞導師係叫 Mercy Charles, 係咪呀?
3	W:	Yes.	係吖。
4	I:	Yes.	Yes.
5	C1:	During the first time you were employed by the first defendant before your accident, how would you describe your relationship with her?	During the first time you were employed by the first defendant before your accident, how would you describe your relationship with her?
6	I:	When you were hired by the first defendant, and before the happening of this accident, OK, how would you describe the relationship between you and this instructor?	響呢你受僱於第一被告人嘅時候,同埋呢響發生意外之前,吓,你點樣形容你同呢位導師之間嘅關係呢?
7	W:	Hmmm . . .	唔 . . .
8	I:	How would you describe it? The relationship between you and her?	你會點形容呢?彼此嘅關係。
9	W:	The relationship between me and her?	彼此嘅關係呀?
10	I:	Yes.	係呀。
11	W:	First, she was the ballet mistress.	首先佢係芭蕾舞團嘅導師啦。
12	I:	We know that already.	我哋知道啦。
13	W:	Right, right.	係啦,係啦。
14	I:	First of all, she was the instructor of . . .	First of all, she was the instructor of . . .
15	W:	[*simultaneously*] My relationship with her, right?	[*simultaneously*] 咁我同佢嘅關係呀?

16	I:	. . . the ballet company.	. . . the ballet company.
17	W:	I quite respected her.	我都幾尊重佢吖。
18	I:	I quite respected her.	I quite respected her.
19	W:	She . . . the relationship is like the ballet mistress prepared a "class" for us, and we attended the class.	佢唔 . . . 即係個關係就係芭蕾舞團導師做一個 "class" 俾我哋咁我哋去上堂咁嘅關係囉。
20	I:	It . . . It's a set of relationship that the ballet mistress conduct, conducted a class for us to attend. That . . . that sort of relationship.	It . . . It's a set of relationship that the ballet mistress conduct, conducted a class for us to attend. That . . . that sort of relationship.
21	C1:	Right. So it is very much like teacher and pupil, and this is a teacher you respected.	Right. So it is very much like teacher and pupil, and this is a teacher you respected. 即係類似呢吓，呢種關係呢類似呢一個老師同一個學生嘅一個關係啦，同埋呢就你身為一個學生嘅時候啦，你就尊重老師咁樣，呢一類嘅關係啦。
22	I:	So it's like, this relationship is like a relationship between a teacher and a student, and you as a student, you respect your teacher. It's like this kind of relationship.	
23	W:	It's not student. We are professionals. So . . .	唔係學生，咁我哋係職業㗎，咁 . . .
24	I:	No, I would not say pupil because we are professional.	No, I would not say pupil because we are professional.

Despite the legal myth of the conduit model, court interpreters in Hong Kong do not translate each and every word said by the witness. They sometimes explicate and elucidate in an attempt to satisfy the criteria of meaningfulness in juridical formalism. That interpreters sometimes intrude, consciously or unconsciously, with their authorial input is commonplace.[12] This need for expansion sometimes arises from grammatical differences between English and Cantonese, because Cantonese grammatical categories are less explicit than English ones. Linguists have suggested that the grammatical categories of a given language determine which precise aspects of an experience must be expressed in that language.[13] As we saw in Chapter 4, in the process of translating a (less explicit) Cantonese utterance into a (more explicit) English text, interpreters are frequently compelled by the structure of English grammar to draw additional data from the context and incorporate them into the text. It is, for example, common knowledge among linguists that Cantonese grammar lacks distinctions of tense as such—that is, past, present, and future have to be expressed lexically and are not encoded grammatically by forms of the verb (Matthews and Yip 1994).[14] Another common example is with third-person singular pronouns (*him, her*), because Cantonese pronouns do not differentiate along gender lines. Here is a short example from the same trial.

Cross-Examination of a Witness (W) Through an Interpreter (I)

Gloss	Original
W: Let me go back to describe the situation. That person got the contract. Since we went to see [the management] one by one, one by one, and since the person came out unhappy, I saw him/her* unhappy. I asked the person what had happened?	話番個情況咁嗰個人攞完合約因為逐個逐個見嘅，逐個逐個見，咁佢出到嚟唔開心，睇到佢唔開心啦咁，問佢發生咩事？
I: Was this person man or woman?	呢個男定女?
W: Woman.	女。

But the interpreter's tendencies to explicate often go beyond the minimal requirements of grammatical reformatting. In the following excerpt, there is an episode of Cantonese side conversation between the interpreter and the witness right after the second question from Khilnani. For clarity of presentation, let me omit the original Cantonese and reproduce only my gloss of this side conversation.

---

*In Cantonese, there is a generic third-person pronoun that can be "him" or "her."

Side Conversation (Gloss Only) Between Ada Chan (W) and Interpreter
Rebecca Ma (I) During the Cross-Examination of Chan by Defense
Counsel Gautam Khilnani (C1)

5 C1: During the first time you were employed by the first defendant before your accident, how would you describe your relationship with her?

6 I: When you were hired by the first defendant, and before the happening of this accident, OK, how would you describe the relationship between you and this instructor?

7 W: Hmmm . . .

8 I: How would you describe it? The relationship between you and her.

9 W: The relationship between me and her?

10 I: Yes.

11 W: First, she was the ballet mistress.

12 I: We know that already.

13 W: Right, right.

14 I: First of all, she was the instructor of . . .

15 W: [*simultaneously*] My relationship with her, right?

16 I: . . . the ballet company.

17 W: I quite respected her.

18 I: I quite respected her.

19 W: She . . . the relationship is like the ballet mistress prepared a "class" for us, and we attended the class.

20 I: It . . . It's a set of relationship that the ballet mistress conduct, conducted a class for us to attend. That . . . that sort of relationship.

21 C1: Right. So it is very much like teacher and pupil, and this is a teacher you respected.

Explication and erasure often coexist in practice. They are, as shown in the transcript, complementary mechanisms that underlie the process of repragmatization. In order to explicate, Ma first has to fend off what appears to be irrelevant or even confusing replies from Chan. The process of eliciting the "right" answer from Chan is at one and the same time a process of *erasure*. Erasure refers to a process in which linguistic practices that are inconsistent with a preset ideological scheme are either rendered invisible or get explained away (Gal and Irvine 1995; Irvine and Gal

2000). Interpreters often purge what they think is meaningless digressive mumbling on the part of witnesses. Here Ma, in an act that is not uncommon among the court interpreters I observed, erases a witness's semantically empty, phatic "Hmmm" (para. 7) in her interpretation. Nor does she translate Chan's semimonologic repetition of "The relationship between me and her." Ma appears to take the repetition as a reflection of Chan's uncertainty about the question; she therefore assures Chan with a simple yes (para. 10) in an effort to elicit more from Chan. When Chan finally answers by saying, "First, she was the ballet mistress" (para. 11), the reply is subtly interesting for its noticeable lack of interiority. But Ma's initial response is dismissive; instead of translating the reply, she tries once more to elicit a proper answer from Chan by telling her, "We know that already" (para. 12). We can see that here Ma is fishing for a statement from Chan with semantically explicit new information.

What Ma does, through explication and erasure, is instill a specific kind of coherence—not the kind of general coherence commanded by the target language's grammar in the process of interpreting but a social, audience-focused coherence that measures the witness's utterance against the evidential standards to which judges and counsel subscribe (Blum-Kulka 1986).[15] We can say that the interpretation of a Cantonese utterance here involves deciphering the prescriptive norms underlying the statement-and-reply structure. Thus the utterance "We know that already" is a metapragmatic comment that makes explicit to the witness what is considered a reply and what is not, laying bare the hitherto invisible but nonetheless salient threshold that separates evidence from nonevidence.

From the witness's perspective, the interpreter's transformation into an inquisitor is inconspicuous. There is no shift of voice between the counsel's question and the interpreter's own elicitation. Any breaks between the questions are obliterated by the use of the first-person plural pronoun 我哋 [ngo5 dei6] (similar to *we* in English).[16] It is noteworthy that the first-person plural pronoun 我哋 [ngo5 dei6] here is what grammarians would call an exclusive "we"—that is, a "we" that excludes the addressee (Chan). The use of the Cantonese exclusive we presupposes the solidarity of the court regulars: the judge, the barrister, and the interpreter herself. Together they form the amici curiae, friends of the court.[17] The pronoun allows the interpreter to structure the deictic relationship in such a way that she not only assumes the voice of the questioning counsel but also the collective voice of the court. But the courtly we in an adversarial court is precarious, to say the least. In moments of dramatic conflict, the interpreter may break off from this imagined unity and draw a line between herself and an attacking counsel.

Taking her cue from Ma, Chan finally makes a courteous remark, saying in Cantonese that she respected Charles (para. 17). Ma translates accordingly (para. 18). But Chan then continues to stay "on the surface" in her next line: "She . . . the relationship is like the ballet mistress prepared a 'class' for us, and we attended the class" (para. 19). Interestingly, Chan also uses the same Cantonese plural pronoun 我哋 [ngo5 dei6] but for different reasons. By describing the relationship as one that exists between Charles and "us" (all the ballet dancers), Chan implies she did not have a personal relationship with Charles.[18]

The episode underlines the obvious differences between cross-examination and casual conversation. In casual conversation, where meanings are usually much more contextualized, what is said only appears to take on significance in reference to what is left unsaid. Thus Chan's hesitation and reluctance to comment would likely have invited curious follow-ups if it had occurred in the middle of a casual conversation. English courtroom interactions in Hong Kong, however, take place with a statement-and-reply structure that privileges constative statements above other speech acts. Hence things must be explicitly said to count as evidence. But there is another reason inherent in the objectives of cross-examination itself that explains why cross-examination proceeds with such a closed interactional logic. Everyday casual interactions feature a more elusive narrative flow; their guiding interactional logic is dialogic and open-ended.[19] A person decides on the spot what to say in response to an utterance just said and in anticipation of a reply to her own utterance. The interval of anticipation is usually short; there is often no preset finishing line for the parties to cross, and much depends on highly local interactional dynamics. Testing and probing, false starts, and repairs are frequent in a casual conversation. So if the transcribed interaction took place between two colleagues near an office soda machine, Khilnani could say, "You don't seem to like her that much," and wait to see whether Chan is willing to say more.

Cross-examination differs from daily conversation in the crucial sense that the questioner's anticipation covers the entire dialogue, as he tries to effect a kind of closure we seldom find in daily conversations. In other words, whereas a participant in a casual conversation anticipates only the next turn, the counsel in cross-examination anticipates the end point of a cross-examination and usually has it literally scripted out. This is why cross-examination, although dialogic in form, is monologic in its underlying drive. Cross-examination is not so much governed by local interactional dynamics as by the logic of counsel's hidden script, a point that I made in Chapter 4. A barrister plots and aligns his questions backwards from the scripted end point. Like the architect of a domino topple who carefully sets up thousands of dominoes so that they are successively tipped over in a particular way, the questions are scripted to lead to, ideally, a foregone conclusion in support of the lawyer's version of the facts. Of course in practice the answers offered by a witness differ from or contradict a lawyer's written script; in such cases, the cross-examination never achieves the closure that the lawyer intends. There is therefore at the end a procedure known as putting one's case, in which the discrepancies between the factual dots drawn from a witness's testimony and the hidden dots implicit in the leading questions are brought out into the open. Putting one's case is usually done at the end of a cross-examination when counsel produces a series of questions that begin with the formulaic phrase "I put it to you that . . ." (Wilkinson et al. 2007: 306), the purpose of which is to give a witness the opportunity to openly disagree with the fact theory of the opposing counsel. It is an English practice, which the courts in Hong Kong follow (but which has not been adopted in the United States; cf. K. Evans 1998).

VERBIGERATION

Back to the ballerina's cross-examination episode. After a couple of questions to get Chan to agree that Charles is no longer employed by the ballet company (Chan readily agrees; not shown in the transcript in the interest of space), Khilnani shifts his focus to Charles's evaluation of Chan. As the following segment shows, Khilnani now tries to get Chan to admit that Charles evaluated her in good faith, even though, given the critical nature of the evaluation, Chan would likely disagree with its content.

Cross-Examination of Ada Chan (W) by Defense Counsel Gautam Khilnani (C1) Through Interpreter Rebecca Ma (I) (Continued)

	Gloss	Original
25	C1: You see, she will say that when you were given your chance to perform in a solo spot, she said you did not live up to expectations or achieve the standard required. Do you not accept that that is a bona fide view which she holds, whether or not you agree with it, but it is a bona fide view she holds?	You see, she will say that when you were given your chance to perform in a solo spot, she said you did not live up to expectations or achieve the standard required. Do you not accept that that is a bona fide view which she holds, whether or not you agree with it, but it is a bona fide view she holds?
26	I: Now this instructor, "Mercy Charles," will say, the company offered you an opportunity to dance solo. Her evaluation of you, her assessment—she will say that when there was an opportunity offered to you, you did not achieve the requirements they asked, which means you did not achieve the standard, did not achieve the standard. Now, this is what she says, this is what she says. Do you agree or not, not your agreeing or not, now this is what she says. Do you accept or not this is a very sensible, reasonable, and legitimate kind of opinion? We are not asking you to agree with her or disagree with her, you know. Do you accept or not that she can say so?	嗱呢個導師 Mercy Charles 佢會嚟講，話呢當公司俾你一個機會吓係嚟到跳一個獨舞嘅時間呢吓，咁佢對於你嘅評價吓，個評語吓，佢就會話呢係，有咁嘅機會俾你嘅時間呢，但係呢你就唔能夠達到佢哋個要求，意思係呢即係達唔到個水平吓，達唔到個水平，咁樣呢呢個係佢講嘅，呢個係佢講嘅，咁你同唔同意話呢吓，唔係話同唔同意，嗱呢個係佢講嘅，你接唔接受呢就係話呢個係佢一個即係佢可以係好合情合理合法所講嘅一個佢嘅意見出嚟，咁我哋唔係問你話要需要同意佢或者係唔同意佢咁樣吓，咁你接唔接受佢話佢都可以咁講？

27 C1: Do you understand the
        question?

28 W: She is, she is entitled to express
        her assessment of anybody.

29 I: Right, that means she can . . .

30 W: Her assessment of anybody.

31 I: Well, I think she's entitled
        to express her views or her
        assessment about anybody.

32 C1: And my point is not only she's
        entitled to do it, but you accept
        that her assessment in this
        situation was given in good
        faith. Whether or not you agree
        with her assessment is one
        matter, but my question is, Do
        you agree her assessment was
        given in good faith?

    Do you understand the
    question?

    佢有, 佢有權講任何人嘅評價。

    係啦，即佢可以 . . .

    佢對任何人嘅評價。

    Well, I think she's entitled
    to express her views or her
    assessment about anybody.

    And my point is not only she's
    entitled to do it, but you accept
    that her assessment in this
    situation was given in good
    faith. Whether or not you agree
    with her assessment is one
    matter, but my question is, Do
    you agree her assessment was
    given in good faith?

At this point of the transcript, the cross-examination is briefly interrupted when Chan's counsel challenges the direction Khilnani is heading. After a brief explanation by Khilnani, Judge Pitt accepts the relevancy of this line of questioning. I want to focus on Ma's interpretation, however. Her interpreted lines build a semantic redundancy into the text that is absent in the original. The interpretation accretes rather than proceeds. Ma appears to try to defer the blow to Chan by meandering about with repetitive phrases and conjunctions, as shown in my English gloss of her Cantonese interpretation. The interpretation's repetitive syntax is most obvious when one notices that the phrase "this is what she says" is repeated three times in the middle of the interpreted question (para. 26). Ma is clearly searching for an appropriate Cantonese phrase for "bona fide," repeating phrases and using Cantonese vernacular fillers such as 咁樣呢 [gam2 joeng5 ne1] or 咁樣吓 [gam2 joeng5 haa5] (both can be roughly translated as "so this is") to buy her time before she eventually offers an uncharacteristically loose interpretation of "bona fide" as 合情合理合法 [hap6 cing4 hap6 lei5 hap6 faat3] (meaning "sensible, reasonable, and legitimate"). When the question is finally put to Chan, it is watered down: "Do you accept or not that she can say so?" (para. 26).

Here we can see that the use of interpreters, while offering counsel even greater dominance over witnesses in terms of narrative capability, nevertheless lessens their control of the pragmatic force of the questions put to witnesses. Every time an English question is put through an interpreter, the question has to be repragmatized in the voice of Cantonese. Here, it is clear that Ma is looking for ways to dull the blade of Khilnani's question. Semantically, the interpreted question is quite messy in Cantonese as well. It is, of course, very different from the original: "Do you not accept that it is a bona fide view which she holds?" The semantic gap between the two is obvious enough to prompt Khilnani to ask the witness, "Do you understand the question?" One can ask, albeit conjecturally, whether Khilnani is really directing his question to Chan or is trying to launch a backhanded criticism of the adequacy of the interpretation. It is more likely that Khilnani's question is, as Bakhtin would term it, doubly oriented. It appears that the interpreter gets this second sense of the question because she erases it from the Cantonese interpretation. Unfortunately, the semantic gap between the two questions creates a trap into which Chan has already fallen. When Chan replies that Charles is entitled to express her opinions about anyone, that in itself is a rather direct answer to the interpreted question "Do you accept or not that she can say so?" But the reply now appears to be an attempt to dodge the counsel's original question "Do you not accept that it is a bona fide view which she holds?"

COURT INTERPRETER AS BUFFER

Khilnani tries to put the same question to Chan for the second time. He now rephrases and downscales the formality of his question by switching from the Latin phrase "bona fide" to the English phrase "in good faith."

Cross-Examination of Ada Chan (W) by Defense Counsel Gautam Khilnani (CI) Through Interpreter Rebecca Ma (I) (Continued)

		Gloss	Original
33	CI:	Madam Chan, that is her view. She is entitled to it. Now whether or not you agree with it is another matter. But my question is this: Do you accept that in this case, in your case, her view has been given in good faith?	Madam Chan, that is her view. She is entitled to it. Now whether or not you agree with it is another matter. But my question is this: Do you accept that in this case, in your case, her view has been given in good faith?
34	I:	Now, let's go back to the question just mentioned. OK? You've already said she could make any comments; she has the right to do so, right? Now, first thing first, we try not to ask whether you agree or not, which means we don't discuss whether you agree or not first, OK?	嗱咁就再講番剛才嗰個問題啦吓，咁樣呢你都你都話呢佢可以作任何嘅評語，有權咁樣做吖，係咪先? 咁我哋啫係首先唔試吓講話呢你同唔同意，啫係唔講同唔同意呢樣嘢先，吓。
35	W:	Yes.	係。
36	I:	So, now she has already said so, do you accept or not, you know, when she said this, she did not have any ill will at that time; she still was making goodwill criticism. Do you accept or not this way of putting it?	咁樣呢，佢既然咁樣講咗出嚟。咁你呢就接唔接納呢就係話佢咁樣講呢一番說話嘅時間呢，當時嚟講呢佢係並無惡意嘅，即都係有，係善意嘅批評嚟嘅，你接唔接納呢個呢個講法。
37	W:	You mean the things she said in her witness statement?	佢響口供所講嘅嘢係咪?
38	I:	The things just mentioned. That opportunities have been provided to you to perform, but you were not up to the standard, you see. This kind of	即係頭先所講話有機會俾你演出呀，咁但係你就達唔到嗰個要求水平呀咁樣樣，即係呢番嘅批評，呢番嘅批評，吓，咁唔理你同唔同意啦吓，我可能唔同意可能

		criticism, this kind of criticism, OK, now let's not bother with whether you agree or disagree. You may disagree or you may agree, right? We don't discuss that. We only discuss at the time when she made such criticism, OK. Do you accept this was criticism out of goodwill?	同意吖係咪，我哋唔好講呢樣嘢咧，我哋剩係講話當時佢作出咁樣嘅批評嘅時間，吓，你接唔接納佢係一個即係善意嘅批評呢？
39	W:	[*sobbing*] I've never heard her criticize me in any way.	[*sobbing*] 我未聽過佢對我有任何批評先。
40	I:	I see. You've not heard this.	哦，你無聽過。
41	W:	Not before I injured myself.	以前我受傷前，我受傷前未聽過。
42	I:	OK.	OK。
43	W:	I only heard her say to me I danced very well.	我剩係聽過佢同我講我跳得好好
44	I:	OK, I see, OK.	OK，得，吓。
45	W:	Since I . . .	由我 . . .
46	I:	Wait wait, wait wait, wait wait. Wait, OK, don't get emotional, don't get emotional.	等等，等等先，等等先，等吓，唔好激動，唔好激動，吓。
47	W:	I'm not emotional, I'm hurt. I can't believe she said this. I've never heard her say these words to me in person.	我唔係激動，我係傷心，我估唔到佢咁樣講，我未聽過佢同我親口講呢句說話。
48	I:	[*simultaneously*] Right, OK, OK, OK.	[*simultaneously*] 係，OK，得，得。
49	W:	Before the accident, I have never heard such comment from her. Personally I mean.	Before the accident, I have never heard such comment from her. Personally I mean.

Khilnani is using "bona fide" or "in good faith" in a nontechnical manner here (para. 33). "Good faith," or "bona fides," is of course a continental legal principle that many common law lawyers find too abstract to apply.

Khilnani here is using "bona fide" more or less as a bookish way to refer to honesty.[20] But Ma is clearly flustered by the semiotic grandeur that the Latin term commands. She tries to match it with a stylized triplet phrase in Cantonese—"sensible, reasonable, and legitimate" (para. 26). But she clearly focuses too much on form over content, and the translation is a far cry from the common semantic meaning of "good faith." Khilnani, who understands some Cantonese, certainly notices this, and he rejects the interpreter's translation in a discreet way—by offering to rephrase his own question (rather than telling the interpreter bluntly that she got it wrong).[21] The interpreter takes the cue accordingly; she drops the stylistic triplet "sensible, reasonable, and legitimate" when she translates the question for the second time and uses instead the Cantonese phrase 善意 [sin6 ji3], roughly meaning "goodwill," for the English term "good faith." Meanwhile, Chan is checking the witness statement contained in the case document bundle to see what precisely Charles said. When the interpreter puts the question across for the third time, "Do you accept this was criticism out of goodwill?" Chan begins to weep.[22]

What follows shows the gendered role that court interpreters in Hong Kong play in the system. In Hong Kong, as in other places, court interpreting is often considered a woman's job. Although court interpreters are officially deemed *voiceless* (i.e., conduit pipes), in practice they often interact with litigants in a gendered voice. Most of the full-time court interpreters are women, and they often play the role of confidant to litigants facing hostile counsel (cf. Morris 1999). Some even assume a maternal role to contain and calm down litigants during moments of breakdown. Counsels and judges whom I interviewed frankly admit that witnesses are more "manageable" when they have to speak through an interpreter (see Chapter 7 for further details). As one can see from the transcript, there are moments when Ma exerts what Berk-Seligson (1990) calls linguistic coercion, asking Chan to wait (等等先 [dang2 dang2 sin1]; para. 46) in order to stop Chan from a full-blown outburst. And then Ma also gently asks Chan not to get emotional (唔好激動 [ng4 hou2 gik1 dung6]; para. 46) or asks her to slow down and pause for her to catch up. Ma saw Chan break down twice on the previous day of the trial, and it is up to her to make sure that the young woman remains in an interpretable state. Meanwhile, the judge, the three barristers, and their instructing solicitors—like the legal professionals in other trials I observed—retain a sense of businesslike aloofness. Like many courtroom regulars, they do not appear to be surprised at all by Chan's emotions.[23]

Court interpreters in Hong Kong also serve as linguistic marshals. They are an integral part of juridical formalism in Hong Kong. And the linguistic control required to maintain this interaction order can come in many forms. Sometimes it comes in the benign form of plead and advice, as when Ma displays maternal sympathy toward Chan; at other times, a poker-faced interpreter simply instructs a witness to pause, telling him that she will not be able to interpret his every word if the witness keeps talking (as in an example later; and as we will see, Ma says the same thing to Chan later).

Yet there are tensions between the ideal of the conduit and the de facto role of court marshal that court interpreters play. Such tension is mani-fested linguistically and so has to be erased linguistically. As we can see, in her bid to keep Chan in an interpretable state, Ma initiates another Cantonese side conversation that is left untranslated (paras. 42–48). To undo her own intervention, Ma ignores in her interpretation what she considers to be Chan's reply ("I'm not emotional. I'm hurt"; para. 47) to her own pleading ("Don't get emotional"; para. 46). Here we can see how Ma erases her very real presence by removing all her back-channeling feedback to Chan in the official transcript of the trial proceedings. The anguish-filled utterance "I can't believe she said this" (para. 47) is also left out. What remains in the official transcript, the one that the judge and counsel refer to, is the constative statement, "I have never heard such comments from her" (para. 49), stripped of all the emotions that came with the original utterance.

THE IDEAL OF COURT INTERPRETATION

Chan's tearful reaction gives Khilnani a good reason to query the "ac-curacy" of the interpretation. Interestingly, though, he chooses not to question the translation of the phrase "bona fide" or the translation of the subsequent English phrase "good faith," a phrase that Smith has also noticed the interpreter has trouble translating. Khilnani instead questions

Ma's choice of the term 批評 [pai1 ping4], which he says means "criticism" in Cantonese, to represent his words "her view" in his original question, which, as he explains to the judge, sounds more like "assessment."

Interactions Between Defense Counsel Gautam Khilnani (C1), Plaintiff's Counsel Peter Smith (C2), and Judge Pitt (J)

50 C1: My Lord, may I invite your interpreter to confirm that when she translated, the word 批評 [pai1 ping4] was used, which to my limited understanding of Cantonese, it's interpreted as criticism, and I mean the thrust of my question is not really a criticism directed at her by Ms. Charles, but it's really just an assessment which Ms. Charles made. I don't know if that makes a difference to this witness. [*At this point, Smith tries to interrupt but Khilnani ignores him.*] But I think when one uses the word "criticism," the interpreter did the best she can. But trying to understand the witness, and we're trying to, when one uses the word "criticism," it instinctively invites a defensive reaction.

51 J: Yeah.

52 C1: But what I'm saying is that was not the thrust of my question and . . .

53 C2: Is my learned friend trying to refer to the interpretation of the words "good faith"?

54 J: No, I think . . .

55 C2: I don't know.

56 J: . . . "assessment," and in fact is interpreted so it sounds more like "criticism," even though in English we use the word "criticism" in a much wider, ha ha, sense.

57 C1: It's not necessarily negative.

58 J: Yeah. Hmm, is there a way to translate it so that it is more neutral?

59 C2: Perhaps the interpreter herself, since she is the court interpreter, can confirm that's the way she translated it.

60 C1: Well, ha ha, my learned friend need not be so concerned because I think . . .

61 C2: There is . . . there is a proper way of matters being interpreted, and it is through the court interpreter, not through counsel . . .

62 C1:... I think my learned friend can rest assured that I have sufficient experience to understand this [*inaudible*] and I certainly have an advantage over him in my understanding of Cantonese.

63 C2: Moot point.

64 J: Let's, let's go back to the interpreter.

65 C1: And I think, my Lord, that was how I started my point. Would your interpreter consider that the word 批評 [pai1 ping4] in Cantonese as, is "criticism" and does not carry the same English connotation?

66 J: Is that right, interpreter? Is there a way of translating it that says not, certainly assessment rather than criticism?

[*A long silence, about 10 seconds*]

67 J: You see the witness appears to, to think that, that she's been asked about criticism of her rather than neutral assessment.

68 C2: My Lord, I am instructed that the words used, the whole phrase used was "sin yee pai ping," which apparently is a criticism in a kind manner.

69 J: All right. Well . . .

70 C2: So it's not quite off.

71 J: No, I couldn't say that.

72 J: Can we deal with this in some other way?

73 C1: I would like to say I, I, I do just that.

74 J: Yeah.

75 C1: I would like to say I do just that.

76 J: Yeah.

This episode is revealing because it is precisely at such moments of interpretational breakdown—between "criticism" and "assessment"—that the parties bring into the open their model of interpretation, in the form of elaborate disquisitions or, more precisely, explicit metapragmatic statements. Khilnani suggests that the Chinese words 批評 [pai1 ping4] carry different connotations from what he wants to convey to Chan; he thus invokes a distinction between explicit referential denotation and implicit evaluative connotation and claims that the connotations of the Cantonese words chosen by the interpreter are unfaithful to the spirit of the original English. In more general terms, Khilnani is suggesting that interpretational failure occurs when the interpreter fails to secure a state of equivalence between individual words in both denotation and connotation. This is often an impossible task, as the judge acknowledges when he comments, "even though in English we use the word 'criticism' in a much wider, ha ha, sense" (para. 56). But the model of conduit, which envisions Cantonese words one by one piped from the interpreter's mouth into the empty space of the courtroom, endorses this mechanical, dictionary-like, and impossible model of interpreting.

It is interesting to see that Ma is criticized for the translation of one word, given that her interpretation has been filled with liberal amplifications and erasures up until that point. It shows that legal professionals have two attitudes toward court interpretation, one official and one unofficial. Officially, court and judges accept that court interpretation involves merely the recoding of evidence from one language to another. Unofficially, they acknowledge that, in real life, court interpretation is more complex than what the conduit model envisions. When a counsel thinks that the input of a court interpreter has done a disservice to his case, he would appeal to the conduit ideal to ask a court interpreter to redo the interpretation, as in the case here.

Is it really misleading to interpret Charles's assessment as *criticism*? Or should one instead ask whether it is misleading to call Charles's criticism an *assessment* in the first place? What kind of accuracy is Khilnani after here? It would add much weight to Charles's eventual testimony if even Chan, the plaintiff herself, endorsed Charles as an honest witness and a trustworthy critic. Even though Khilnani has recapped for Chan what Charles said, the use of the term "assessment" is a move that in effect temporarily dissociates the contents of Charles's remark from the speaker's intention. This allows him, like a magician on stage, for a brief interactional moment (which is all that is needed) to misdirect Chan toward the decoy question (about Charles's honesty) while the subject matter, the criticism itself, is masked under the neutral cover of the term "assessment." So long as Chan finds Charles's character agreeable, it is not important whether Chan finds the content of the comments agreeable or not. For one thing, one is never an objective evaluator of one's own artistic talent; and for another, Charles is by far the more seasoned and established ballerina of the two. She was the ballet mistress of the company and was in a position to evaluate younger dancers. Ma ruins Khilnani's carefully orchestrated misdirection when she brings the contents of the assessment back into the question (which Khilnani carefully frames as a question only about Charles's honesty) by using the term "criticism." So understood, Ma's "mistake," if it can be called that, occurs when she takes the liberty of offering an all-too-honest gloss on Khilnani's "lawyer-speak," thus unveiling the trick for Chan.

Furthermore, even though Khilnani does not contest the translation of the term "bona fide," it is interesting to note that the term has taken on new meanings as the parties continue to *try* to find an exact equivalent in Cantonese; Ma translates it into Cantonese as 善意批評 [sin6 ji3 pai1 ping4] (roughly meaning "criticism made with a kind heart"), which is then retranslated back by Smith (on the advice of his instructing solicitor) into English as "criticism in a kind manner." In the protracted process of searching for an exact equivalence of "bona fide" in Cantonese, a question of "heart" has now become a question of "manner."

VOICING

Ma, who has hitherto subsumed her voice under the courtroom "we," stops serving as the faithful echo of Khilnani by shifting the deictic frame as soon as Khilnani raises the question, albeit politely, about the accuracy of her interpretation.

Cross-Examination of Ada Chan (W) by Defense Counsel Gautam Khilnani (C1) Through Interpreter Rebecca Ma (I) (Continued), with Comments from Plaintiff's Counsel Peter Smith (C2) and Judge Pitt (J)

	Gloss	Original
77	C1: Ms. Chan, I appreciate you're very sensitive to these issues, and, please rest assured that it is not my intention to belittle you in any way.	Ms. Chan, I appreciate you're very sensitive to these issues, and, please rest assured that it is not my intention to belittle you in any way.

78   I: The barrister said he knew that you are relatively, relatively sensitive to this question, this kind of questions. But then you must believe, you must feel relieved, he was not trying to belittle you, to say that you are not good. That wasn't what he did.   大律師話呢佢都知道呢你對於呢個問題，呢一方面嘅問題呢你較為，較為啫吓，較為敏感嘅，咁但係呢，你一定要係啫係相信呢，好安心吓，佢唔係話呢想話係貶低你嘅，話係你唔好㗎。佢唔係咁呀吓。

79   W: No, now I want to tell him that I've never heard it from her own mouth. The only thing I heard from her is her praise. She said I was good, well done.   唔係呀，依家我係話，話想話番俾佢聽我從未聽過佢親口對我講，我剩係聽過佢讚我好呀，做得好呀。

80   I: [*simultaneously*] "OK." Wait. Wait.   [*simultaneously*] OK。等等

81   W: I never. The first time I saw this, I felt, [*sobbing*] the first time I saw this, I was really emotional.   我未，我第一次見到呢份嘢我就覺得，[*sobbing*] 我我第一次睇呢份口供我就真係激動囉。

82   I: You wait first, wait first, OK? You told me so many things, but I can't remember them all. OK?   你等等先。等等先，吓，你你講晒俾我聽咁多我都記唔得咁多。OK, 吓。

83   W: First of all, I have never heard, I have never personally heard from her such words. The . . .   First of all, I have never heard, I have never personally heard from her such words. The . . .

84   J: What words?   What words?

85   I: So what words?   即係聽佢咁講講咩呀？

86   W: I mean the things she said in the statement, her assessment of me.   即係份口供講嘅嘢，對我嘅評價。

87   I: The content contained in the statement in relation to her views on me, or her assessment of me. The only . . .   The content contained in the statement in relation to her views on me, or her assessment of me. The only . . .

88   J: OK. Next one.   OK. Next one.

89 I: The only, the only comment I received from her was that she said that I was doing very, very well.

        The only, the only comment I received from her was that she said that I was doing very, very well.

90 C1: Madam Chan, I understand . . .

        Madam Chan, I understand . . .

91 W: But when I saw her statement, I was really . . .

        但係睇到佢份嘢我就真係 . . .

92 C1: Madam Chan.

        Madam Chan.

93 C2: The witness should be allowed to answer the question, my Lord. She is being interpreted . . .

        The witness should be allowed to answer her question, my Lord. She is being interpreted . . .

94 C1: That's my very point. There's no question for her to answer . . .

        That's my very point. There's no question for her to answer . . .

95 J: [*inaudible*] Let me clarify this. You weren't being asked whether she had . . . you ever heard her say what she's saying now. You were merely being asked, really in a negative way, whether you know any reason why she should make these . . .

        [*inaudible*] Let me clarify this. You weren't being asked whether she had . . . you ever heard her say what she's saying now. You were merely being asked, really in a negative way, whether you know any reason why she should make these . . .

96 C1: No.

        No.

97 J: No, we are getting that wrong again, aren't we?

        No, we are getting that wrong again, aren't we?

98 C1: May I just step backward? May I step backward?

        May I just step backward? May I step backward?

99 C2: [*inaudible*] Can we move forward?

        [*inaudible*] Can we move forward?

100 C1: I think the difficulty is the witness understandably is sensitive to these issues and she understands our question in such a way . . .

        I think the difficulty is the witness understandably is sensitive to these issues and she understands our question in such a way . . .

101 J: [*simultaneously*] I took that, yes.

        [*simultaneously*] I took that, yes.

102 C1: . . . [*inaudible*] and than the way we would have liked. But that is not my question. And Ms. Chan I'm going to put my question again. She has made an assessment, and she said you did not live up to expectation when you performed solo.

103 J: Let's put it at a time [*inaudible*] and wait for the interpreter. This isn't a question. It's just a statement to start with.

104 I: The instructor, OK, she made an assessment. She said when you performed solo, you were not up to the required standard, which means the standard they thought you were capable of achieving, but you were not up to it. Now, this was an assessment she made, an assessment she already made, OK? No question yet. OK?

105 J: Let's go on.

106 C1: Now if she did express this view, do you agree it is not surprising because you yourself say that the views are not relayed to the dancers? Can I get that out of the way? My Lord, we established that on her evidence, that is, before assessments are not relayed [*inaudible*]. So I just want to get that out of the way.

. . . [*inaudible*] and than the way we would have liked. But that is not my question. And Ms. Chan I'm going to put my question again. She has made an assessment, and she said you did not live up to expectation when you performed solo.

Let's put it at a time [*inaudible*] and wait for the interpreter. This isn't a question. It's just a statement to start with.

個，個導師呢吓佢就做咗一個評估出嚟，佢話呢你跳獨舞嘅時候呢吓，你未能達到嗰個要求，嗰個水平，吓，即係佢哋諗住你可以去到嗰個水平嘅，但係你達唔到咁吖，呢個係佢作出嚟嘅一個評估，佢已經作出嚟嘅一個評價，吓，未有問題住呀，吓。

Let's go on.

Now if she did express this view, do you agree it is not surprising because you yourself say that the views are not relayed to the dancers? Can I get that out of the way? My Lord, we established that on her evidence, that is, before assessments are not relayed [*inaudible*]. So I just want to get that out of the way.

107 J: So she wouldn't have been necessarily told that assessment.

108 C1: That's right. Had been made after the solo dance. That's right.

109 J: Does, does she agree she wouldn't necessarily have been told of the assessment of Charles? The witness.

110 I: Lord, I'm lost.

111 J: If the . . . what's her name, the . . . she's the ballet mistress isn't she? If the ballet mistress had made her personal assessment of her ability after her solo performance, she wouldn't necessarily, Madam Chan wouldn't necessarily have been told of that assessment.

112 C1: I am grateful.

113 I: If the ballet mistress had made a certain assessment of your performance, certain evaluation let's say, but she wouldn't necessarily have to tell you about her assessment. Even if she made a certain assessment, she didn't always tell you, right?

114 W: Yes. Whether it's good or not good she didn't have to tell me.

115 I: Either way, whether we did well or vice versa.

116 W: Unless she thought there was a need. Otherwise she would tell me only if she chose to do so.

So she wouldn't have been necessarily told that assessment. That's right. Had been made after the solo dance. That's right. Does, does she agree she wouldn't necessarily have been told of the assessment of Charles? The witness.

Lord, I'm lost.

If the . . . what's her name, the . . . she's the ballet mistress isn't she? If the ballet mistress had made her personal assessment of her ability after her solo performance, she wouldn't necessarily, Madam Chan wouldn't necessarily have been told of that assessment.

I am grateful.

若然呢吓呢個芭蕾舞導師咁佢對你嘅表現呀吓作出一個某樣嘅，作出咗一個某樣嘅評估，或者評價咁先算吖吓。咁你哋身為一個嘅舞蹈員嘅時間呢吓，唔一定話要話俾你哋聽㗎，就算佢哋有啲咩嘢評價，作出咩嘢評價，唔一定講俾你哋聽嘅，係咪吖？

係吖，好定唔好都唔一定要講俾我聽。

Either way, whether we did well or vice versa.

除非佢覺得有需要啦，佢自己講，佢自己選擇講先講之嘛。

151

| 117 | I: | Unless, unless the instructor found that there was a need to let us know. | Unless, unless the instructor found that there was a need to let us know. |

When interpreting Khilnani's courtesy consolation toward Chan, Ma drops the courtroom we and introduces Khilnani's statement with the title 大律師 [daai6 leot6 si1], "The barrister said he knew . . ." (para. 78). She is, for the moment, neither part of the courtroom we nor the faithful echo of Khilnani. Juxtaposing the Cantonese neuter third-person pronoun 佢 [keoi5] ("S/he") is a hidden 我 [ngo5] ("I"). Ma's deictic shift turns the interaction into a three-way exchange, which is immediately taken up by Chan, who takes up the same Cantonese third-person pronoun 佢([keoi5]) in reference to Khilnani: "Now I want to tell him (佢 [keoi5]) . . ." (para. 79).

Through deictic shifts, Ma realigns the interactional footing and her relationship with both Chan and Khilnani (see Goffman 1981; Schiffrin 1990). However, by her deictic reframing, Ma also makes herself visible in the linguistic space of Cantonese. That creates a problem for Ma: Ma the interpreter, as a mere conduit, is, as I said, a nonperson; she is not supposed to have a presence in the trial. How can she reconcile the fact that she *is* linguistically visible in the Cantonese space with her official mandate to be invisible? Ma's solution to this dilemma is a *pragmatic self-erasure* that realigns the deictic footing in her English interpretation. Because the use of the Cantonese third-person pronoun presupposes the shadowy presence of a first person "I" (i.e., the interpreter) and because Ma, the invisible ventriloquist, is not supposed to assume a voice in the conversation, Ma unsurprisingly edits herself out of the English interpretation when she reverts to the original deictic frame to eliminate any reference to Khilnani as "S/he" (佢 [keoi5]). Meanwhile, Smith tries to put a stop to Khilnani's cross-examination. It is at this point that the judge decides to intervene and restore the interactional order of the cross-examination. The judge for a moment becomes a second interpreter, whose native language is English, trying to clarify the question for the English-speaking counsel. But his attempt ends in frustration: "No, we are getting that wrong again, aren't we?" (para. 97). After that, Khilnani does not go back to his original question; instead he asks Chan whether she agrees that whatever assessment Charles made about her performance might not have been known to her. Chan agrees, adding that it was up to Charles whether to tell her or not.

The excerpt also shows how the counsel is in a position of dominance because of his knowledge of the rules of the game. When Khilnani rebukes Smith's intervention, "That's my very point. There's no question for her to answer" (para. 94), he aims at crucial constraints on Chan's narrative license, so to speak, delimiting her role as a witness and not a storyteller. Khilnani also retains and exercises his authority to offer metalinguistic commentary on the process of cross-examination, suggesting that it is Chan's sensitivity—strong enough to make her bend the meaning of his question—that gives rise to the communicative impasse.

It should now be clear that there are really two conversations taking place in the cross-examination—one a sometimes intense, glib English war of words between the two barristers and the other a slow-paced Cantonese question-and-answer sequence between the interpreter and the witness. Not only does the interpreter choose not to interpret her Cantonese inner dialogue with Chan into English, but she also does not interpret the crossfire between Khilnani and Smith, and the judge's eventual intervention, to Chan. Among the key participants involved, only Ma, Khilnani (who understands Cantonese), and another bilingual counsel So (counsel for the first defendant) "hear" the trial in its entirety. The others only get one of the two interpretations (i.e., English and Cantonese, albeit differently edited) offered by Ma.

PUTTING THE QUESTION ACROSS

The moment after the judge's intervention, the interpreter immediately returns her deictic footing back to the courtroom "we," as seen in the question put to Chan yet again.

Cross-Examination of Ada Chan (W) by Defense Counsel Gautam Khilnani (C1) Through Interpreter Rebecca Ma (I) (Continued), with Comments by Plaintiff Counsel Peter Smith (C2) and Judge Pitt (J)

		Gloss	Original
118	C1:	My Lord, may I take the point established?	My Lord, may I take the point established?
119	J:	Yeah.	Yeah.
120	C1:	Now may I move on? And I want to ask you this. Perhaps a simple direct answer would be helpful. She has expressed this assessment of your performance in that solo spot, and she said you did not live up to expectations or achieved the standard. Now, whether or not you agree that's another matter. My question is, Do you accept that her view is given in good faith? It's as simple as that.	Now may I move on? And I want to ask you this. Perhaps a simple direct answer would be helpful. She has expressed this assessment of your performance in that solo spot, and she said you did not live up to expectations or achieved the standard. Now, whether or not you agree that's another matter. My question is, Do you accept that her view is given in good faith? It's as simple as that.
121	C1:	Or honestly if you like.	Or honestly if you like.
122	J:	Don't try to complicate things.	Don't try to complicate things.
123	I:	Now Charles was your ballet mistress. She made an assessment of you, OK? This was on your solo performance, OK? She said you were not up to the level they expected you to achieve, which means you were not up to that level, OK? This was an, an, an assessment she made, an evaluation. Whether you agreed or not, this is another matter. You can agree, you can disagree; this is another matter.	咁呀 Charles 呢佢係你嘅導師呀，佢就已經表達咗佢對你嘅一個評估啦，吓，即係嗰次你跳獨舞嘅時間，吓，佢就話呢你係未有呢係能夠呢係達到佢哋期望你嘅嗰個水平，即係唔及到嗰個水平啦吓，呢個係佢作出嘅一個嘅 . . . 嘅 . . . 嘅評價㗎嘅，評估㗎嘅，至於你同意抑或唔同意呢，呢個係另外一回事，你可以同意，可以唔同，可以唔同意吖，呢個另外一回事。

124	W:	Yes, yes.

係，係。

125	I:	But we want to ask you when she, do you . . . you think that when she made a certain evaluation, or this kind of comment, she was at that time very honest? That is to say, she said honestly what she regarded as facts. Do you think so or not?

咁但係呢就我哋想問你呢吓，當佢，你 . . . 覺唔覺得呢佢作出一個某樣嘅評估，或者一個咁樣嘅評語嘅時候呢吓，咁佢當時呢係好忠誠地即係將嗰個佢覺得係嗰個事實嘅忠實地嚟到講出嚟，你覺唔覺得係呢？

126	W:	No.

唔 . . . 係。

127	C1:	No, I, I think we got lost again [*sigh*] because the last part of my, of the interpreter's question "Do you think so?" was inviting an agreement or a disagreement to the assessment. The simple point is, Do you accept that her assessment was given in good faith? I'm not troubled whether she agrees with that assessment or not.

No, I, I think we got lost again [*sigh*] because the last part of my, of the interpreter's question "Do you think so?" was inviting an agreement or a disagreement to the assessment. The simple point is, Do you accept that her assessment was given in good faith? I'm not troubled whether she agrees with that assessment or not.

128	I:	The question, ask . . . you once more.

個問題，再 . . . 問你一次。

129	W:	Ask again.

再問一次。

130	I:	It's not whether you think so or not. The question asks you whether you accept or not, you accept or not, you accept or not.

唔係問你覺唔覺得啦，而係問你接唔接納喇，你接唔接納，你接唔接納。

131	W:	Can you repeat? I'm sorry.

再之前講多次先，唔好意思吓。

132	I:	Do you accept this assessment? The assessment of you, that she made it honestly?

你接唔接納呢佢嗰個評語呢？咁樣對你作出嘅評語呢吓，佢係好忠誠地作出嘅？

133	W:	I don't accept.

唔接納。

134	I:	No.

No.

135 C1: OK. So it's your evidence that she for some reason is giving an assessment in bad faith—dishonestly, if you like.

OK. So it's your evidence that she for some reason is giving an assessment in bad faith—dishonestly, if you like.

136 I: So you said you didn't accept. So do you think that when she made this kind of assessment of you, she, on the contrary, was not very, was not very honest, was not faithful? That what she said was not the fact? Is that what you think of her?

而你，嘩你話唔接受吖吓，唔接受，咁你是否呢就覺得佢作出咁樣嘅對你嘅評價嚟講呢吓，佢呢，相反嚟講啦，就唔係好唔係好，唔係好忠誠啦，吓，唔忠實咧，講出嚟即係唔係係實情咧咁樣，係唔係呀？你覺得佢？

137 W: On this particular issue?

咁呢件事嚟講？

138 I: The assessment is of your solo performance, OK?

個評價佢話你話你跳獨舞吖嘛。

139 W: This is not the fact.

唔係實情喎。

140 I: Not the fact.

唔係實情。

141 W: Not the fact.

唔係實情。

142 I: That is correct.

That is correct.

143 W: Because she came to me that time and told me in person that I did it quite well.

因為佢親口走嚟同我講話我幾好喍嘛喗次。

144 I: OK.

OK。

145 W: After I danced, she came in person with the artistic director and told me.

跳完之係佢親口同埋 artistic director 走嚟同我講，係囉。

146 I: OK. Wait, wait first.

OK。等等先，等等先。

147 W: She said it with her own mouth. I have no reason after hearing it . . .

親口對我講嘅嘢我無理由聽完之後 . . .

148 I: I got it, OK.

得，OK。

149 W: I disagree because on that occasion after I have performed the solo dance, she and also the artistic director, both of them,

I disagree because on that occasion after I have performed the solo dance, she and also the artistic director, both of them, came to me personally and told me that I had done a very good job.

150 C1: Oh, we have to hear about that. Did you really expect them to come to you and tell you you've done a very poor job and you will never dance again? Is that what you are telling the court that you expect them to say?

151 I: Then did you or not, did you or not think . . .

152 C2: My Lord . . .

153 C1: I'll leave it, my Lord.

154 J: Yes, I think we are getting off the track on this.

155 C1: It's more comment.

156 J: Hmmm.

157 C1: I'll leave it.

came to me personally and told me that I had done a very good job.

Oh, we have to hear about that. Did you really expect them to come to you and tell you you've done a very poor job and you will never dance again? Is that what you are telling the court that you expect them to say?

咁你係咪你係咪諗住 . . .

My Lord . . .

I'll leave it, my Lord.

Yes, I think we are getting off the track on this.

It's more comment.

Hmmm.

I'll leave it.

It is interesting to note that Ma utters 評價 [ping4 gaa3], the Cantonese term for "assessment," with great hesitation, as it is preceded by the long filler 嘅 [gei3] (para. 123); she then immediately supplements her interpretation with a similar Cantonese term, 評估 [ping4 gu2], in an anxious attempt to buy herself, as it were, linguistic insurance (paras. 123 and 125). The incantatory repetitions I identified in her previous interpretation persist. Still, Khilnani is not happy with the question "Do you think so or not?" (para. 127). He suggests that it is too broad in inviting Chan to describe the contents of Charles's assessment. He wants the question to be more specific, focused only on Charles's motive: "Do you accept or not that her assessment was given in good faith?" Upon Khilnani's query, Ma tells Chan, "It's not whether you think so or not. The question asks you whether you accept or not, you accept or not, you accept or not" (para. 130). This seems to further confuse Chan. She then asks Ma to repeat the question one last time (para. 131).

So, after an hour of planned misdirection, imperceptive redirection, and heated contestation, not to mention a display of the advocate's domination, hostile undercutting between the counsel, with tears shed and anguish displayed, the question is finally put to Chan one last time: "Do you accept this assessment? The assessment of you, that she made it honestly?" (para. 132). Chan replies: "I don't accept" (para. 133). But even so, it is not entirely clear whether Chan means that she does not accept that Charles has made the assessment honestly (as an answer to the second question) or that she does not accept what Charles specifically said in the assessment of her (as an answer to the first question). In any case, Khilnani intends to leave no doubts for the judge by stamping his interpretation on Chan's answer: "OK. So it is your evidence that she for some reasons is giving the assessment in bad faith—dishonestly, if you like" (para. 135). Here's another question from Khilnani that sets up a difficult yes or no. For Chan to say yes, she would appear to be too defensive; but for her to say no, she would acknowledge that Charles's comment was made in good faith. Ma, however, unsuspectingly offers Chan a lifeline when she interprets Khilnani's question as: "You said you didn't accept. So do you think that when she made this kind of assessment of you, she, on the contrary, was not very, was not very honest, was not faithful? *That what she said was not the fact?* Is that what you think of her?" (para. 136). It is of course much easier to say no to Ma's interpreted question ("That what she said was not the fact?") than to pick a yes or no to reply to Khilnani's original question. It is easier to say that what was said by Charles was not true than to accuse Charles the person of being dishonest. Chan then elaborates that she was praised by Charles, in person, right after the performance.

In response, Khilnani makes a dismissive remark about Chan: "Oh, we have to hear about that" (para. 150). He does not dispute that Charles once praised Chan but puts it in a context that significantly reduces the gravity of the comment—that is, Charles was forced by the circumstances (right after a performance) not to say something bad to Chan. "Did you really expect them to come to you and tell you you've done a very poor job and you will never dance again? Is that what you are telling the court that you expect them to say?" (para. 150). This question, although rhetorical in its nature, is one that Chan should at least have an opportunity to respond to, according to the rules of cross-examination; however, as Ma begins to interpret the question, Khilnani "concedes" that "it's more comment" (para. 155) and decides not to pursue it further. The question, as a result, is left untranslated in part and Chan does not get a chance to listen and respond to it.

THE QUESTION OF ACCURACY

For reasons I referred to in Chapter 4, equivalence of meaning on the basis of a textual model is particularly emphasized in the common law system of Hong Kong, a system in which many judges are not bilingual as required by law.[24] But a textual understanding of the work of court interpretation does not take into account the wider Cantonese-English diglossic divide in the background. As the transcript illustrates, court interpreters, in their drive to produce statementlike evidence, often must confront the gap in the linguistic habituses (taken-for-granted default contexts) of English and Cantonese, two languages that are drastically different in terms of where and when people use them. Court interpretation is thus the site where Cantonese and English, often segregated into their own linguistic habituses, are forced to encounter each other interactionally face to face, where the irreducible differences between the two are negotiated and models of legal language are erected or erased.

I therefore suggest that court interpretation in Hong Kong is far from a simple process of recodification of linguistic texts. A more socially grounded way to conceive of the work of court interpreters is to see interpretation as a process of repragmatization, by which I mean pragmatic features of witnesses' *utterances* in Cantonese are translated into pragmatic characteristics of English-language *evidence*. This process is part of a broader project of producing a "unitary language" for the law, an attempt to control "the conflicting usages and differently oriented accents of social dialogue" (Goodrich 1986: 188). Translating Cantonese utterances into English is, at the same time, a process of situating Cantonese heteroglossia under the analytical gaze of the law. Court interpretation systematically mutes the ambiguous, expressive, and emotional aspects of witnesses' utterances while amplifying their semantic, descriptive, and propositional aspects. This is so despite the fact that, in the legal common sense shared among lawyers and judges, court interpreters merely play the role of a semantic conduit and are effectively invisible in the process of law.

The use of court interpreters also means that the rigidity of the statement-and-reply structure I described in Chapter 4 is justified as a practical necessity in interpreted trials. In the presence of a court interpreter, it takes some really assertive and savvy witnesses to insist on answering questions at their own pace. That said, most judges are aware of the inconvenience created by court interpretation. During the course of my fieldwork, I came across some witnesses who made it known to the court that they preferred to speak in Cantonese (sometimes a bilingual opposing counsel might, for tactical reasons, prefer to use English; see Chapter 7). When such a preference is openly expressed to the judge, the witnesses often put the court in a defensive position. Despite their official power to decide the language of a trial, many judges in Hong Kong are aware that an English trial could have been conducted in Cantonese instead.

In the next example, a witness resists the segmentation of his narrative and insists on finishing his answers in one go. His act draws the ire of the court interpreter, who tells him that this will make it impossible for her to interpret. Refusing to back down, the witness shoots back that he prefers to have the trial conducted in Cantonese (para. 9; which means that the court interpreter has to leave the courtroom) and tells the court interpreter that she is the reason he forgot his answer.

A Witness (W) and a Court Interpreter (I) in an English Trial

		Gloss	Original
1	W:	That's because I had a wife in Mainland China in the past.	因為呢我之前國內有個太太。
2	W:	I registered with her.	同佢註咗冊嘅。
3	I:	[*simultaneously*] At that time I had a wife . . .	[*simultaneously*] At that time I had a wife . . .
4	W:	I had asked . . .	我就問過 . . .
5	I:	. . . in Mainland . . .	. . . in Mainland . . .
6	W:	. . . before I . . . I knew May.	我 . . . 我未識阿 May 之前。
7	I:	Wait, wait, wait.	等,等,等。

8 I:	I have to interpret the things you said. You go nonstop . . .	你講啲嘢我要譯嘅。 你一輪咀講出嚟 . . .
9 W:	We can just speak Cantonese!	咁咪講廣東話囉！
10 I:	[*simultaneously*] You . . .	[*simultaneously*] 你 . . .
11 I:	You take it slowly. I have to interpret every line you said. Do you understand?	你慢慢嚟吖。 你講咗每一句說話呢我都要譯嘅。 你明唔明呀？
12 W:	But . . .	但係 . . .
13 I:	[*simultaneously*] Give me a chance to speak.	[*simultaneously*] 你俾機會我講吖。
14 W:	. . . But after I stopped, I forgot. Stop and go, stop and go, right? I want to speak Cantonese.	但係停咗之後我，我唔記得啦又，斷斷續續，係咪先？我要講廣東話講吖嘛。
15 I:	I've got, I've got a wife living in Mainland China, and, eh, eh, and that was before I came to know May, and I informed the, eh, Housing Authority at that time.	I've got, I've got a wife living in Mainland China, and, eh, eh, and that was before I came to know May, and I informed the, eh, Housing Authority at that time.
16 I:	What follows?	跟住點呀？
17 W:	I forgot.	我唔記得咗啦。
18 I:	I forgot.	I forgot.

The job performance of court interpreters, especially part-time court interpreters, has in recent years drawn the attention of the mass media and of politicians in Hong Kong (Hong Kong Judiciary 2004b). This followed the revelation that a part-time interpreter of Indonesian had been exposed for coaching and fabricating evidence given by a witness in front of a magistrate who happened to know the language. Policymakers and politicians commonly assume that the quality of interpretation (and of the interpreters) can be addressed by improving the linguistic skills of court interpreters in general. Some have called for a system of accreditation similar to the Australian model (C. K. Lau 2000) as a method of quality control. Of course, adequate linguistic command of the languages involved is a must, but the difficulties of courtroom interpretation run deeper than a simple matter of language comprehension and grammar. The episode in this chapter shows that it is highly unrealistic to blindly stick to the conduit model of court interpretation. If we set our sights on what court interpreters actually *do*, it is clear that far from being invisible, they often have to insert themselves into dialogic interactions (cf. Wadensjö 1998). To wit, court interpreters are an integral part of the practices of juridical formalism in Hong Kong. The nature of consecutive interpretation means that there is an extra layer of institutional control on how freely a witness can tell her story or interact with the questioning counsel. Consecutive interpretation requires the speaker to pause at regular intervals—in Hong Kong usually every one or two sentences—to give the interpreter time to interpret aloud his speech into the target language (e.g., Chinese into English, or vice versa). Court interpreters, standing at the linguistic border, are given the impossible task of turning raw utterances in Cantonese into "admissible" evidence in English. Courtroom interpretation is never simply word-for-word translation. Often in Hong Kong the interpreted version of a witness's answer is more literate, coherent, and precise. In the process, court interpreters unknowingly proceed through erasure and explication, as I hope the circuitous path that one single question put to the witness in my example has shown. Interpreters use a more formal register, reflected in the choice of lexicon, and they avoid contradictions and will cohesion into witnesses' and counsel's utterances by filling in gaps with explanatory phrases.

But the presence of court interpreters, as the nature of English in Hong Kong requires, is only one feature that explains the extremely rule-governed nature of the English-language trials. As we saw in some of the examples in Chapter 4, even without the presence of court interpreters, juridical formalism has a commanding presence in the medium of English. In the next chapter I shift focus to Cantonese courtrooms, where we will see the very different dynamics of interaction triggered by the use of Cantonese.

CHAPTER 6

Cantonese Courtrooms
Formalism in Flux

IN THE LAST TWO CHAPTERS I showed that the English-language courtrooms in Hong Kong are highly structured spaces within which juridical formalism is instantiated through the role-specific interactions among the actors. The live performances of witnesses are rendered as purely constative through the testimonial ideal of statement making endorsed by the machinery of cross-examination. English in Hong Kong, powerful, businesslike, and untethered from the quotidian, gives juridical formalism a fitting voice. When litigants choose to speak through court interpreters, the interpreters' presence keeps the narrative of witnesses in check. The use of English affects the interactional dynamics of the courtroom in two related but analytically distinct ways. The first is institutional. It is the easier dimension of the two to identify. The elite status of English means that lay litigants most often resort to the aid of court interpreters when testifying in English-language trials. The impact of two-way interpretation on courtroom dynamics is simply impossible to overlook, as I attempted to show in Chapter 5. Consecutive interpretation means that evidence has to be delivered in small segments.

The second, more elusive and yet more important way that English affects the interactional dynamics of the courtroom is social-structural. This is the spellbinding language effect that I attempted to pin down in Chapter 4. Even in the absence of court interpreters (in some trials or in some sections of trials where no court interpreters are used), speaking in English continues to mean something different to the actors who participate in otherwise identical courtroom dramas. The evidence suggests that the use of English alone, in the absence of procedural interventions such as the use of court interpreters, brings about the kind of controlled linguistic transaction that juridical formalism prescribes. Facts amenable to legal analysis are generated from within the statement-and-reply structure. This power of language that I want to get at is less direct and in your face and is almost impossible to accurately appraise without the aid of comparative cases (in our case, Cantonese); it is, however, more persistent, because it is not sustained by explicit institutional rules. It is a form of power, embedded in people's beliefs to see a language in a certain light and in people's habits to use a language in some particular ways, that can be traced back to the earlier social history of English in Hong Kong. This effect of English is something that cannot be changed easily by means of institutional adaptation (of course, from the standpoint of juridical formalism, why change it?); it is instead part of the environment that even an institution as seemingly autonomous and powerful as the legal system has to live with, to take it as it is. It is precisely the presence of this diffuse power of language that calls for a sociolegal perspective that goes beyond the narrow realm of institutional rules and arrangements, a perspective that calls for a study of law *in* society. I will address this social power of English again from the subjective side, by looking at the evaluations of the language by counsel and judges in Chapter 7. Suffice it to point out here that the use of English in the here and now of Hong Kong courtrooms establishes for the actors a particular relation to law that even the presence of court interpreters cannot fully account for. This picture will become clearer once we also get the Cantonese half of the picture, to which I now turn.

SOCIAL DEMOGRAPHY OF THE
CANTONESE COURTROOMS

It is undeniable that the availability of Cantonese as an official language in the courts of Hong Kong has made the system more accessible (in fact, too accessible for some legal professionals). The colonial English-only system was highly inconvenient. Many litigants would need lawyers to literally speak for them in the English-only courts. But legal services in Hong Kong were and still are expensive; this, coupled with the "loser pays" principle used for allocating the costs of litigation, means that under the English-only system, people would acquiesce instead of taking their cases to court, given the high financial stake of civil litigations. The availability of Cantonese makes no change to the threat of "loser pays"; however, it means that lay litigants can choose to speak for themselves if they so wish or if they cannot afford the cost of professional legal representation. Based on my observation, and confirmed by the lawyers I talked to, it is clear that unrepresented litigants in Hong Kong overwhelmingly choose to pursue their cases in Cantonese (for further discussion, see Chapter 8), given its status as the everyday language in Hong Kong. That, of course, does not mean that unrepresented litigants stand a good chance of winning their cases, especially when their opposing parties are legally represented. In principle at least, juridical rules and trial procedures remain technical and complex in Cantonese trials. The formidable task of arguing law for themselves in an adversarial trial, however, does not deter desperate litigants from arriving at the doorstep of the courts in Hong Kong without lawyers. But unrepresented litigants are also a burden for judges in an adversarial system designed to be dominated by opposing counsel from both sides. A presiding judge in a trial of unrepresented litigants has to assume a greater responsibility in interrogating witnesses, overseeing the production of relevant documents and exhibits, and identifying the relevant law for the lay litigants to focus on.

The presence of Cantonese influences the working juridical formalism in many ways: the increased presence of unrepresented litigants, the turning of judges in some cases from adjudicators into interrogators, and the elimination of court interpreters. But all these visible changes involve the institutional adaptation of juridical formalism to the new social reality brought forth by the bilingual arrangement. Would the choice of Cantonese over English, or vice versa, still matter if we were to compare the interactions between the two languages in the same institutional platform, that is, a good old-fashioned adversarial trial in an open court? My answer is yes. To make such a controlled comparison of the two languages valid, here I exclude Cantonese trials in which unrepresented litigants face off in the absence of counsel. The decision to confine myself to cases involving litigants with legal representation is not to gainsay the significance of unrepresented litigants but to facilitate a more controlled comparison of the English and Cantonese courtrooms. In fact, plenty of interesting and emotional examples might be found of litigants who, for different reasons, represent themselves in the Cantonese courtrooms. In one case, for example, a litigant stood up and said to the judge, "Objection!" (in English) in the midst of the other party's cross-examination, only to be told by the judge that he had watched too much American TV! All the excerpts in this chapter involve interactions between litigants and counsel (or judges) in Cantonese during cross-examination and will allow us to identify the embedded social effects of Cantonese on juridical formalism.

BILINGUALISM AND THE PRESERVATION
OF THE COMMON LAW

The procedures of Cantonese trials are specified by the same rules that apply to English trials in Hong Kong. During the trial, a judge hears submissions from counsel representing the plaintiff and the defendant and also testimonies from witnesses. Examination of a witness includes the same three procedural stages of examination-in-chief, cross-examination, and reexamination described in Chapter 4. Roles are supposedly specified and differentiated in the same way—counsel (own or opposite) questions, witnesses answer. The same procedural rules are also supposedly in force in Cantonese and in English courtrooms. The judiciary in Hong Kong has been adamant in stressing this point to both local and overseas audiences. Senior judges and legal administrative officials reiterate that the common law has not even been slightly overwritten by Chinese law since 1997; the old colonial system is preserved under the principle of "one country, two systems." Hong Kong's legal system is a *bilingual* system with Chinese and English as the two official languages, not a *bilegal* system in which Chinese courtrooms run a set of laws different from those used in English courtrooms, which was the case with legal dualism in some British colonies, including Hong Kong itself in the past.[1] In official discourse, bilingual law works like one computer software program in two different languages; it is still the same program, recognizing and processing commands in exactly the same way, or so we are told. If institutions such as the judiciary in Hong Kong have their way, variations in shifting from English to Cantonese, or vice versa, will be kept to a minimum, if they occur at all. Hence any differences between the two types of courtrooms, if identified, are all the more impressive, given that adversarial trial procedures in the common law are highly circumscribed, not to mention that the publicized political will is to make the system bilingual but not bilegal.

One feature of Cantonese trials that makes it easier for us to identify the direct contribution of language to courtroom practice is the absence of court interpreters in Cantonese trials.[2] The convenience and efficiency of direct interaction among all parties is the main reason that many magistrates in Hong Kong generally prefer Cantonese over English, because the pressure of crowded case dockets is most intense in the lowest levels of the court hierarchy. Cantonese is used only in trials when all parties are capable of speaking in Cantonese (and agree to do so), which in practice virtually means an all-Chinese cast, although Chinese migrating to Hong Kong from other parts of China might choose to speak in Putonghua or other regional dialects.[3] During my fieldwork, I did not see any English-speaking litigants, aided by court interpreters, appearing in Cantonese trials.

CANTONESE IN THE HONG KONG LEGAL SYSTEM

To further facilitate comparisons, I have selected cases from the Court of First Instance and the District Court, just as I did for the cases in English, even though the magistracies are where Cantonese is most frequently used. A more detailed justification is given in the Appendix. It is difficult to offer a qualitative account of the Cantonese courtroom that is equivalent to the "statistical average" in quantitative analysis, whatever the term in fact means. However, I have tried to avoid relying on moments that were more indicative of the idiosyncrasies of individual judges and concentrated on some interesting but more representative features found in the Cantonese courtrooms. Of course, the determination of what is general and what is idiosyncratic requires the evaluation of the ethnographer at the site. Judges, as individuals, have their own style and temperament. The same can be said of counsel and litigants. I therefore focus on moments, some more dramatic and some less so, that show how things can, and in fact do, proceed differently in Cantonese courtrooms, in ways that are, even by counsel's own admissions, unheard of or seldom seen in the English courtrooms. To encapsulate the social acts that cause juridical formalism to burst at the seams, I attempt to illustrate different ways in which the statement-and-reply structure is challenged, undermined, and on some occasions overthrown by litigants speaking in Cantonese.

The speech act of statement making is disrupted by other culturally recognizable speech acts that people do in Cantonese. The problematic moments in the Cantonese trials are diagnostic of the Cantonese challenge to the common law system in Hong Kong. Of the judges and counsel I talked to, almost all of them agreed that the differences between English and Cantonese trials are palpable. The usual way they describe it is to say that the atmospheres between the two are different. What I want to provide here is an analytical narrative that may articulate the phenomenon to which the foggy term "atmosphere" alludes. The argument made here is not a linguistic one. In another place, to be sure, English, and arguably any language for that matter, can be as colorful and boisterous as Cantonese, but what I compare here are English *in* Hong Kong and Cantonese *in* Hong Kong. This is why understanding the power of the two languages within their respective social histories is so important; otherwise I would be slipping into a form of linguistic determinism.

A DIFFERENT ATMOSPHERE

In Chapter 4, I described how the English courtroom environment is carefully built to foster an iconic semblance of the vision of juridical formalism. Cantonese trials take place in exactly the same physical setting (no separate courtrooms for Cantonese trials) with exactly the same costume (judges and counsel wear the same wigs and gowns) and supposedly the same serious and respectful mannerism, only this time Cantonese is used to play out the drama. The simple switch of language, however, shakes the courtroom out of the once tightly wrapped world of cultural anachronism found in the English courtrooms. The tone of the legal drama is slightly less serious when played out in Cantonese, at times driven by an excess of melodrama, at other times disrupted by displays of lèse majesté. What seems to happen is that when Cantonese replaces English, it undermines the coherence of the anachronistic context it stages. The overall choreography of the courtroom drama known as adversarial cross-examination becomes a bit out of joint. This is hardly surprising, because the efficacy of the staged anachronism rests on a historical and cultural isomorphism of its components—the modern adversarial courtroom, the regalia and the etiquette, and above all, the use of British-accented English language, all of which are deeply connected to the colonial history of Hong Kong and make the use of Cantonese out of place.

If anachronism is the theme in the English-language courtrooms, the transmutation of social space when Cantonese is used is, to say the least, incomplete. Speaking in Cantonese while dressing up in seventeenth-century English wigs and gowns comes together as Hong Kong–style postcolonial hybridity in action. Another way to get a grip on this tension is to see how counsel address each other and how they address the judge in Cantonese. There is no "learned friends" or "My Lord." In a Cantonese courtroom, counsel and judges simply give up the idea of re-creating the same exquisite manner that English exudes. There is no standardized way to say the common phrase "learned friend" in Cantonese. I have heard some barristers use a literal translation, that is 博學嘅朋友 [bok3 hok6 ge3 pang4 jau5] in Cantonese; but even among counsel the translation comes across as awkward, pedantic, and pompous, as many of them attest. Some barristers address opposing counsel as "colleague" (同事 [tung4 si6]). This is strange, however, because in an adversarial system such as Hong Kong's, the relationship between opposing counsel is putatively anything but collegial. Some simply use the Cantonese term 大狀 [daai6 cong4] as a title, which is a colloquial Chinese term that Hong Kong people use to translate the word *barrister*. So, a barrister whose last name is Chan is addressed in Cantonese as "Chan Daai Cong" (in Chinese, the title of a person is suffixal rather than prefixal). But the term itself suggests an image quite different from that of an English lawyer. The term *Daai Cong* derives from the term 狀師 [cong4 si1], which means in Chinese "plaintmaster," or litigation master. The address, however, was not taken as a compliment. Government officials in Imperial China used the term to refer to a type of renegade second-rate literati who manipulated the legal system (Bodde and Morris 1967; Macauley 1998); they were the Chinese equivalent of ambulance chasers in contemporary American context.

The ritualistic elaborateness seen in the English courtrooms has an added sense of awkwardness when inserted into a Cantonese context. Speaking in Cantonese, counsel and judges are reluctant to reproduce the elaborate nomenclature of address used in the English courtrooms. To make things easier, the judiciary of Hong Kong simplifies the system and recommends in its published guidelines that all judges at different levels of court be addressed as 法官閣下 [faat3 gun1 gok3 haa6], which can be roughly translated as Sir (or Madam) Judge. But because the address itself is a new synthetic title not rooted in everyday Cantonese, many litigants and even some lawyers find it awkward to use the title to address judges. Many instead prefer to use the colloquial honorific title 法官大人 [faat3 gun1 daai6 jan4], literally "Judge, Your Big Man (Woman)"—a traditional title used to address judges in Imperial China, which actually is closer to "Your Excellency" than "Sir/Madam Judge" in English.[4]

In a circumspect way, the difficulty of coming up with appropriate translations of often used titles reveals the gap between the English legal space and the everyday world where Cantonese dominates. Cantonese poses the challenge of carrying out the law in the language that makes up the outside world and in the process accentuates how far away the English legal tradition is from, for want of a better expression, the legal sensibilities of the locals. Also, the fact that the colloquial deferential title "Faat Gun Daai Jan" is used despite the official recommendation of the alternative "Faat Gun Gok Haa" is a telltale sign of how juridical formalism fails to seal its own space. It is the first sign of a process in which local cultural practices seep into the legal domain through the new official language.

THE PRECARIOUSNESS OF THE STATEMENT-AND-REPLY STRUCTURE

How is cross-examination conducted in the Cantonese courtrooms? The questioning has a sense, however vague, of the tenuousness of the hold of juridical formalism on the trial process that is not found in the English courtrooms in Hong Kong. Procedural rules that are close to axiomatic in English courtrooms now have to be made explicit to be effectuated; they become more visible and hence precarious. In the most extreme cases (which show how far this disruption can go), cross-examination turns into a hubbub of talking, if not shouting, past each other. In response, counsel and judges have to persistently remind witnesses of the rules and sometimes even restart the disrupted process to keep litigants in check. When litigants begin to contest or even ignore the rules, juridical formalism cannot sustain its own momentum through tacit obedience to its procedures. Its artificiality becomes too easily noticeable—the waning of the doxa—through cycles of breaking and reinstating of procedural rules.

Although trials do not always turn into chaos, order in Cantonese courtrooms is more tenuously in place compared to the firm entrenchment of rules in the English courtrooms. The faster pace of Cantonese trials (in the absence of interpreters) is often offset by big chunks of irrelevant excursion during "proper" cross-examination; witnesses and sometimes even counsel veer off on tangents. Judges and counsel have to *work* to keep their preferred interaction order—that is, statement and reply—in place, with much effort and labor, and sometimes even that may not be sufficient to avoid confrontations with witnesses. This is a crucial distinction between the courtrooms in English and the courtrooms in Cantonese. Nowadays, some judges in criminal trials run their courts using a strong disciplinarian style; I once saw a judge bark at a person sitting in the public gallery (apparently a friend of the defendant in the case) to uncross his legs and sit up straight.[5] And I have also heard a judge shout from the bench, questioning whether a witness was playing tricks with her; the witness, frightened, replied in the soft tone of a repentant schoolgirl, 法官大人我唔敢 [faat3 gun1 daai6 jan4 ngo5 ng4 gam2] ("Judge, Your Big Woman, I dare not"). In Cantonese courtrooms, the easy orderliness of English cross-examination becomes a precarious quality and must be defended for it to last.[6]

A cross-examination that lives up to the ideal of juridical formalism relies on the statement-and-reply structure to brand all responses that fall short of being a direct reply as irrelevant. This is most obvious when barristers and sometimes judges explicitly request a witness to answer the question (translation: "Your response is not considered a proper reply here"). This is also why lawyers are taught to make their questions as specific as they can, almost to the point of tediousness. Experienced counsel cultivate the habit of avoiding open-ended questions that begin with a simple "Why?" or "How?" in cross-examination (more acceptable in examination-in-chief) because these questions, so often used in casual conversations, customarily hand over too much to the discretion of the answerer (K. Evans 1998: 89). The idea, as mentioned in Chapter 4, is to mold all utterances into constative statements through the rigid structure of statement and reply. But when responses, not just direct replies, are allowed to slip into the flow of a cross-examination, they bring out what Goffman calls the flexibility of talk common in daily conversation (1981: 52). In the next section, I examine some examples in which litigants *perform* in Cantonese. I show how through the performance of culturally recognizable speech acts, litigants at times disrupt and undermine the efficacy of juridical formalism.

DISRUPTING THE STATEMENT-AND-REPLY
STRUCTURE OF CROSS-EXAMINATION
Reversing the Rules

A recurrent feature of the verbal wrangling unique to Cantonese trials is the occasional interjection of witnesses answering a question with a question. When that happens, the question in reply (as an answer) often poses a challenge to the legitimacy of the original question raised. In the context of cross-examination, questioning the questioner is a sanctioned act, for the act itself pushes the role assignment of the questioner and the questioned out of the clearing. True, witnesses in English-language trials may occasionally veer away from the straight sequence of questions and answers, but they are quickly ushered back to follow the line of questioning. The situation is subtly different in Cantonese trials. I have seen in some trials extended episodes in which witnesses and counsel switched roles. Rules, and the roles prescribed by the rules, are reversed when a witness's response subverts the assigned roles of the questioner and the questioned in the process of cross-examination.

The following excerpt is taken from a District Court trial that involved a dispute about the severance payment owed to eight female workers who worked for the same knitting factory. A crucial question in the trial that the judge had to determine was whether the factory ownership or the former leader of the mending department who supervised the eight workers, Ms. Tam Wan Sheung, should be responsible for the unpaid salaries. Tam is a key witness (she is also a defendant in a multiparty matrix). Counsel disagreed about her legal status at that time—Tam's side argued that she was an employee of the factory; the factory's side argued that she was a subcontractor (and hence responsible for the severance payment for her "own" employees). The excerpt shows Tam being cross-examined by the counsel representing the factory, Mr. Kenneth Chiu. Chiu tries to prove that what Tam actually did amounted to giving her the status of subcontractor (another instance of legal fact). That is the conclusion to which Chiu intends his line of questioning to be driven. Tam, on the other hand, said she did what she did out of empathy and compassion. She also mocks Chiu for his lack of life experience. In the excerpt, Chiu asks Tam why she once paid the workers their salaries in advance, demonstrating the "fact" that Tam was not merely a superior in the line of command but an employer, at least as far as these workers were concerned. In response, Tam says she did that on the eve of the Chinese New Year because she understood the hardship that these workers had to endure, the same hardship that she herself endured to make it in Hong Kong.

Cross-Examination in Cantonese Between Tam Wan Sheung (W) and Counsel Kenneth Chiu (C)

		Gloss	Original
1	W:	Altogether, I gave them altogether. They needed money to spend for the New Year. So I advanced the money.	一齊 . . .一齊俾佢吖嘛,佢哋等錢過年吖嘛,即係我出住先吖嘛。
2	C:	Yes.	係。
3	W:	They needed money to spend for the New Year, they said to me.	佢哋等錢過年吖嘛,佢哋提出。
4	C:	That means you at that time . . .	即係你嗰陣時係咪 . . .
5	W:	Sometimes there weren't many jobs for people to do. Their lives were very miserable. [*sigh*] That's so true. Workers didn't have money to spend for the New Year. They needed money to buy their food. Mr. Barrister, do you know?	有時係無咩嘢做吖,人地啲生活好慘㗎,唉真係,工人過年無錢使㗎,羅米㗎,你知唔知呀大律師?

6	C:	I think I do know.	我諗我都知嘅。
7	W:	[*laugh*] What?	[笑] 吓?
8	C:	I think I'm more miserable. [*Laughter from the workers*]	我諗我慘啲嘅。[眾笑]
9	W:	So, so [*laugh*] . . .	咁樣,咁樣 [笑] . . .
10	JUDGE:	You two shouldn't keep doing this here . . .	你兩個唔好響度係咁呀 . . .
11	C:	I'm sorry.	唔好意思吖。
12	W:	[*simultaneously*] Is that right?	[同時] 係咪呀?
13	C:	Sorry. I just hope that from now on we can . . . No, Madam Tam, it's really simple, because you, I understand, because you already paid them the salaries, but at that time you had to wait until February the sixth before you would have received the second-half installment for January, right?	對唔住。即係我 . . .我希望之後大家可以 . . .唔係,阿譚女士,即係好簡單嘅啫,因為呢你喺,我明白即係你係俾咗,咁但係嗰陣時候呢要二月六日呢,你先呢係收埋一月下期嗰個數嘅,係咪呀?
14	W:	Yes, let's just say I lent them the money. Can't I?	係啦,我當借俾佢地好唔好,咁得唔得先?
15	C:	Of course you can.	得,當然啦。
16	C:	You can of course be nice.	你好人梗得。
17	W:	[*simultaneously*] What?	[同時] 吓?
18	W:	[*sigh*]	唉,真係。

Tam does not deny that she paid the salaries to the workers (a piece of evidence that gives weight to the theory that she was an independent subcontractor who hired her own staff), but she questions the questioner by firing a question at him. In reversing the role assigned to her by the rules in cross-examination, Tam deviates from standard statement making and questions the moral sense of the question Chiu raises. The sarcastic comeback question that Tam asks draws from the popular imagery of this hardworking older generation of Hong Kong, many of whom spent long hours in factories to support their families. Tam, herself in her 60s, asks her question in an exaggerated raised tone, an unmistakable mark of sarcasm in Cantonese. People in Hong Kong describe this way of talking as 講嘢有骨 [gong2 je5 jau5 gwat1], meaning "having bones in speech." One can easily choke on language bones if one is not careful. In defying her role as the witness, her question is as much a challenge in the form of a question as a question in the form of a challenge, implying that Chiu, a "Mr. Barrister," or literally "Mr. Big Lawyer" (大律師 [daai6 leot6 si1]), in his 30s, does not have the life experience to understand what it meant to be a factory worker in the old days. She is calling out Chiu not in his institutional role as a cross-examiner but in his social role as a young barrister short on life experience. This is precisely the kind of revealing moment that powerfully shows that the institutionally preassigned structure of role inhabitancy can be disrupted and reversed in the unfolding of interactions.

So here Chiu, the questioner, becomes the questioned. To everyone's surprise and against the rules, Chiu answers back. In trying to defend himself, Chiu uses a bit of self-deprecation, telling Tam that he is not talking down to her or to any other factory workers listening in the courtroom and that he doesn't enjoy cross-examining Tam at all (he describes himself as more miserable). Tam, and the workers (who otherwise do not like Tam), laugh, apparently finding Chiu's assertion that *he* is the miserable one amusing. The dialogue is soon broken up by the judge, who by that point must have realized that the exchange had completely morphed into a different kind of activity. Tam's challenge is carried through by her question at the end: "Can't I?" Chiu is once again left on the defensive.

This episode gives us a look at how Cantonese, from the standpoint of juridical formalism, presents a problem. In the face of a witness who Chiu would later describe to me as "very difficult," the statement-and-reply structure so easily maintained in English courtrooms has been turned upside down. Cantonese, because of its outsideness in relation to the common law system, makes it easier for litigants to step *outside* the space of juridical formalism and reflexively challenge its rules. The struggle to maintain statement-and-reply interactions is reflective of the precariousness of juridical formalism in the Cantonese environment. This precariousness means that from the standpoint of juridical formalism, participants are well aware, in fact too aware, of the role-playing quality of the whole game. A game can always be called out as merely a game if some parties are not happy with the way the game goes.

Tam comes to enact the role of someone who cares for the livelihood of a group of aging workers with meager salaries. These workers sat through the whole trial, which lasted 10 days. Legally, they sued the company and Tam, and it was up to the court to decide whether the factory or Tam should pay. None of the workers were willing to testify against Tam, however, because, as I learned from them, they wanted to avoid direct confrontation with their former leader. They did not like her, but they had worked together for a long time. Tam was certainly an imposing figure among these women workers, all in their late 50s and 60s at the time of the trial. Their refusal to testify allowed Tam to speak on their behalf. She thus came to inhabit the role of an elderly worker who knows the world and cares about the livelihood of her subordinates. The proof of the effectiveness of her moral challenge is in Chiu's immediate reply to Tam's challenge (not just once, but twice; see also para. 15). It was an exceptional act given that barristers are taught not to engage in personal arguments with witnesses (especially when the witness initiates the argument by *questioning* the counsel) (Hyam 1999). It is difficult to imagine that Chiu, an otherwise reserved and experienced barrister, would concede to Tam the exclusive right of questioning if, at least for a moment, her questions bring into being a social space that stands outside juridical formalism, a space where Chiu feels the need to defend his moral sense.

Breaking of Rules

In some dramatic moments, the rules that give shape to the statement-and-reply structure can completely break down, something that is clearly much more common in Cantonese trials than in English trials. In terms of interaction, the things that go without saying in English-language trials— the settling down of interactional turns into a perceptible question-and-answer sequence, the domination of counsel in the topics cross-examined, the peeling apart of gaps and holes in a witness's testimony—suddenly become practices that are highly contested by some litigants who may now complain in Cantonese.

In another excerpt taken from a different day of Tam's trial, it is left to another counsel, Eddie Tong, representing the factory workers, to cross-examine the defiant witness (this questioning takes place after Chiu has finally finished his difficult cross-examination of Tam). Tong, younger and more aggressive, decides to adopt a more heavy hitting approach in dealing with Tam. He indicates to Tam that she has been evasive. Her responses did not amount to replies. In the excerpt, Tong asks Tam why she chose to fill out profit tax forms and not salary tax forms during her years with the factory, another piece of evidence that indicates that she already knew then that she was in fact a subcontractor. Tam continues to play to her image as an old factory worker with little education. She tells Tong that she was simply following the instructions of the factory's accountant. He presses Tam for a yes or no answer by repeating his questions several times. But the cross-examination is getting nowhere. Finally, Tam erupts.

Cross-Examination in Cantonese Between Tam Wan Sheung (W) and Counsel Eddie Tong (C)

		Gloss	Original
1	C:	That is to say, your eldest daughter wrote the report. In fact it was you who asked her to fill out the tax form according to your instructions, right?	即係話你個大女寫嗰份報告書，報稅表其實係你叫佢填，即係照你嘅意思去做嘅，係咪？
2	W:	According to the instructions of Ms. Yu [the factory accountant].	照 . . .照 . . .照余小姐嘅意思去做嘅。
3	C:	So did your eldest daughter . . .	咁吖你個大女 . . .
4	W:	[*simultaneously*] Not according to my instructions.	[同時] 唔係照我去做。
5	C:	Did Lai Sze Ki [Tam's daughter] contact Ms. Yu before she filled out the tax form?	黎思琪 [譚大女] 填報稅表之前有冇同余小姐接觸過呀？

6   W: Of course not. She too said, I've
       been telling you for so long. She
       too said this was not something
       that, mom, you were supposed
       to do.

7   C: If no, then . . .

8   W: She said this was not something
       you were supposed to do,
       mom, not something you were
       supposed to do. So I said, you
       earned a twenty-two hundred
       dollar allowance from them. You
       have to do this, my dear, please
       help me. Are you satisfied?
       This is true. These are all facts.
       [*Waving the oath card on the
       witness table*] If I tell, tell lies, I
       tell you, may heaven and earth
       destroy me. May I die without
       a place to bury my body. If I lie,
       I tell you. You can ask her to
       come out and ask her if this is
       the case. I filled out that, that,
       that form, that tax form myself?
       It has so many darn words; the
       words are so small and blurred.
       I went to school for only three
       years, two or three years only.
       They always asked me to do
       things I didn't know how to
       do? Do you understand? I had
       to earn my living. I wanted to
       support my children. That's why
       I did that for her. Satisfied?

梗係無啦，佢都話同你講咗好耐，佢都話呢啲嘢唔係你做嘅阿媽咁囉。

咁如果無，咁即係 . . .

佢話唔係你做嘅，阿媽，呢啲嘢唔係你做㗎，咁。咁我話呢，你賺人二千二蚊津貼，就要做呢啲嘢啦，女，幫下我啦咁，滿意未呀？真㗎，呢啲事實㗎；[手揮宣誓卡] 若果我有講，有講大話呀，我話俾你聽吖，吖，天誅地滅呀，吖死無葬身之地呀．若果我有講大話呀，我話俾你聽噃；吖，你可以叫佢出嚟問下佢係咪咁樣先。我揸住填嗰啲嘅咩咩咩表吖，報稅表，咁鬼多字，細細隻矇查查，我讀三年書咋，兩三年書咋，專叫我做埋晒我唔識做嘅嘢。明唔明吖？我要搵食呀，我要為咗養仔女，所以我就同佢做。滿意未呀？

9   C: Madam Tam, you've got to get this clear. You've got to understand, there's no need for you to view me with such hostility. I'm just carrying out my responsibility.

譚女士，你攪清楚一樣嘢先，即係你你要明白，你唔需要咁敵視我嘅，我只係盡緊我嘅責任。

10   W: I am not discriminating against you. [Tam apparently misheard the Cantonese term 敵視 (dik6 si6) (meaning "view with hostility") as 歧視 (kei4 si6) (meaning "discrimination").]

我唔係歧視你，

11   C: [*simultaneously*] No . . .

[同時]唔係 . . .

12   W: I really don't understand what you are really asking. You need to ask . . . You need to make me understand. Why was filling out the tax form such a big deal? She asked me to do some work for her, and I helped her to do the work. Was that an offense? She gave me an allowance of twenty-two hundred dollars. She even gave Ms. Cheung's share to me. Before that I only got half of the allowance. What's wrong when I helped her to do some extra work? I don't understand. I don't understand. Even now, I don't understand what you are really asking, what you are doing. OK, I went to school for three years only. I quit school at Grade 3 in the Mainland. I came down here

你事實問啲問題我都唔明你究竟講乜嘢嘅，你要問 . . .你要令到我明你講乜嘢先得㗎，填嗰張報稅表乜嘢咁大件事先得㗎。佢叫我做嘢咁做佢唔係有罪啫係咪嘛？佢有二千二蚊津貼俾我過嘞，連 . . .連張姑娘嗰份都俾埋我過嘞，以前我得一半咋嘞。咁幫佢做多啲嘢咁又又點樣唔啱呢，我又唔明。我唔明喎，我都直到依家我都唔明你究竟係問乜嘢，做乜嘢。嗱我讀咗三年書啫，最 . . .升咗三年級我已經無得讀喇係大陸，落嚟捱世界吖，我係香港捱到今時今日 [拍枱]，係咪要咁樣嚟對我先！

to work my butt off to earn my
living. I've worked my butt off
in Hong Kong until this very
day [*hand slapping the table*]. Is
that your way of treating me?

13   JUDGE: Hmm.   嗯。

14   W: [*sobbing*] I've worked for   [哭]我做咗幾十年嘞，你想問乜
      several decades. What do you   先？
      want to ask?

15   C: Your Honor, I wonder if we   法官閣下，我唔知係咪需要俾呢
      should give some time to the   個時間俾證人 . . .
      witness to . . .

16   W: [*simultaneously*] I tell you, I   [同時] 我同你講，我俾呢個社會
      have given this society; I tell you   呢，我話俾你聽 . . .
      . . .

17   C: Your Honor, perhaps we should   法官閣下，我哋或者稍為小休，小
      take a short break of five, ten   休一兩個字吖。係。
      minutes. Yeah.

18   W: I've worked in Hong Kong for   我係香港做咗四十幾年嘞，我係
      40-odd years. Do I deserve this   咪要有咁嘅懲罰，[哭] 咁問，咁
      kind of punishment? [*sobbing*]   問，講極都係咁問，你問乜嘢先
      You keep asking me this, you   得咯。
      keep asking me this. Whatever
      I said, you keep asking me this.
      What are you really asking?

Tong, at the time of the event in his late 20s, is clearly flustered by Tam's outburst. He attempts to repair the situation by telling Tam that his repeated questioning is merely an act of carrying out his duty, trying to impose some distance between himself and his role as the cross-examiner. This further brings the artificial contrivance of juridical formalism into the foreground. Just as no magic trick survives an explanation, no performance survives a reminder from its performer that it is merely an act. Tong lets everyone know that he is aware of his role and he is acting his role, albeit reluctantly. From that point on, Tam takes the stage and performs in full force. Tam says she did what the factory accountant (Ms. Yu) told her to do and that as a poorly educated factory worker, she did not know whether it was legal or not. Tam then relates her experience in the courtroom to her 40 years as a factory worker in Hong Kong. It is here that Tam couches her response in a well-known speech act known as "speaking bitterness" (訴苦 [sou3 fu2]). Speaking bitterness as an oral performance has its roots in traditional Chinese village culture; it was radically reworked in China during Mao's era to adapt the Marxist theory of revolution to the essentially agrarian context of China (Anagnost 1997: 30; cf. Hinton 1966). The meaning of speaking bitterness took yet another turn in the context of Hong Kong society. Stripped of the Maoist lexicon of class antagonism, it is politically less mobilizing but still culturally potent. It is very much a weapon of the weak, often used by people, especially the older generations, in a bittersweet way to refer to the hardships they suffered in helping to transform Hong Kong from a small fishing port into the prosperous city it is today.

We can see how the episode itself becomes a distinct, recognizable interactional stretch through which Tam turns the passive experience of being cross-examined around into a vivid performance of speaking bitterness. In speaking bitterness, her utterances have shifted deictically from the here and now of the cross-examination to the then and there of her life as a factory worker.[7] The shift is easy to identify in Cantonese and can be picked up quite easily even from the English gloss of the excerpt, because in Cantonese the way a speaker facilitates a deictic shift is done not through grammatical indexes (e.g., by changing tense) but by means of explicit lexicalization. Tam tells her young questioner and the judge that she received only three years of formal education and came to Hong Kong to 捱世界 [ngaai4 sai3 gaai3], to labor, to make a living, or more literally, to endure the world. By speaking bitterness to the judge and the opposing counsel, Tam displays to everyone in the courtroom, including the women workers in the audience, the social power conferred to her as a hardworking albeit uneducated elderly individual in a Chinese society, who pulled herself up by her bootstraps and contributed to society along the way. This social power enables her to reflexively question what is going on during the cross-examination. The message is loud and clear—that she was doubted and cross-examined by two young counsel was already a punishment she does not deserve, after 40 years of hard work in Hong Kong! This is a powerful speech act, partly because it is made in a society where the Confucian virtue of reverence for the elderly still commands symbolic power and partly because it is made in a society where being tagged as a defendant in a lawsuit is enough to be considered a bitter and shameful experience, but mostly because it is made in a society where the familiar form of the act shimmers with stirring echoes that hark back to many memorable instances of speaking bitterness in the living practices of Cantonese in the everyday world.

The dissolution of the cross-examination framework is so dramatic and yet so subtly realized that it is truly transformative—once again, no longer is Tam the examined and Tong the examiner. Instead, Tam has become a grand elderly figure lecturing a young man who does not know the world, harking back to social identities she has been invoking since her earlier session with Chiu. She is, in the fullest sense of the phrase, having her day in court. In my interview with her afterward, Tam, ever defiant, repeated the same message to me. She said Hong Kong as a society should pay more respect to the elderly people like her who contributed to building Hong Kong into a world-class city. She also said the government made the mistake of spending too much money on "all those new immigrants" from China. She said she had to pay part of the legal fees out of her own pocket, because the legal aid provided by the government did not cover everything.

What Tam did, of course, according to the orthodox view of juridical formalism, was merely *commenting*; she did not recount what had happened but offered her opinions on how she was questioned. Judges and counsel loathe disruptions of this sort for what some of them consider the "vulgarity" they bring to the courts. It is therefore not surprising to see that many of them believe rough emotions and Cantonese tend to go hand in hand and that many in fact explicitly attribute the emergence of a disorderly courtroom culture to the use of Cantonese (see Chapter 7). And, so as not to provoke the witness further, judges usually allow the witness to let it all out, to dissipate their emotional energy in what they see as rhetoric that does not mean much. After an outburst, the presiding judge, either at his own initiative or at the request of counsel, usually allows a break and then the trial resumes as though the outburst never took place. Episodes such as the one between Tam and Tong are taken by counsel as aberrations better left ignored. Information from these episodes is almost invariably left out in the decisions judges eventually deliver. These Cantonese speech acts have too much undigested life for the court. The intense performances are incommensurate with and indeed inimical to the pristine constative statements on which juridical formalism builds.

Like their counterparts in Western common law jurisdictions, court regulars and legal professionals in Hong Kong view rants such as Tam's as "silly" and "irrelevant" and as "hollow" posing.[8] Tong, for example, rolled his eyes in disbelief when Tam lectured him. But so simple a distinction between facts and opinions, relevancy and irrelevancy, does not adequately capture what someone like Tam achieves through her performance. She did, after all, say that she filled out the tax form herself, in ways that might indicate she was an employer of the workers. That "statement," however, was deeply embedded in the act of speaking bitterness. And it is clear that Tam did not see herself as merely commenting ("These are all facts," para. 8). She took her telling of "facts" so seriously that she even performed a "poisonous oath," to swear, in the most solemn and deadliest way that she knew, to the truth of what she said ("If I tell lies . . . , may heaven and earth destroy me. May I die without a place to bury my body," para. 8). It is just this kind of performative colloquialism, precisely because it draws its authority from social sources from without (needless to say, there is no "poisonous oath" in the common law of Hong Kong), that inevitably further undercuts the authority of juridical formalism. Tam's utterance of the poisonous oath during which she was *already* under legal oath inevitably demeaned the solemnity of the legal oath.

If I have succeeded in the previous chapters in showing that no statements, however conforming to the rules of juridical formalism, are purely constative, then in the discussions in this chapter so far I aim to reveal the impossibility of the dichotomy from the opposite side. Tam's speaking bitterness and swearing of a poisonous oath, however performative, are not totally devoid of descriptive truth or falsity. It is just that her statements—rough, coarse-grained, and all wrapped up in the visceral performance—do not come near the pristine form of neutral statements that are of most assistance to juridical formalism. When a witness breaks away from the statement-and-reply shackles and launches into narrative overdrive, the contents of what is said can no longer be properly "examined," juridically speaking. This does not necessarily mean that the narratives are intrinsically less true or false. What it does mean is that the very process of legal rearticulation in juridical formalism is rolled back. What these performances accumulatively achieve is the re-embedding of an inchoate legal case, be it a breach of contract, a dispute of probate, or a case of personal injury, into the social context from which the dispute first arose, so much so that the case at stake is no longer just a breach of contract, just a dispute of probate, or just a case of personal injury.

In the course of my fieldwork, I often found it easier to discern the "real" dispute beneath the legal surface in Cantonese trials, because disputes in Cantonese trials are often talked about in moral, commonsensical categories with which people are all too familiar, be it family feuds, love betrayed, or friendship turned sour. It is in this sense that we can say that there are facts in English and there are facts in Cantonese, one predominantly legal and the other mixed, eclectic, and at times highly moralistic.

In the end the judge ruled in Tam's favor; Tam was found to be an employee of the factory and was thus not responsible for the severance payments of the other workers. She was also entitled to obtain her own severance payment from the factory. In the judgment, the judge did not mention any of the dramatic highlights of Tam's performances; instead, he focused primarily on the available documentary evidence (receipts, expenditure reports, tax forms, etc.). He mentioned in passing that Chiu described Tam as an "unreliable" witness but added that he considered her reliability by and large irrelevant for determining the outcome of the case (because according to the judge, the factory clearly concealed its employer-employee relationship with Tam).

Consider the following example drawn from a mixed-language trial (evidence is given in Cantonese but legal deliberation is in English; see Chapter 8). It involves an emotional dispute of an "indigenous" family in the New Territories of Hong Kong—that is, families whose ancestors were inhabitants in the New Territories long before Hong Kong became a British colony.[9] The case involves an application by the patriarch of the family, Au Kam Ming, to set aside a transaction that would effectively give away as gifts his houses to three of his grandsons, all sons of the defendant couple, Au Yiu Tong and Melissa Poon. In legalese, it is a case about whether or not the two defendants have exerted "undue influence" on the old man. The senior Au, who was over 90 years old at the time of the trial, suffered from dementia and was deemed unfit to testify.[10] Apparently, the old man regretted the transaction and wanted to take back the family house and give it to his younger son and daughters. The younger son, Au Wai Tong, initiated the lawsuit on his father's behalf against his brother and sister-in-law. Two other daughters also testified in court against the couple. From early on in the trial, the judge, Charles Shen, urged Au Yiu Tong and his wife to settle with other family members.

The explosive speech in the transcript that follows was made at a critical moment in the trial, in the middle of a long cross-examination that did not go well for Au Yiu Tong. It was at this point that Au, a self-described man of few words, gave the longest speech of the whole trial, a kind of speech that I have never seen and would not expect to see in any English trial. Like Tam, Au also speaks bitterness to the judge, and in the performance he takes a stab at the other family members who turned their backs on him, in particular his ex-wife. During the performance, he summons his authority from traditional patriarchy to attempt to justify the inequalities in status between men and women that he had choked back from saying until that point, and in the process he dismisses the rights of all five of his sisters to inherit family properties. Au is further infuriated by the sight of his first wife, who still maintains a close relationship with the rest of the extended family, sitting among the audience. This is a cross-examination in name only; in substance, it is a one-man monologue by Au. Neither counsel nor judge interrupt or ask any questions.

A Second Example of Speaking Bitterness: Au Yiu Tong (W)
Speaks to Judge Charles Shen (J)

Gloss	Original
W: That is to say, I very much agree with what Your Excellency has said. The pressure I experienced today, the pressure I experienced, the attack targeted at me, some of them were fabrications. I sincerely, sincerely say this—so many people work against me; I really feel that myself.	即係呢我好同意你法官大人你講嘅嘢,我今日所受嘅壓力呢,所受嘅壓力,俾人攻擊呀,有啲係無中生有呀其他嘢呢,我好 . . .好衷心咁樣講,即係咁多人嚟對付我,我自己亦都身同感受.
J: I see.	係。
W: I know best if I did something wrong, right? I am the eldest son. When the life of my papa wasn't good, when he didn't feel happy, in fact, when they really didn't go and see him, he came to me. He came to me to tell me what I said before the court today. He said everything; I didn't twist a word. No, not at all. If those of you in the audience really want the house . . .	即係我自己有無做錯我自己知,喍唔喍呀?我做個大仔嘅,我爸爸過得唔係好好,過得唔開心,事實上當佢地真係冇去見佢嘅時候,佢就要搵我,搵我就係講我今日在庭嘅嘢,一路講晒出嚟,我無泥橫折曲,我一啲都無,若果係在座咁多位,佢係要嗰間屋嘅 . . .
J: Hmm.	嗯。
W: . . . I can give it back to you with both hands, if only these people apologize to me in the newspaper. Because when I received the newspaper, I endured much pressure. When friends in Canada saw that copy of *Economic Times* . . .	我可以雙手奉送番俾佢地,只要佢地登報紙同我道歉,因為我新接到呢份報紙嘅時候,我亦都受到好多壓力,而加拿大啲朋友見到嗰份《經濟日報》 . . .
J: Hmm.	嗯。

W: . . . "Wow! What happened?"
they said. And then, those women
who married out—now I'm not
reasoning, now I'm really not
reasoning . . .

J: I see.

W: . . . Women who married out really
have no right to say one thing or
another on our ancestry properties,
right? I'm not reasoning.

J: I see.

W: Right?

J: I see.

W: What rights does my divorced
wife still have? Why does she even
come to this court? Even when my
mother died, she dared not step
onto the shrine. She still asked me
if she could. She has recently seen
my papa.

J: I see.

W: But before that my papa kept
sending her away, right?

J: Hmm.

W: Did I leave my family for this wife?
I'm telling you my family affairs,
Your Excellency. Did I leave my
family for this wife? Was she the
third party?

J: Hmm.

W: No, she wasn't, she wasn't at all.
When my Au Wan Man was very
young, very young, I held his hand;
he was six or seven years old.

J: Hmm.

嘩，乜呀，攪到咁大劑，咁樣。再唔
係，嗰啲外嫁女，即係我打橫嚟講㗎
啦吓，依家我打橫嚟講 . . .

係。

我外嫁女根本就無權去過問我地祖
先遺留落嚟嘅物業，係咪呀？即係
我打橫嚟講.

係。

啱唔啱呀？

係。

我離婚嘅太太仲有乜嘢權，仲走嚟
呢個庭呀？甚至乎我媽媽死，佢呀都
未必敢上去嗰個祭堂，都要問過我。
佢到目前最近都有去見我爸爸.

係。

之前係一路我爸爸都趕佢走嘅，係
咪吖？

嗯。

我係咪識咗呢個太太嘛，嘩我依家
講家事俾你聽呀，法官大人。我係咪
識咗呢個太太，佢係第三者？

嗯。

唔係，一啲都無。阿區允文好細個，
好細個，拖住佢，六、七歲。

嗯。

187

W: I began going out with her [Melissa Poon], going out with her.

J: Hmm.

W: We were colleagues. If I lie a single word, may I die a terrible death. My current wife has gone to persuade this Fung Mei Tsang [his ex-wife], has persuaded her. She was definitely not a good wife, in my mind. I was just scratching the surface.

J: Hmm.

W: At home . . . What do I mean by scratching the surface? My mom saw me iron my own shirts and stuff. My mom cried. I ironed my own shirts, because I had to wear a tie when I worked in Jebsen. That pile of garbage; it was still there after a week. At that time, there were no public, no, no private water toilet. There was only a spittoon. She had my youngest sister to take out her excrements. What kind of person is she? You can see how I feel. [turning toward his former wife] Today you still have the face to sit here, to blacken me. I'm telling it all. I tell you, my two houses, I'm not really concerned about the house. My . . . ting house is now gone. I have a good wife. Every time I . . . drove pass the house, I cried. My wife

嗰陣時我識佢，識佢吖。

嗯。

係大家同事。我講半點假話嘅，我唔會得好死。我呢個太太，去勸過呢個馮美珍，勸過佢嘅，佢一一定唔係好嘅老婆，在我心目中。我係蜻蜓點水。

嗯。

喺屋企呀，乜嘢叫做蜻蜓點水？我媽媽見到我，自己熨衫，自己成，我媽媽都流眼淚。我自己返工自己熨呢，因為要打呔喺 Jebsen 做嗰時候，嗰堆垃圾喺度，嗰堆垃圾喺度，一個禮拜仲喺度。我地嗰陣時無公，無 . . . 無私家水廁，係有一個用痰罐，佢嘅大便仲要我最細嗰個妹同佢倒，你話係唔係人？你可想而知我嘅感受係點樣。[望庭內前妻]今日你仲有面走嚟坐喺度，抹黑我，我依家就數出嚟。我講俾你聽，我呢兩間屋，我唔係志在呢間屋，我 . . . 嗰間丁屋都無咗囉，我有個好太太，我見到我 . . . 我渣車經過我就喊，我太太勸我，佢話有條命，你驚無咩？係佢 support 我，直至到我爸爸要咁樣，要咁樣做，原因喺邊度，我爸爸知道佢地咁多人係對我唔好呢，係攻擊我嘅，我條村啲人都話，佢話你媽咪死咗你就無運行，就講呢啲說話。

188

consoled me. She said, "As long
as you live, what makes you fear
you won't get another house?"
It was she who supported me.
Until my papa decided to do this,
decided to do this. Why? My
papa knew all these people were
treating me bad; they attacked
me. Even people in my village
said, they said my luck would
run out the day my mom died.
That's all I said.

Although this speech was made in an open court, I felt very much like an intruder when I was listening to it in person. The speech itself was a yowling discharge of emotions, loaded with moral indignation, from a man who has no qualms defending gender inequality in the name of indigenous customs. Au raised his voice at certain junctures during the speech. The air inside the courtroom was unbearably heavy, punctuated only by the hushed sighs, sardonic smirks, and angry tears of some family members in the audience.

Unlike Tam, Au did not win his case. In the decision handed down immediately on the final day of the trial, Judge Shen concluded that Au and Poon had exercised undue influence over the plaintiff and thereby had voided the transactions in dispute. Au's performance appears to have backfired; Shen depicts Au and Poon in a way that must be considered highly morally colored according to the standards of Hong Kong judges. The judge comes down on the dubious character of Au, describing him as "a man who has been undoubtedly defeated by many failures of adventures in his life" and calling him the "black sheep of the family." But the harshest criticism from the judge comes when he describes Au and Poon as a contemporary "Macbeth and Lady Macbeth." The judge said, "They are what I regret to call a horrible pair. I do not therefore in any way find him an acceptable or credible witness. If there is anything that they have said which are [sic] not supported powerfully by independent contemporaneous reliable evidence, I will not accept their oral evidence." Here we see the East meets West hybridity of Hong Kong on display. Shen, an England-educated judge, invokes the famous Shakespearean character—a cynic about life and usurper who tried to disrupt succession—to describe Au, a man who appealed to indigenous customs to excuse himself. The judgment itself is as much an application of legal rules as an exercise in moral vocabulary, its concern as much about truth as about truthfulness. The judgment is probably the most morally loaded one among the trials I attended in the course of my fieldwork; it turns juridical formalism upside down when law and morality are mingled and not kept apart.

Playing with the Rules

At other times, the disruption of the legal rearticulation process in juridical formalism does not necessarily involve the display of boiling emotions. On some of the less intense, less dramatic occasions, even when the rules of cross-examination are ostensibly being followed, one can find subtler forms of playing within the rules, a kind of what Goffman calls "keying" (1974: 40–82) of the original act of statement making, in an apparently identical interaction.

In terms of structure, one can hardly tell any difference between the following sequence and a standard cross-examination, as both display an orderly question-and-answer sequence. Yet the questioning proceeds in a different key, and the tone of the interaction is subtly changed. The following example is taken from a libel trial I attended. The plaintiff, Ms. Fung Sze Ming, is suing the defendant, Mr. Yip Man Sang, for libel, alleging that he distributed defamatory letters to residents of the building where they both lived. The excerpt is taken from the cross-examination of Yip by Fung's counsel, Mr. Kit Li. Yip has accused Fung of perjuring herself before the court by describing herself as a teacher; Yip argues that she was not a teacher but only a private tutor. The whole debate in fact turns on a play of words because "teacher" in Cantonese, 教師 [gaau3 si1], and "private tutor," 補習教師 [bou5 zaap6 gaau3 si1], both contain the same Cantonese words 教師 [gaau3 si1]. Yip alleges that his opponent lied about her real occupation when she talked herself up as a teacher. In defense of his client, Li tries to show that Yip is splitting hairs. Yip, however, rebuts by insisting on the lexical difference between the terms "teacher" and "private tutor" in Cantonese.

Cross-Examination in Cantonese Between Yip Man Sang (W)
and Counsel Kit Li (C)

Gloss	Original
C: So what did you mean when you said she [Fung] made a false oath? Who did you think she could not be?	咁就 . . .你話[馮]發假誓嘅意思呢，就應該佢人唔係一個點樣嘅人話？
W: "Teacher" means teacher—registered teacher, in my mind.	Teacher 就係教師，註冊教師，喺我嘅心目中。
C: In your mind.	喺你心目中係嘅。
W: Yes, registered teacher.	係，註冊教師。
C: Registered teacher.	註冊教師。
W: It should also be so in ordinary people's mind.	喺普通人心目中都應該係咁樣。
C: How do you know? Perhaps it is only in your mind.	你點知㗎？可能剩係你心目中係咁。
W: No. Lawyers generally mean registered lawyers. If you say you are a member of the Federation of Hong Kong Industries, you must be a registered functional organization; then you can call yourself a member. If I say I'm a member of the Industry Association but I'm not registered, don't you think I'm making a false oath?	唔係㗎。律師，一般都係指註冊嘅律師，工業總會會員一定係喺工業總會註咗冊，功能團體，先可以做稱為會員。如果我話工業總會會員，但我又無註冊，你話係咪發假誓呢？
C: Are solicitors and barristers both lawyers? [In Cantonese, 律師 (leot6 si1) is the term for solicitor, and the term for barrister is 大律師 (daai6 leot6 si1), literally meaning "big lawyer."]	律師同大律師係咪都係律師呀？

W: Solicitors and barristers are, are both registered lawyers of Law Society; of course they are, are different, but both are registered. The difference is registered and nonregistered.

律師大律師同樣都係 . . . 係 . . . 呀律師公會註冊嘅律師，當然係 . . . 係唔同，性質唔同，但係都係註咗冊嘅，分別係註冊與唔註冊。

C: Are solicitors and barristers both lawyers?

律師同大律師咁係咪都係律師吖？

W: Yes, they are both lawyers.

係律師吖。

C: Are the Land Tribunal and the High Court both law courts?

土地審裁處同埋高等法院原訟庭係咪都係法庭吖？

W: Yes.

係。

C: Don't you think that a tutoring teacher, a piano teacher, and a school teacher are all responsible for instilling knowledge in their students?*

你唔覺得補習教師、鋼琴教師、學校教師都係嘅責任就係向學生灌輸知識咩？

W: I disagree. Yes, they all instill knowledge; but there is a big difference, registered and not registered.

我唔同意，係灌輸知識，但係有個分別，最大嘅分別，註冊與唔註冊。

Here we can see how the semantic meaning of an utterance can be contested with the same intensity but in a different way. The exchange between Li and Yip has turned into a tricky call-and-response sequence known in Cantonese as catching fleas in words (捉字虱 [zuk1 zi6 sat1]), a slightly mischievous version of parsing words. Here, both Li and Yip show off a form of "cunning intelligence" reminiscent of the style of the litigation masters of Imperial China. Old Chinese novels and operas often describe how litigation masters use their cunning intelligence to subvert the Imperial court system. In Hong Kong, the stories of famous litigation masters have been made into movies and TV dramas numerous

---

* The Cantonese words for "teacher" and "tutor" are both 教師 [gaau3 si1]. The phrase 補習教師 [bou5 zaap6 gaau3 si1] is used for private tutor, literally "tutoring teacher."

times. In fact, when people think of lawyerspeak in a Chinese society such as Hong Kong, they don't think of the obscure legalese of the common law; they think of the kind of shrewd but playful talk that famous litigation masters deploy. This is why litigation masters are known as tricky in Cantonese.

In the excerpt, we see how the interaction between Li and Yip quickly turns itself into a competition of mischievous word tricks that clever litigation masters used to wiggle out of the legal charges against their clients. The game takes the form of verbal sparring that is superficially logical but profoundly silly when participants deliberately turn a blind eye to the context of words and playfully focus on their literal meanings, often in the ruthless advancement of their own little arguments. The sequence comes close to a parody of a proper cross-examination because it displays an unsettling twist on the obsession with semantic transparency we saw earlier in the English trials. Yip accused Fung of lying because Fung was a private tutor, not a registered teacher. For Yip, a teacher must be a registered teacher. To counter that, Li insists that his client is a teacher, because the words for "private tutor" in Cantonese, literally translated, are "tutoring teacher" (hence, with the word "teacher"), even though unlike schoolteachers, they are not certified. Li then makes reference to similar examples: Solicitors ("lawyers") and barristers ("big lawyers") are both lawyers; the Land Tribunal and the High Court are both law courts. The purpose is to prove that Fung can rightly be called a teacher.

Later that day, Li orchestrates a verbal comeback by questioning Yip's own professional qualifications. Yip says he is an engineer; Li asks the same question Yip asked him minutes ago about his client—whether he is a registered engineer. Yip then says he is an engineer of his own company. Once again, the act of cross-examination is turned into a bouncy, impish sequence of catching fleas in words, nested in a pattern of one-upmanship. The verbal ping-pong proceeds in a crisp tempo that is rarely seen in English-language trials in Hong Kong. The development of the conversation hinges very much on the flow of the moment. Again, from the judicial standpoint, the exchange is absolutely trivial. But for both Yip and, yes, Li, the focus here is on the battle (one-upmanship) rather than on the war (the trial), a sentiment nicely captured by Yip's statement at the end: "But I'm a boss" (但係我係老細 [daan6 hai6 ngo5 hai6 lou5 sai3]) (i.e., "I'm even better than an engineer"). It is a comment that is apparently innocuous, but truly vicious in context.

Cross-Examination in Cantonese Between Yip Man Sang (W) and Counsel Kit Li (C)

	Gloss	Original
C:	First of all, you said that the cost of an elevator wouldn't be as high as $800,000, right?	你第一就話，好喇一個電梯呢，就嘅價錢就唔會八十萬咁高嘅，係咪呀？
W:	It definitely couldn't be the case.	肯定唔會啦。
C:	But could it or could it not be the case that the cost varies from building to building? For some buildings, it costs less. For some buildings, it costs more.	但會唔會每間大廈嘅情況唔同呀？有啲大廈平啲，有啲大廈貴啲呀？
W:	There shouldn't be a big difference.	相差唔會好大嘅。
C:	Is that right?	係咪吖？
C:	Are you an expert? May I ask?	你係咪呢方面嘅專家呢？請問？
W:	I've been working in the engineering business for 20 years.	我做廿年工程。
C:	I see.	吖。
W:	I've seen more than a few of all different elevators.	大大話話所有電梯睇咗唔少。
C:	Are you an engineer?	你係咪工程師呀？
W:	What?	吓？
C:	Are you an engineer?	你係咪工程師呀？
W:	You can say I am an engin . . . engineer of Lung Coeng Engineering.	可以講龍翔工程…工程工程師。
C:	You're an engineer?	你係工程師？
W:	Yes, an engineer.	係工程師。
C:	Are you registered? With professional qualification?	有冇註冊呀，專業資格嗰啲呀？

W:	I am an engineer of Lung Coeng Engineering.	呃，我係龍翔工程嘅工程師。
C:	I see. I'm not asking you this. First things first, are you an engineer? Those who are registered?	哦。我唔問你呢樣。第一，你係咪工程師先？註冊嗰啲？
W:	I'm not a registered engineer.	我唔係註冊工程師。
C:	You're not.	唔係嘅。
W:	Hmm.	嗯。
C:	Yes.	吓。
W:	But I'm a boss.	但係我係老細。
C:	That's a different matter.	咁就第二件事。
W:	I can hire many engineers.	我可以請好多工程師。
C:	But that's a different matter.	咁就第二件事㗎。
W:	Hmm.	嗯。

In these examples I hope to convey the peculiar Cantonese voice I heard in these trials. There is something about it that is quite different from the stiff and dry style of the English voice. Sometimes the voice jumps out in direct defiance of the rules of cross-examination; sometimes it simmers underneath the surface of the perfunctory observance of rules. From a performative standpoint, speeches are thicker, in the sense that the relationship between what one says and what one means becomes complicated. Tam's responses, for example, are sarcastic: saying one thing while meaning the opposite to mock and ridicule. Or, for example, the verbal ping-pong between Yip and Li is parodic: saying the same thing in imitation while meaning something different. In literary parlance, litigants speaking in Cantonese are *troping* on the plain meanings that the speech act of statement making aspires to produce, and in so doing, they turn meaning into anything but plain. To describe it in the colloquial Cantonese terms that people in Hong Kong use, there are many "bones" in between the lines. The increasing salience of these tropes is evidence that the tight entrenchment of the statement-and-reply structure that secures a dominance of constative meanings has been undermined.

In terms of the change in interactional ground rules, what happens in Cantonese courtrooms is that the statement-and-reply structure is often interrupted enough to give way to a more open, looser structure known as call and response. Again, I am here drawing on the distinction Goffman made in "Replies and Responses" between what is known as a response on the one hand and a reply on the other (Goffman 1981).

To recap, a statement-and-reply structure confines exchanges of live utterance within a rigid textual model to facilitate the speech act of statement making described in the previous chapters. A reply is an answer to the immediately preceding question in an interactional sequence. It addresses the semantic core of the prior question or statement in the sequence. A response, however, is not so much a direct reply, and its relation to the prior statement is often more ambiguous. So defined, a response is a concept that covers a much wider scope than that of a statementlike reply. A response does not take up the antiperformative guise of statement making, in the sense that the speaker does not ostensibly confine herself to describing the information that the questioner is seeking but is *doing* something in the course of interaction (cf. Lyons 1995: 238). If we move outside the courtroom context, we can see that often a reply is only one of many socially recognizable responses possible in an interactional episode. In other words, there are many possible ways to respond to someone's prior utterance without directly replying to the person's question or statement. A call-and-response structure allows for more spontaneous and performative responses to the prior calls. In Goffman's description, "As long as the respondent can make listeners understand what he is responding to and ensure that this expression is ritually tolerable, then that might be all that is required" (1981: 43).[11]

SOCIAL CREATIVITY IN LANGUAGE

Why do litigants break up or disrupt the institutional frame of cross-examination and come up with their own performances in the Cantonese courtrooms? The question is not too difficult to answer. It starts with an institutional structure weakened by the unique diglossia of Hong Kong. The period of colonial governance that created the diglossic situation also stifled the development of an appropriate register ready to be used in legal courtrooms. Trapped in the witness box, with their money, reputations, and entitlement to justice on the line, litigants speak in what they see as the most persuasive way to speak in Cantonese. Cantonese, in the words of Johannes Fabian, reminds its users of "a ridiculous precariousness," even when the relation between the users is one of domination and control (1986: 135). The distance created by English for the sense of aloofness and authority required by juridical formalism is gone. It prompts litigants to reach over the four walls of the enclosed courtroom to bring in performative speech acts that they are so familiar with in their everyday lives, hence allowing the clamoring voices of the locals to intrude on the once hermetically sealed space of juridical formalism.

But the more puzzling question is why lawyers, and sometimes even judges, break frame, given their familiarity with the legal system and above all their loyalty to the system. The puzzle itself is particularly troubling if one subscribes to a purely utilitarian approach to the use of language (i.e., language is an instrument that is completely at our disposal). The comparative evidence from the bilingual system in Hong Kong suggests the inadequacy of an agentive, individualized model in understanding language practice. In Chapter 3, I described how historically the institutional-*cum*-social segregation of the use of Cantonese and English contributes to the emergence of two linguistic habituses that are minimally overlapped (Bourdieu 1977, 1991).[12] Each of these habituses sets out its own principles for the generation and structuring of linguistic practices. They each define the rules that come to be taken for granted, the common sense that a speaker knows without explicit reasoning. Shifting from one language to another, then, has the effect of altering witnesses' sense of what is appropriate and acceptable by reconfiguring the felicity conditions of different speech acts. As Austin (1962) points out, the performative derives its force from the social conventions that govern a speech act. In Hong Kong, the historical English-Cantonese diglossia creates two incommensurate sets of conventions along the language divide. In discussing how different professional genres within a language emerge, Mikhail Bakhtin interestingly remarks: "It is in fact not the neutral linguistic components of language being stratified and differentiated, but rather a situation in which the intentional possibilities of language are being expropriated: these possibilities are realized in concrete, particular, and are permeated with concrete value judgments;

they knit together with specific objects and with the belief systems of certain genres of expression and points of view peculiar to particular professions" (1981: 289).

What Bakhtin calls the intentional possibilities of language are a form of structural intentionality, realizable when one finds oneself in a situation in which such "possibilities of language are being expropriated." The word *possibility* in the quote captures how speaking in one language or speaking in one particular register of a language nudges actors toward certain performative possibilities and steers them away from others. Hence, litigants who speak in Cantonese suddenly are ready-tongued to speak bitterness or to catch fleas with words—speech acts that are speakable and doable in the new bilingual institution. It is these seemingly oxymoronic structural intentional possibilities that I want to pin down in my analysis of the speech acts that litigants do in the Cantonese courtrooms. It is only oxymoronic if one subscribes to the notion that performative creativity is deemed possible only at the remove of the social. But performative creativity does not spring up ex nihilo—for the purpose of interaction, total creativity is communicatively ineffective, an argument most famously articulated by Wittgenstein (1953) in his "private-language" argument. For it to be socially effective, performative creativity must be the pouring of old wine into new bottles. Cantonese allows litigants to invoke familiar speech acts to bend, break, and rekey the activity of statement making.

WRESTLING WITH THE COMMON LAW
IN CANTONESE

For many of the suddenly eloquent litigants, dominating the little Cantonese battles in verbal combat is a different thing from winning the adversarial war in the common law. Although it is difficult to empirically verify whether such performances help or hurt a litigant's cause, my impression is that a free rein in Cantonese is often a mixed blessing for lay litigants (I return to this question in Chapter 9). By and large, counsel I interviewed are indifferent to, if not skeptical of, litigants who act out.[13] The structural discrepancies between the emotional sensibilities in Cantonese performances and the rules of juridical formalism mean that the best performance one can give in Cantonese is often taken by legal professionals as "irrelevant," "off-the-wall," "emotional," or just "crazy."[14] Many litigants, especially those unaccompanied by lawyers, do not know that their best performances in Cantonese often do not help, and in some cases in fact hurt, their legal cause.

PART THREE

Legal Bilingualism and the Rule of Law

CHAPTER 7

Language Ideology and Legal Bilingualism

FOR THE LEGAL PROFESSIONALS and in fact the educated middle class of Hong Kong, the question of Chinese is an especially vexing one. Although the influence of the British on the economic and political fronts has quickly faded since the end of colonial days in 1997, the desire to maintain or even strengthen the presence of English remains strong among the educated middle class. It might be a stretch to say that Hong Kong people typically enjoy speaking English, but many of them revere the global outlook and metropolitan feel that English brings to the city (cf. Pennycook 1998). Elites see the lingering presence of English in Hong Kong as a feature that distinguishes their society from other parts of China, in fact, the rest of East Asia. The sentiment itself is a vivid display of the complex tension between colonialism and postcolonialism; postcolonialism often posits itself as progress from colonialism, whereas colonial legacies so often provide the substance from which many post-colonies carve their identities. It is perhaps no coincidence that Hong Kong is commonly compared to Singapore in Southeast Asia, not simply because of their similarly small geographic sizes, predominantly urban populations, and tropical to subtropical climates but because of their similar fate of having once been British nonsettler colonies. In a number of crucial ways, however, Hong Kong is different from Singapore. Unlike Singapore, Hong Kong did not become a sovereign state after the end of colonialism. And for related historical reasons, English did not remain the main official language in Hong Kong, as was (and still is) the case in Singapore. Hong Kong's overnight change in 1997 from a British colony to a city of China meant that the political premise that once sponsored the dominance, if not exclusivity, of the English language has since been extinguished. Today, the retreat of English is most rapid and visible in the realm of politics in Hong Kong; senior government officials and legislators now speak predominantly in Cantonese in public. By any standard, this has to be taken as a rapid shift if one takes into consideration that, as recently as the first half of the 1990s, government officials and most leg-islators still used English by default in public and on formal occasions.

The legal domain, however, is where the stronghold of English re-mains undiminished. Why is that the case? Why does English continue to dominate in law when its status as the dominant language is rapidly retreating in some other power domains, such as the political domain and, to a lesser extent, the business and commercial sectors? The an-swer has much to do with the contrasting ways that legal professionals conceptualize the relationship between the common law and the two languages in question as well as with how English and Chinese are dif-ferently embedded in the institution of the common law. In this chapter I focus on the first aspect by looking at how counsel and judges under-stand the meaning of legal bilingualism in practice on the basis of their assessments of the nature of the two languages. I use the word *Chinese* here because the ensuing discussion involves not just the assessment of Chinese (i.e., Cantonese) as an oral medium but also its current use and future potential as a written language of record. My goal is to determine what forms of language ideology and strategies of reasoning counsel and judges consciously use to convince themselves that English and Chinese are different and that the two languages should play different roles in the common law system, despite the political decree that makes them abso-lutely equal in the constitution of Hong Kong. In the next chapter I will look at the institutional consequences, which create a form of linguistic division of labor that accentuates the believed differences between Eng-lish and Chinese.

EVALUATING CANTONESE AND ENGLISH AS LANGUAGES OF THE COURTS

Even the most cynical critics of legal bilingualism would find it difficult to object, in principle, to the use of Cantonese. Of all the lawyers and judges I have interviewed, I have yet to come across one who would flatly oppose the use of Cantonese in the courts. But, yet again, not all, in fact, not even most barristers (to some extent, one might say the same about judges) in Hong Kong embrace the new era of legal bilingualism with enthusiasm, if legal bilingualism is taken to mean a form of symmetric bilingualism in which two languages are interchangeably used in the same system. This important point is often overlooked because of the many ways the term *legal bilingualism* is casually used. For courtroom regulars, legal bilingualism does not mean that legal Chinese is just the doppelganger of legal English, or vice versa. In practice, legal bilingualism assumes specific meanings for counsel and judges. These specific meanings qualify the scope of legal bilingualism in Hong Kong. It has much to do with their preference for preserving the use of English in some areas and avoiding the use of Chinese in others.

How do counsel and judges react to the arrival of Cantonese as an official language in the courts? To answer the question, I approached counsel who appeared in the trials I attended and asked their views on legal bilingualism. Interviews create an interactional setting in which people can make explicit their ideas and evaluations of the two languages of the bilingual system. In other words, my focus here is on the metalinguistic discourses on the nature of English and Cantonese. These metalinguistic statements rationalize not just the use of one language over another but the use of a particular language in one way over another way. Scholars point out that reference to the essence of language, or language ideology, is often a powerful tool to valorize or denigrate specific linguistic practices (Gal 1998; Mertz 1992; Woolard 1998; Woolard and Schieffelin 1994). My focus is therefore on the effects of language ideology—to see how my interviewees deploy their own thematic articulations about the nature of English and Chinese to describe, interpret, and justify the contrasting courtroom performances in English and Cantonese.

The rest of the chapter draws heavily from my interviews with these courtroom regulars. The group that plays the most important role in determining which language to use in a trial is counsel from both sides. Although in principle it is the presiding judge who has the authority to decide which language is used in a trial (see Chapter 3), lawyers are the group who de facto decide the language of a trial, at least in most cases where the involved parties are all legally represented. At the pretrial stage, counsel from both sides indicate to the judiciary which language they prefer to use in court, and in most cases the registrar will accede to the requests of counsel.[1]

As a group, counsel are obviously the ones with vested interests. The difference between Cantonese and English is too important to be overlooked by the people who use language every day to do many things—to narrate, to question, to persuade, and to argue—in the courts. They are also the group whose interests are most immediately affected by the legal language policy. The quality of counsel's advocacy hinges greatly on their mastery of the language chosen for a trial. As Martin Shapiro (1990: 709) puts it, lawyers are at root "specialists in a particular language." All expatriate counsel without exception and still a significant number of Chinese senior counsel (even when they could converse in Cantonese in daily conversations) advocate in English and only in English. Even though the system itself is said to be bilingual, not all legal personnel, judges, and counsel are bilingual for the purpose of the law. In fact, among the 1,000 barristers in Hong Kong,[2] about 150 of the current expatriate barristers would be immediately out of business if English were no longer an option. Here we can see why it is unrealistic to treat English and Chinese as equals in actual legal practice. Although the lack of knowledge of Chinese could amount to a practical inconvenience, it is feasible to practice without any knowledge of Cantonese; a Queen's Counsel from London can fly into Hong Kong overnight to take over a big case (and indeed it is not an uncommon practice). The same, however, cannot be said of English, or the lack of knowledge of it. No person can practice law in Hong Kong without an adequate knowledge of spoken and written English, however well versed they are in Chinese.

Besides barristers who appear in the trials I attended, I also talked to judges who agreed to be interviewed. Some of them presided over the trials I observed; others were involved in various facets of the development of legal bilingualism. Judges in Hong Kong are generally more reluctant to be interviewed. Like many professional judges in other common law jurisdictions, they are more reluctant to express their own views on important judicial topics. By design, I interviewed more Chinese judges than expatriate judges, not only because Chinese judges are now the majority group but also because their experience of presiding over trials in both English and Cantonese makes it easier for them to make comparisons. Furthermore, I approached and sought to interview prominent members of the local bar association who had expressed their views on legal bilingualism in the press before. To allow my interviewees to speak candidly on the subject, I told them I would not use their real names.[3] Hence, except for the people whom I interviewed in their official capacity, which included then bar association chairman Alan Leong and former chief justice Sir Ti Liang Yang, I assigned pseudonyms to protect the interviewees' anonymity.

The interviews were loosely structured. The questions I used were mostly open-ended (e.g., "Could you tell me your thoughts about using Chinese to conduct trials?"). My objective was to see how judges and barristers evaluated the emergence of legal bilingualism and to learn how they envisioned the future of the legal system in Hong Kong. In the course of developing their own reasoned assessments (after all, lawyers and judges are trained to offer reasoned explanations), my interviewees inevitably talked about the nature of the two languages in question, English and Chinese. They offered reflexive discourses on the nature of English and Chinese language practices (in many instances when only the oral context was referred to, specifically, Cantonese).[4] It is clear from the interviews that, when they were assessing the current situation and the future direction of the legal system, judges and barristers often built from the tissue of ideas associated with what they thought were the essential natures of the languages of Chinese and English.

WHAT IS LEGAL BILINGUALISM?

One thing that baffled me in the course of my fieldwork was the apparent contradiction in the many interviewees between their verbal support of legal bilingualism on the one hand and their indifference or even opposition to the greater use of Chinese in the legal process on the other. Why would someone say he supports legal bilingualism when he seemingly does not care whether or not more judgments or legal arguments are made in Chinese? It is not the case that many of the lawyers I interviewed are insincere; most of the people I interviewed are deeply concerned about the use of Chinese in the legal system. The contradiction, as I later found out, suggests that the term *legal bilingualism* carries specific meanings for many lawyers and judges in Hong Kong.

Legal bilingualism, in the interpretation of my many interviewees, is not a project of developing the common law in Chinese on top of the existing one in English. Their understandings are constructed through a stereotypical characterization of what English and Chinese are good at and bad at, as I came to understand from their answers on how lawyers and judges go about constructing and negotiating the meaning of legal bilingualism in Hong Kong.

Instead of distilling a uniform, monologic picture from different barristers' takes on legal bilingualism, the style of my presentation here is juxtaposition. Hong Kong barristers are far from monolithic in their attitudes toward legal bilingualism. In the course of my field-work, I ran into counsel who held different outlooks, perspectives, and priorities. No uniform view emerged from the counsel I interviewed. The bar in Hong Kong today is in fact a diverse group. The old image of the bar in the colonial period as a homogeneous, elitist caste, par-ticularly before the 1990s, is of little relevance today. Unfortunately, the absence of any but the most general surveys means that it is impos-sible to offer an accurate picture of the income variance among Hong Kong barristers. But judging from what I gathered from informal dis-cussions with them, there appears to be a huge gap between the haves and the have-nots. A reputable local silk can command a brief fee in the range of HK$300,000–$500,000 (about US$38,000–$64,000) for a one-day case, and a daily refresher fee of HK$80,000–100,000 (about US$10,000–$12,800), but other barristers may struggle to take enough cases to break even (e.g., barristers have to pay the expenses of their chambers out of their own pockets).

What Heinz et al. (2005) found in the American legal profession also applies to the bar of Hong Kong: It is a highly stratified profession with a wide income hierarchy separating the top from the bottom. Although Hong Kong does not have an English system of Inns of Court (profes-sional barrister associations) that own and rent the places where counsel establish their chambers, star counsel (those who frequent the Court of First Instance and the Court of Appeal) almost invariably reside in cham-bers situated in the most upscale commercial buildings. These chambers, located in the heart of Hong Kong's downtown business district, simply known as the Central, are also in close proximity to the High Court Building. Lesser established barristers can be found in sets of chambers located in older, less expensive buildings in the west end of the Central, farther away from the High Court Building. Further down the ladder one can find barristers who are confined to small chambers situated in the crowded commercial districts in Kowloon, far removed from the legal center of Hong Kong. Barristers there serve a clientele predominantly made up of working-class defendants in criminal cases. Some of these less glamorous members of the bar have to keep their legal careers alive by occasionally taking nonlegal part-time jobs (e.g., teaching, private tutorship, small private businesses, sales).

At the pinnacle of the prestige hierarchy are counsel who acquire the status of social celebrity in Hong Kong, very much in the classic sense defined by C. Wright Mills—that is, the names that need no further identification (1956: 71–72). In terms of star power, lawyers easily outshine other professionals in Hong Kong. As influential as professionals such as architects and medical doctors might be in their own professions, that influence can hardly be cashed in in the social arena. Lawyers are different; they, particularly barristers, are unique in their ability to translate their occupational prestige into social and political capital. As in other former British colonies, the bar is a breeding ground for charismatic and popular politicians in Hong Kong.

I mention this because, although lawyers' opinions concerning legal bilingualism are ostensibly based on reasoned arguments one way or the other, their attitudes reflect at least in part a division between those who are well established in the upper circuit of the court system and those who are making ends meet or cutting their teeth in the magistrates' courts. In short, when discussing the future of English and Chinese, barristers of different income brackets, seniority, and professional prestige come to hold contrasting views. Hence I resist the temptation to create a semblance of uniformity in my account. My goal instead is to present the diversity of opinions among what I see as four different groups of counsel within the Hong Kong bar, whose attitudes toward English and Cantonese are distinct. The four groups are the elitists, the strategists, the white wigs, and the mavericks.[5]

CANTONESE OR ENGLISH AS THE
LANGUAGE FOR ADVOCACY

Most local barristers who are able to speak both Cantonese and English have in their professional careers practiced in both languages. They have experienced firsthand the stark differences between English and Cantonese as the language of the court. What would they say about the two languages? Which language do they prefer? How do they conceive of the relations between law and language?

The Elitists

More experienced barristers, who came of professional age before the late 1980s, have a consistent distrust of the ability of Cantonese to become a viable means of advocacy. They are the most experienced practicing barristers in Hong Kong today, and their advocacy service often comes with the highest price tag. Most of them are now in their 50s, and some are well into their 60s and 70s. As a group, they came from middle- and upper-class family backgrounds. Some studied in England for their legal degree, well before university legal education became available locally in Hong Kong. Others were among the earliest graduates of the university law program of the prestigious Hong Kong University, at a time when receiving a university education was considered an unmistakable mark of social distinction.[6] Although some early graduates of the University of Hong Kong came from working-class families, the structural conditions of the profession have for a long time discouraged people of more humble backgrounds from joining the bar. It is a profession of delayed rewards; in sociological parlance, it is a profession where the Matthew effect ("For unto every one that hath shall be given, and he shall have abundance: but from him that hath not shall be taken away even that which he hath"), à la Robert Merton, is most prominently in play. Unlike solicitors, who mostly work for a legal firm and are thereby salaried, a barrister is always self-employed. It takes at least a few years for novice barristers to earn enough to sustain their own practices. Family support in some cases is not just a comforting psychological insurance but a necessity for early survival. This accounts for why many experienced barristers in Hong Kong today came from well-off families.

The most successful of the elitists have become the cream of the profession today; some of them have risen to the esteemed rank of senior counsel. During my interviews, they expressed skepticism about the desirability of having Cantonese serve as a legal language. The fact that most of them speak Cantonese themselves does not change their view of Cantonese as primarily a dialect of uncouthness and bad taste and, for some, even vulgarity and sharp dealing. In their view, Cantonese threatens chaos. A senior counsel, Katherine To, conveys the general negative feeling shared by many elite counsel in Hong Kong.

Cantonese dialect in fact is rather colloquial and also not very respectful and proper. It doesn't have the decorum that is necessary or the solemnity for serious occasions as required by court language. Very often, you want the members of the public to respect the legal principle or the particular issue that is at stake. But then if you use colloquial way of expressing it, very often the whole importance of the issue is diminished. It brings the dignity of the court down.

Another senior counsel, Billy Cheung, remarked, "If you ask me, my personal view is that the use of Chinese is not conducive to the proper development of our legal system at all, it doesn't help. It's a shortcut to enable more people to properly understand what's happening in courts."

The counsel I interviewed believe that Cantonese and the vulgarity of local street life that it inherits undermine the solemnity and respect of the courts. Cheung makes an explicit linkage between the rowdy atmospheres of Cantonese courtrooms and the crude nature of the language.

Cantonese is a dialect. It is debatable if one can treat Cantonese as a language. It is definitely not a precise language, not a language that articulates things in the abstract. Cantonese can only handle questions of fact, and the only advantage of using Cantonese in courts is its accessibility to the members of the public; it makes the judicial process more accessible. When there is a dispute of law, English is inevitable. The native language of the common law is English.

These barristers, who began practicing in the 1970s and 1980s, indicate a clear preference for English over Cantonese. They no doubt practice what they preach—some can count their Cantonese appearances on one hand; others never use Cantonese in court. They say that there is a sense of "courtliness" that only English can bring. For them, deliberating the law, as they call it, is a speech act best done in English. Some elite counsel would go so far as to say that it is impossible not to think in English when arguing law. Cheung made the following remark when I asked him if he thinks about the law in English or in Cantonese: "It's of course in English. We received our legal education in English; our English textbooks are all in English. All the cases we read are in English." Katherine To added, "I really don't pay much attention to the Chinese translation of a legal term. I use English most of the time. When I really, really have to use Chinese, I'll call up my friends in the last minute for help."

For Cheung and To, a part of the common law culture, a really important part indeed, will disappear if Chinese replaces English. Jackie Lo, who has practiced for 13 years and who always prefers to use English when he has a choice, remarked how difficult it is to translate the English court etiquette into Cantonese. "When I hear someone translate 'learned friend' literally into Cantonese as 博學嘅朋友 [bok3 hok6 ge3 pang4 jau5], I break out in goose bumps. I think if a man on the street hears that, he would wonder whether the person who uses the expression really lives in this day and age."

These experienced counsel are also critical of how some judges succumb to the crude colloquialism of Cantonese when they interact with litigants. Cheung remarks:

Unfortunately, there are judges who use colloquial Cantonese. When somebody hears a judge use that kind of expression, they tend to lower their expectations of the authority of the judge. Some judges use very, very rough colloquial Cantonese like 有冇搞錯 [jau5 mou5 gaau2 cok3] [a colloquial expression, roughly meaning "What the hell is going on?"]. . . . It doesn't help to promote the rule of the law.

One counsel jokingly suggests that to really capture the solemnity of the English-language court in Chinese, one should try to revive classical Chinese verse, which many Chinese still consider the most elegant texts that the Chinese language has to offer. Only the language of Confucius and Mencius, Li Bai and Su Shi, the language of China's belle époque can squarely match the solemnity that modern English bestows.[7] The comparison of English to classical Chinese is indeed revealing. I referred to the work of George Steiner when I discussed the formalistic context of the English courtrooms in Hong Kong as anachronistic (see Chapter 4). Here, I want to refer to Steiner's view on distance and translation. Steiner points out that archaism (i.e., a reversion to an obsolete style) is a move frequently deployed when translators labor to secure a natural habitat for the alien presence that they have imported into their own tongue. By archaizing their own style, they produce a sense of déjà vu; the foreign text is felt to be not so much an import from abroad as an element out of one's native past (Steiner 1998: 365).

As we saw in Chapter 4, counsel in Hong Kong preserved with vigor the peculiar mannerisms of courtroom English. But even in England and Wales, the artificial politeness of legal English has been criticized by both insiders (e.g., Pannick 1987) and outsiders (e.g., Berlins 2003).[8] By this standard, there is no doubt whatsoever that Hong Kong is a haven for juridical formalism. As I have already pointed out, the ideal language for a highly formalistic system is a language that is better heard from a distance. Hence courtroom English in Hong Kong, in its arcane and exotic moments, is revered as humble and solemn. And counsel in the elitist group, whose career development dovetailed with the golden age of English advocacy in Hong Kong, are among the staunchest supporters of this language tradition. Like other social elitists, they are conservative in culture and stand against the destruction of old practices and standards. They worry that Cantonese, clearly in their view a dialect too colloquial to be deemed respectable, will one day replace English as the dominant language of the courts. For them English represents precisely what Cantonese is not: solemn, respectful, civilized—in short, naturally the "natural" language of the court. To some of them, speaking English is not just a professional necessity; it is a way of life. Their endorsement of English is not simply a rational decision based on vested interests but a visceral commitment to the way of life that the voice of English loudly indexes. Many came of professional age during, if not before, the 1970s and 1980s, an era before the rapid expansion of the legal profession took place. The bar then was a more homogeneous group compared with the bar today. It was one intimate, close-knit circle where everyone knew everyone. In a Cantonese society, English became a proud group marker for this group of elites—to advocate in courts, communicate in chambers, or mingle with other members of the legal fraternity in clubs and resorts such as Beaconsfield House and the Dragon Boat Bar. Not many of the local elites in Hong Kong are culturally anglophile, but some of the elite Chinese counsel of this era come close, in a sort of china and sterling flatware kind of way. Conservative in outlook and impervious to the influences of local Cantonese culture, they are conscious of their own separateness from the rest of society. Inside prestigious sets of chambers in Hong Kong, back then and still today, English remains the default language of communication. Here is how Billy Cheung responds when asked what language he chooses to use in talking with other people in his chambers.

Invariably, we speak in English. Well, I shouldn't say invariably. Ninety-five percent of the time we speak in English. In chambers here, normally we speak English. Of course, when you speak with the messengers or the secretaries, sometimes you have to speak in Chinese, but mostly we speak in English. And that's how I would tell everybody, even people who come in, our pupils, I would tell them, "Look, you are expected to speak English."

The elites are also the group who adhere to a strong culturalist thesis of language—language embodies and reflects the character of a culture—and argue that the common law, itself an English product, cannot be talked about in another language. This culturalist view comes close to a lay version of Whorfianism, the belief that the qualities inherent in a language determine the breadth and depth of its speakers' cognitive capacities. On such interpretation, the affinity between the common law and the English language goes beyond the tight institutional connections the two already enjoy. The belief is that embedded in the English lexicon and grammar are distinctions not found in other languages that most faithfully express the conceptual complexities and logical precision of the common law. Underlying the claim that the common law expressed in another language is no longer the *same* common law is a particular notion of the law that prescribes English as a defining feature.[9] The English language is taken to be the perfect linguistic tuning fork used to discern, with uncanny precision, subtleties of the common law that are indecipherable in other languages. This is especially so when English is compared to Chinese, an old, monosyllabic, nonalphabetical, and noninflectional language limited in its capability to express subtle conceptual variants. It is through such ideological articulation of the connection between English and the common law that justifies the predominant use of English over Chinese in so-called legal matters. The chairman of the bar association at the time of my fieldwork, Alan Leong, makes the following comparison:

English, compared with Chinese, is a relatively more precise language. English has a high level of precision. Chinese has a very low level of precision, relatively speaking. Chinese depends more on implied meaning. If you want to achieve the same standard of precision in Chinese, you have to engage maybe three or four times more words. You have to rule out other possibilities.

Leong further explains:

If you want to express the law in Chinese, you have to express it in a redundant way; the Chinese used must be, by literary standards, bad Chinese. You won't use thirty Chinese words to express what can be expressed in only four words in Chinese. But when you use four words in Chinese, you have to depend on the implied meanings of the words. The law leaves no room for imagination. When it says something, it means exactly that something.

Despite their concern about the nature and character of Cantonese, the elitists do not publicly speak strongly against its use in law. They also know that the colonial period in which they grew up is a bygone past, and so is the once exclusive dominance of English. Besides, it is against their sensibility to oppose Cantonese in a more outspoken and political way. Their reaction to the project of legal bilingualism is instead a form of quiet indifference. In their practices, elitist counsel continue to prefer English over Cantonese.

The picture that emerges from the elitists' metalinguistic discourses could hardly be clearer. English has come to be conceived as the iconic embodiment of the essence of the common law. Cantonese, on the other hand, is considered colloquial, impetuous, and sometimes cunning; it does not have the quality to be deemed a language proper. For the elitists, the appearance of Cantonese as an official language in the courts of Hong Kong is an unfortunate unintentional consequence of the change of sovereignty in 1997.

The Strategists

The second group of counsel are the strategists. Like the elitists, the strategists also prefer English over Chinese, but their preference is more instrumental. They like English because they see English as a tool that can give them an extra edge over witnesses in an adversarial setting. This group of barristers is most attracted to the ability of English to mystify and to intimidate. They note that the open disdain displayed by witnesses today, such as the derisive smirk and the constant fidgeting described in earlier chapters, not to mention the unruly swearing at judges and defiant display of physical force (such as throwing shoes at a judge), was simply unheard of before the introduction of Cantonese.[10] P. F. Lee, a veteran counsel who has practiced for more than 25 years, interestingly compares English to a veil put on the courts in Hong Kong and sees the use of Cantonese in courts as the act of lifting a veil. "In the past, you wouldn't find people representing themselves in person, even with the use of an interpreter. You didn't see people talking back to judges in the old days. How would someone dare to confront an English-speaking judge?"

Although Lee may have exaggerated, it is true that the use of Cantonese has deepened and hastened the change in the atmosphere of Hong Kong courts.[11] As recently as the 1980s, judges, if they so wanted, could easily command fear not just among witnesses but among counsel as well. One example is the following account by two counsel of their experience appearing before a judge with a feisty style in the 1980s.

Upstairs, Garcia J. cross-examined many defendants giving alibi evidence in defence of the charges brought against them. When papers placed before him were not to his liking, he was prone to throw them on the floor or at the practitioner presenting them, purely to keep the bar on its toes, of course. We believe this was case management in an embryonic form. One member of the bar, a recipient of his style of justice who is now himself a High Court Judge and heavily involved in case management, happily does not show any signs of repeating such behaviour which, although not the norm then, was certainly not unheard of. (Remedios and Bharwaney 2000: 58)

More litigants talk brashly to judges in trials nowadays than in the past. The impertinence displayed by litigants can be found not just in the lower courts such as the magistrates' courts but also in some of the higher courts of the system. The difference between the past and the present is not so much that order cannot be maintained in Cantonese courtrooms. Of course it can; a judge today can exert the full force of law against any defiant witness if he so wishes, as when, for example, a worker who swore at a judge was sentenced to two months in prison.[12] But it is the laborious efforts required to sustain order in Cantonese courtrooms that irk many veterans who have seen the "good old days." As pointed out in earlier chapters, formalism as an institutional form is more often questioned and challenged when courtroom exchanges are conducted in Cantonese. Barristers of higher seniority described this development as a lack of respect for the courts and decried the new "Cantonese style" as demeaning. Fanny Mak, a veteran counsel who practiced for more than 20 years, said, "I can't tell you why this is the case. But when you use Cantonese, the witness often behaves as if he is prepared to argue with you." Mak is in fact one of the few interviewees who is candid about her own disgust at using Cantonese in courts: "It's OK to be mundane; it's OK to be tedious; but I hate it to be undignified. But when you use Cantonese in courts, that's unfortunately the case. It's often undignified."

The strategists' predominant concern is maintaining order and control in court. Strategists believe that an English courtroom with the presence of a court interpreter is most advantageous from an advocate's standpoint. Although outsiders might think that barristers would prefer the faster and more dynamic pace that Cantonese would bring in cross-examination, the strategists, many of them accustomed to cross-examining in English, prefer the slower and more deliberate pace of interpreted cross-examination. They believe that involving court interpreters in the flow of cross-examination (as in many English trials) plays to their advantage. The goal is getting the job done, even if it means that the process has to be more drab and arid than it already is (without the presence of interpreters).

During interviews, some counsel in the strategist group suggested that the key to a successful cross-examination from an advocate's standpoint was to gain control over witnesses as well as control over their own utterances. The fact that the presence of interpreters often keeps a witness's otherwise uninhibited performance on a leash is definitely an institutional advantage that counsel like to possess. Other counsel said that they prefer to have interpreters when they cross-examine, because the arrangement can eke out a few more seconds for them to think ahead (while the interpreter is interpreting). The strategists, of course, are well aware that in Hong Kong many witnesses who choose to speak through an interpreter understand English exchanges on their own, despite the fact that they feel more comfortable speaking in Cantonese. Hence the practice of court interpretation should also benefit witnesses by giving them a few extra seconds to think about their answers. That said, counsel in the strategist group said that a few extra seconds mean a lot more to a practiced player than to a novice. Even with more time, the strategists believe, a lay witness usually would have a hard time figuring out the different components of a legal maze and say the right thing.

Keith Leung, a young barrister who prefers the use of English, explained to me why English is better for him: "You can give witnesses all the time they want to think about what their answers should be, but often they trick themselves by thinking too much. The fact is many lay people just don't really know the law enough to understand what should be said and what should not be said from a legal standpoint."

In justifying their preference for English over Cantonese, the strategists emphasize more the function of English as an instrument of control and manipulation in their metalinguistic discourses. The use of English, coupled with the presence of a court interpreter, gives counsel the upper hand to box in a witness in the cat-and-mouse game of cross-examination. Cantonese, according to the strategists, can become a dangerous weapon for resistance in the mouths of some recalcitrant witnesses.

The White Wigs

Another group of counsel began their legal careers around the time or even after Cantonese was introduced as an official legal language in Hong

Kong. I would describe them as the "white wigs."[13] Those counsel who fall into this group are not necessarily younger in age (although some are), but they are usually at an earlier stage of their careers. The white wigs differ from the elitists and strategists in their receptiveness toward the use of Cantonese in court. Many of them believe that the introduction of Cantonese can make the legal system more accessible. Less established in their practices, the white wigs are also the group that stands to gain the most from the additional number of litigants that a more accessible bilingual system brings.

In terms of class backgrounds, the white wigs differ from the elitists in being a much more diverse group. Many of them graduated from the two local law schools (University of Hong Kong and City University of Hong Kong) in the 1990s or later, when the then colonial government finally decided to expand the legal profession at a much faster rate than ever before. Expansion weakened exclusivity, which in turn dampened the elitist spirit. The white wigs lack the invincible élan of the more senior barristers. They are less attached to English in the ways that the elitists and even the strategists are. English is less a marker for them to feel like members of the bar. Their young careers mean that unlike the more senior counsel, who started their practices in the English-only era, their practices have been bilingual since day one. In fact, many white wigs are still honing their advocacy skills in the magistrates' courts and use more Cantonese than English to cross-examine in court. Much to the chagrin of the elitists, the white wigs generally take a more detached attitude toward English in their professional lives. For example, many do not speak English in their chambers (unless speaking to an expatriate chambers-mate); nor do they choose to speak English in professional gatherings if they have a choice.

Some younger, greener white wigs are cognizant of the fact that the old bar culture is oddly at variance with that of the larger society. Their belief in accessibility means that many of them are supportive of measures that give litigants greater rights to speak in their own language, be it Cantonese or something else. In their interviews, some of the white wigs said that promoting Cantonese in cross-examination had genuine merit. They want the system to be more transparent, and allowing court proceedings to be conducted in Cantonese is a crucial step toward greater transparency. The white wigs are the ones who experience firsthand the defiant behaviors of some litigants in Cantonese; but some said that Hong Kong is now a different society than it was two or three decades ago, and it is natural that people are now more outspoken.

As mentioned, the white wigs are the group that stands to gain the most from more litigants. Unlike their senior colleagues, they are less established in their legal careers and have yet to reach a point in their careers where they are sought after by big clients. Salina Chu, a young counsel who has been practicing for five years, remarked, "I like to cross-examine in Cantonese. I think it's more direct and efficient. Cross-examining in English just slows down the whole process."

Like many other white wigs, the faster tempo of cross-examination is what they like about using Cantonese. When I told Chu that other counsel preferred English because of the imposing effect it has on witnesses, she responded, "I don't think you have to intimidate witnesses with English in order to crush them. In fact, for someone like me, it works better if I can disarm a witness by playing nice. And I can do that so much better in Cantonese. With English, often you have to speak through an interpreter and that [disarming] is difficult to do."

For Chu, the less intimidating persona brought out by her Cantonese speech works to her advantage. By adopting a more congenial and casual style, she can be a more effective cross-examiner. In this sense, Chu's comments that using Cantonese can disarm a witness can be seen to be similar to the strategists' justification of using English in courts, although for Chu, using Cantonese is not strategically inferior but in fact better.

Tim Chan, another young counsel with five years of practice, also prefers Cantonese: "I like to use Chinese. There's no question about it. It's quicker; it's more accurate. . . . I know courtroom Chinese in Hong Kong is still in a state of flux. It's not standardized. But eventually it will be."

Chu, Chan, and other white wigs who came of professional age around and after 1997 know that the courtroom culture has been changing since Cantonese was recognized as an official language in the courtrooms of Hong Kong. In my interviews with them, they were quite open to the new changes, and, as noted, many prefer Cantonese for its immediacy and convenience. Here we see a different articulation of the nature of

Cantonese; instead of being viewed as vulgar and impulsive, Cantonese is taken to be direct and crisp. White wigs in general value efficiency over control and order. Their views suggest that Cantonese trials might not be as solemn as English trials in Hong Kong, but they are also not as drab, dull, and long.

But the white wigs agree with the elitists and the strategists in one important area. When it comes to so-called matters of law (i.e., deliberation of legal arguments, the deployment of case law and statutory law, and the use of legal references), the views of the three groups are in unison. The elitists, the strategists, and the more liberal white wigs all agree that English is still the primary language to be used to discuss legal matters and should remain so in the future. Chu, for example, although she prefers to use Chinese to cross-examine, says that she prefers English for her legal deliberation. Together the three groups form a mainstream view on how English and Cantonese should be used in the bilingual system. This linguistic division of labor turns on the common law–fact distinction, a point that I discuss in further detail in Chapter 8. The crux of the consensus is that, although English should remain the language of legal argumentation, Cantonese can take over as the language of evidence elicitation. It is noteworthy to point out that because of the virtual absence of civil juries in Hong Kong, the potential advantage of Cantonese as a more direct language for persuading the jury is not relevant for counsel's consideration in most cases. Hence, when barristers say that they support legal bilingualism, often they mean an asymmetric form of bilingualism in which Cantonese and English assume different and unequal roles. Legal bilingualism means only the copresence of two languages in the same system; it does not guarantee congruity between the role of English and the role of Cantonese in the system. Most counsel see no contradiction in supporting legal bilingualism on the one hand while expressing doubts on using Chinese to discuss legal concepts and to deliver judgments on the other.

Why should English continue to remain the language of the law? The standard answer is one that Billy Cheung gave in my interview with him: English is the native language of the common law. Although the strategists and the white wigs would not couch their support of English in the culturalist terms used by the elitists, they too see the common law as indissolubly bound up with the English language, so much so that if the common law were no longer argued in English, one might question whether it could still be called the common law. Counsel therefore consider the question of preserving English as synonymous with the question of preserving the common law in Hong Kong.

Kenneth Chiu, whom we met in Chapter 6 from his cross-examination of Tam, believes that Chinese is more convenient for cross-examination but that English is undeniably the better language for the purposes of legal argumentation and conceptual dissection. He prefers to see English continue as the primary language of the system: "I think if we want to continue to use the common law, English should stay. We have concepts that are developed in English, precedents that are written in English. Our connections with other common law jurisdictions would be weakened if we gave up English."

Chiu and other counsel who came of professional age in the 1990s and afterward (many had practiced for less than 10 years at the time of my fieldwork) represent a new breed of barristers in the bilingual legal environment in Hong Kong. When they appear in the District Court and the Court of First Instance, they seem to prefer Cantonese to cross-examine witnesses, but they also seem to prefer English to argue the law before a judge. During my fieldwork, the white wigs were the ones who were most likely to appear in mixed-language trials (see Chapter 8). This kind of half-Cantonese, half-English way of practicing law is frowned on by the older elitists and strategists. Some elitists attributed this half-baked style to what they see as the declining standard of English among younger counsel. But more white wigs are engaging in mixed-language practice, and judges appear to condone it (see the section on judges later in this chapter).

Metalinguistically, the hybrid practice of the white wigs suggests that Cantonese is seen as a factual language, or, more specifically, legal-factual language, for the gathering of facts in court, whereas English remains the pure law language. Although a couple of white wigs I interviewed use the word *accurate* to describe the advantage of using Cantonese, it is clear that most of them justify the use of Cantonese for the faster pace and greater efficiency it brings into the courtroom. Meanwhile, English is seen by the white wigs as a technical, conceptual language that is ideal for legal deliberation but too abstract and clumsy for elicitation of factual evidence.

The Mavericks

As we have seen, even the more liberal white wigs, the group who are much more receptive to the use of Cantonese in court, believe in and support the unshakable dominance of English in matters that are strictly legal. One might ask whether there are barristers who believe in a more radical form of legal bilingualism in which Chinese assumes an equal role not just in matters of fact but also in matters of law. The answer is yes; there are counsel who view the English-only legal system with a degree of frustration and, in some cases, disillusion. For them, the technicality of English constitutes the social mechanism of distinction that makes law an exclusive and obscure venture. The language of Chinese, they believe, if given time, can become as capable a language of the common law as English is. Some in this group are prepared to push ahead with the idea of a Chinese common law, even, if necessary, at the cost of severing the ties between Hong Kong's common law system and other common law jurisdictions.

When I was a reporter in the early 1990s, I had a short conversation with a Hong Kong politician who also had a full-time job as a solicitor. He was not a highflier but made enough money in a small local firm to allow him to pursue a political career. He told me, jokingly, that after 1997, he could easily become a Queen's Counsel, if he so wanted. What the politician said was meant to be a joke, but wrapped up in it was a common sentiment shared among the less glittering members of the bar: "It's the English language, stupid!" I use the label "mavericks" to describe this final group of barristers, not just because of their minority views on English and Chinese but also because of their self-perceived identity as outsiders. Many of them believe that they have good enough legal knowledge to compete with the best of the profession, but their inferior command of English is their Achilles' heel. They believe that they are the exploited in a system where the social capital of English fluency was, and to some extent still is, disproportionately magnified. Under the old system, proficiency in English (specifically, courtroom English) was too often confused with excellence in law. Some mavericks believe that English is the invisible wall that keeps them remote from the center of the profession. In an important sense, they are the exact opposite of the elitists. Furthermore, unlike the white wigs, they endorse Cantonese not so much because they are used to cross-examining in the language but because of their defiance toward English and the old era that the dominance of English symbolizes. Some of them are old hacks who have become disillusioned with their own profession. From a distance, they cast a more critical gaze on the phenomenon of English dominance that is absent in the mainstream view. They associate the mainstream's adherence to English with an arrogance that forms a part of their elitist identity.

Certainly, some mavericks have a great mastery of the English language, but for political beliefs or other reasons they have rejected the mainstream vision. Like the white wigs, they praise the accessibility that the official status of Cantonese can bring to the legal system. Kevin Lam, who has practiced for 11 years, has this to say:

Our profession in the past gained respect from others because it spoke a language that common people did not speak. Thus, there is a certain mystique when barristers speak English in courts. However, the court is a mechanism for dispute resolution. At the end of the day, it is a question of the strength of the legal institution. Is it really the case that in a Chinese society like ours, the court has to use English in order to be solemn and respectful? I really can't see how this has to be so.

Although the elitists and the strategists describe the atmosphere of Cantonese trials as demeaning, Lam says that they are "vivid and lively." He says it is questionable in principle for barristers to prefer to use English simply because they believe they might avoid the defiant acts of Cantonese-speaking litigants. For someone like Lam, who wants Cantonese in the courts despite its potentially disruptive nature, accessibility and transparency trump solemnity and respect.

But perhaps the most provocative suggestion made by Lam is his questioning of the allegedly inextricable connection between legal thoughts and the English language. Lam sees a difference between "thinking in

English" and "thinking in Cantonese with the use of occasional English terms." According to Lam, many of the local Chinese counsel misdescribe what they do, that is, "thinking in Chinese with occasional English terms," as "thinking in English":

Sometimes I ask myself, when a local born barrister says he thinks in English, what does he actually mean? I really don't understand what the phrase "thinking in English" means in this context. I, for one, think in Chinese. If English is your second language, I don't understand how you can say you "think" in English. You of course think in Chinese, and then translate your thought to English.

He adds:

I still remember when I studied law [in the late 1980s], all the study groups I participated in discussed in Chinese. Clearly people who grew up in Hong Kong think in Chinese. *Of course you use English terms in the process of thinking in Chinese, but that is a different thing from thinking in English.* (emphasis added)

Implicit in Lam's message is the allegation that many Chinese lawyers talk up the importance of English as a way to defend its continued dominance in the legal system. If what counsel do, that supposed act of thinking in English, is merely thinking in Chinese with some English terms, then English, contrary to the claims of many, should not be taken as the fabric of common law reasoning. Thinking in Chinese with English terms implies that Chinese is already providing the skeleton of legal reasoning for counsel and can eventually completely take over the job of legal argumentation without the assistance of English, once a set of legal terms of art in Chinese have become widely standardized through repeated use.

Lam's comments raise an important question: Do counsel in Hong Kong, many of whom use Cantonese as their everyday language, *really* think in English? It is true that some counsel in Hong Kong have difficulties recalling the Chinese terms for legal concepts that they refer to on a daily basis in English, concepts such as easement, consideration, or duty of care, just like many legal professionals in other colonial settings (cf. Fabian 1986). The question, however, remains: Does such an inability to recall legal technical terms in Chinese imply that one is, by default, thinking in English? Perhaps the *real* question, in the context of Hong

Kong, is, What exactly is thinking in English? As an example, I once heard a counsel arguing in a Chinese trial. He code-mixed extensively, making utterances such as the following: "Agent 呢只係 principal 嘅一隻 手嚟" ["Agent" ne1 zi2 hai6 "principal" ge3 jat1 zek3 sau2 lai4], which can be glossed as "An agent is only a hand of the principal." As we can see, the two legal concepts of agent and principal are uttered in English, but the rest of the sentence is in Cantonese. Is the sentence an example of thinking in English? Or is it just an example of code mixing in practice, thinking in Chinese with English terms?

Let me also use myself as an example. I think of myself as someone similar in educational upbringing to many of the younger barristers I interviewed—born and raised in Hong Kong, received my education there (from elementary school to college), got my Ph.D. in the United States, and now write and teach primarily in English. I think that I think in an eclectic mix of Cantonese and English words. I frankly do not know if it is more "accurate" to describe my thinking activity as thinking in English or thinking in Cantonese. Likewise, counsel in Hong Kong mostly do not communicate exclusively in English when they discuss legal questions among themselves, nor do they communicate exclusively in Cantonese. The language they practice, their parole, à la Saussure, is a hybrid speech popular among the younger college graduates in Hong Kong, a heavily code-mixed form—that is, people switching back and forth between English and Cantonese, often in the middle of a sentence, in their conversations.

My purpose is not to question some counsel's claim that they think in English. My point here is about metalinguistic descriptions of our language practices. To say that we either think in English or think in Cantonese presupposes a bright line that we cannot cross if we are to say that we think in a particular language, a bright line that is difficult to delineate in an environment like Hong Kong, where code mixing is common. In such a case, the label "thinking in English" is no neutral description; it is used as a metalinguistic tag by some to forge a link between legal thinking and the language of English and is contested by others who question the link.

Other mavericks say that historically the exclusive use of English imposed the brutal cost of injustice on some unfortunate litigants. Tommy

Chik, a veteran barrister who became disenchanted with the legal profession, equated the promotion of Chinese with the promotion of justice. He saw injustices done to the locals who failed to understand the legal procedures that were conducted in English. It is not that the mavericks do not see the practical challenges involved in promoting the more radical form of legal bilingualism. Many of them said it would take a long time. But they are far more sanguine about the future of a legal system that features Chinese as the main language.

Like the successful elitists and the practical strategists, the mavericks acknowledge that English is the more respectful language. But for the mavericks, English is more respectful only because it is not often used in the streets of Hong Kong. By the same token, they question whether the vulgarity described in Cantonese courts is a consequence of the Cantonese language itself or rather a consequence of the policy that for years excluded Cantonese from the legal arena. Chik made the following comment:

Cantonese is much closer to life, perhaps too close to have the foreignness in English and the subsequent sense of intimidation that English brings. When English is used, it is measured and dignified. Court English is calculatingly formal, but when Cantonese is used, you feel free—actually too free. Many people get carried away by this sudden freedom. That's why you find vulgar talk, inappropriate expressions in Cantonese courtrooms.

The way Chik describes English is not that different from the account given by the elitists and the strategists. What stands in contrast to the views of the other two groups is the reasoning Chik offers in accounting for the differences that Cantonese produces. According to Chik's formulation, the differences between English and Cantonese are attributed more to the different social roles that the two languages play in Hong Kong. As Chik explains, Cantonese is vulgar not because Cantonese *is* vulgar but because it is "much closer to life." The quotes here point out what sociolinguists would call the lack of a specific legal-formal speech register in Cantonese. The problem with Cantonese, according to Chik, is that there are no widely adopted, well-rehearsed set phrases and trade expressions in Cantonese that distinguish lawyerspeak from lay speech. This explains why native Cantonese speakers find it difficult to argue law in Cantonese with authority and grace; it is not so much their lack of competence with the language or the alleged inferiority of the language per se but the lack of a history in the practice of law in Cantonese and hence the retarded development of an appropriate legal register. To get out of the feedback loop that consistently pushes down the role of Chinese in the law, mavericks insist that Chinese must be used more, aggressively more.

To summarize, the metalinguistic discourses of the mavericks paint English and Cantonese in ways that are different from those offered by the other three groups. A distinct feature found in the discourses of the mavericks is their insistence on tying the characters of the two languages to the colonial history of Hong Kong. English is seen as the historical instrument of domination and even oppression; Chinese was made inferior because of the English-only policy in the past. The mavericks, a minority in the legal profession, are the only group who question whether Chinese as a language is intrinsically incapable of becoming the primary vehicle of the common law in Hong Kong. They are also the group who favor a more radical form of legal bilingualism.

Judges

I have so far described how counsel, arguably the most important regular players in the adversarial trial process, think of English and Cantonese as court languages. I now move on to discuss how judges in Hong Kong view the issues of legal bilingualism. Judges, like barristers, have their work influenced by the choice of language in a trial. In theory, judges are the ones who decide the language of a particular trial, although they usually take into consideration, and when practicable follow, the preferences of the parties. As a group, judges tend to pay more attention to the future development of legal bilingualism and its impact in the long term. After all, judges, especially the senior ones, are the people responsible for judicial policies. Probably for this reason, the judges I interviewed are more reserved and are cautious not to express strong opinions on legal bilingualism (except their general support). The issue of language is a potentially divisive one among judges—one's ability to speak, read, and write Chinese or lack thereof is now the criterion used to separate so-called bilingual judges from monolingual judges.[14] In reality, bilingual judges in

Hong Kong are all ethnic Chinese judges.[15] Likewise, so-called monolingual judges are judges initially recruited from England and other common law jurisdictions such as Australia, New Zealand, and South Africa; others began their legal careers in Hong Kong as expatriate counsel before joining the bench. For this reason, I made an effort to talk to both bilingual and monolingual judges in the course of my fieldwork.

All the judges I interviewed support legal bilingualism, whether they themselves speak and read Chinese or not. However, like the barristers, different judges have different visions of the future of legal bilingualism. This vision ranges from some use of Chinese within a primarily English system to a system that gives equal roles to English and Chinese. Also, all the judges I talked to, including those who do not speak Cantonese, acknowledge the convenience that the language brings to the courts. The question for them is to what extent the court should value practical convenience. Among judicial personnel of all ranks, magistrates are the ones who most treasure the efficiency of Cantonese. I talked to only a few magistrates (or barristers who once worked as magistrates), and they were all ethnic Chinese, but the impression I got is that magistrates, at least among those who are bilingual, are strong supporters of using Cantonese in court, in part because they often deal with cases conducted in Cantonese already (for statistics, see Chapter 8). Magistrates see Cantonese as direct, convenient, and cost saving. Above the magistrates' courts, as my interviews with the white wigs have already indicated, bilingual judges at the District Court and the Court of First Instance now condone an eclectic approach of allowing both languages to be used in the same trial—Cantonese for eliciting evidence and English for legal deliberation. As is evident from my interviews, this is a developing trend that in part reflects the preference among younger counsel to use Cantonese in a limited fashion. Many judges seem to agree with the mainstream view of the bar—it works to the benefit of the common law in Hong Kong if a form of linguistic division of labor between English and Chinese can be established within the system.

With expatriate judges, obviously it is difficult for them to compare the two languages in court. The focus of my interviews was therefore on how they viewed the future of English in Hong Kong. Monolingual judges, most of them non-Chinese, can see that English is retreating in Hong Kong. As one expatriate judge, Eugene Burton, said: "More and more, Chinese is used as the first language of court." This is also reflected in the demography of new judges hired after 1997; these judges are predominantly bilingual Chinese. "No expatriate has been recruited to the magistracy for some years. So, certainly at the bottom level, you will get Chinese, I think, certainly being very much the norm and it is almost the norm now," Burton commented.

But Burton, like most expatriate judges, believes that English should remain the main legal language in Hong Kong. The point here is well rehearsed by counsel who support the use of English: English is the language of the common law; a jurisdiction that conducts its business in another language cannot remain a common law jurisdiction. Judge Tom Harper, another expatriate judge, said, "English must be retained for a significant number of cases. I think it is unavoidable if you are part of the common law system. You've got to use English in certain cases. The source of the law is English. And I don't know of any other common law system that abandoned English and yet remained a common law system." According to Harper, the use of English also allows the common law in Hong Kong to remain one that interacts with other common law jurisdictions in the world. For a small society like Hong Kong, he believes that English is the window to the world.

I think what happens then you are cutting off the umbilical cord with the rest of the common law. Your system then is going to evolve away from the common law system. Of course, one of the strengths of the common law system is that you are not just dependent on what happens in your own country or your own territory, but you got the benefit of the law of other jurisdictions. That is a great strength. . . . I think it would be very unfortunate if you were not to retain that link with the other common law jurisdictions.

Judges are careful to spell out the importance of English without undermining the importance of the right of litigants to testify and argue in Cantonese. They instead use the common law to justify the continued use of English. Here, then, is the question: Must Hong Kong remain a common law system? Even today, the question would sound merely rhetorical if ever posed to a lawyer in Hong Kong. The common law is so well entrenched in Hong Kong that it is considered an immovable horizon of the city's legal landscape. For this reason, the whole issue of legal indigenization was never a serious topic among the legal professionals in Hong Kong. As I pointed out in Chapter 1, this eagerness for Hong Kong to remain a common law system must be seen not only in the context of British colonialism but also in the context of what happened in China during the Cultural Revolution, when political mobilization replaced law as the mode of governance. In the face of the political turmoil and legal anarchy in China, legal professionals in Hong Kong, and the general public for that matter, embraced insulation from the social and legal changes that took place in China, so much so that the promise that Hong Kong's legal system would remain unchanged was explicitly written down in the Basic Law, the constitution of Hong Kong. The belief, then, was to ensure continued integrity of Hong Kong's legal system rather than to create a mixed jurisdiction of the common law and Chinese civil law.

Today, however, with the idea of the rise of China as a global power having taken on a warm glow, there are bilingual judges, very much still in the minority in Hong Kong, who have begun to see the future of Hong Kong's legal system not so much as a minor player in the common law family but more as a pioneer in the evolving legal system of China. Although these judges believe that it is important for Hong Kong to remain a common law system in the foreseeable future, they have also begun to see the future of Hong Kong's legal system as tied ever more closely to the legal development of China. For them, Hong Kong has a bigger role to play in showcasing Western legal concepts and ideas for China. Through the lens that projects this emerging vision, Hong Kong is posited to become a source of influence in shaping the legal reform of a new world power. Throughout the twentieth century, China's legal scholars had looked primarily to civil law countries for innovations. Since its economic reform in the 1980s, China has been increasingly looking to common law jurisdictions, Hong Kong included, for models of law, particularly in those areas concerning commercial and economic affairs (Epstein 1989: 39). But doing so means that Chinese has to be used more in Hong Kong, not simply as an oral medium for the purpose of convenience but also as the language of judgments and records. A bilingual judge, Timothy Lau, makes the following remark:

We cannot ignore the practical reality. What's going to happen ten years from now? Even though China is said to adopt the civil law, and Hong Kong the common law, but if you look at the ways China's legal system developed in the past few years, their civil law is not growing further and further away from Hong Kong's common law. In fact, the two are becoming more and more similar. In some aspects, they are exactly the same. For example, in the area of evidence, they basically adopt common law's ideas on the questions of the burden of proof and the standard of proof. To some extent, the Chinese legal system today is influenced by the Hong Kong legal system.

Lau then explains:

I think many aspects of their [Chinese] system are now influenced by the common law. To a certain extent, Hong Kong can be a place [that] China can use as a reference. Hong Kong can be a beneficial influence for China here. I personally think that when it comes to legal system, Hong Kong has a more mature and better system. If we can influence China, that's a good thing. How can we influence China? Of course, there are many bright people in China who are proficient in English. But many people do not understand the common law in English. If we can use more Chinese in the common law, we can exert an influence [on China].

Despite his tentative tone, Lau is expounding an idea that would have been unthinkable before the recent rapid rise of China as an economic and political power. What Lau and some Chinese judges suggest is that, although Hong Kong should remain a common law system for now, closer integration with the legal system in China is a development that Hong Kong cannot avoid and should not try to avoid in the long run.

This point was also brought up in my interview with Sir Ti Liang Yang, the first Chinese chief justice of Hong Kong, who retired from the post in 1995 (see Figure 3). Yang acknowledged that the common law was a foreign system brought to Hong Kong by the British colonial government. He said it had been proven to work well in the city. But how

FIGURE 3. *First Chinese chief justice Sir Ti Liang. Courtesy of Ming Pao.*

Hong Kong's legal system is going to develop in the long run is difficult to tell. For Yang, it is as much a matter for Hong Kong to decide as it is a matter for China to decide.

I think fifty years from now, the law then will be much different from the law now. Today, the fountain of our law is still in London. We still refer to English precedents. . . . They are many QCs [Queen's Counsel] coming from London to appear in the courts of Hong Kong. Many people study law in London. And there are still many expatriates practicing in Hong Kong. . . . What will happen in the future much depends on the future legal developments of the two places [Hong Kong and China]. We people in Hong Kong of course want the common law, a system which we are familiar with and have faith in, to stay. But China the sovereign state will consider it from its own perspective. It remains a question whether China will allow a different system of law in an island with a population of a few million people to continue to operate.

I also asked Yang what would happen if, one day, Chinese eventually replaced English as the only legal language of Hong Kong. Yang was quite philosophical in his reply. He said that if that happened, it would then be time to rethink whether Hong Kong should still continue with the common law system. Implicit in Yang's answer is an assessment shared by many that the common law persists in Hong Kong to this day because of the isolation that English provides. For many lawyers in Hong Kong, the day English is no longer used will also be the day Hong Kong makes a break with the common law.

CHAPTER 8

Institutional Adaptation to Legal Bilingualism

L EGAL BILINGUALISM in Hong Kong is institutionally asymmetric; its practices do not favor an equipoise of Chinese and English. The two languages are equal only in an "equal but different" sense, because their roles and functions are identifiably different. In Chapter 7 I discussed how counsel and judges understand legal bilingualism on the basis of their metalinguistic assessments of English and Chinese. Here, I turn to the institutional arrangements that stem from and reinforce that language ideology. We will see how the existing beliefs that English *stands for* the abstract common law and that Chinese *stands for* factual everyday mundaneness guide the use of Cantonese as a legal language in the operation of the bilingual system. Understanding the institutional enactment of legal bilingualism requires us to chart out the line of fragmentation in the actual practices of the courts to see how the asymmetry between English and Chinese is played out.

Together, Chapters 7 and 8 underline the linkage between language ideology and language practice. In his relatively unknown article "The Arrangement Between the Sexes" (1977), Erving Goffman describes this spiral reinforcement between beliefs and practices as "institutional reflexivity." The insight here is that self-fulfilling prophecy is often the consequence of the pursuit of cognitive coherence. Social institutions work *reflexively* with reference to their declared beliefs in ways that ensure that these beliefs are "true" (Goffman 1977: 301).[1] Modern law is perhaps the most reflexive of social institutions. Max Weber believed that legal rationality is the archetypical rationality of modern institutions. It is reflexively built on reasoned rules; hence the requirement for procedural specificity is elevated to the iconic status of the rule of law. It is for this reason that discussions of any major changes to the procedural aspects of the legal system (e.g., legal bilingualism) often take on a deliberate ideological cast— the question of the development of Chinese in the legal system becomes a question of the nature of the common law in Hong Kong.

How is the preference for English over Chinese negotiated in the actual practices of legal bilingualism? In the everyday operation of legal bilingualism, four key practices restrain the role of Chinese in Hong Kong's legal system: (1) linguistic asymmetry across the hierarchy of courts, (2) mixed-language trials, (3) the making of case precedents, and (4) statutory interpretation. Together, these practices reproduce along different planes of the legal machinery a resolute linguistic division of labor in Hong Kong–style legal bilingualism, a unique legal bilingualism that merges English and Chinese with the traditional fact-law distinction.

LINGUISTIC ASYMMETRY ACROSS COURT HIERARCHY: ENGLISH ABOVE, CANTONESE BELOW

The phenomenon of the linguistic division of labor is most manifest in the ways that Chinese and English are asymmetrically allocated across the court hierarchy. The distribution of Cantonese across the hierarchy is almost exactly an upside-down image of the distribution of English. As a medium for oral communications in court, the bottom-heavy distribution of the use of Cantonese inversely corresponds to the top-heavy pattern of courtroom English. The first decade of the bilingual common law was marked by a surge of Cantonese in the magistrates' courts, the lowest tier of the court hierarchy; at the same time, however, the magistrates' courts are by far the busiest courts in terms of volume of business.[2] Bilingual magistrates, who are now in the clear majority, mostly conduct their business in Cantonese. It is clear that the magistrates' courts are the place where Cantonese has made its headway. This is especially so in minor summons cases, where no charge and arrest is involved. In 2006, for example, up to 95 percent of all summons cases in the magistrates' courts were conducted in Cantonese (Hong Kong Judiciary 2007c). Judges and lawyers in Hong Kong said cases there were concerned with factual disputes; not much law was involved in the cases heard in the magistrates' courts.[3] What they meant was that cases tried in the magistrates' courts seldom involved discussions of complex legal concepts. It is for this reason that today, as it was in the past, magistrates are the only judicial personnel who are not customarily required to give written reasons for their decisions, whereas judges presiding over higher courts must offer reasons for their decisions in the form of written judgments.[4] The magistrates' courts in Hong Kong handle the greatest caseloads on the criminal side of the law in Hong Kong. But decisions of the magistrates' courts remain seldom reported (i.e., published in professional law reports).

As a case moves further up the court hierarchy, the likelihood of its being heard in Cantonese decreases. Conversely, the presence of English exhibits an inverted pyramidal distribution. English is de facto the only language used in the Court of Final Appeal, the highest court of the jurisdiction. At the time of this writing, no appeal has been heard in Chinese in the Court of Final Appeal. Five judges are impaneled in a Court of Final Appeal hearing. It is doubtful that there are enough Chinese-speaking judges to form a group of five to preside over Chinese proceedings.[5] English is also the dominant language of the Court of Appeal. English retains a reasonably strong presence in the Court of First Instance and the District Court (see Figure 4). The institutional pattern is that Cantonese is the language of the lower courts and English is the language of the higher courts.

Such a pattern of course does not happen in a social vacuum. Rich litigants represented by accomplished lawyers involved in high-stakes lawsuits are often advised by their counsel to have trials conducted in English; on the contrary, unrepresented litigants almost universally prefer to try in Cantonese. Although rich litigants are prepared to take their cases to appellate courts and are financially capable of doing so if necessary,

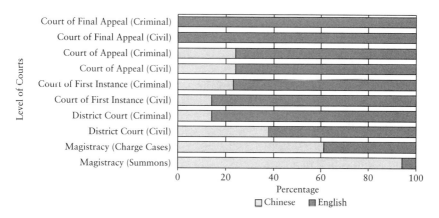

FIGURE 4. *Cases heard in Chinese and English in Hong Kong Court (2005). Data from Hong Kong Judiciary (2007c).*

unrepresented litigants would most likely abandon their claims if ruled against. The high cost of civil litigation in Hong Kong means that, even with a (somewhat limited) system of legal aid, only resourceful litigants serviced by experienced counsel are daring enough to play the game of legal poker at the level of the appellate courts. The lawyer-dominated nature of adversarial trials, in Hong Kong as elsewhere, means that the relative economic wealth and legal sophistication of litigants are the key factors that determine how far a civil case can go in a legal system; and the group that is most financially prepared and legally savvy is also the group that is most likely to pick English over Cantonese for trial proceedings, in anticipation of possible appeals.

The pattern here suggests that, taken as a whole, the mainstream view of the superiority of English over Cantonese is implicitly operant in the very process that shapes the linguistic division of labor vertically across the hierarchy of courts. Because Cantonese appears mostly in the magistrates' courts, its use in the legal domain is associated with factual disputes and trivial arguments (from the perspective of legal professionals). Meanwhile, English is increasingly becoming the pure language of legal argumentation. This trend will only continue because the magistrates' courts are filled mostly with bilingual personnel. Together with the lack of exposure to the higher courts, such a linguistic division of labor reflexively justifies the belief that Cantonese is iffy for the abstract argument of the law but convenient enough for gathering brute facts.

MIXED-LANGUAGE TRIALS:
THE INVISIBLE "CANTONESE" TRIALS

But just looking at the official statistics can be misleading. My fieldwork in the Court of First Instance and the District Court suggests that cross-examination in Cantonese (without the aid of court interpreters) is in practice more prevalent than the official statistics suggest. The gap between official statistics and actual practices arises because Cantonese cross-examination at times appears in trials that are officially categorized as English trials. In the Court of First Instance, for example, a substantive number of trials are conducted in neither English nor Cantonese alone but in a mixture of both. The same is true with trials in the District Court. This is the eclectic mode of mixed-language trials that, as mentioned in Chapter 7, bilingual judges condone. Mixed-language trials are driven by the same belief that English is better for law and that Cantonese is convenient for facts. Here we begin to see how the binary fact-law distinction is reproduced on diverse planes, not just vertically across the court hierarchy but inward within the unit of a single trial.

The procedures of the simplest civil trial can be broken down into four main parts: opening statements, evidence elicitation, closing statements, and judgment. In theory, the judiciary has to decide early on, during the pretrial stage, what language to use as the official language of the trial. Again, in theory, once either English or Chinese is chosen, the language of choice is supposed to be used throughout the entire course, from gavel to gavel.[6] Furthermore, when an appeal is launched against a decision, the language used for the appeal proceedings is by default the same language used in the original hearing, for the obvious reason of saving the cost of translation. However, in the new mixed-language trials, Cantonese is reserved for evidence elicitation, and the rest of the proceedings are conducted in English.[7] In short, courtroom regulars speak in Cantonese when they interact with witnesses; they switch to English when they interact among themselves (even when judges and counsel are bilingual).

Officially, the language of a trial is determined by the language in which the judgment is written. Mixed-language trials are thereby lumped into the category of English trials, because judgments in these trials are delivered in English. For this reason, accurate statistics on the prevalence of mixed-language trials are unavailable. Statistically, mixed-language trials are strictly an invisible category. The reason is not so much that judges want to hide the use of Cantonese in the higher courts of Hong Kong but more that judges do not view the use of Cantonese as consequential enough to categorize mixed-language trials separately from English trials. According to the official interpretation, which tends to perpetuate the narrow understanding of law as "black letter law," what really matters is the language of a judgment because the judgment is the very materiality that turns a case into case law. Based on my own observations, among the trials tried by bilingual judges and represented by bilingual counsel in the Court of First Instance, I would say that as many as half of them resorted to the mixed-language mode. Certainly, some counsel (mainly the elitists and the strategists) prefer to cross-examine in English, but younger counsel are choosing the mixed-language mode in the name of practical convenience, and this could well be the trend of the future. Judges with an overloaded docket sometimes also encourage the mixed-language mode, because English trials often require court interpretation, which in turn means more court time spent on a single trial.

The mixed-language trial format epitomizes the unique form of legal bilingualism in Hong Kong. The arrangement is a vivid example of how beliefs about language interact with the day-to-day practice of the common law in Hong Kong. It is these beliefs about the ineradicable link between English and the common law that promote the emergence of mixed-language trials in Hong Kong. The high versus low distinction between English and Cantonese in the court hierarchy fractally re-presents itself in the well-recognized form of the fact-law distinction at the level of a single trial. Counsel cross-examine witnesses entirely in Cantonese but then, in presenting their legal arguments, pick and choose relevant pieces of evidence and translate them into English. Judges do the same, hearing evidence from both sides in Cantonese but delivering their judgments in English. This arrangement, even on the terms of juridical formalism, is not without its problems. Translation errors can be committed by bilingual counsel and judges when they translate Cantonese evidence that they heard into factual accounts described in their judgments. After all, judges and lawyers are not court interpreters. And because without court interpretation there are no verbatim transcripts of the evidence in English, an appellate judge who does not know Chinese will have no way to go back to the original evidence in a review.

Still, even if one puts aside the concern with potential translation discrepancies in mixing English and Cantonese, are mixed-language trials, merely because their judgments are produced in English, any different from English trials? My argument is yes, they are. To follow through with the argument that I make in this book, the juridical character of mixed-language trials is only the same as that of English-language trials if the facts generated in both cases are of the same nature. My comparison of the machinery of cross-examination in English and Cantonese courtrooms in Hong Kong, however, suggests that facts in the voice of English and facts in the voice of Cantonese are different; facts presented in English are deeply entrenched in the speech act of statement making, and facts presented in Cantonese are embedded in a heteroglossic spectrum of local speech acts. In other words, if, as we have seen, the process of rearticulation in Cantonese is different from that in English, then the use of Cantonese, even if solely for evidence elicitation, undoubtedly will change the character of a common law trial in Hong Kong in the long run. I come back to this point in Chapter 9.

THE "TRANSLATED" NATURE OF CHINESE STATUTES

Another key practice that limits the role of Chinese in Hong Kong's legal system is the contrasting significance assigned to the Chinese and English versions of local statutes. As in other common law jurisdictions today, statutes have become a key source of law in Hong Kong.[8] One would imagine that it is easier to treat Chinese and English statutory law as congruent, given the fact that a statute is not linked to other statutes in the same way that a case is to other, prior cases, and hence can be read as a stand-alone text. Indeed, as an extension of the principle of Article 9 of the Basic Law (that both Chinese and English are the official languages used by the executive authorities, legislature, and judiciary of Hong Kong), section 10B of Hong Kong's Interpretation and General Clauses Ordinance of 1997 stipulates that the English and Chinese texts of Hong Kong's statutes are equally authentic. However, in practice, statutory interpretation tends to favor the English text, so much so that a statute printed in English is taken by counsel and judges as the de facto original. In contrast, a statute in Chinese is not treated as the same piece of law in another language; it is seen by the court more as a derivative of the English original.

A piece of statute is only as authentic as people are willing to take it. Most lawyers (solicitors and barristers included) see a statute written in Chinese as a document stringing together a list of coded symbols rather than as a law written in a language with its own dynamics. Treating a Chinese statute as a combination of coded symbols gives rise to a totally different attitude when it comes to interpreting the statute. The meaning of the statute is not to be construed by referring to the conventional meanings of the Chinese words that appear in it. Instead, the statute can be construed only in accordance with the common law meaning of its terms, that is, its legally designated meaning derived from its equivalent in English. Suppose I designate two Chinese words 隨機 [*sui ji* in Putonghua; *ceoi gei* in Cantonese] to represent the concept of contract in a Chinese statute. Such a designation is, of course, misleading because readers of Chinese would know that the words conventionally mean "arbitrary" in Chinese. There are obviously better alternatives, something closer to the meaning of "contract" in Chinese. But a bad translation actually better illustrates the point here. Under the existing interpretative policy of bilingual statutes, it does not really matter whether or not a term's *conventional meaning* closely resembles its *legally designated meaning.* When lawyers in Hong Kong interpret the meaning of a Chinese statute, they do not approach it by trying to understand what it conventionally means in Chinese. Instead, their strategy is to read it as a string of code, more precisely, translated code. To go back to our hypothetical example, although the Chinese words 隨機 [sui ji] conventionally mean "arbitrary," their authentic legal meaning is not derived from their conventional usage in Chinese; instead it is derived from the equivalent English words they are designated to represent. Hence if the Chinese words *sui ji* are legally designated to mean the English word *contract,* then "contract" it is (see Table 5).

It is this underlying codelike nature of Chinese statutes that explains why lawyers in Hong Kong always look up the English text of a statute when, ironically, they want to understand what the Chinese text means.

TABLE 5 *Difference between the interpretation processes of nonlegal and legal texts written in English and Chinese in Hong Kong*

Language	Object	Interpretative mechanism
English	Nonlegal text (e.g., a newspaper article)	Meaning of the words/expressions in conventional usage *in* English
	Legal text (e.g., a statute written in English)	Meaning of the legal terms in the common law plus the common meaning of nonlegal English words/expressions used
Chinese	Chinese text (e.g., a newspaper article)	Meaning of the words or expressions in conventional usage *in* Chinese
	Legal text (e.g., a statute written in Chinese)	Meaning of the legal terms in the common law plus the common meaning of the nonlegal *English* words/expressions that the Chinese text denotes

Sometimes, one can somehow intuit the meaning of a Chinese statute without looking at the English version when the conventional meanings of the words used in the statute more or less resemble their legally specified meanings (although this is uncommon); more often, however, the legal meaning of a Chinese statute is impossible to read from its conventional meanings, as in my own deliberately misleading example. Under the current interpretative philosophy adopted by the judiciary of Hong Kong, a judge would still say that *sui ji* is "contract," despite the obvious gap between this and the conventional meaning of the term, which shows that a Chinese statute is not interpreted as a legal text that stands on its own. Law students learn in their first year of law school that different rules govern prudent statutory interpretation, such as golden rules or the mischief rule or the literal rule. But when it comes to written Chinese statutes in Hong Kong, the only rule that matters is the English rule. Such an official interpretative strategy is inscribed in the local Interpretation and General Clauses Ordinance. Section 10C(1) of the ordinance reads:

[W]here an expression of the common law is used in the English language text of an Ordinance and an analogous expression is used in the Chinese language thereof, the Ordinance shall be construed in accordance with the common law meaning of that expression.

This preference for determining the meaning of a Chinese word by first mentally translating it back into English is endorsed by Tony Yen, Hong Kong's law draftsman (Yen 1997, cited by T. L. Ng 2000). Yen's justification is that the English terms in particular are rooted in the sociocultural context in which the English legal system evolved (i.e., the relation is indexical). By contrast, it is not always possible to find an identical equivalent Chinese expression for a common law concept (i.e., the relation can only be symbolic). Thus, when a term has its history in the common law tradition, as all legal terms of art do, it is the common law and therefore the English statutory meaning that prevails. This point is further clarified by the Hong Kong Department of Justice.

What should be noted is the fact that when a Chinese term is used to express a common law concept, the full meaning behind the term cannot be grasped by merely taking the literal meaning of the term or deciphering its morphemic elements in the Chinese language. Reference must be made to the meaning as it is found in the common law. The common law must be taken as the semantic reference scheme. (Hong Kong Special Administrative Region Government, Department of Justice 1999: 39)

To capture the unique common law meaning of a legal term, drafters frequently coin new Chinese terms that are unintelligible to Chinese speakers themselves. In passages loaded with legal terms of art, a translated Chinese text often reads like an unending stream of half-sense produced by Internet translation software, as the practice of translation gives way to transliteration in the name of legal accuracy.

Despite the stated goal of rooting the common law in the Chinese language (Hong Kong Special Administrative Region Government, Department of Justice 1999: 41), most lawyers find the Chinese versions of the statutes robotic, opaque, and impenetrable. "If you take a look at some of the Chinese statutes, you would agree with me that they are not written in Chinese, at least not the Chinese we know. In some of the worst cases, you don't understand even a single word of an ordinance," said Alan Leong, senior counsel and chair of the bar association at the time of interview. The problem is that the asymmetric importance of the two language versions in practice means that local law drafters, almost without exception, draft the English version of the text first and then develop the Chinese text by translating the English text.[9]

What I have described so far applies to words or phrases that have a history in the common law tradition (e.g., "contract," "chattels," "equity," "recklessness"). As we have seen, law drafters defend such practices by appealing to legal consistency; that is, both the English and the Chinese versions of a statute should present the same set of legal terms and concepts. However, in the process of interpreting a statute, the practice of privileging English over Chinese does not merely apply to words and phrases with established common law meanings. It applies to virtually each and every word contained in a statutory text, even words that are not legal terms of art. Such spillover effects find their clearest expression in cases involving apparent discrepancies between Chinese and English versions of the same statute.

In principle, when there is a discrepancy alleged between the Chinese and English versions of a statute, the law requires reference to both versions to arrive at a common meaning. Section 10B(3) of the Interpretation and General Clauses Ordinance states that "the meaning which best reconciles the texts, having regard to the object and purposes of the ordinance, shall be adopted." The actual practice, however, is a one-way process that accords an authentic status only the English text. In *R. v. Tam Yuk Ha*,[10] a case that drew the attention of legal scholars in Hong Kong, a fishmonger running her business in a public fresh food market was convicted before a magistrate on two counts of permitting an "addition" to the approved plan of the shop without written permission from the local governing council (the Urban Council). The alleged additions were metal trays containing fish for sale, a chopping block, and a table outside the shop. The relevant bylaw (Bylaw 35 of the Food Business [Urban Council] Bylaws [Cap. 132 sub leg.]) reads as follows:

After the grant or renewal of any licence, no licensee shall, save with the permission in writing of the Council, cause or permit to be made in respect of the premises to which the licence relates—

(a) any alternation or addition which would result in a material deviation from the plan thereof approved under by-law 33.

The words corresponding to the term "addition" in the Chinese text of the by-law read 增建工程 [zeng jian gong cheng], which commonly means additional work or construction. The fishmonger appealed the decision to the Court of First Instance. The judge there adopted the principle that it "is the English language text and the Chinese language text of an Ordinance *together* which make up the legislation enacted by the Legislative Council" (*R. v. Tam Yuk Ha*, at 612; emphasis added). The same judge concluded that "[no] one who understands the Chinese language would, by any stretch of the imagination, come to the conclusion that the placing of metal trays and other items in front of the shop would be a *zengjian gongcheng*" (*R. v. Tam Yuk Ha*, at 611). Because the English term *addition* was ambiguous and the Chinese term *zeng jian gong cheng* was, according to the opinion of the trial judge, more specific, the Chinese term was adopted and the convictions were quashed.

The case was subsequently appealed. In the higher Court of Appeal, the panel of judges adopted a different, in fact, contrary, approach. The appellate judges privileged the more abstract notion of "addition" in the English text over the plain meaning in the Chinese texts; that is, the Chinese term *zeng jian gong cheng* was reinterpreted abstractly to conform with the meaning of the English term *addition*, even though this line of interpretation defied the conventional meaning of the Chinese words in a situation where the words themselves are not legal terms of art.[11]

The implication of the Court of Appeal decision is striking. It prescribes an interpretative method that basically says that whenever there are doubts over the meaning of a particular term in the statute book, be it a legal term of art or an everyday term used in the text of a statute, its meaning is defined by the English text and the English text alone. So understood, it is unnecessary to refer to the plain meanings of the Chinese text, however concrete and clear they may be. The Chinese language text is authentic, but its authenticity is derivative. The conceptual reach of a Chinese term can be arbitrarily expanded or reduced by the English term it is supposed to denote. Under such an interpretative theory, Chinese is a second-order object language denoting a first-order legal language expressed in English, and the meaning of an object word (in Chinese) should be determined by referring back to the object (in English) it denotes. The association between a word in Chinese and a legal concept in English is thus established by institutional stipulation.

A Chinese legal term, whether it is borrowed from the existing Chinese lexicon or a neologism, is incorporated into the common law lexicon by its denotational link to an existing English term (the ideal is to achieve a one-to-one denotational correspondence). As a legal sign, the meaning of a Chinese legal term can be completely disconnected from the usual everyday meanings of the words the term is made up of, because its meaning is completely dependent on the existing English term that it is designated to denote.

In fact, it can be deceptive, as the appellate court's decision in *Tam Yuk Ha* shows, to focus too much on the conventional meanings of Chinese legal terms. What the appellate judges promoted in their judgments was an interpretative stance that is willing to completely dislodge Chinese words in statutes from their everyday meanings. Opposite meanings can be forced on a word. In practice, the Chinese statute is at best an obscure, imperceptive gloss of the English original.[12]

R. v. Tam Yuk Ha effectively declares the second-class status of the Chinese version of Hong Kong statutes. Since then, subsequent cases involving apparent discrepancies between the English and the Chinese versions of an ordinance have continued to privilege the English version as the ultimate authority.[13] In a later case, *Chan Fung Lan v. Lai Wai Chuen*, the judge simply declared that the Chinese text was inaccurate because it did not correspond to the English text.[14] No attempt was even made to try to reconcile the two versions.

THE USE OF ENGLISH AND CHINESE IN JUDGMENTS

Besides its authoritative status in statutory law, English also continues to assume its role as the predominant language of record for case law in Hong Kong. Most bilingual judges I interviewed said they are far more accustomed to writing judgments in English than in Chinese. Judges, without exception, are far more familiar with legal terminology in English. Switching to Chinese in judgment writing does not save time, unlike cross-examination in Chinese does. "When I first started [writing judgments in Chinese], I would say the time it took for me to write a Chinese judgment was about four times as much as that for writing an English judgment. It's better now, but still it takes me longer to write a Chinese judgment," a Court of Appeal judge said.

Judges indicated in their interviews that they are also more accustomed to the judicial voice they learned by reading and writing English judgments. They say it is awkward to import the narrative style in English into Chinese writing. Stylistic idiosyncrasies aside, judges, Chinese and expatriate, all model their English judgments after the same corpus of precedents. Judgments from the courts of Hong Kong, a small jurisdiction by any standard, are by far more homogeneous than judgments from the courts in larger jurisdictions, such as the higher courts in the U.S. federal court system. The overall writing style of Hong Kong judgments can be described as terse, matter-of-fact, and highly structured. But such stylistic uniformity is less obvious among the even smaller number of Chinese judgments available. Apparently, judges are still experimenting with their own style and voice in Chinese judgment writing. The lack of authoritative legal reference books in Chinese also makes the job of writing Chinese judgments more difficult.

Indeed, Chinese legal judgment is such a different genre that many judges have to learn it afresh. Since 1999, Hong Kong judges have regularly attended summer courses on Chinese judgment writing held at the prominent Tsinghua University in Beijing.[15] But the most time-consuming aspect of writing judgments in Chinese is the work required to translate quotes from previous judgments and established legal reference books, all without exception in English, into Chinese. Counsel said that translating a couple of pages from a reference book such as *Chitty on Contracts* may take days of work. To get around translating quotes from English precedents, some judges simply directly quote in English in the middle of their judgments, which has now become a common practice in Hong Kong–style Chinese judgments.

Despite individual efforts, written Chinese plays an all but negligible role in the panoply of legal texts that make up the body of Hong Kong case law. Much more so than in other legal systems, the body of the common law, or as jurists might regard it, the body of writings that provide authority for and bear witness to what the common law can be said to be, is made up of past decisions of the courts.[16] Most of the judgments above the level of the magistrates' courts are still delivered in English. Since its inception in 1997, the Court of Final Appeal delivered 962 judgments in the first decade of its existence (1997–2006). All these judgments were handed down in English. Only 39 of them (i.e., about 4 percent) have so far been translated into Chinese (Hong Kong Judiciary 2003, 2007a). More depressing is the fact that the pace of translating important judgments into Chinese has in fact slowed down in recent years. Of the meager 39 judgments with Chinese translations, 37 of them were produced between 1997 and 2002. Recently, the rate of translating judgments handed down in the Court of Final Appeal into Chinese declined precipitously, almost coming to a halt; from 2002 to 2006, only 2 more Court of Final Appeal judgments have been translated into Chinese. It seems that the early effort to establish a Chinese corpus of case law has mostly fizzled out.

The judiciary has apparently given up on the idea of building a Chinese corpus of law (on the other hand, the few more important Chinese judgments have been translated into English). Lawyers and judges believe that it is impracticable to translate a substantial amount, let alone all, of the existing English judgments into Chinese.[17]

If we take a look at the judgments handed down by the Court of Appeal, the next highest court within the jurisdiction of Hong Kong, important judgments that were later appropriated as precedents on substantive areas of law are almost without exception delivered in English. Chinese judgments are considered by many counsel I interviewed to be unimportant in terms of their reference value. This is not just because judges in general prefer to deliver their judgments in English, but also because important cases where parties employ the services of top counsel tend to be conducted in English. When given a choice of language, judges often prefer to write their judgments in English. Besides the relative ease of writing in English, judges also know that the potential reference value of a particular judgment is much higher in English than it is in Chinese, all other things being equal. The lack of precedent-setting Chinese judgments means that lawyers in general do not think it is necessary to refer to Chinese casebooks, even if they existed, on different substantive areas of law.[18] The likelihood of the more lasting influence that the English medium offers means that when Chinese is chosen by bilingual judges, it is often out of practical necessity, as in cases when either or both parties are unrepresented. Because litigants in person without exception argue for themselves in Cantonese in court, judges are virtually left with no choice but to write Chinese judgments for the convenience of unrepresented litigants. This is especially the case in the Court of Appeal, where judgments are predominantly given in English. For example, in 2004, of the 82 Chinese civil appeal decisions given out by the appellate court, all but just 5 of them (77) involved litigants without counsel. In 2005, 75 out of 87 cases involved unrepresented litigants; in 2006, the number of cases involving unrepresented litigants was 73 (out of a total of 75).[19] As mentioned earlier, cases involving litigants who represent themselves are often derided by lawyers as "garbage cases." Many of them are either dismissed as frivolous or quickly ruled against for lack of rigorous factual and legal justification. The judgments that come out of these cases are often brief in description and short in argument. Some counsel I interviewed describe Chinese judgments as "legally trivial" in general. In many cases, the judgments are no more than quick dismissals of the claims made by unrepresented litigants.

The barristers and judges I interviewed agreed that English is still the predominant choice of record, a trend that they think will remain unchanged for the foreseeable future. It is here that we can see the indelible link between English and the common law at the height of its power; even the most steadfast supporters of the Chinese language concede that there is a long way to go before a decent case law in the Chinese language can be developed. Many would simply say that it is virtually impossible to turn the legal system of Hong Kong into a truly bilingual system, because of the simple fact that the common law expressed and recorded in a language other than English is no longer the common law people recognize. Billy Cheung, the celebrated barrister who expressed concern about the use of Chinese in Chapter 7, had this to say:

English is the medium used for our legal system for the past hundred years. It also inherits from England a much longer history. We have judicial reports dating back to the fifteenth or even the fourteenth century. It is an immense body of learning which is recorded in English form. And there's no other alternative. It is impossible to translate that body of learning and reporting into another language. So that I think the first thing we must realize is that if we are to keep our legal system, as indeed we are, then it is impossible to conduct all judicial proceedings in Chinese, or in Chinese only.

That lawyers view Chinese judgments as lacking in substance and authority is further corroborated by the rarity of their appearance in law reports. Although the common law is traditionally described as *lex non scripta* (i.e., unwritten), the corpus of a common law is practically made up of reported judgments widely circulated among lawyers and judges. Proper law reporting has been established in Hong Kong since the beginning of the twentieth century (Wesley-Smith 1994). There are currently two professional general law reports in Hong Kong: the more established *Hong Kong Law Reports and Digest* and the newer *Hong Kong Cases*. Both are general law reports that report a wide range of cases in various areas of the law. Throughout the first decade of legal bilingualism, the presence of reported Chinese cases in both law reports, and the *Hong Kong Law Reports and Digest* in particular, is, if anything, symbolic. Most Chinese cases remain unreported. This is hardly surprising. As we have seen, Cantonese is openly practiced in so-called unreported courts—that is, courts whose decisions are seldom reported, such as the magistrates' courts—and to a lesser extent in the District Court. In reported courts— that is, courts whose decisions are more often reported—Cantonese is practiced but to some extent invisibly (in mixed-language trials in the Court of First Instance) or just occasionally (as in the Court of Appeal) or never (as in the Court of Final Appeal). This pattern suggests that Chinese has an ephemeral presence under the present institution of legal bilingualism; the great bulk of Chinese practices take on an oral rather than a written form. Chinese in the common law of Hong Kong, despite its substantial use in oral settings, is surprisingly secluded. It leaves little trace in the *corpus juris* of Hong Kong's common law.

The discussion so far has focused on judgments given out by the courts of Hong Kong. It is important to point out that historically, Hong Kong was heavily influenced by English case law and, to a lesser but still significant extent, the case law of such Commonwealth jurisdictions as Australia and New Zealand. Counsel in Hong Kong are accustomed to canvassing cases from other common law jurisdictions, sometimes spending more time studying overseas cases than local ones. During the colonial era, English case law and the decisions of the Privy Council (which was then the court of last resort for Hong Kong) were *binding* authorities for Hong Kong. Today, English precedents are no longer binding, but they are still considered by most judges and counsel as, in legal parlance, persuasive authority, indeed very persuasive authority. A cursory look at judgments by the Court of Appeal and the Court of Final Appeal in Hong Kong would confirm the continued influence of nonlocal authorities, particularly English authorities, after 1997. Despite the severing of formal authority, judgments from England and Wales remain highly valid. As we have seen, lawyers and judges believe that Hong Kong's common law would become unbearably thin and inward-looking if it relied only on local precedents and authorities.

Traditional jurisprudence defines the common law in terms of its ideational sources: custom and equity. But the common law today, in Hong Kong as elsewhere, has little to do with local customs and is far removed from any lay notion of equity and justice. When the lawyers I interviewed said that the common law in another language was not the same common law, they were referring to the common law as a global institution, in fact, one of the first global institutions to make inroads into different parts of the world in the heyday of English colonialism and after colonialism. The law is recognized as a hierarchically organized canon of case precedents, with the overwhelming majority of them written in English, scattered in the legal reports of different English-speaking countries and read and understood by people who share a set of more or less established interpretation techniques. As one of the earliest and still influential global institutions of knowledge, the world common law system features internal movements and transfers of knowledge within the different jurisdictions of the system. Such internal flows of intellectual expertise and personnel, by means of the citation of precedents and the physical movement of legal experts, are not random, however. Their direction is unmistakably from the center to the periphery, of which Hong Kong, a small jurisdiction by any standard, is one.

This sentiment, that only law written and reported in the language of English counts as the common law, is shared by counsel working in everyday civil trials. And the dominance of English is even more complete in other spheres of civil litigation where clients are corporations rather than individuals and legal exchanges are conducted mainly in the form of documentary examinations and exegesis of legal documents. In areas such as commercial and patent disputes, one can hardly perceive a difference in practice between the pre- and post-1997 systems when specialized counsel in these areas discuss relevant statutes, precedents, facts, and law that are deep in the English legal domain.

REDRAWING THE BOUNDARIES
OF JURIDICAL FORMALISM

An examination of how English and Chinese are used in the common law system of Hong Kong shows how the well-known fact-law distinction is carried out with a postcolonial twist. The fact-law distinction is mapped onto the Cantonese-English divide within the bilingual common law system. With the new presence of Cantonese at all levels of the legal system (except the Court of Final Appeal), boundaries between law and fact within the legal realm itself have to be drawn; that is, English-language jurisprudence has been retained in opposition to the procedures through which evidence is gathered in Cantonese. In the discursive universe of lawyers and judges, English stands to Cantonese as law to fact. This distinction reproduces the formalistic gesture that insulates the domain of law from the influences of civil society, but this time the line is drawn inside the four walls of the courtroom. It has been effected by using language to map the formalist distinction between the social and the legal onto the legal distinction of fact (Chinese) versus law (English).

As we have seen, such a "Cantonese fact, English law" division of linguistic labor is applied both horizontally and vertically within the legal system. Vertically, the presence of Cantonese exhibits a pyramidal distribution; Cantonese is used more in the lowest tier of the court hierarchy (the magistracies), where the common perception among lawyers is that cases there are about facts rather than about law (at least not in any way that Cantonese cannot handle). Cantonese is used with decreasing frequency as one moves up the court hierarchy, and it is totally absent in the Court of Final Appeal. In a parallel manner, the presence of English exhibits an inverted pyramidal distribution. English is used less frequently in the lower courts but retains its strong presence in the higher courts. Horizontally, there is a growing practice of mixed-language trials in the Court of First Instance and the District Court. Cantonese is used when witnesses are examined, but English remains the language of choice when law is debated. If the original fact-law distinction were perpetuated in Anglo-American common law to take the decisions of important questions away from juries, the newly devised distinction of English law and Cantonese fact would serve a different but related purpose of shielding the contents of the common law from the local society. What will be the long-term effect of this asymmetric legal bilingualism? How does that relate to the postcolonial development of the society of Hong Kong as a whole? I turn to these questions in Chapter 9.

CHAPTER 9

Legal Bilingualism and the
Postcolonial Dilemma

IN THIS BOOK, I have shown how juridical formalism—the set of institutionalized techniques and practices of order and certainty—became
the dominant form of practice of the common law in Hong Kong. The
formalistic character allows its practitioners to focus more on following the rules than on inquiring about the reasons behind the rules. As
a mechanism designed to resolve social disputes, juridical formalism is
distinguished by its practical techniques to extract apparently universal
statements whose truth values are detached from the context of their
making. The order of the procedures in juridical formalism gives rise to
its rational character. Historically, it was this order and certainty that
established a boundary separating West and East, English and Chinese,
modernity and tradition.

But underneath the self-sufficient, autonomous appearance of juridical
formalism in Hong Kong lies a specific social foundation that sustains its
operation. In the colonial context, the authority of juridical formalism was
derived from the historical dominance of the English language. Formalism as an institutional form thrives on a context that is carefully orchestrated to sustain a bounded, rule-following method of communicating,
understanding, and reasoning. The tacit recognition of the legal context
by the public is linguistically colored in a real sense; historically, the legal
practice is grounded in the English habitus of power in Hong Kong. Like
the common law itself, the legitimizing power of English in Hong Kong
bears a social history of its own, in particular, the English-Cantonese
diglossia that defined colonial governance in the past. The anachronistic
theme created by the English courtrooms accentuates the gap separating
interactions that happen in a courtroom and interactions on the street.
Both the rule-bound regularity and detached modulation of the English
courtrooms are unquestioned because the rules that sustain such a formal style of interaction are displaced onto the articulatory formality of

speaking English, a language that is spoken with the greatest care and seriousness in many situations in Hong Kong. It is such displacement that explains, sociologically, what lawyers would describe as the grandeur, gravity, and solemnity of the English courtrooms. In short, English establishes the mood and demeanor of what a proper law trial should be for its participants long before a given trial commences.

Specifically, the courtroom interactions excerpted in Chapters 4–6 show how the speech act of statement making, on which the generation of legal facts is based, is embedded in contrasting interaction structures in the English and Cantonese courtrooms in Hong Kong. The statement-and-reply structure of English courtrooms brings along a context that facilitates the speech act of statement making. It is through the elicitation of constative statements that the English courtrooms in Hong Kong purport to be a safe haven for dispassionate reason, impartial justice, and objective truth. Although the act of statement making is firmly anchored in the rule-oriented structure of statement and reply in English, it is mixed in with other speech acts in the looser structure of call and response in Cantonese. The use of Cantonese in cross-examination disrupts such a process of legal rearticulation. The entry of Cantonese renders juridical formalism precarious and its procedures shaky. The fact that Cantonese is used in the courtrooms means that local speech acts that do not conform to the pristine constative nature of statement making enter the courtroom through the backdoor of Cantonese. Specifically, intertextual slippages in everyday speech acts occur frequently enough today in the Cantonese courtrooms that they punch holes in the dominance of juridical formalism.

Alongside the use of Cantonese comes a different kind of facts emerging from the courtrooms: moral facts that are undigested from the standpoint of juridical formalism, in the sense that they remain alien to the machinery of legal rearticulation. The life stories told, the moral values articulated, and the hot emotions invoked in addition to the irreverent repartees and the piquant and often sarcastic comebacks are all elements that come from the outside society, which the common law system in colonial Hong Kong was mostly able to immunize itself from. Old-timers look askance at dealing with Cantonese in court. For many of them, the exuberance of Cantonese is too wild and capricious. Many of them continue to cling to English in their own practices. However, younger counsel, especially those who began their practice after the bilingual era began in 1997, are open to the use of Cantonese for cross-examination because of its crispness, directness, and quickness. But even among the younger counsel, the convenience of Cantonese is no substitute for the authority of English in the common law. Within the legal quarters of Hong Kong, legal bilingualism, in its simplest symmetric form in which Chinese would play an equal if not more important role than English (as one may intuit from reading the constitution of Hong Kong), is generally viewed as an inconvenient political decree thrust on the "naturally" English common law system.

Few lawyers and judges take the idea of Chinese common law seriously. Legal professionals generally either respond to the arrival of Chinese (Cantonese in oral form, Standard Modern Chinese in written form) with an attitude of containment (the elitists and the strategists) or resort to a practice of selective use (the white wigs and many bilingual judges). The resulting institutional adaptation is a unique asymmetric division of labor between English and Chinese within the bilingual system. Judges and counsel map the use of Chinese and English onto the conventional fact-law distinction, fissuring within the legal space a Chinese domain of facts and an English domain of law. In Chapter 8, I described in detail how the "Chinese facts, English law" formula is carried out. The trend now is that Cantonese is increasingly used as a front-end language in the lower tiers of the Hong Kong courts. English, on the other hand, is not replaced but instead resides higher up in the court hierarchy to become the dominant language of back-end operations, that is, those operations that are considered by professionals as highly legalistic and hence complex in nature. This trend is reflected in the official statistics on English and Chinese cases across different levels of the courts (see Figure 4). At the level of appellate courts (Court of Appeal and Court of Final Appeal), English remains dominant and shows no sign of waning.

For social, political, and ideological reasons, English remains the dominant language of the laws of Hong Kong (both in case law and in statutes). Chinese, despite its regular appearance in the court system (especially in the magistrates' courts), is confined to the ephemeral realm of orality and is continually shunned in the textual practices of the common law. In Chapters 7 and 8, I tried to show how English is valorized by the legal profession in Hong Kong as the only possible language of the common law—so much so that the common law in entirely another language is considered unthinkable. Such valorization is naturalized by institutional arrangements that entrench the common law in an English environment, both locally and globally.

ACTUAL CONSEQUENCES OF LEGAL BILINGUALISM

How will the "Chinese facts, English law" situation affect the machinery of juridical formalism in the long run? If we take the conventional view that treats language as *merely* a medium of representation through which legal facts are enunciated, then using two different languages within the same system in the judicial process should not constitute a subject for sociological inquiries. My argument aims precisely at the assumed insignificance of such a linguistic division of labor within the bilingual common law system. Even the staunchest opponents among the elitists and strategists tend to equate the Cantonese challenge with a disruption of courtroom atmosphere and order. They see it *merely* as a potential problem of disrespect, epitomized by the sudden presence of vexatious litigants. Their complaints fail to come to grips with the pivotal role of language in the constitution of legal facts. To talk about the Cantonese challenge as a problem of courtroom order trivializes the phenomenon. My perspective is to study the constitution of legal facts not *through* language but *in relation to* language. As I have been arguing throughout the book, a strict demarcation between fact and law obscures the crucial insight that juridical facts are the products of juridical construction and not vice versa. The institutional form of the common law in Hong Kong, a form I describe as juridical formalism, turns on the efficacious execution of interlocking procedural practices that propel the spiraling molding of fact and law. Legal rearticulation does not take place *after the fact*.

Still, one might say that it is plausible for judges, the primary fact finders in a legal system where the civil jury is all but dead, to discern the essential English facts from the white noise of Cantonese in the process of legal consideration. After all, it is for this reason that most of the evidential rules and restrictions, such as the so-called rule against hearsay, do not apply in civil trials in Hong Kong (and in many other Commonwealth jurisdictions for that matter). Judges are considered sophisticated enough to discern the appropriate relevance of different types of evidence. This also seems to be the premise on which the viability of the "Chinese facts, English law" formula rests. Judges, proud of their role as professional fact finders, are confident that they know how to discern the truth (and in some cases, falsity) of witness testimonies amid the white noise of Cantonese. They are confident that proper adjudication will follow once the right law is applied. So, by excluding or at least minimizing the use of Chinese in legal arguments, the integrity of the common law can be maintained. But can it?

My analysis of Cantonese court interactions suggests that the challenge of Cantonese pushes into the fabric of juridical formalism. Unlike the English-language trials, where evidence comes in the highly processed form of legal facts by means of the machinery of juridical formalism, evidence presented in the Cantonese courtrooms in some cases is bound up with the witnesses' stories, word games, and even emotional outbursts. Cantonese—blunt, rough, street-smart—spins out talk that is fast and furious, but perhaps too fast and furious to be taken seriously from the standpoint of juridical formalism. In contrast to the slow, methodical probing of English cross-examination, Cantonese cross-examination is more interactional in the true sense of the word; litigants are equipped with an ample repertoire of speech acts capable of instantaneously unleashing the social feeling and emotion previously wrapped in colonial-style courtroom English and its cultural paraphernalia. In the absence of a well-established legal register, cross-examination in Cantonese must be seen, from the standpoint of juridical formalism, as a venture that is riskier and more experimental. My analyses suggest that the communicative intentions in Cantonese speech acts go beyond the dichotomy of conveying true or false information. It is therefore not always easy to identify legal facts from the surplus of performances given by litigants. Judges and counsel often choose to ignore what is said by witnesses in their performative moments, putting it down to the flippancy of Cantonese.

But if law and facts are, and have to be, interlinked in the machinery of juridical formalism, then the driving of the Cantonese wedge between the two in the crucial process of statement making must have an effect on the outlook of the law. We have seen how in the District Court and the Court of First Instance, the main courts of the civil justice system in Hong Kong, Cantonese evidence is often bound up with the witnesses' stories, word games, and sometimes emotional outbursts. Here I want to go beyond the specific examples I have examined so far and take a broader look at the moral sentiments of the Hong Kong legal system today.

As suggested, Cantonese is now most widely practiced in the magistrates' courts. The impact of Cantonese on the legal system, if any, is likely to be more visible there. What happens there is in line with what we have seen in the Cantonese trials described in Chapter 6. Interactions are more spontaneous; witnesses and defendants are livelier, and at times, livid; courtroom order is weaker compared to the colonial era. What is particularly interesting is the changes one can see in the tone that magistrates give to their own decisions. More than a decade after 1997, magistrates in Hong Kong today, many of them local Chinese, have assumed a more moralistic tone than their predecessors in the colonial era. This is not to say that magistrates in Hong Kong today do not apply the law. They do of course justify their decisions by applying relevant law. They apparently preserve the formalist vision by ostensibly applying the law. But they layer their decisions with moral commentaries, pleadings, and sometimes requirements that together create an image of law that is noticeably different from that of the colonial past. It is noteworthy to point out that magistrates' courts in Hong Kong have historically been more formalistic than even their counterparts in England and Wales. English magistrates' courts are staffed mostly with lay magistrates rather than with professional judges, whereas permanent magistrates in Hong Kong are required to be legally qualified.[1] The idea of a bench of lay magistrates dispensing justice in accordance with local values was something long ruled out by the colonial judiciary.

Experienced counsel compare the morality tales that magistrates like to weave into their oral judgments today with the terse, aloof decisions given by magistrates in the colonial era. The contrast is day and night. Examples are plentiful: A police inspector who was convicted of drunk driving for a second time was asked by his magistrate to publicly pledge in the court that he would never drink again. Of course, a pledge, even made before the court, is not legally binding. But the defendant obliged and was lightly fined for HK$5,000 (besides having his driver's license suspended for two years).[2] Other court news stories often feature moral- ity tales in which magistrates lecture unfilial sons, come down on self- ish gambling husbands, console single mothers, sympathize with lonely octogenarians, and offer repenting young criminals encouragement. Put another way, magistrates discursively turn the litigants they judge into members of the local social categories, be it an unfilial son, a gambling husband, a single mom, a lonely elder, or a remorseful youngster. Their moral narratives cast a different glow over the judicial system. The nature of their comments suggests that some bilingual magistrates are now at the forefront of those whose business it is to reinforce the moral values of the society. Many counsel said that magistrates today have become more parental; the Chinese term used to describe judges of this kind is 父母官 [fu2 mou5 gun1], meaning a "parental judge" who is not hesitant to ar- ticulate personal ethics and morality inside the courtroom.

It is, of course, exceptionally difficult to empirically verify whether magistrates' and judges' decisions are becoming more moralistic because of what happens in Cantonese trials. After all, professional judges, whether they conduct their trials in English or in Cantonese, are well aware of the possibility of appeal and reversal by appellate court judges and of the potential for criticism by other legal professionals for failing to apply legal reasoning. But it is worthwhile to point out that, to go along with the orthodox distinction between law and fact for the moment, the so- called finding of facts is not as binding as the application of case law. The facts of a case, as lawyers would say, have to be determined on a case- by-case basis; and the trial judge is the person who is most qualified to make factual judgments. It is true that the Hong Kong appellate review system, which follows the English model, allows for a greater scope of fact reviewing than, say, the U.S. system (one main reason for this is the extensive use of the jury as fact finder in civil trials in the United States, and decisions of the jury are seldom challenged; cf. Atiyah and Summers 1987). Some factual findings, such as a trial judge's finding of negligence, can be subject to review. But other findings of fact (such as whether or not a key witness is credible) or fact-related judgments (such as the respective weights that a trial judge accords to different facts) are seldom second-guessed by appellate judges in Hong Kong, because the trial judge is the person who has the benefit of actually seeing the witness in the box.

So here is the question: If discretion with reference to factual findings indeed exists, does the infusion of Cantonese speech acts bring about different criteria for factual findings when, alongside the central machinery of testing and examining statements, witnesses are also judged by their performative persuasiveness? That is, do irreverent banter and emotional outbursts, so often seen in Cantonese trials, in fact play a role in judges' assessments of the reliability of the evidence of a witness? Again, it is difficult to gather empirical evidence to answer the question definitively. Officially, judges consider these performances irrelevant, but it is hard to tell whether these performances influence character assessment because many of the assessments take place in judges' heads.

There are two tangential observations I could make based on my observations of trials in the District Court and the Court of First Instance. First, it is commonplace among lawyers (confirmed by some counsel I interviewed) that a trial judge can much more easily justify her own decisions using some formulaic reference to the credibility, or the lack thereof, of a key witness than formally lay out the logical inconsistencies of the person's statements. Assessment of credibility is seldom challenged by appellate judges. Second, although judges in English trials take detailed longhand notes of witness testimonies, they do not seem to do the same, or at least to the same degree, in Cantonese trials. It is obviously much harder to speedily write Chinese ideographic characters than English alphabetical letters. Some bilingual judges write their notes in English even when witnesses give evidence in Chinese. Meanwhile, English trials in Hong Kong usually work to facilitate note taking, because the frequent use of interpreters in English trials slows down the pace of cross-examination and gives judges more time to write their notes.

DILEMMA OF THE COMMON LAW IN HONG KONG

Of course, as I hope I have made clear in this book, the institutional finding of legal facts and the equitable delivery of justice are two different
things. The analyses in Chapters 4 and 5 indicate that the quest for constative meanings can be manipulated to justify counsel's and the court
interpreter's domination of witnesses in courtroom interactions. The
looser format of Cantonese trials, on the other hand, might be further
developed in a direction that is more responsive to substantive justice or
equity, because of the mixture of both legal and moral facts. However,
doing so would involve a wholesale reorientation of the nature of law in
Hong Kong, a move that most legal professionals in Hong Kong consider
too radical to entertain.

The crux of the problem here is that juridical formalism as an institutional form is ill-suited to cope with the more substantive aspirations of the rule of law in its postcolonial manifestations—whether it is
the expansive rights-based discourse of law or the culturally embedded
notion of social justice. This point was implicitly confirmed by the judiciary when Chief Justice Andrew Li recently warned against the expansive use of judicial review, a most public area of law that addresses
the relationship between the state and the individual within the formalist system; Li said judicial review should confine itself to the question of
"what is legally valid and what is not, in accordance with legal norms
and principles" (Hong Kong Judiciary 2008). The sudden availability of
Cantonese by political decree is now pushing juridical formalism to its
limits, if it has not already exceeded them. Historically, colonial governance of Hong Kong depended on a highly concentrated, bounded form
of technical institutionalism of which the common law in Hong Kong
was an integral part. Situated deep in the technical heartland of the
English habitus in Hong Kong, the common law was by design formalistic and inaccessible. After all, the colonial administration was mostly
concerned with the maintenance of law and order. Thus Hong Kong
was and still is characterized by a strong degree of juridical formality
that emphasizes legal predictability, procedural uniformity, and institutional stability, a professionalized system that repeat players such as
large business firms and global corporations embrace for its by-and-large

"legal rational" nature but that lay "one shotters" find too formidable to approach. Clearly, juridical formalism was not a system designed to be responsive to social demands or to provide broad access to promote a more litigious civil society. The presence of Chinese, however, has made the formalist system suddenly much more accessible; the English barrier created by the historical diglossia in Hong Kong on the institutional level has been, at least partly, overcome. Incidentally, this has happened at a time when the rule of law has been appropriated as the banner ideal that defines Hong Kong's distinctiveness. Within the elite discourse, the rule of law is now infused with expansive meanings to accommodate political aspirations toward a more rights-based, if not democratic, governance. It is in this context that the bilingual courts and, more specifically, the civil justice system that this book examines are now forced to deal with an emerging crowd of Cantonese litigants who talk and, more important, talk back.

In the course of describing Cantonese courtrooms in Hong Kong, I have endeavored not to romanticize them. My ethnography suggests that the aspirations of this emerging crowd are different from the aspirations of the rights-based discourse enunciated by local elites. The Cantonese movement is very much a local movement, with its own values and aspirations and prejudices and biases. It is not a well-organized, cause-driven rights movement promoted by law-oriented global nongovernmental organizations (NGOs) ubiquitous in every corner of the world today. Indeed, it is surprising to see how rarely the issue of language rights is put in the spotlight by the global NGOs in Hong Kong. The emergence of Cantonese in the courts has instead been due to a concatenation of otherwise unrelated social and political causes. Certainly people have begun to more readily use the law, and they have become more litigious; but as we have seen, the quest and sometimes resentment arising from these disputes do not exactly fall within the scope of the rights-based agenda enunciated in the 2003 political demonstration.

As a domain of power relations in its own right, the Cantonese courtroom resembles a contested space where litigants negotiate their interests through their lay understanding of what the law is. Although the new voice of Cantonese appeals more substantively to the local sense of justice, it would be utopian to equate the Cantonese legal space with an ideal zone for moral discourse. The Cantonese courtroom is a contested arena in which traditional values and beliefs spurned by juridical formalism come alive again. As we saw in Chapter 6, what happens in the Cantonese courtrooms today is often an awkward mix of aspiration to legality and articulation of traditional Chinese moral beliefs; this kind of awkward mix of legality and culture, I suspect, can be found in other postcolonies as well (cf. Comaroff and Comaroff 2006). Indeed, if the banners and slogans from the 2003 rally represent the high-sounding manifesto of a new vision of the rule of law, what happens in the Cantonese courtrooms represents postcolonial-style litigiousness on the ground. More than anything, we see cultural values, embedded in a hierarchal society and manifested in the litigants' self-identification as an elder or a patriarch, come alive in the common law courtrooms whose values are supposed to enshrine the principles of classical liberalism. It is here that we see the liberal notion of individual rights being transformed on the ground into various traditional understandings of cultural entitlements.

CONCEPTUALISM OF THE LAWS IN HONG KONG

What will be the future of the bilingual common law in Hong Kong? Of course, any answer to the question is by nature speculative. But the temptation to extrapolate from the analysis offered in this book is impossible to resist. And so I am not going to resist it.

The data gathered in this book suggest that legal professionals in Hong Kong are reconciled to holding on to the status quo for as long as they can. For professionals who practice law for a living, there is much to be liked about legal formalism. First, the implementation of any developed formalist legal system, such as the common law system in present-day Hong Kong, requires a body of specialized knowledge about its languages and rules. Furthermore, cases in the common law—not just local cases but precedents from England, Australia, New Zealand, Canada, the United States, and many other common law jurisdictions—are so meticulously classified and documented that even searching for and retrieving the relevant cases requires expert knowledge. In short, a formalist common law system serves well to separate the learned from the unlearned in law. No doubt, for some legal professionals the desire to hold on to English can be related to some sort of unjustified intimidation of litigants that was once available in a colonial society. Second, besides the obvious presence of vested interests, many legal professionals are genuinely concerned that the disappearance of formalism would risk the common law falling prey to everyday unruliness. The judiciary, in its relation to a legislature and an executive that are not fully democratically elected, might also think that formalism offers some kind of respite and security. In the world of Hong Kong politics, with its constant looming sense of uncertainty about its future, formalism in law is considered the best available safeguard against substantive political interference of all forms, including political interference from China. For example, the common law doctrines of stare decisis and *lex non scripta* provide a residual yet significant degree of freedom that allows the courts to circumvent the state's use of legislative intervention to exert political control. Finally, legal formalism also is attractive to the general public of Hong Kong. Its mandatory rule-following character is often contrasted to the "rule of man" in China. The public in Hong Kong expect their government to obey the rules set out, and they themselves exhibit a high degree of voluntary compliance.

But the predictability and stability offered by this formalistic vision of law come with a price. The current formula of "Chinese fact, English law" represents a compromise reached by the judiciary and the lawyers to walk a narrow line between two competing visions of the rule of law— the highly formalistic English rule of law and the more socially embedded Chinese rule of law. It is a de facto act of institutional decoupling, albeit with a linguistic twist. The inevitable reality is that, insofar as lawyers and judges restrict the use of Chinese as a factual language, English will continue to remain the language of the law. This compromised form of legal bilingualism only entangles the law further in the web of specialized English case law, whose development has never reflected the shared experiences and changing dynamics of everyday life in Hong Kong. Chinese, more specifically, the lived experience and the practical sense that the Chinese language entails, continues to play a trivial role in the accumulation of local case law and thus has a limited input into interpreting what the common law means, let alone deciding what the common law should be, in Hong Kong. Perhaps the most profound effect created by the formalistic nature of the common law is that law in Hong Kong will continue to appear as though it is essentially abstract and conceptual. It will appear as a conceptual scheme of right and wrong, truth and falsity, not developing from the ground up but socially a priori, by which I mean that the scheme existed long before it was applied to Hong Kong. This is ironic because the common law has long been heralded precisely for its adaptability to changing needs and circumstances.

So Hong Kong's common law in its hybrid linguistic scaffolding cannot be what it is not: a proxy for democracy and hence a liberating tool in politics. As an institution originally developed to facilitate minimal integration of law and society, it is ill-suited to carry out a form of judicial activism or assertiveness to compensate for the lack of democracy in postcolonial Hong Kong, even from a liberal viewpoint that is sympathetic to such a project. It is difficult to see how any substantive form of constitutional justice, or, in other words, more politicized visions of law, can avoid conflict with the present formalism, whose recognition depends on a language that excludes public understanding and stifles the growth of a civil society.

When Chinese was officially introduced into the legal system in 1997, the great concern was that this would signal the beginning of the end of the common law in Hong Kong. Prominent counsel warned the public then that the two languages might lead to two kinds of jurisprudence—and that the common law system might be under real threat (Buddle 1997). But a full decade has passed, and jurisprudence in Chinese remains, at best, inchoate. If bilingual common law means the development of a common law system that can be debated, discussed in the terms of both English *and* Chinese, then it remains a pipe dream for such a full-fledged form of legal bilingualism to appear in Hong Kong anytime soon. Some judges I interviewed candidly admit that legal bilingualism is merely a more user-friendly way to help the local public gain access to the English-style common law system.

If there is one thing that counsel for and against the continued dominance of English agree on, it is that the common law in Hong Kong requires English to authenticate its identity. This sentiment is well reflected in a speech made by the chief justice of Hong Kong, Andrew Li, when he addressed judges and lawyers in Hong Kong at the opening ceremony of the legal year in 1998.

Administering the law in a language that the parties can understand is important. The use of Chinese in court proceedings is a complex subject and no other jurisdiction has the experience in the use of Chinese in a common law setting to help us. We have in fact built up substantial experience in the lower courts. We need to progress steadily but cautiously. The tradition of the common law has its roots in English and its literature is mostly in English. We have to ensure that the common law in its full vigour is maintained and developed, and that our jurisprudence is accessible to and respected in the international common law family.[3]

At the heart of this sentiment is the view, reflected in earlier chapters, that a Chinese common law, if it ever exists, matters little to the legitimacy of Hong Kong as a common law system in the world. For a unique and yet fragile society that is obsessed with its place in China and the world, Hong Kong is most concerned with not letting itself slip into the international legal backwaters. Here, one finds a rather poignant twist to the old adage "Justice should not only be done, but should be seen to be done." Being outwardly respectable requires a corpus of case law that is open to view, and in the common law world that requires case law to be recorded in English. The underlying message is that if a lawyer wavers in this acceptance of the hermeneutic authority of English, the legal system of Hong Kong will be disconnected from the family of common law systems. The reluctance among legal professionals in Hong Kong to use Chinese to record the law is most evident in the prevalence of the mixed-language trials, in which evidence is given orally in Cantonese but re-presented in English in judgments.[4] The hybrid trial itself emblematizes the contrasting views on English and Chinese that the legal system holds—where the transient, contingent flow of utterances is carried out in Cantonese but the immemorial words of law are reported in English. Karl Llewellyn, the famed legal realist, once remarked that the first rule of killing off a precedent is to confine it to its exact facts (1960b: 87). One might add in the context of bilingual legalism that confining the use of Chinese to mainly facts alone is a good method of making it invisible in the common law.

It is therefore no accident that the people who want a greater role for Chinese in the law of Hong Kong are also those who are psychologically prepared for, or at least open to, the possibility of seeing Hong Kong's common law give way to other forms of legal system in the future (see Chapter 7). The first decade of legal bilingualism in Hong Kong does not mean the death of English common law in Hong Kong. If anything, it means the premature death of the idea of Chinese common law. Despite the official policy of legal bilingualism, many of the lawyers I interviewed believe that a Chinese common law is an impossible project. Of course, that does not mean that the presence of Chinese has no effect on how court trials are practiced in Hong Kong. It only means that case law as a body of knowledge remains entrenched in the domain of English. Between the steady dose of morality tales in Cantonese courtrooms on the one end and the endless rows of English judgments derived from the formalist application of law on the other, we find a stunningly incoherent imagery in the status quo of the common law of Hong Kong. This suggests that the linguistic diglossia that defined the character of colonial Hong Kong is still at work today. As true today as in the past, there are two Hong Kongs—the Hong Kong of the global English metropolis and the Hong Kong of local Cantonese communities—and the two Hong Kongs coexist and work alongside each other but do not interact much.

The real question for the legal future of Hong Kong is no longer whether the common law should be conducted in English or in Chinese. The real question for the future that lawyers and judges seem to have in mind is whether the common law in the voice of English should continue or whether a different non–common law system in the voice of Chinese should be introduced in the future. One thing that can be said with certainty, if one day the law in Hong Kong is comprehensively and independently voiced in Chinese, is that it will not be voiced in Cantonese but instead in the official language of the People's Republic of China, that is, Putonghua. That Chinese law will probably not be the common law either. There is a much better chance that Putonghua will gradually replace English as the elite language (including the legal language) in Hong Kong than that Cantonese will grow to become an elite language. Some of the judges I interviewed are look forward to the pioneer role that Hong Kong can play in developing a common law–influenced hybrid system in China. But more lawyers and judges in Hong Kong today are still ambivalent toward the idea of Hong Kong's legal system being a part of Chinese law; this ambivalence stems from their eagerness and aspiration to move Hong Kong closer to the center of an emerging world power and from their reluctance to give up the isolation and protection that English is able to offer in the still grim shadow of the fragility of law in China.

Reference Matter

Methodology

THIS STUDY is based mainly on my fieldwork in Hong Kong in 2001 and 2002. From October 2001 to September 2002, I observed civil trials that took place in the Court of First Instance and in the District Court of Hong Kong. More specifically, the cases that I selected and analyzed are general (noncommercial) civil cases, that is, torts (such as personal injuries actions and libel actions), claims in equity, probate, and trust, and employment and labor claims. As mentioned in Chapter 1, these cases were ideal for my research purpose because they dealt with normative questions (such as how common standards of conduct can be established for members of a society) or with the scope of a person's responsibility as a member of society. The interaction between law and culture, if any, would be most prominently on display in these civil cases.

I observed 30 trials during the period. A typical day for a trial at the Court of First Instance begins at 10 a.m. and ends at 4 p.m. with a lunch break in between. The length of a trial varies. I have seen trials that were quickly wrapped up in a single morning, when the parties decided to settle instead of pressing on, and I have seen trials in which parties decided to pursue their case to the bitter end, which could take months or, in some extreme cases, years.

Trials were selected in the following way. First, on the eve of the day when I planned to start attending a new trial, I would go over the daily cause list issued by the Hong Kong Judiciary to identify cases that fell within my selected categories of torts and equity. When more than one case on the list fell into these categories, I gave preference to cases based on the following two criteria: (1) legal diversity and (2) judicial diversity. For the legal diversity criterion, I would pick a case that was different in legal nature or party makeup from the cases I had already heard up to that point. For example, in the early months of my fieldwork, I attended a number of personal injury cases that involved individuals suing their employers for compensation. I later made it a priority to attend other cases outside the category of personal injuries, such as probate action. For the judicial diversity criterion, I gave preference to new cases presided over by judges whom I had not previously observed. My purpose was to observe trials presided over by as many different judges (and counsel, although this was not much of a problem) as possible. I hoped that observing a number of judges would reduce the possibility of basing my analysis on the idiosyncrasies of a few individuals. In the end, I observed 15 judges and more than 50 counsel in action.

In the ideal situation, I would have attended all the cases I chose from gavel to gavel. However, because this was a one-man project (which I consider an advantage for ethnographic work and an important part of my empirical research), sometimes it was impossible for me to attend the opening or the concluding submissions (usually the first day and the last few days) of a trial. This only happened if another trial I intended to attend overlapped with the trial I was already attending (e.g., when a new trial I planned to attend began on the last day of a trial that I was already observing). However, I made it a rule for myself not to skip any days of a trial when counsel cross-examined witnesses (the most crucial part of the trial process for the purpose of my project). I might also add that, even though I attended many of the open-court sessions of the cases I selected, an open trial is only a part, albeit the most important part, of a long process of legal adjudication. Most civil trials have at least one pretrial review session, which is usually held in chambers for counsel from both sides to meet with the trial judge or a master to settle outstanding matters and tie up any loose ends. The review session might result in decisions on interlocutory applications, decisions on application for a jury trial, fixing a trial date, and so on. For more complicated trials, two or even more pretrial reviews can take place.

SITE SELECTION

All the cases I analyzed in this book were tried in either the Court of First Instance or the District Court. Both courts enjoy original jurisdiction in civil actions. The selection of these two courts as my ethnographic sites was guided by two considerations.[1] First, they are the main courts for civil cases in Hong Kong. In general, the court system in Hong Kong is a simple four-tier system. At the lowest level are the magistracies that handle mostly minor violations of the criminal laws. The next two levels, in ascending order, are the District Court and the Court of First Instance. At the top of the judicial system are the two appellate courts: the Court of Appeal and the Court of Final Appeal. The common legal categories that the courts use to classify the civil cases they handle include contractual disputes; company laws; bankruptcy; intellectual property; torts (with personal injury by far the most common subcategory); claims in equity, probate, trust, specific performance, relief against fraud or mistake; disputes involving land titles; and employees' compensation. For the cases I selected, the main difference between the jurisdictions of the Court of First Instance and the District Court lies in the amount of money involved in the legal dispute. As a middle-level court, the District Court has limited jurisdiction so far as the monetary value of a case is involved. At the time of my fieldwork, the District Court could handle a contract or tort claim that involved an amount no greater than HK$600,000 (US$77,000).[2] Cases with a larger value at stake are handled by the Court of First Instance, which enjoys unlimited jurisdiction over all civil matters. One might argue, in the name of simple comparability, that I should have focused only on cases that were heard in the Court of First Instance. At the end of the day, I decided to also include the District Court because using both courts allowed me to observe the greatest number of trails during my fieldwork. Furthermore, the judicial system of Hong Kong is not a particularly big institution by common standards; using two courts as my field sites allowed for greater variance and representativeness in terms of judicial and legal personnel.

Second, given that my research purpose was to compare Cantonese and English-language trials in Hong Kong, I believed it was the best practice to conduct my fieldwork in courts where both English and Cantonese were used extensively. That is the other major reason that the District Court and the Court of First Instance were selected as my sites. Also, for the same reason, I did not include the magistracies as a field site, despite the fact that the magistrates' courts are where Cantonese is most frequently used. Magistrates' courts in Hong Kong are primarily criminal courts, and it would have been impossible to study civil trials if I made the magistrates' courts my focus. Furthermore, because most of the summons cases in the magistrates' courts are now conducted in Cantonese, I decided that the other two courts offered a better comparative angle.

COURTROOM ETHNOGRAPHY

I took extensive notes of the trials I attended. My notes provide good outlines of the interactions of the trials that I subsequently analyzed. However, I do not know English shorthand and Chinese is a particular difficult language to write speedily (because of the ideographic characters). Together that means that my notes did not achieve the level of detail and accuracy required for my analyses. The Hong Kong Judiciary does not allow third-party tape recording of any of the proceedings in the courtrooms of Hong Kong. The Judiciary itself records all open court proceedings through its own digital recording system. Toward the end of my fieldwork in 2002, I requested and obtained permission from the Judiciary to purchase official tapes of the trial episodes that I analyzed at length. The availability of these tapes allowed me to produce accurate transcripts to back up and supplement the notes I had taken at the trials I selected. That said, I consider being able to be physically present at the trials a great strength of my project. There is a difference between being there and listening to the tapes or reading the transcripts afterward. I was able to see firsthand how actors in a trial interacted with each other, both at the trial and during tea and lunch breaks. These unobtrusive observations informed my analyses directly in Chapters 4, 5, and 6 and indirectly in the remaining chapters. I was also able to get a good sense of the actors' demeanor, gestures, and mode when they spoke in court (some of which is recorded in the transcripts given in the book); all these crucial paralinguistic details would have been missed (particularly in some of the Cantonese trials where people were in performative mode) if I had not been physically present at the scene. Initially, when I started my fieldwork in 2001, I entered the courtrooms of Hong Kong with a long checklist prepared for my analysis, including items such as speech style, body language, narrative plot, linguistic competence, assumptions, norms shared by speaker and hearer during interactions, and so on. In the end, these issues are addressed as part of my discussion on the pragmatics of juridical formalism. As a rule, except for cases where I cite directly from court judgments, pseudonyms are used to protect the identities of the individuals described in this book.

It is also important to note that, although Chinese and English are the two official languages of the court, they are not the only languages one might hear in all the courts of Hong Kong. I saw, for example, witnesses testify in German and Thai in the course of my fieldwork. The judiciary has recruited part-time interpreters of a wide range of languages, for example, Igbo, Indonesian, Sinhala, Swahili, Hausa, Twi, Tigrinya, Outer Mongolian, and Portuguese.[3]

INTERVIEWS

I interviewed many of the plaintiffs, defendants, lawyers, and presiding judges who appeared in the trials I observed. Plaintiffs and defendants were the most accessible, but they were also the ones who had the least to say when asked to compare the two languages. When asked to comment on using Cantonese or English in courts, most of them offered me terse answers. They did not have much to say even when I prompted them to elaborate. They were not reluctant to speak to me as a researcher (many had a lot to say about their opponents and what they thought the outcome should be, for example); but clearly legal language was a topic that somehow slipped their minds. Perhaps this is not too surprising given the purpose of my interviews. My interviews were not set up to collect speech samples for analysis or to serve as a laboratory to probe people about the ways they use language in courts. In the interviews, I was not interested in knowing *how* people used language or *what* they did with language. I was interested in their more systematic and conscious beliefs or ideas about using a particular language, be it Cantonese or English, in court. For most of the litigants I interviewed, however, going to court was a one-off experience. The lack of a basis for comparison (fortunate for them but a problem for my research), I believe, explains why people offered prosaic accounts of the perceived advantages or disadvantages of using Cantonese or English in court. In a way, the reticence displayed by the litigants confirms my thesis: When it comes to language, it is easier just to talk than it is to talk about talk. For the litigants I interviewed, using the language they picked is so much a foregrounded *practice* that it is beneath their own reflexive radar. When asked, most litigants said tersely that they just felt more comfortable speaking in the language they chose. I therefore do not think that my interviews with the litigants are especially useful for the purpose of addressing my research question.

The situation is different with my interviews of counsel. Most of the local barristers (with the exception of some senior counsel) already had a fair amount of experience practicing in Cantonese, not to mention English, at the time of the interviews. I use the term *barristers* because Hong Kong, following the traditional English model, has a "split profession." Barristers are lawyers who specialize in advocacy. The other group of lawyers, known as solicitors, plays a lesser role in court advocacy. Barristers in Hong Kong have the right of audience at all levels of courts in Hong Kong; solicitors, on the other hand, have the right of audience in the District Court and magistracies only.

Counsel, as I found out, had no problem articulating and explicating their reflexive assessments of English and Cantonese as legal languages. Because I was interested in how counsel evaluated the emergence of legal bilingualism and how they understood the relation between the two languages (English and Chinese) and the common law, I gave precedence to interviewing people who had experience with using both Chinese and English in courts, which in practice meant locally born, ethnic Chinese lawyers. Hence, by design, I interviewed more local counsel than expatriate counsel (from English, Australian, New Zealand, and other English-speaking jurisdictions) who did not practice in Cantonese. Locally trained Chinese barristers are also the majority group among the legal professionals in Hong Kong today; they make up more than 80 percent of the 1,000-strong bar. That said, I made an effort to interview some expatriate counsel to get a sense of their views on the policy of legal bilingualism.

Naturally not all the counsel whom I saw in courts agreed to be interviewed, but many of them did. I managed to interview about 40 barristers with a wide spectrum of experience; some were experienced counsel who had practiced for more than 20 years, and others were relatively young counsel who had practiced for only 5 or 6 years.

Besides interviewing counsel who appeared in the trials I attended, I also surveyed past issues of *Hong Kong Lawyer* (the official magazine of the Hong Kong Law Society) and the "Bar's Column" that appears in three Chinese newspapers in Hong Kong to identify lawyers who had expressed opinions on the topic of legal bilingualism. Finally, I interviewed the then chairman of the Hong Kong Bar Association, Alan Leong, and other prominent senior counsel, some of them well-known public figures in Hong Kong.

The interviews were loosely structured. The questions were mostly open-ended. These interviews represent my attempt to compile statements of reflexive assessment made by my interviewees on the nature of Chinese and English as a legal language. I asked counsel to comment on the differences, if any, between the English and Cantonese trials in areas such as atmosphere, etiquette, perceived authority, efficiency, and order. In the course of answering my questions, my interviewees talked extensively about their respective opinions of English and Chinese, what they saw as the strengths and weaknesses of the two, and the character and nature of the two languages. I found my interviews with counsel loaded with justifications of why English is better than Cantonese, and in some rare cases, vice versa.

Besides barristers who appeared in the trials I attended, I also talked to judges who agreed to be interviewed. Some of them presided over the trials I observed; others were involved in various facets of the development of legal bilingualism. As a group, judges were more reluctant to be interviewed. As with professional judges in other common law jurisdictions, they tended to be more reserved when asked about their own views on a policy that has grave consequences for their judicial practices. I eventually managed to interview eight judges (some barristers I interviewed also had the experience of serving as a recorder, that is, a temporary judge), including former chief justice Sir Ti Liang Yang and other senior incumbent judges.

Again by design, I interviewed more bilingual judges than judges who preside over English-only trials, because the bilingual judges' experience with both Chinese and English made it easier for them to make comparisons. Some of the judges I interviewed were responsible for and were therefore perhaps more enthusiastic about the policy of legal bilingualism (which was why they agreed to be interviewed in the first place) than a typical judge in Hong Kong. These judges' views on Chinese might also be more sympathetic than a typical judge's in Hong Kong. That said, if they were biased, they were biased in ways relevant to the nature of my inquiry. As I described in Chapters 7 and 8, during the interviews, even for the most sympathetic judges, Chinese was seen as performing a subordinate role in the legal system compared with English.

To make sure that my interviewees spoke candidly on the subject, I informed them that I would not use their real names. I told them that I would tape-record the interviews to ensure accuracy but that I would not do so if they were uncomfortable with having their interviews taped. In general, I do not consider legal bilingualism a topic that counsel consider so sensitive as to shy away from expressing their opinions. Some of my interviewees said that they did not mind being quoted by their real names. For the sake of consistency, however, I decided to adopt pseudonyms unless an interviewee was interviewed in his or her public or official (including former official) capacity.

Interviews ranged in length from 45 minutes to about 2 hours. With the exception of one case, all interviewees agreed to have their interviews tape-recorded. In most cases, the interviews were conducted in the chambers of counsel and the antechambers of judges. In a few cases I interviewed counsel in cafes and restaurants. The lists of questions I used for my interviews with judges and counsel are included in the following pages. I should add that the lists are only a reference; they did not become the "schedule" that I used for individual interviewees (i.e., the actual list of questions). My interviews were basically of the open-ended type; even though I had in mind the questions to be discussed, I did not have a scripted questionnaire to follow. For example, when I interviewed judges and counsel who appeared in the trials that I attended, I would often begin or end the interviews by asking them what they thought about some of the dramatis personae featured in the trials. Often, they were also curious to know what I thought about *their* trials.

Basic Questions Used in Interviews with Hong Kong Barristers

1. Personal Information
    a. Educational background?
    b. Born in Hong Kong? Years in Hong Kong?
    c. Years of practice?
    d. Field of specialty?
    e. Levels of court most frequently appear in

2. Cross-Examination and the Trial
    a. What do you want to achieve in cross-examination?
    b. Is it good to provoke a witness?
    c. What makes a good witness? What makes a lousy witness?
    d. Is there a difference between a good cross-examiner and a good debater in daily conversations?
    e. How do you gauge a person's credibility in trial? Is it coherency of the witness's testimony? The person's demeanor? Or something else?
    f. Do you think being theatrical helps or hurts in Hong Kong?
    g. Do the differences among judges' styles matter? If yes, in what ways?
    h. Do you know if you are winning/losing a case?
    i. How much contact do you have with your clients before the trial?

3. Language
    a. Have you done both English and Cantonese trials?
    b. Do you prefer to use Cantonese or English in trials?
    c. Are there any differences in presentation between an English and a Cantonese trial?
    d. Are there any differences in court etiquette?
    e. Is there any difference in atmosphere between English and Cantonese trials? Examples?
    f. Is it an advantage or a disadvantage to witnesses when they are allowed to speak in Cantonese?
    g. Do you sense a difference in the ways people interact in Cantonese and English trials?
    h. Which is more efficient as a trial language, English or Cantonese?
    i. What, for you, are the strengths and weaknesses of the two languages as a court language?

4. Bilingualism Policy
    a. Are you in support of legal bilingualism?
    b. Do you agree that litigants should be given the right to speak the language they choose?
    c. Do you think only English can be the language of the common law?
    d. Do you think that Cantonese will overtake English in the local legal sector in, say, 10 or 20 years?
    e. What about Putonghua as another alternative?
    f. Is it possible for Hong Kong to develop a decent set of Chinese case law?

5. Legal Profession
    a. Do you think it is time for barristers to get rid of their colonial costume, that is, wig and gown?
    b. What is your view on unrepresented litigants?

Basic Questions Used in Interviews with Hong Kong Judges

1. Personal Information
   a. Educational background?
   b. Born in Hong Kong? Years in Hong Kong?
   c. Years serving on the bench?
   d. Field of specialty?
2. Cross-Examination and the Trial
   a. How do you judge whether a person is telling the truth?
   b. What makes a good witness? What makes a lousy witness?
   c. What makes a good interpreter?
   d. What are the qualities of a good translation?
   e. How do you form your judgment?
3. Language
   a. Have you presided over English and Cantonese trials?
   b. Do you prefer to use Cantonese or English in trials?
   c. Are there any differences in presiding over a Cantonese trial (vis-à-vis an English trial)?
   d. Are there any differences in terms of court etiquette between Cantonese and English trials?
   e. Are there any differences in court atmosphere? Could you describe? Examples?
   f. Is it an advantage for local witnesses to be allowed to speak in Cantonese?
   g. Do you sense a difference in the ways people interact in Cantonese and English trials?
   h. Which is more efficient as a trial language, English or Cantonese?
   i. What, for you, are the strengths and weaknesses of the two languages as a court language?
4. Bilingualism Policy
   a. Are you in support of legal bilingualism?
   b. Do you agree that litigants should be given the right to speak the language they choose?
   c. Do you think only English can be the language of the common law?
   d. Do you think that Cantonese will take over English in the local legal sector in, say, 10 or 20 years?
   e. What about Putonghua (Mandarin) as another alternative?
   f. Is it possible for Hong Kong to develop a decent set of Chinese case law?

Abbreviations

CFA	Court of Final Appeal
CLR	Commonwealth Law Reports
DC	District Court (Hong Kong)
HKC	Hong Kong Cases
HKCLR	Hong Kong Criminal Law Reports
HKLJ	Hong Kong Law Journal
HKLR	Hong Kong Law Reports
HKLRD	Hong Kong Law Reports and Digest
HKLY	Hong Kong Law Yearbook
HKSAR	Hong Kong Special Administrative Region
KB	Law Reports, King's Bench Cases
LC	Legislative Council (Hong Kong)
LHK	Laws of Hong Kong
PRC	People's Republic of China
QB	Law Reports, Queen's Bench Cases
QC	Queen's Counsel
R	Regina (The Queen)
SC	Senior Counsel
SMC	Standard Modern Chinese
WLR	Weekly Law Report

Notes

CHAPTER I

1. I say "semirealistic" because most Queen's Counsel from London who come to practice in Hong Kong are men.

2. Jeremy Bentham, the famed British Utilitarian philosopher, is known for his strong opposition to all forms of natural law, that is, theories that justify law by means of moral reasoning (cf. Postema 1986).

3. Article 9 of the Basic Law, the constitution of Hong Kong, provides that "[in] addition to the Chinese language, English may also be used as an official language by the executive authorities, legislature and judiciary of the Hong Kong Special Administrative Region." The legal ban on the use of Chinese in the higher courts of Hong Kong was lifted in 1995, when the then colonial government changed the law to anticipate the bilingual requirement stipulated in the Basic Law. See Official Languages (Amendment) Ordinance of 1995. The first Chinese trial in the High Court of Hong Kong was not conducted until 1997, however.

4. I understand that it is potentially confusing for me to switch back and forth between the terms *Cantonese* and *Chinese*. The problem here is that the people I studied (and people in Hong Kong in general) do not write the way they speak, with the exception of producing verbatim court transcripts. Many of the spoken words in Cantonese have no standardized written characters. When the people of Hong Kong have to write down words, they often write in homophones. More often, people write in Standard Modern Chinese, which is by and large the written form of Putonghua (Mandarin). Hence, in the rest of this book, unless otherwise specified, I use the term *Chinese* to refer to the use of both Cantonese in oral settings and Standard Modern Chinese in written settings. I use the term *Cantonese* to refer only to the use of Cantonese in oral contexts.

5. I borrow this meaning of *revolution* from Jonathan Lear's *Love and Its Place in Nature* (1990).

6. "Jobless Man Calls Judge 'Lackey,'" *Ming Pao*, March 20, 2001 (in Chinese).

7. "Robber Throws Shoe at Judge; Ruled Contempt of Court," *Ming Pao*, March 17, 2001 (in Chinese); "Criminal Curses Judge; Three More Months in Jail," *Ming Pao*, November 9, 2001 (in Chinese).

8. W. Richard Scott, in his popular book on the topic, defines institution as "consist[ing] of cognitive, normative, and regulative structures and activities that provide stability and meaning to social behavior" (Scott 1995: 33).

9. Of course, a language is a dialect with an army and a navy, to quote the famous aphorism shared among linguists. Here, as in the rest of the book, I use the terms *language* and *dialect* in a decidedly phenomenological fashion, bracketing any intrinsic linguistic qualities that might distinguish language from dialect. In other words, I am concerned only with the way language is distinguished from dialect at the level of social discourse.

10. The colonial Official Languages Ordinance (now repealed) provided that pro-

ceedings in the Court of Appeal, the High Court (renamed the Court of First Instance after 1997), the District Court, and any other nonscheduled court had to be conducted in English. In scheduled courts—magistrates' courts, coroners' inquiries, juvenile courts, labor tribunals, and immigration tribunals—proceedings could be in either language, at the discretion of the court.

11. Many locals of course often spoke in Cantonese then, but their words were translated by court interpreters into English. In all the official records and judgments, English was the only official language. In the case of magistracies, Cantonese has been allowed to be used as a spoken language in courts since 1974; see Chapter 3.

12. Article 8 of the Basic Law, the constitution of Hong Kong, provides that the "laws previously in force in Hong Kong, that is, the common law, rules of equity, ordinances, subordinate legislation and customary law shall be maintained, except for any that contravene this Law, and subject to any amendment by the legislature of the Hong Kong Special Administrative Region." I should also add that this is in fact a rarity among British ex-colonies. English remains the sole language of the law in many other former colonies, from India and Singapore in Asia to Kenya and Nigeria in Africa, not to mention former settler colonies such as Australia and New Zealand.

13. Bourdieu refers to habitus as the dispositions and habitual behaviors embedded in the routinized structure of everyday life that are not necessarily open to reflective evaluation (Bourdieu 1977, 1984).

14. The notion of comprehensiveness can be compared to the notion of justiciability in English jurisprudence. In his recent discussion of formality, Stinchcombe (2001) also raised the importance of comprehensiveness, or what he termed "cognitive adequacy," as a crucial feature of efficient formality.

15. The particular cutoff date varied by colony. In Singapore it was 1826; in Australia, 1828; and in New Zealand, 1840. Cf. Dupont (2001).

16. *Li Chok Hung v. Li Pui Choi*, 6 HKLR 12 (1911), at 53, per C. J. Piggot, cited by D. M. E. Evans (1971).

17. According to the Confucian classic text *Li Chi* (The Book of Rites), the ceremonies for a valid customary marriage consisted of "Three Covenants and Six Rites" (Chiu 1966).

18. In 1971, with the passing of the Marriage Reform Bill, the legal distinctions that marked the dual system finally disappeared.

19. For a vivid sense of the frustration experienced by colonial judges in ascertaining the specific content of Chinese customs, see J. Macfee in *Lui Yuk Ping v. Chow To*, HKLR 515 (1962). For a more personal and dramatic account, see Coates (1968).

20. See Application of English Law Ordinance (No. 2 of 1966). See also Supreme Court Ordinance (No. 15 of 1844).

21. See *Belilios v. Ng Li-shi*, HKLR 202 (1969).

22. *Wong Yu-shi v. Wong Ying-kuen (No. 1)*, HKLR 420 (1957), 442–443, cited by Wesley-Smith (1994: 136).

23. Judicial Committee Acts of 1833 and 1844.

24. See *de Lasala v. de Lasala*, HKLR 214 (1979).

25. The Privy Council (the Judicial Committee) and the House of Lords (the Appellate or the Appeal Committee), although institutionally different, are constituted by virtually the same group of English law lords.

26. In torts, for example, the guidelines for the awarding of damages for personal injury in Hong Kong were different from the guidelines adopted in England.

27. As I pointed out earlier, the promise was written into the Basic Law (Article 8); see note 12.

28. At the time of this writing, half of the 60 seats of the Legislative Council of Hong Kong were determined by geographic direct elections; the remaining half were returned by what was considered functional constituency indirect elections, in which representatives were elected from different functional constituencies, such as education, legal, labor, agriculture and fisheries, finance, and commercial and industrial. The chief executive of Hong Kong is not elected by universal suffrage but by an 800-member electoral college known as the election committee. More than half of the members of the election committee are nominated by and come from the same functional constituencies from where half of the Legislative Council's seats are indirectly elected. There are also representatives from other "special constituencies," religious organizations, and 96 ex officio members taken from the Hong Kong Special Administrative Region government.

29. "The Long March," *Time* (Asia Edition), July 14, 2003, 162(1).

30. "Rebellion," *Economist*, July 10, 2003.

31. The Basic Law writes that the special administrative region shall enact laws "on its own" to implement Article 23, which seeks to ban acts of treason, subversion, sedition, and theft of state secrets. There were widespread fears that the bill to implement Article 23 would undermine freedom and civil liberties. The proposed bills were eventually indefinitely deferred in the face of tremendous public resistance, and at the time of this writing no new proposal had appeared on Article 23.

32. A few highly publicized events since 1997 have confirmed the impossibility of separating economic rights from political rights. For example, in 1999, the rule of law was emphasized in the controversial right of abode case, which involved migrant children from mainland China born to permanent residents of Hong Kong. At the center of the controversy was the government's decision to seek a reinterpretation of the Basic Law from China's National People Congress Standing Committee (NPCSC) to reverse a ruling by the local Court of Final Appeal on the issue. The move was criticized by local lawyers as a mockery of the rule of law and a blow to judicial independence. On June 30, 1999, in protest of the "interpretation" adopted by the NPCSC, about 650 barristers and solicitors walked in mourning dress from the High Court Building to the Court of Final Appeal Building.

33. *Laws of Hong Kong*, Cap. 241 (1964 ed.).

34. One may even disagree whether such restraints based on political considerations can be described as a manifestation of the rule of law. Ronald Dworkin, perhaps the leading jurist in liberal legal theory today, defines the rule of law as a practice that "insists that force *not be used or withheld*, no matter how useful that would be to ends in view, no matter how beneficial or noble these ends, except as licensed or required by individual rights and responsibilities flowing from past political decisions about when collective force is justified" (1986: 93, emphasis added).

35. Again, the Utilitarians did not believe that elaborate checks and balances were suitable in the colonial context (cf. Hussain 2003: 35–68).

36. In 1985, indirect elections were first introduced to the Legislative Council, the colonial law-making body. Altogether 24 members of the 57-member council were indirectly elected (12 were indirectly elected by the members of the district boards and municipal councils, and 12 by functional constituencies composed mainly of the economic and professional sectors of Hong Kong society).

37. Cf. Tai (1999: 49, esp. n. 46). For the principle of Wednesbury unreasonableness,

see *Associated Provincial Picture House Ltd. v. Wednesbury Corporation,* 1 KB 223 (1948).

38. Despite Tai's (1999: 54) loose definition of judicial review, it is clear that the total number of judicial review cases before 1990 was small.

39. According to the Letters Patent, the constitutional document of Hong Kong during the colonial era, Article XVIA stipulated that a judge could be removed from office "for inability to discharge the function of his office (whether arising from infirmity of body and mind or from other cause) or for misbehavior."

40. Cf. Her Majesty's Attorney General in and for the *United Kingdom v. South China Morning Post Ltd. and Others,* HKLR 143 (1988), cited by Tai (1999: 48).

41. In his *Introduction to the Study of the Law of the Constitution* (1898), Dicey suggests three constitutive features of the concept of the rule of law. First, individuals can be punished for a breach of the law only through the courts; second, "every man was subject to ordinary law administered by ordinary tribunals"; and third, the general principles that governed rule and rights were themselves the result of specific court decisions and their value as precedent. How to interpret Dicey's formulation of the rule of law is a huge topic in jurisprudence. Legal scholar David Dyzenhaus (2000) recently suggested an interesting interpretation that views Dicey's formulation as caught in an irresolvable tension between formalistic positivism and judicial antipositivism.

42. A survey conducted in the 1980s showed overwhelming public support for the legal system of Hong Kong in general and for the different values related to the rule of law in particular (cf. Hsu 1992: 60–95).

43. Of course, local liberals should not be blamed for turning law into politics. The Basic Law, passed by China's National People Congress as the constitution of Hong Kong, promotes, at least on paper, the rule of law with provisions protecting personal and economic rights. The Basic Law reflects China's desire to provide a legal framework with enough certainty and predictability (in the form of rights protection) for the continued operation of capitalism in Hong Kong (Ghai 1993). The problem, of course, is that it is impossible to identify just what rights are sufficient for the market economy alone.

44. See, for example, the submission paper by the Hong Kong Bar Association to the Committee on International Human Rights of the Association of the Bar of the City of New York and the Joseph R. Crowley Programme in International Human Rights of the Fordham School of Law. This paper can be found at http://www.hkba.org/whatsnew/submission-position-papers/2001/20010913.htm (accessed March 1, 2004).

45. The full text of the speech can be found at http://www.hkba.org/whatsnew/chairman-corner/speeches/2003/opening_of_legal_year-13.1.03.doc (accessed February 29, 2004).

46. *Secretary for Justice v. Ma Kwai Chun,* 1 HKLRD 539 (2006).

47. The ruling meant that Ma was enjoined from attending at court buildings. In a later meeting with an official from the Department of Justice to air her grievances, Ma happened to run into the government counsel who was involved in the injunction proceedings. When Ma attempted to engage her in conversation, the government counsel turned her back to make her way toward her office. Ma subsequently grabbed her by the hair and collar and pulled her backwards, causing her neck pain and loss of hair. Ma was later convicted of assault and sentenced to a fine of HK$500 or three days imprisonment should the fine not be paid. The Hong Kong Special Administrative Region government applied for a review of sentence, arguing that the fine was manifestly inadequate and did not reflect the gravity

of the offense. The application for review was refused by the Court of Appeal, however. See *Secretary for Justice v. Ma Kwai Chun* 5 HKC 1 (2008).

48. The Chinese subjects that Bloom tested scored poorer than their American counterparts in terms of the ability of theoretical thinking. Bloom attested this result to the Chinese lacking certain linguistic devices that are present in English and supposed to be critical in performing theoretical thinking (Bloom 1981).

CHAPTER 2

1. As Weinrib points out, legal formalism can be understood in the tradition of both natural law and positive law. For those who understand it from within the natural law tradition, law, although formal, cannot be disentangled completely from morality. This also seems to be the way Roberto Unger understands formalism in his famous critique of formalism (1983: 561). This understanding of formalism is distinguished from the "thinner" positivistic notion of formalism, which, among other things, asserts the "separability thesis" regarding the relationship between morality and law (Weinrib 1988: 949).

2. In a frequently cited passage in *Economy and Society*, Weber writes: "The disappearance of the old natural law conceptions has destroyed all possibility of providing the law with a metaphysical dignity by virtue of its immanent qualities. In the great majority of its most important provisions, it has been unmasked all too visibly, indeed, as the product or the technical means of a compromise between conflicting interests" (Weber 1978: 874–875).

3. Here, Weber's position comes close to the famous "separability thesis" (Coleman 1982: 139; Hart 1961: 263) of legal positivists, which asserts that the substantive or moral value of law, if any, cannot be a condition of its legality. In fact, if we were to use the terminology of modern-day jurisprudence to try to pigeonhole Weber, we would find that he was not just a legal positivist but an exclusive legal positivist. He believed not only that morality was irrelevant to legality but also that its presence could be considered detrimental to legality, because moral considerations would contaminate the purity of legal rationality (Coleman 2001; Dyzenhaus 2004; Waluchow 1994).

4. Weber's reluctance to consider common law as a form of formal-rational law is well known. This is the so-called England problem in Weber's story of the development of capitalism. For Weber, England is an anomaly to his general argument that the development of formal-rational law is a prerequisite for the emergence of capitalism. Yet England underwent the first major historical development of capitalism, albeit with a system of common law that Weber describes as of a "highly archaic character" (1978: 787). Weber points out that the English lawyer system maintained a system of education by apprenticeship that discouraged abstract reflection and favored practical flexibility (Weber 1978: 789, 976). He regarded the precedent system as an example of "empirical justice" that was inferior to "rational adjudication" (Weber 1978: 976). Weber also considered the jury trial and the use of lay magistrates as two additional "irrational" elements of the English system. For Weber, the formal-rational interpretation of law can be attained only through the process of legal codification; it is only through codification that law can develop into a gapless system of rules (Weber 1978: 656). Weber did not believe that the common law could develop into a similar system of rules through a different process of natural linguistic formalization. Other people—Pierre Bourdieu, for example—believe that the inductive method of case law is comparable to the self-referential system of formal rationality. Thus Bourdieu sees the rule of stare decisis (to stand by things decided) as the legal corollary of Durkheim's

precept, "Explain the social by the social"; it is another way of asserting the autonomy and specificity of legal reasoning and legal judgments (Bourdieu 1987: 832).

5. This was so even though Weber himself noticed that the notion of "fact" in the common law was highly processed: "English and American laws have developed so much more numerous and detailed rules of law than the systems of the Civil Law" (Weber 1978: 896n8).

6. 1 WLR 527 (1977).

7. *Miller v. Fenton*, 474 US 104 (1985), at 113.

8. *Lochner v. New York*, 198 US 45 (1905).

9. In Hong Kong, "grievous bodily harm" is mentioned in the Offences Against the Person Ordinance of 1997, Cap. 212, secs. 17, 19, 22, and 31.

10. One English judge commented, in the context of a tort case, that the maxim "possesses no magic qualities: nor has it any added virtue, other than that of brevity, merely because it is expressed in Latin. When used on behalf of a plaintiff it is generally a short way of saying: 'I submit that the facts and circumstances which I have proved established a prima facie case of negligence against the defendant.'" See *Roe v. Minister of Health*, 2 QB 66 (1954), per L. J. Morris.

11. The underlying idea is to see fact-finding not so much as a probing of the world out there but as an activity of "worlding" (the work of constructing and sustaining a world) itself (Pollner 1987: 7).

CHAPTER 3

1. Goffman distinguishes three aspects of a social encounter: rules of irrelevance (properties of the situation that should be considered irrelevant), realized resources (the full set of locally realizable events and roles that can be generated by the encounter), and transformation rules (inhibitory and facilitating rules that guide actors in modifying an external pattern of properties within the encounter).

2. In terms of absolute numbers, Cantonese-first, English-second bilinguals clearly outnumber English-first, Cantonese-second bilinguals. However, it is hard to gauge the proportion of the latter group among the existing English-speaking population in Hong Kong. It is clear that expatriates of high socioeconomic status generally lack the impetus to learn Cantonese systematically to make it an acquired language. Historically, the South Asian minorities living in Hong Kong were the English-speaking group who were most proficient in Cantonese. More recently, a large group of expatriates from the Philippines (approximately 170,000 in 1999; cf. Bolton 2002c: 43), who work mainly as domestic helpers in Hong Kong, use English as their working language but also pick up Cantonese, because many of them reside in their employers' homes.

3. The Executive Council, until its disbandment in 1997, had consisted only of members appointed by the colonial governor. The Executive Council never had elected members. The same was true for the Legislative Council until 1988, when indirect elections of representatives of a number of functional consistencies were allowed. In 1991, a limited number of directly elected seats were added to the legislature.

4. These elites, of course, bore little resemblance to the traditional Confucian elitist ideal of literati.

5. Received pronunciation (RP) is commonly considered the standard accent of British English. It is the standard despite the fact that only 3–5 percent of the population of England use it as their native accent. RP is the accent that is used most often in radio and television

broadcasts in England. In Britain, it is considered a regionless accent; that is, if speakers have an RP accent, their listeners cannot tell which area of Britain these speakers come from. However, RP is saliently marked for class and is associated with the upper-middle and upper classes in Britain (Trudgill and Hannah 2002: 9–16).

6. Some Hong Kong linguists have recently challenged the "monolingual myth" of Hong Kong, that is, that Hong Kong is essentially a monolingual Cantonese-speaking society (Bacon-Shone and Bolton 1998; Bolton 2002c). I very much agree that as a global metropolis, Hong Kong is more linguistically diverse than most local people perceive. In the courts of Hong Kong, for example, litigants who speak in a language that is neither English nor Chinese (e.g., French, German, Indonesian, Japanese, Nepali, Tagalog, just to name a few) occasionally appear. Others also speak Chinese dialects other than the vernacular Cantonese and the increasingly popular *Putonghua*, such as *Shanghainese*, *Foo Chow* dialect, *Amoy* dialect, and other common southern dialects that can be heard in Hong Kong (e.g., *Chiu Chow* dialect, *Haklo* dialect, *Hakka* dialect, and *Toishan* dialect) (Hong Kong Judiciary, 2004b). That said, I am of the opinion that it is fair to say that the majority, even overwhelming majority, of the population in Hong Kong today use Cantonese as their usual language.

7. A relatively small group in Hong Kong (mostly middle-class families of South Asian descent and middle- to upper-class ethnic Chinese whose parents sent them to local elite or international schools) have become what linguists describe as coordinate bilinguals; that is, they develop both languages at a young age but nevertheless associate English and Cantonese with different domains.

8. For example, in the early 1980s, the government commissioned a team of foreign experts to review the education system. The subsequent report, commonly known as the Llewellyn report, recommended that the colonial government provide more resources to Chinese-language schools and introduce a quota system to ensure that some proportion of Chinese-language secondary school graduates be admitted to higher study and the civil service. The recommendation was, not surprisingly, not taken up by the government (Lin 1997).

9. In reality, between the elitist schools that insist on teaching all subjects in English (except Chinese, Chinese literature, and Chinese history) and the so-called Band Five schools at the lowest rank that use Cantonese for teaching most subjects, many schools in the middle practice a mixed mode of instruction that features much code switching between English and Cantonese in the interactions between teachers and students (Johnson 1983, 1994; Lin 1997, 2000).

10. As pointed out by many scholars, the uniformity provided by Standard Modern Chinese is achieved at the expense of nonnative speakers of Northern Mandarin. It is more difficult for speakers of southern dialects (e.g., Cantonese) to acquire SMC than it is for speakers of northern dialects to do so. Indeed, the choice of Northern Mandarin as SMC was not without opposition when the decision was made to replace *wenyan* (cf. P. Chen 1999).

11. It goes without saying that how this colloquial English is perceived by English guardians and educators is a totally different matter.

12. The first comprehensive account of Cantonese grammar, written by two Hong Kong–based linguists, Stephen Matthews and Virginia Yip, was published in 1994 (cf. Matthews and Yip 1994).

13. The evidence is thin and inconclusive here. Pierson et al. (1980), in their survey of

secondary school students, suggested that the use of Cantonese reinforced local identity among the surveyed Hong Kong students.

14. "Report of the Working Group on the Use of Chinese in the Civil Service," cited by C. K. Lau (1995).

15. The motion in its entirety reads as follows: "That, as an excellent command and the extensive use of English is pivotal in maintaining and enhancing Hong Kong's status as an international city and centre of trade, commerce and finance, this Council urges the Government to adopt comprehensive measures to improve the standard of English as well as increase its use in Hong Kong; such measures include better training and development of local teachers of English, promoting and encouraging the learning and extensive use of English in schools, the business and professional sectors, government departments and the community" (Hong Kong Legislative Council 1999).

16. The term *foreign language* is used to highlight the fact that English in Hong Kong is not taken to be what linguists would call a first or second language (Kachru 1990; Wilkins 1972). Some linguists in Hong Kong also describe English as an *auxiliary language*, that is, something between a foreign language and a second language (Luke and Richards 1982).

17. In my recent visits to Hong Kong, I noticed an emergent phenomenon of talking in English among some middle-class parents. They deliberately use English to communicate with their children. In doing so, they turn family talks into practices of conversational English with their children.

18. Bolton and Kwok (1990) suggest that when only male respondents are considered, almost half (46.7 percent) of them picked "Hong Kong bilinguals" as their desired model of English. They went on to suggest that some Hong Kong men do wish to speak like "Hong Kong men." But other studies have suggested that the status rating of Hong Kong English was significantly lower than that of RP English (Gran 1988).

19. Government publicity stated that the campaign was meant to improve the English skills of junior staff in Hong Kong businesses, including secretaries, clerks, frontline service personnel, receptionists, and telephone operators—who collectively account for about one-third of the workforce. The campaign also gave a language-learning kit, containing a booklet and two compact discs or cassette tapes, to Hong Kong's 40,000 full-time taxi drivers. But apparently few taxi drivers are improving their English (Wong 2000).

20. The colonial government began to enact ordinances in both English and Chinese in 1989. Pre-1989 ordinances were translated into Chinese and authenticated by an appointed committee known as the Bilingual Laws Advisory Committee.

21. Securities and Futures Commission Ordinance.

22. The point here was confirmed in my interview with then chairman of the Hong Kong Bar Association, Alan Leong. Mainland legal scholars told Leong that they could not comprehend the Chinese version of many Hong Kong statutes.

23. According to then Hong Kong law draftsman Tony Yen, English text is usually first prepared because drafting instructions from the government's administration are invariably prepared in English. Also, most of the more experienced draftsmen in the government are not bilingual lawyers (Zhao 1999: 38).

24. Butterworths has published separate Halsbury's series for other common law jurisdictions, including the British colonies of Australia, India, and former Singapore.

25. According to the Official Languages Ordinance (1974), the "courts" in which Chinese could be used were the magistrates' courts, coroner's courts, juvenile courts, labor tribunals, small claims tribunals, and immigration tribunals.

CHAPTER 4

1. Katherine Fischer Taylor's (1993) study of the Palais de Justice in Second Empire Paris is an interesting study of how the architecture of the Palais reflected the ideal of the criminal justice system of the period.

2. In the terminology of American philosopher Charles Sanders Peirce, the courtroom architecture is both *iconic* (formal resemblance) and *indexical* (spatiotemporal connection) to formalism in practice.

3. The bauhinia was chosen, after much deliberation, as the official emblem for the Hong Kong SAR by a decision-making body known as the Basic Law Drafting Committee. But local critics have drawn attention to the fact that the plant is a sterile hybrid that can reproduce only by artificial propagation and that the flower is also extremely "cheap" (J. Chen 1997).

4. For a detailed empirical study of modern English courtrooms from a sociological perspective, see Rock (1993).

5. My description here basically applies to courtrooms in the High Court Building in Hong Kong. Courtrooms in the District Court are similar but not entirely the same—for example, there is no jury box and the public seating faces the judge at the back of the room.

6. Although I am not sure that this is the motive behind the design, the effect of locating the entrance on the side is that the presiding judge is less distracted by people coming and going from the courtroom. I was told by some judges that they are often not aware of who is in the public audience.

7. Among architects, the courtroom is often seen as a "sign system through which a society tries to communicate its ideal model of a relationship between judges, prosecutors, juries and others involved in judicial proceedings" (Gutman 1972: 229, cited by Greenberg 1976: 424).

8. Barristers in Hong Kong, following their English counterparts, prefer to be called counsel. The term is a bit misleading because it suggests that they act as a friend or confidant (cf. Pannick 1987: 152); in reality, barristers in Hong Kong generally maintain a strictly businesslike relationship with their clients.

9. In the District Court, the clerk's table and the counsels' row are set close to each other; judges have to rely on other means to establish social distance from everyone else in the court.

10. The Queen's Counsel is called a silk because his or her black gown is made of silk.

11. Unlike many jurisdictions, Hong Kong does not build different courtrooms for civil and criminal trials.

12. On the use of juries, the United States is in fact an exception among common law jurisdictions throughout the world (cf. Vidmar 2000).

13. The jury seats are found only in the courtrooms in the High Court Building; there are no jury trials in the District Court and the magistrates' courts.

14. In the District Court, two courtrooms share one sound lobby.

15. It seems to be an accepted practice (at least I saw it more than once during my fieldwork) for opposing counsel in the same trial to have lunch together in the lawyer canteen while their clients eat separately outside in the public canteen.

16. After much debate and delay, judges in England and Wales finally abolished the traditional wigs and gowns in the courts in October 2008 (see Dyer 2008). It would be interesting to see whether the English decision will prompt a change in the judicial attire in Hong Kong.

17. This view is, for example, advocated by Audrey Eu, a senior counsel and a popular politician in Hong Kong. See Eu (2002).

18. During the course of my fieldwork, I saw the address bestowed by some barristers to solicitors on some occasions.

19. Some barristers I saw acted in a theatrical fashion, so long as theatricality did not leave the audience with the impression that they were, in Goffman's words, "out of character" (Goffman 1959).

20. I am aware of the difficulties that historians face in discussing feudalism as a sufficiently coherent concept to be applicable to different periods and societies. All I suggest is that there are certainly titles available in Chinese that resemble the apparent meaning of the word *lordship* in English.

21. On the reasons for the use of pseudonyms, see Chapter 7.

22. Yu then suggested "politely and tactfully" to the presiding judge that the court interpreter might have inadvertently omitted the word *social* before the word *intercourse*. According to Yu, the interpreter acknowledged almost immediately that the word *social* should have been added in the first place (Yu 2002: 147).

23. Certainly, some counsel use English in a way that outsiders might take as locally unique. One example is the strong preference shown by lawyers in Hong Kong for initialisms. For example, two policemen who gave evidence for the prosecution in a criminal case would often be addressed as PW1 and PW2 in deliberations and judgments.

24. I am here loosely following the distinction made by linguist John Lyons (1995: 235), who suggests that the term *utterance* can be used either to refer to the activity of uttering or to the products of that activity. Utterances in the former sense are referred to as speech acts; utterances in the latter sense are referred to as utterance-inscriptions.

25. That is precisely the point made by linguistic anthropologists such as Bauman and Briggs (1990), Silverstein (1992), and Mertz (2007) and by philosopher Hilary Putnam in his famous article "The Meaning of Meaning" (1975).

26. In English evidence law, this is known as the Hayes test, following the English case *R. v. Hayes*, 1 WLR 234 (1977).

27. A statement of facts in the legal context, as Elizabeth Mertz points out, contains a highly determinative epistemological claim. The use of the label "facts" indexes the definitive social power entailed in the process of legal storytelling (Mertz 2007: 67).

28. In the law of evidence, this is translated into the interrelated topics of relevance, admissibility, and weight (probative force).

29. As mentioned in Chapter 1, except for cases where I cite directly from court judgments, pseudonyms are used to protect the identities of the individuals described.

30. Goffman developed the statement-and-reply concept in part as his wholesale critique of conversation analysis. It is not my intention to examine the disagreements between Goffman and conversation analysis scholars. My purpose here is simply to appropriate both the statement-and-reply sequence and the call-and-response sequence for heuristic purposes. For a defense of the conversation analysis methodology in light of the critique made by Goffman, see Schegloff (1988).

31. The witness gave her answers originally in Cantonese. In the interest of space,

I present only the English answers translated by the interpreter. I discuss in detail the problem of interpretation in Chapter 5.

32. In Hong Kong, examination, cross-examination, and reexamination constitute a three-stage process. If a counsel forgets to ask a particular question, he then must seek the judge's permission to restart his cross-examination. In the United States, the rule is less stringently applied. As Keith Evans pointed out, "The examination in most jurisdictions can continue on the basis of 'direct,' 'cross,' 're-direct,' 're-cross' and so on until everyone is content that everything has been elicited from the witness" (1983: 120).

33. As Bokhary (1975) noted, "There are occasions when one wonders if the natural reserve, so to speak, of local women, particularly young girls, causes them to testify so hesitantly of sexual offences against them that some magistrates and District Court judges form an unjustifiably dubious view of their credibility" (p. 189).

CHAPTER 5

1. The latest official figures suggest that there are 167 full-time court interpreters operating within the Hong Kong Judiciary, a figure that is comparable to the number of court interpreters in the 1990s (Hong Kong Judiciary 2007c). Regular court interpreters provide interpretation between English, Cantonese, and Putonghua (Mandarin). The Judiciary also has a pool of 395 part-time interpreters who speak various Chinese dialects and foreign languages (Hong Kong Judiciary 2004a).

2. In one of the personal injury cases I observed, a university lecturer appearing as a witness for the defendant chose to testify in Cantonese. I asked him why he preferred Cantonese; he said he wanted to be absolutely comfortable with the language he used when he testified before the judge, so he picked Cantonese, his mother tongue. Indeed, of the few Chinese whom I saw testify in English, all had gone abroad to English-speaking countries in their early adolescence, some even when they were children.

3. The court interpreter doing dockside interpretation is expected to interpret only the gist of the English conversation going on in the courtroom. Moreover, so as not to disturb the conversation between the judge and counsel, the court interpreter can only whisper the interpretation to the defendant (Lee 1994: 31). It is, of course, an open question how much a litigant can hear, not to mention understand, under such circumstances.

4. 43 Cr App Rep 90 (1958).

5. HKC 182 (1977–1979).

6. HKLY 301 (1985).

7. HKLY 284 (1988).

8. 1 HKCLR 56 (1992).

9. 4 HKC 564 (1996).

10. 104 CLR 419 (1960).

11. Chan's story is that the floor was slippery and therefore unsafe to dance on and that her former employer was in breach of an "implied term" of her contract of employment to take all necessary precautions for her safety at work, to not expose her to the risk of injury they reasonably ought to have anticipated, and to provide her with a safe place and safe training regimen. Her case against the Urban Council charges it with failure to discharge the common duty of care owed to her under section 4(2) of the Occupier's Liability Ordinance in Hong Kong, Cap. 314.

12. When I began to work as a journalist in the early 1990s, I was sent by my newspaper to the courts to cover some legal stories. One of my initial impressions was

that court interpreters played a much more active role than merely serving to bridge the language gap between Cantonese-speaking witnesses and English-speaking counsel and judges. This sense is shared by many court reporters and barristers.

13. In the literature of legal anthropology, another interesting example concerning the information required by grammatical categories found in Goldman's (1993) study of the notions of coincidence and cause among the Huli of Papua–New Guinea. Huli is a language that exhibits the property of ergativity—that is, nouns and pronouns that are the subjects of transitive verbs are grammatically marked in relation to nouns and pronouns that are intransitive subjects. In this sense, English is not an ergative language. So although Huli encodes the notions of accident and intention in its grammatical forms, English explicitly lexicalizes the notions with such words as *accidentally* or *intentionally* (Goldman 1993).

14. In the absence of explicit tense marking, temporal relations are expressed by a combination of adverbials, aspect markers, and contextual factors. For a detailed discussion, see Matthews and Yip (1994: 195–228).

15. Another obvious example is that, unless required by the presiding judge, court interpreters do not translate any utterances that are out of order, for example, occasional "pleadings" by the attending parents of a defendant who is found guilty (cf. Luk 1999: 8).

16. There is no verb agreement or case marking in Cantonese; the only coding property is position in the clause (Matthews and Yip 1994). In other words, the verb does not change form depending on the number or gender of the subject, and neither nouns nor pronouns change their form depending on whether they serve as the subject or the direct object.

17. The Latin term *amicus curiae* literally means "a friend of the court." In a legal context, it refers to someone who calls the attention of the court to some point of law or fact that would appear to have been overlooked. In Hong Kong, the amicus curiae is almost without exception a counsel appointed by the Secretary for Justice (known as the Attorney General in the colonial period) to assist the court when one party is unrepresented (without a lawyer) and the judge thinks that it serves the cause of justice to have a counsel present any points that could be made on behalf of that unrepresented party.

18. Cantonese does not make a distinction between the forms of a personal pronoun in the subjective case and the objective case.

19. Dialogic not in the formal-structural sense of taking turns but dialogic in the sense of internal to a given utterance (Bakhtin 1981; Volosinov 1986).

20. The bona fides principle is traditionally a continental legal principle. For an interesting discussion of how the principle is reinterpreted in the English common law context, see Teubner (1998).

21. Counsel in Hong Kong are cautious not to confront a court interpreter directly even if they disagree with the interpretation. It works against their advantage to alienate a court interpreter (see K. H. Ng 2009).

22. I do not know whether or not a Chinese translation of Charles's witness statement (which was in English) was provided in the document bundle; but Chan, who finished high school in Hong Kong, knows enough English to read the comments in English, especially comments offered by one ballerina to another, given that Chan is familiar with the terms of ballet dancing.

23. A female solicitor from Smith's side did approach Chan and console her when the judge eventually decided to take a break.

24. Figures released by the Judiciary Administration suggest that about 30 percent of judges at all levels of the courts cannot speak Chinese (Hong Kong Judiciary 2007c). At

the higher levels of the Court of First Instance and the Court of Appeal, the figure reaches a level of about 50 percent (Hong Kong Judiciary 2004c).

CHAPTER 6

1. Recently, in a speech given at an international conference of chief justices in Asia and the Pacific, Chief Justice Andrew Li used the opportunity to emphasize that the common law system in Hong Kong has continued to develop and thrive since the territory's return to China (Hong Kong Judiciary 2007b).

2. I use "direct" in much the same sense as quantitative variable-based analyses uses it in the term "direct effect"—that is, an effect not mediated by any intervening variable. In an important sense, the effect of the presence of court interpreters in the English-language trials is caused by the use of English, for it is because of the elite status of English in Hong Kong that many lay litigants need to testify through an interpreter.

3. The judiciary and the legal sector in general have a visibly different demographic makeup. At the time of writing, about 35 percent of judges at all levels of the Hong Kong courts could not speak Chinese (and there is a sizable population, some estimate 20 percent, of expatriate barristers and solicitors practicing in Hong Kong).

4. This is understandable because there was no separation of powers in Imperial China; a judge was also an official sent by the central government.

5. Most of the trials I attended were civil trials. I did attend a few criminal trials at different levels of the court hierarchy just to get a sense of criminal trial proceedings.

6. Other judges adopt an opposite, laissez-faire approach, hoping that litigants will become more cooperative once they settle down. That approach seems to work better than the disciplinarian approach.

7. Deictic or indexical expressions are expressions that depend on the context of an utterance for their meanings. For example, the deictic *tomorrow* refers to the next day after the day when the utterance is made. By the same token, words such as *this* and *that* are deictic; the contrast between them is measured in terms of nearness to or distance from the speaker. Indeed, tense and demonstratives are both deictic categories that allow the speaker to locate events described in times and places remote from the here and now of the utterance itself (cf. Lyons 1995; Kearns 2000).

8. Legal professionals in the United States also react in similar ways to the performance of trouble-making litigants, as reported by Greenhouse et al.'s (1994: 140) study of courtroom interaction in three American towns.

9. On July 1, 1898, the New Territories were leased by China to Britain for 99 years by the Convention of Peking. Special rights were given to male indigenous residents to honor their tradition and customs, the most important of which is the right enjoyed by male indigenous residents to build and inherit "small house" (*dingwu* in Putonghua; ding1 uk1 in Cantonese) in their villages.

10. This particular fact was not mentioned in the judge's decision. It was, however, raised in the trial that I observed. The mother of the extended family, who was said to have a soft spot for the eldest son, died a few years before the trial began.

11. In "Replies and Responses," Goffman famously comes up with many different responses to the question "What time do you have?" (1981: 68–70).

12. Even the overlapping areas are mostly newfangled phenomena; for example, within the government's bureaucracy, English and Cantonese did not begin to coexist until the early 1970s.

13. William O'Barr (1982: 32), in his survey of widely used trial practice manuals in the United States in the 1970s, concluded that the writers of these manuals often view angry, antagonistic witnesses as less convincing. Legal professionals in Hong Kong whom I interviewed seem to hold similar views.

14. Clearly, the label "emotional" itself is political. It indicates an out-of-place quality from the standpoint of someone who uses the label. As Susan Bandes writes, "Emotion tends to seem like part of the landscape when it's familiar, and to become more visible when it's unexpected" (1999: 11). In the context of the United States, scholars such as Greenhouse et al. (1994), Merry (1990), and Yngvesson (1993) have written extensively on how emotionally stirring performances often secured for litigants a reputation of being "crazy" or "unreliable" among court regulars in the United States.

CHAPTER 7

1. This point was confirmed in my interview with the registrar of the High Court, Christopher Chan. One noticeable exception is the much-publicized case of *Re Cheng Kai Nam, Gary* 1 HKC 41 (2002), when a well-known politician challenged the court's decision to assign a judge who spoke only English to hear his case.

2. According to the figures released by the Hong Kong Bar Association, as of March 2007, there were 993 practicing counsel in Hong Kong (78 senior counsel and 915 junior counsel) (http://www.hkba.org/the-bar/aboutus/index.html, retrieved May 1, 2007).

3. Some of them subsequently mentioned to me that they did not mind being quoted by their real names. However, I decided to adopt pseudonyms unless the interviewee was interviewed in his or her public or official (including former official) capacity.

4. Among linguistic anthropologists, these reflexive discourses are often known as metapragmatic discourses.

5. Of course, even presenting the views of the bar in a four-group format is inevitably stereotypical. There are, for example, counsel with elitist backgrounds who do not hold a typical elitist attitude; and there are white wigs who side with the views of the strategists.

6. Before this first generation of locally trained lawyers, anyone who studied law in the 1950s and the 1960s almost without exception obtained his or her law degree in England. Studying abroad then was not a realistic option available to most locals in Hong Kong. Hence people who became lawyers in Hong Kong in the 1950s and the 1960s mostly came from wealthy and pedigreed families.

7. A century ago, classical Chinese was abandoned because of its inadequacy for contemporary Chinese society. It was criticized by Republican intellectuals such as Chen Dushou and Hu Xi for its literature that was separated from life, for being an elite language that walled off ideas that ordinary languages could communicate simply (Levenson 1968: 127). Ironically, the reasons offered by counsel for holding on to courtroom English are precisely the same reasons that classical Chinese was abandoned by Republican intellectuals—the language in question isolates its subject matter from everyday life.

8. In England, for example, longtime legal journalist Marcel Berlins of the *Guardian* commented in his column: "Why are appeal court judges known as Lord or Lady Justice when they aren't peers at all? Why are mere high court judges addressed as My Lord or My Lady when they're even further away from a peerage than appeal judges? Why do we still use the ridiculous 14th-century title master of the rolls (once translated by a bemused French judge introducing an incumbent of the job as 'le maître des petits pains'). Why do we

still say Mr. or Mrs. Justice when almost every other English-speaking country manages, without affronting its dignity, to refer to them as Justice or Judge?" (Berlins 2003).

9. But the view that English is the natural language of the common law is nevertheless a rather recent invention. Even a cursory reading of the history of the English law shows that both French and before it Latin were once thought to be the natural language of the law (Mellinkoff 1963). As late as the eighteenth century, the celebrated English barrister Roger North could say that "the law is scarce expressible properly in English, and when it is done, it must be *Françoise*, or very uncouth" (North 1824; cited by Mellinkoff 1963: 125).

10. There are often reports in newspapers about disgruntled litigants sentenced to imprisonment because of open contempt of court. See, for example, "Worker Who Cursed Judges Sentenced Two Months in Jail," *Apple Daily*, July 19, 2006 (in Chinese).

11. When I was a reporter, I occasionally covered the courts in the early 1990s. I recall that already in the newspapers there were reports of angry litigants confronting judges; most of those incidents took place in the magistrates' courts, where Cantonese was already allowed.

12. "Worker Who Cursed Judges Sentenced Two Months in Jail," *Apple Daily*, July 19, 2006 (in Chinese).

13. The brand-new wigs of young counsel are generally shinier and whiter than the wigs of the so-called old hacks.

14. It is somewhat misleading to describe the non-Chinese judges in Hong Kong as monolingual; some of them, in their private lives, are bi- or multilingual. For the purpose of the law, however, they are not able to conduct judicial business in Chinese.

15. Not all ethnic Chinese judges are bilingual (some grew up and were educated abroad), but virtually all bilingual judges are ethnic Chinese.

CHAPTER 8

1. In the essay, Goffman accounts for how members of our society "do" gender. Central to his claim is that there is "an integrated body of social beliefs and practices" that allow certain innate sex differences to be articulated and put forward as a warrant for our social arrangements. Institutional reflexivity refers to the fact that "deep-seated institutional practices have the effect of transforming social situations into scenes for the performance of genderisms by both sexes, many of these performances taking a ritual form which affirms beliefs about the differential human nature of the two sexes even while indications are provided as to how behavior between the two can be expected to be intermeshed" (Goffman 1977: 325). The concept is thus used to capture the swirling spiral in the perpetual dance between institutional practices and its sponsoring ideologies. The insight here is that a lot of actual work can be done to make a self-fulfilling prophecy fulfill itself. One may find that the notion of institutional reflexivity is very much functionalistic. In many ways, it is, a point that Goffman himself acknowledges (1977: 302), but at the same time the focus on the interplay between beliefs and practices means that the path taken to fulfill a function is not structurally predetermined, molded, and shaped by the guiding ideologies involved.

2. The magistrates' courts are a unique institution in English-style court systems. They have a wide and varied jurisdiction. In Hong Kong, they are the courts where all defendants in criminal cases make their first appearance in the trial process. The magistrates' courts are involved in virtually all criminal prosecutions; the courts also hear cases concerning young people (under age 16, when constituted as the Juvenile Court). Minor offenses such

as hawking, traffic contraventions, and littering are heard in the magistrates' courts by special magistrates (Dobinson and Roebuck 2001; Heilbronn 1998).

3. Of course, being the originating court in the criminal justice system, even the most serious criminal cases have to make their "first appearance" in the magistrates' courts for arraignment, when the charges against a defendant are formally read to him.

4. For example, section 80 of the District Court Ordinance (Cap.3 36) requires that a District Court judge should give the reasons for the verdict and any sentence either orally or in writing within 21 days after the trial. But under sections 28 and 34 of the Magistrates Ordinance (Cap. 227), magistrates are required only to give minimal explanations in the minutes of the proceedings (cf. Heilbronn 1998: 253). One noticeable exception to this norm is when a party appeals a magistrate's decision (as stated in sections 105 and 113 of the Magistrates Ordinance).

5. There have been cases in which litigants appeared before the Court of Final Appeal in person and made submissions in Chinese. One well-known example here is *HKSAR v. Ng Kung Siu and Another* (3 HKLRD 907 [1999]), in which the litigant, who was prosecuted for desecrating the national flag of the People's Republic of China and the regional flag of the Hong Kong Special Administrative Region in a prodemocracy public demonstration in 1998, made a speech on liberty in Cantonese before the court.

6. This is strictly figuratively speaking. A judge in Hong Kong usually does not use a gavel to impose court order.

7. Without exception, mixed-language trials are used when the counsel and judges are bilingual and can speak and understand both English and Cantonese without the aid of interpreters. These trials switch to Cantonese when litigants give evidence; as mentioned before, many litigants in Hong Kong request the aid of an interpreter when testifying in English. Cantonese is chosen as a matter of practical convenience. From a legal point of view, there is a potential problem of accuracy. Unless one goes back to listen to the official tape recording, it is impossible to determine whether the counsel and judges "translated" the evidence correctly when they argued and summarized in English because the evidence under such an arrangement was originally given in Cantonese.

8. This is so especially after the promulgation of the Basic Law, the constitution of Hong Kong.

9. This is according to a conversation I had with a lawyer who once worked as a law drafter.

10. 3 HKC 606 (1996).

11. *HKSAR v. Tam Yuk Ha*, 2 HKC 531 (1997).

12. The way that a Chinese common law term is interpreted (i.e., it is both a symbol *and* taken as a symbol), makes it, in Peircean terminology, an *argument*. An argument, for American philosopher Charles Sanders Peirce (1998: 289–299), is the highest kind of semiotic entity, which further explains why it is theoretically impossible to misinterpret the common law in Chinese; or, more precisely, if there is a misinterpretation, the misinterpretation is not due to translating the common law from English to Chinese. The only problem here is that the same interpretative strategy also makes Chinese common law concepts parasitic upon their English counterparts (see Chapter 6).

13. *R. v. Tam Yuk Ha* later became *HKSAR v. Tam Yuk Ha* when the case was heard before the Court of Appeal after the political changeover in 1997.

14. 1 HKC 1 (1997). For a comparison of the interpretative methods used in the *Tam Yuk Ha* case and the *Chan Fung Lan* case, see Fung (1997).

15. According to the statistics released by the Hong Kong Judiciary, 5 Tsinghua University Chinese writing courses were organized between 1997 and 2003. Furthermore, 14 local Chinese writing courses have been organized internally by the Civil Service Training Development Institute and have been made available to bilingual judges (Hong Kong Judiciary 2004c).

16. This is because the common law is taken to be unwritten by authors of classic jurisprudence, such as Blackstone, who in his famous *Commentaries on the Laws of England* describes the common law as "unwritten law."

17. Furthermore, although a translated judgment in Chinese is said to have a "very high referential value," the fact remains that it does not have the same authority and legal status as the English judgment does (Hong Kong Special Administrative Region Government, Department of Justice 2003).

18. To address this problem, the Hong Kong Judiciary has entered into an agreement with a legal reference book publisher to publish a new series of Hong Kong casebooks, with the requirement that Chinese translations of excerpts from frequently cited judgments be included in these casebooks. At the time of this writing, only three titles in the series— the first on criminal law, the second on land law, and the third on employment law—had been published. Yet the Chinese translations are only excerpts; the full texts of the English judgments remain untranslated (Hong Kong Judiciary 2003).

19. The figures are based on my own counting of the judgments listed in the official judgment database of the Hong Kong Judiciary (http://www.judiciary.gov.hk/en/legal_ref/judgments.htm).

CHAPTER 9

1. Magistrates Ordinance (Cap. 227), Sections 5AA (1) and (2).

2. "Judge Asks Police Inspector Pledge Not to Drink Again," *Ming Pao*, June 6, 2008 (in Chinese).

3. Andrew Kwok Nang Li, "The Chief Justice's Address at the Opening of the Legal Year 1998." Retrieved March 15, 2007, from http://sc.info.gov.hk/TuniS/www.judiciary.gov.hk/en/other_info/speeches/legal_yr_cj.htm.

4. Indeed, a good trick question on evidence law would be to see whether a judge really can quote a witness verbatim in his judgment in a mixed-language trial—on the one hand, Chinese quotes are not supposed to exist in an English judgment, but on the other hand, can a translated quote in English be said to be "verbatim"?

APPENDIX

1. I spent a full week in two of the magistrates' courts in Hong Kong. I went there mainly to get a sense of what magistrates' courts in Hong Kong were like after 1997. I did not use cases from the magistrates' courts in this book.

2. On December 1, 2003, the civil jurisdictional limit of the District Court was increased to HK$1 million (approximately US$129,000).

3. The full text of the recruitment notice can be found at http://hkucsb.hku.hk:8080/csb/advertsys/ejob/jobdetail?id=4750&version=E, accessed March 12, 2004.

Cases Cited

Associated Provincial Picture House Ltd. v. Wednesbury Corporation, 1 KB 223 (1948)
Attorney-General v. Phung Van Toan, 1 HKCLR 56 (1992)
Belilios v. Ng Li-shi, HKLR 202 (1969)
Chan Fung Lan v. Lai Wai Chuen, 1 HKC 1 (1997)
de Lasala v. de Lasala, HKLR 214 (1979)
Gaio v. R., 104 CLR 419 (1960)
HKSAR v. Ng Kung Siu and Another, 3 HKLRD 907 (1999)
HKSAR v. Tam Yuk Ha, 3 HKC 606 (1996)
HKSAR v. Tam Yuk Ha, 2 HKC 531 (1997)
Li Chok Hung v. Li Pui Choi, 6 HKLR 12 (1911)
Lochner v. New York, 198 US 45 (1905)
Lui Yuk Ping v. Chow To, HKLR 515 (1962)
Miller v. Fenton, 474 US 104 (1985)
Paul v. Constance, 1 WLR 527 (1977)
R. v. Attard, 43 Cr App Rep 90 (1958)
R. v. Hayes, 1 WLR 234 (1977)
R. v. Ip Chiu, 1 HKC 182 (1977–1979)
R. v. Li Kin Wai, HKLY 301 (1985)
R. v. Tam Kwok Yeung, HKLY 284 (1988)
R. v. Tam Yuk Ha, 3 HKC 606 (1996)
R. v. Thakoen Gwitsa Thaporn Thongjai, 4 HKC 564 (1996)
Re Cheng Kai Nam, Gary, 1 HKC 41 (2002)
Roe v. Minister of Health, 2 QB 66 (1954)
Secretary for Justice v. Ma Kwai Chun, 1 HKLRD 539 (2006)
Secretary for Justice v. Ma Kwai Chun, 5 HKC 1 (2008)
United Kingdom v. South China Morning Post Ltd. and Others, HKLR 143 (1988)
Wong Yu-shi v. Wong Ying-kuen (No. 1), HKLR 420 (1957)

Bibliography

Abbott, Andrew. 1988. *The System of Professions: An Essay on the Division of Expert Labor*. Chicago: University of Chicago Press.

Abimbola, Kola. 2002. "Questions and Answers: The Logic of Preliminary Fact Investigation." *Journal of Law and Society* 29(4): 533–559.

Allen, Christopher. 2004. *Practical Guide to Evidence*, 3rd ed. London: Cavendish.

Allen, Ronald J., and Michael S. Pardo. 2003a. "Facts in Law and Facts of Law." *International Journal of Evidence and Proof* 7: 153–171.

———. 2003b. "The Myth of the Law-Fact Distinction." *Northwestern University Law Review* 97: 1769–1807.

Anagnost, Ann. 1997. *National Past-Times: Narrative, Representation, and Power in Modern China*. Durham, NC: Duke University Press.

Anscombe, G. E. M. 1958. "On Brute Facts." *Analysis* 18(3): 69–72.

Arendt, Hannah. 1963. *On Revolution*. London: Faber.

Atiyah, P. S. 1985. "Common Law and Statute Law." *Modern Law Review* 48(1): 1–28.

Atiyah, P. S., and Robert S. Summers. 1987. *Form and Substance in Anglo-American Law*. Oxford: Clarendon.

Atkinson, J. Maxwell, and Paul Drew. 1979. *Order in Court*. London: Macmillan.

Au, Kenneth Kim-lung. 1996. "Chinese as a Legal Language of Hong Kong in the Run-up to 1997." *Hong Kong Linguist* 16: 21–32.

Austin, J. L. 1962. *How to Do Things with Words*, 2nd ed. Cambridge, MA: Harvard University Press.

Axler, Maria, Anson Yang, and Trudy Stevens. 1998. "Current Language Attitudes of Hong Kong Chinese Adolescents and Young Adults." In *Language in Hong Kong at Century's End*, Martha C. Pennington, ed. Hong Kong: Hong Kong University Press, 329–338.

Bacon-Shone, J., and Kingsley Bolton. 1998. "Charting Multilingualism: Language Censuses and Language Surveys in Hong Kong." In *Language in Hong Kong at Century's End*, Martha C. Pennington, ed. Hong Kong: Hong Kong University Press, 43–90.

Baker, J. H. 1978. "A History of English Judges' Robes." *Costume: The Journal of the Costume Society* 12: 27–39.

Bakhtin, Mikhail M. 1981. *The Dialogic Imagination*. Austin: University of Texas Press.

Bandes, Susan, ed. 1999. *The Passions of Law*. New York: New York University Press.

Bar-Hillel, Yehoshua. 1954. "Indexical Expressions." *Mind* 63: 359–379.

Bauman, Richard, and Charles L. Briggs. 1990. "Poetics and Performance as Critical Perspectives on Language and Social Life." *Annual Review of Anthropology* 19: 59–88.

Bennett, W. Lance, and Martha S. Feldman. 1981. *Reconstructing Reality in the Courtroom: Justice and Judgment in American Culture*. New Brunswick, NJ: Rutgers University Press.

Benton, Lauren. 2002. *Law and Colonial Cultures*. Cambridge, UK: Cambridge University Press.

Berk-Seligson, Susan. 1990. *The Bilingual Courtroom: Court Interpreters in the Judicial Process*. Chicago: University of Chicago Press.

Berlins, Marcel. 2003. "Let's Drop the Lords and Ladies." *Guardian*, September 30. Retrieved June 16, 2008, http://www.guardian.co.uk/world/2003/sep/30/law.theguardian.

Blommaert, Jan. 2001. "Context Is/As Critique." *Critique of Anthropology* 21(1): 13–32.

Bloom, Alfred H. 1981. *The Linguistic Shaping of Thought: A Study in the Impact of Language on Thinking in China and the West*. Hillsdale, NJ: Erlbaum.

Blumberg, Abraham S. 1967. "The Practice of Law as a Confidence Game." *Law and Society Review* 1(2): 15–40.

Blum-Kulka, Shoshana. 1986. "Shifts in Cohesion and Coherence in Translation." In *Interlingual and Intercultural Communication: Discourse and Cognition in Translation and Second Language Acquisition Studies*, Juliane House and Shoshana Blum-Kulka, eds. Tubingen, Germany: Gunter Narr, 17–35.

Bodde, Derk, and Clarence Morris. 1967. *Law in Imperial China*. Cambridge, MA: Harvard University Press.

Bokhary, Kemal. 1975. "Judicial Notice and Other Facts of Life in Hong Kong." *Hong Kong Law Journal* 5(2): 178–191.

Bolton, Kingsley. 2002a. "Chinese Englishes: From Canton Jargon to Global English." *World Englishes* 21(2): 181–199.

———. 2002b. "Hong Kong English: Autonomy and Creativity." In *Hong Kong English: Autonomy and Creativity*, Kingsley Bolton, ed. Hong Kong: Hong Kong University Press, 1–25.

———. 2002c. "The Sociolinguistics of Hong Kong and the Space for Hong Kong English." In *Hong Kong English: Autonomy and Creativity*, Kingsley Bolton, ed. Hong Kong: Hong Kong University Press, 29–55.

Bolton, Kingsley, and Helen Kwok. 1990. "The Dynamics of the Hong Kong Accent: Social Identity and Sociolinguistic Description." *Journal of Asian Pacific Communication* 1: 147–172.

Bourdieu, Pierre. 1977. *Outline of a Theory of Practice*. New York: Cambridge University Press.

———. 1984. *Distinction: A Social Critique of the Judgment of Taste*. Cambridge, MA: Harvard University Press.

———. 1987. "The Force of Law: Toward a Sociology of the Juridical Field." *Hastings Law Journal* 38: 814–853.

———. 1991. *Language and Symbolic Power*. Cambridge, MA: Harvard University Press.

Brown, Gillian. 1982. "The Spoken Language." In *Linguistics and the Teacher*, R. Carter, ed. London: Routledge & Kegan Paul, 75–87.

Brown, Gillian, and George Yule. 1983. *Discourse Analysis*. Cambridge, UK: Cambridge University Press.

Buddle, Cliff. 1997. "Rapid Changes 'Threaten' Justice." *South China Morning Post*, January 14, p. 1.

Cameron, Nigel. 1991. *An Illustrated History of Hong Kong*. Hong Kong: Oxford University Press.

Carlen, Pat. 1976. *Magistrate's Justice*. London: Robertson.

Carroll, John M. 2005. *Edge of Empires: Chinese Elites and British Colonials in Hong Kong*. Cambridge, MA: Harvard University Press.

Chanock, Martin. 1985. *Law, Custom, and Social Order: The Colonial Experience in Malawi and Zambia*. Cambridge, UK: Cambridge University Press.

Chen, Albert H. Y. 1985. "1997: The Language of the Law in Hong Kong." *Hong Kong Law Journal* 15(1): 19–47.

Chen, Jackie. 1997. "Hong Kong 1997: Deconstructing Symbols." *Sinorama*, July 1997.

Chen, Ping. 1999. *Modern Chinese: History and Sociolinguistics*. Cambridge, UK: Cambridge University Press.

Cheung, Anne S. Y. 1996. "The Paradox of Hong Kong Colonialism: Inclusion as Exclusion." *Canadian Journal of Law and Society* 11(2): 63–85.

Cheung, Eric T. M. 2000. "Bilingualism: Where Are We Heading?" In *Reform of the Civil Process in Hong Kong*, Michael Wilkinson and Janet Burton, eds. Hong Kong: Butterworths Asia, 241–252.

Cheung, Y. S. 1984. "The Uses of English and Chinese Languages in Hong Kong." *Language Learning and Communication* 3(3): 273–283.

Chiu, Vermier Y. 1966. *Marriage Laws and Customs of China*. Hong Kong: New Asia College, Chinese University of Hong Kong.

Clarke, W. S. 1990. "The Privy Council, Politics, and Precedent in the Asia-Pacific Region." *International and Comparative Law Quarterly* 39(4): 741–756.

Coates, Austin. 1968. *Myself a Mandarin: Memoirs of a Special Magistrate*. Hong Kong: Oxford University Press.

Cohn, Bernard. 1989. "Law and the Colonial State in India." In *History and Power in the Study of Law*, June Starr and Jane F. Collier, eds. Ithaca, NY: Cornell University Press, 131–152.

———. 1996. *Colonialism and Its Forms of Knowledge*. Princeton, NJ: Princeton University Press.

Coleman, Jules. 1982. "Negative and Positive Positivism." *Journal of Legal Studies* 11(1): 139–164.

———. 2001. *The Practice of Principles*. New York: Oxford University Press.

Collins, James. 1995. "Literacy and Literacies." *Annual Review of Anthropology* 24: 75–93.

Comaroff, Jean, and John L. Comaroff, eds. 2006. *Law and Disorder in the Postcolony*. Chicago: University of Chicago Press.

Conley, John M., and William M. O'Barr. 1990. *Rules Versus Relationships: The Ethnography of Legal Discourse*. Chicago: University of Chicago Press.

———. 2005. *Just Words: Law, Language and Power*, 2nd ed. Chicago: University of Chicago Press.

Cooke, Robin. 1983. "Divergences: England, Australia, and New Zealand." *New Zealand Law Journal*, 297–303.

Cottrell, Jill. 1996. Review of *The Law of Tort in Hong Kong*, by D. K. Srivastava and A. D. Tennekone. *International and Comparative Law Quarterly* 45(2): 502–503.

Cottrell, Jill, and Yash Ghai. 2001. "Between Two Systems of Law: The Judiciary in Hong Kong." In *Judicial Independence in the Age of Democracy*, Peter H. Russell and David M. O'Brien, eds. Charlottesville: University Press of Virginia, 207–232.

Crooker, Constance E. 1996. *The Art of Legal Interpretation: A Guide for Court Interpreters*. Portland, OR: Portland State University, Continuing Education Press.

Damaska, Mirjan R. 1997. *Evidence Law Adrift*. New Haven, CT: Yale University Press.

Danet, Brenda, and Bryna Bogoch. 1980. "Fixed Fight or Free-for-All? An Empirical Study of Combativeness in the Adversary System of Justice." *British Journal of Law and Society* 7(1): 36–60.

Dasgupta, Probal. 1993. *The Otherness of English: India's Auntie Tongue Syndrome*. New Delhi, India: Sage.

De Jongh, Elena M. 1992. *An Introduction to Court Interpreting*. New York: University Press of America.

Dicey, A. V. 1898. *Introduction to the Study of the Law of the Constitution*. London: Macmillan.

Dobinson, Ian, and Derek Roebuck. 2001. *Introduction to Law in the Hong Kong SAR*, 2nd ed. Hong Kong: Sweet & Maxwell Asia.

Downey, Bernard. 1976. "Editorial: Judicial Independence of Hong Kong." *Hong Kong Law Journal* 6(1): 1–2.

Drew, Paul. 1990. "Strategies in the Contest Between Lawyers and Witnesses in Court Examinations." In *Language in the Judicial Process*, Judith N. Levi and Ann Walker, eds. New York: Plenum, 39–64.

———. 1992. "Contested Evidence in Courtroom Cross-Examination: The Case of a Trial for Rape." In *Talk at Work*, Paul Drew and John Heritage, eds. Cambridge, UK: Cambridge University Press, 470–520.

Du-Babcock, Bertha. 1998. "An Analysis of Code-Switching or Mixing in Cantonese Business Meetings." In *Proceedings of the 11th European Symposium on Language for Special Purposes: LSP Identity and Interface Research, Knowledge, and Society*, Lita Lundquist, Heribert Picht, and Jacques Qvistgaard, eds. Copenhagen, Denmark: Copenhagen Business School, Faculty of Modern Languages, Center for Terminology, LSP Center, v. 2, 555–561.

Dupont, Jerry. 2001. *The Common Law Abroad: Constitutional and Legal Legacy of the British Empire*. Littleton, CO: Fred B. Rothman.

Duranti, Alessandro. 1994. *From Grammar to Politics: Linguistic Anthropology in a Western Samoan Village*. Berkeley: University of California Press.

Dworkin, Ronald. 1986. *Law's Empire*. Cambridge, MA: Belknap.

Dyer, Clare. 2008. "Judges' New Bare-Headed Designer Look Unveiled." *Guardian*, May 13. Retrieved June 16, 2008, http://www.guardian.co.uk/uk/2008/may/13/law.fashion.

Dyzenhaus, David. 2000. "Form and Substance in the Rule of Law: A Democratic Justification for Judicial Review?" In *Judicial Review and the Constitution*, Christopher Forsyth, ed. Oxford, UK: Hart, 141–172.

———. 2004. "The Genealogy of Legal Positivism." *Oxford Journal of Legal Studies* 24(1): 39–67.

Ede and Ravenscroft. 2007. "Legal: Frequently Asked Questions." Retrieved August 9, 2007, http://www.edeandravenscroft.co.uk/Legal/(e20a1k45xkztqp4503pygp45)/StaticPages/Faq.aspx.

Edlin, Douglas E., ed. 2007. *Common Law Theory*. Cambridge, UK: Cambridge University Press.

Edwards, Alicia. 1995. *The Practice of Court Interpreting*. Philadelphia: John Benjamins.

Epstein, Edward J. 1989. "China and Hong Kong: Law, Ideology, and the Future Interaction of the Legal Systems." In *The Future of the Law in Hong Kong*, Raymond Wacks, ed. Hong Kong: Oxford University Press, 37–75.

Eu, Audrey. 2002. "大律師服飾顯重任" [Barrister's Costume Manifests Solemn Responsibility]. *Apple Daily*, May 15. Retrieved December 30, 2008, http://www.audreyeu.org/public/contents/article?revision_id=13182&item_id=13181.

Evans, D. M. Emrys. 1971. "Common Law in a Chinese Setting: The Kernel or the Nut?" *Hong Kong Law Journal* 1(1): 9–32.

———. 1973. "The New Law of Succession in Hong Kong." *Hong Kong Law Journal* 3(1): 7–50.

Evans, Keith. 1983. *Advocacy at the Bar*. London: Blackstone.

———. 1998. *The Language of Advocacy*. London: Blackstone.

Evans, Stephen, and Christopher Green. 2001. "Language in Post-Colonial Hong Kong: The Roles of English and Chinese in the Public and Private Sectors." *English World-Wide* 22(2): 247–268.

Evans-Pritchard, E. E. 1976. *Witchcraft, Oracles, and Magic Among the Azande*. New York: Oxford University Press.

Ewick, Patricia, and Susan Silbey. 1998. *The Common Place of Law*. Chicago: University of Chicago Press.

Fabian, Johannes. 1986. *Language and Colonial Power*. Cambridge, UK: Cambridge University Press.

Faure, David. 2003. *Colonialism and the Hong Kong Mentality*. Occasional Papers and Monographs 150, Centre of Asian Studies, University of Hong Kong, Hong Kong.

Felstiner, William L. F., Richard L. Abel, and Austin Sarat. 1980. "The Emergence and Transformation of Disputes: Naming, Blaming, Claiming." *Law and Society Review* 15: 631–654.

Ferguson, Charles. 1959. "Diglossia." *Word* 15: 325–340.

Fishman, Joshua A. 1965. "Who Speaks What Language to Whom and When?" *La Linguistique* 2: 67–88. Reprinted in *The Bilingualism Reader*, Li Wei, ed. London: Routledge, 89–106 (2000).

———. 1972. "Bilingualism With and Without Diglossia: Diglossia With and Without Bilingualism." *Journal of Social Issues* 23(2): 29–38.

———. 1980. "Bilingualism and Biculturalism as Individual and Societal Phenomena." *Journal of Multilingual and Multicultural Development* 1: 3–17.

Fitzpatrick, Peter. 1992. *The Mythology of Modern Law*. London: Routledge.

Fung, Spring Yuen-ching. 1997. "Interpreting the Bilingual Legislation of Hong Kong." *Hong Kong Law Journal* 27(2): 206–228.

Furnivall, J. S. 1948. *Colonial Policy and Practice: A Comparative Study of Burma and Netherlands India*. Cambridge, UK: Cambridge University Press.

Gal, Susan. 1979. *Language Shift: Social Determinants of Linguistic Change in Bilingual Austria*. New York: Academic Press.

———. 1998. "Multiplicity and Contention Among Language Ideologies: A Commentary." In *Language Ideologies*, Bambi B. Schieffelin, Kathryn A. Woolard, and Paul V. Kroskrity, eds. Oxford, UK: Oxford University Press, 317–331.

Gal, Susan, and Judith T. Irvine. 1995. "The Boundaries of Languages and Disciplines: How Ideologies Construct Difference." *Social Research* 62: 967–1001.

Galanter, Marc. 1974. "Why 'the Haves' Come Out Ahead: Speculations on the Limits of Legal Change." *Law and Society Review* 9: 95–127.

Garfinkel, Harold. 1956. "Conditions of Successful Degradation Ceremonies." *American Journal of Sociology* 64: 420–424.

Ghai, Yash. 1993. "The Rule of Law and Capitalism: Reflections on the Basic Law." In *Hong Kong, China, and 1997: Essays in Legal Theory*, Raymond Wacks, ed. Hong Kong: Hong Kong University Press, 343–366.

Gibbons, John. 1987. *Code-Mixing and Code Choice: A Hong Kong Case Study*. Clevedon, UK: Multilingual Matters.

Glofcheski, Rick. 2002. *Tort Law in Hong Kong*. Hong Kong: Sweet & Maxwell Asia.

Goffman, Erving. 1959. *The Presentation of Self in Everyday Life*. New York: Doubleday, Anchor Books.

———. 1961. *Encounters*. New York: Bobbs-Merrill.

———. 1974. *Frame Analysis*. New York: Harper & Row.

———. 1977. "The Arrangement Between the Sexes." *Theory and Society* 4(3): 301–332.

———. 1981. *Forms of Talk*. Philadelphia: University of Pennsylvania Press.

Goldman, Laurence. 1993. *The Culture of Coincidence: Accident and Absolute Liability in Huli*. Oxford, UK: Clarendon.

Goodpaster, Gary. 1987. "On the Theory of American Adversary Criminal Trial." *Journal of Criminal Law and Criminology* 78: 118–153.

Goodrich, Peter. 1986. *Reading the Law*. Oxford, UK: Blackwell.

Goodwin, Charles. 1987. "Unilateral Departure." In *Talk and Social Organization*, Graham Button and John R. E. Lee, eds. Philadelphia: Multilingual Matters, 206–216.

Gran, Betty Jean. 1988. "A Study of Language Attitudes in Hong Kong: Cantonese Speakers' Response to English and Cantonese on the Telephone." Working Paper in Linguistics and Language Teaching, Language Centre, University of Hong Kong, Hong Kong.

Greenberg, Allan. 1976. "Selecting a Courtroom Design." *Judicature* 59(9): 422–428.

Greenhouse, Carol, Barbara Yngvesson, and David M. Engel. 1994. *Law and Community*. Ithaca, NY: Cornell University Press.

Grey, Thomas. 1983. "Langdell's Orthodoxy." *University of Pittsburgh Law Review* 45: 1–53.

———. 1999. "The New Formalism." Working Paper 4, Stanford Law School, Stanford, California.

Grice, H. Paul. 1975. "Logic and Conversation." In *Syntax and Semantics*, Peter Cole and Jerry L. Morgan, eds. New York: Academic Press, v. 3, 41–58.

Gutman, Robert. 1972. *People and Buildings*. New York: Basic Books.

Habermas, Jürgen. 1996. *Between Facts and Norms*. Cambridge, MA: MIT Press.

Harris, Peter. 1978. *Hong Kong: A Study of Bureaucratic Politics*. Hong Kong: Heinemann Asia.

Harrison, Godfrey, and Lydia K. H. So. 1997. "The Background to Language Change in Hong Kong." in *One Country, Two Systems, Three Languages: A Survey of Changing Language Use in Hong Kong*, Sue Wright and Helen Kelly-Holmes, eds. Philadelphia: Multilingual Matters, 8–17.

Hart, H. L. A. 1961. *The Concept of Law*. New York: Oxford University Press.

Haydon, E. S. 1962. "The Choice of Chinese Customary Law in Hong Kong." *International and Comparative Law Quarterly*. 11: 231–250.

Heilbronn, Gary N. 1998. *Criminal Procedure in Hong Kong*, 3rd ed. Hong Kong: Longman.

Heinz, John P., Robert Nelson, Rebecca Sandefur, and Edward O. Laumann. 2005. *Urban Lawyers: The New Social Structure of the Bar.* Chicago: University of Chicago Press.

Hinton, William. 1966. *Fanshen: A Documentary of Revolution in a Chinese Village.* New York: Vintage.

Hirsch, Susan. 1998. *Pronouncing and Persevering: Gender and the Discourses of Disputing in an African Islamic Court.* Chicago: University of Chicago Press.

Hohfeld, Wesley Newcomb. 1923. *Fundamental Legal Conceptions as Applied in Judicial Reasoning and Other Legal Essays.* New Haven, CT: Yale University Press.

Holm, John. 2000. *An Introduction to Pidgins and Creoles.* Cambridge, UK: Cambridge University Press.

Hon, May Sin-mi. 2001. "'No Rules' on Language at Meetings." *South China Morning Post,* November 17, p. 6.

Hong Kong Bar Association. 2000. *Hong Kong 50th Anniversary.* Hong Kong: Sweet & Maxwell Asia.

Hong Kong Government. 1971. "The Third Report of the Chinese Language Committee." Hong Kong: Government Printer.

Hong Kong Government, Attorney General's Chambers. 1986. "Discussion Paper on the Laws in Chinese." Hong Kong: Government Printer.

Hong Kong Government, Civil Service Branch. 1995. "Report on the Use of Chinese in the Civil Service." Hong Kong: Civil Service Branch, Hong Kong Government.

Hong Kong Judiciary. 1993. "Report of the Working Party on the Use of the Chinese Language in the District Court." Hong Kong: Hong Kong Judiciary.

———. 2002. "Use of Official Languages for Conducting Court Proceedings." LC Paper CB(2)415/02-03(01). Paper prepared for the Legislative Council's Panel on Administration of Justice and Legal Services, December 13, 2002. Hong Kong: Hong Kong Judiciary. Retrieved March 15, 2004, http://www.legco.gov.hk/yr02-03/english/panels/ajls/papers/aj1125cb2-415-1e.pdf.

———. 2003. "Replies to Written Questions Raised by Finance Committee Members in Examining the Estimates of Expenditure 2003–04." Hong Kong: Hong Kong Judiciary. Retrieved April 20, 2004, http://www.judiciary.gov.hk/en/other_info/fc_questions/fc_questo304.htm.

———. 2004a. *Hong Kong Judiciary Annual Report 2003.* Retrieved April 20, 2004, http://www.judiciary.gov.hk/en/publications/annu_rept_2003.htm. Hong Kong: Government Printer.

———. 2004b. "Performance of Court Interpreters." LC Paper CB(2)1592/03-04(01). Paper prepared for the Legislative Council's Panel on Administration of Justice and Legal Services, February 2004. Hong Kong: Hong Kong Judiciary. Retrieved April 21, 2004, http://legco.gov.hk/yr03-04/english/panels/ajls/papers/ajo322cb2-1592-1e.pdf.

———. 2004c. "Use of Official Languages for Conducting Court Proceedings." LC Paper CB(2) 1416/03-04(03). Paper prepared for the Legislative Council's Panel on Administration of Justice and Legal Services, February 2004. Hong Kong: Hong Kong Judiciary. Retrieved March 17, 2004, http://www.legco.gov.hk/yr03-04/english/panels/ajls/papers/ajo223cb2-1416-03-e.pdf.

———. 2007a. "Follow-up Actions Arising from Issues Discussed at Previous Meetings." LC Paper No. CB(2) 878/06-07(01). Paper prepared for the Panel on Administration of Justice and Legal Services, January 15, 2007. Hong Kong: Hong Kong Judiciary.

Retrieved March 6, 2007, http://www.legco.gov.hk/yr06-07/english/panels/ajls/papers/ ajo122cb2-878-1-e.pdf.

———. 2007b. "HK Common Law System Thriving: CJ." Retrieved June 15, 2007, http:// www3.news.gov.hk/isd/ebulletin/en/category/lawandorder/070604/html/070604en08001 .htm.

———. 2007c. "The Judiciary Administrator Replies to Written Questions Raised by Finance Committee Members in Examining the Estimates of Expenditure 2007–2008." Retrieved June 15, 2007, http://www.judiciary.gov.hk/en/other_info/fc_questions/ pdf/ja_e_0708.pdf.

———. 2008. "CJ's Speech at Conference on Effective Judicial Review: A Cornerstone of Good Governance." Retrieved December 27, 2008, http://www.info.gov.hk/gia/ general/200812/10/P200812100125.htm.

Hong Kong Legislative Council. 1999. "Official Record of Proceedings, Wednesday, 26 May 1999." *Hong Kong Hansard*, May 26. Retrieved April 10, 2004, http://www.legco.gov .hk/yr98-99/english/counmtg/hansard/990526fe.htm.

Hong Kong Special Administrative Region Government, Census and Statistics Department. 2007. *2006 Population By-Census: Summary Results*. Hong Kong: Census and Statistics Department, HKSAR Government. Retrieved January 2, 2009, http://www .bycensus2006.gov.hk/FileManager/EN/Content_962/06bc_summary_results.pdf.

Hong Kong Special Administrative Region Government, Department of Justice. 1999. "The Common Law and the Chinese Language." *Hong Kong Lawyer*, February, 39–42.

———. 2003. "Translation of Court Judgments." LC Paper CB(2) 2566/02-03(01). Paper prepared for the Legislative Council's Panel on Administration of Justice and Legal Services, June 2003. Retrieved April 20, 2004, http://www.legco.gov.hk/yr02-03/ english/panels/ajls/papers/ajo623cb2-2566-1e.pdf. Hong Kong: Department of Justice, HKSAR Government.

Hong Kong Special Administrative Region Government, Information Technology Services Department. 2004. "HKSCS Questions and Answers." Retrieved December 26, 2008, http://www.ogcio.gov.hk/ccli/eng/structure/cli_faq.html#hkscs.

Hsu, Berry Fong-Chong. 1992. *The Common Law System in Chinese Context*. New York: M. E. Sharpe.

Hung, Tony T. N. 2002. "Towards a Phonology of Hong Kong English." In *Hong Kong English: Autonomy and Creativity*, Kingsley Bolton, ed. Hong Kong: Hong Kong University Press, 119–140.

Hussain, Nasser. 2003. *The Jurisprudence of Emergency: Colonialism and the Rule of Law*. Ann Arbor: University of Michigan Press.

Hyam, Michael. 1999. *Advocacy Skills*, 4th ed. London: Blackstone.

Hymes, Dell. 1972. "On Communicative Competence." In *Sociolinguistics*, J. Pride and J. Holmes, eds. Harmondsworth: Penguin, 269–293.

Irvine, Judith T., and Susan Gal. 2000. "Language Ideology and Linguistic Differentiation." In *Regimes of Language: Ideologies, Polities, and Identities*, Paul V. Kroskrity, ed. Santa Fe, NM: School of American Research Press, 35–84.

Johnson, Robert Keith. 1983. "Bilingual Switching Strategies: A Study of the Modes of Teacher-Talk in Bilingual Secondary School Classrooms in Hong Kong." *Language Learning and Communication* 2(3): 267–283.

———. 1994. "Language Policy and Planning in Hong Kong." *Annual Review of Applied Linguistics* 14: 177–199.

Jones, Carol. 1999. "Politics Postponed: Law as a Substitute for Politics in Hong Kong and China." In *Law, Capitalism, and Power in Asia*, Kanishka Jayasuriya, ed. London: Routledge, 45–68.

Kachru, Braj B. 1990. *The Alchemy of English: The Spread, Functions, and Models of Non-Native Englishes*. Urbana: University of Illinois Press.

Kearns, Kate. 2000. *Semantics*. New York: St. Martin's Press.

Kennedy, Duncan. 2001. "Legal Formalism." In *The International Encyclopedia of the Social and Behavioral Sciences*, N. J. Smelser and P. B. Baltes, eds. New York: Elsevier, v. 13, 8634–8638.

Kronman, Anthony T. 1983. *Max Weber*. Stanford, CA: Stanford University Press.

Langbein, John H. 2003. *The Origins of Adversary Criminal Trial*. New York: Oxford University Press.

Laster, Kathy, and Veronica Taylor. 1994. *Interpreters and the Legal System*. Sydney, Australia: Federation Press.

Latour, Bruno. 2004. "Scientific Objects and Legal Objectivity." In *Law, Anthropology, and Constitution of the Social*, Alain Pottage and Martha Mundy, eds. Cambridge, UK: Cambridge University Press, 73–114.

Lau, Chi Kuen. 1995. "What Will Become of English in the Territory After 1997?" *South China Morning Post*, September 18, p. 19.

———. 1997. *Hong Kong's Colonial Legacy*. Hong Kong: Chinese University Press.

———. 2000. "Need That Begs to Be Translated into Action." *South China Morning Post*, March 26, p. 11.

Lau, Siu-kai, and Kuan Hsin-chi. 1988. *The Ethos of the Hong Kong Chinese*. Hong Kong: Chinese University Press.

Law Society of Hong Kong. 2000. "Independent Judgment" (interview with Mr. Justice Gerald Godfrey). *Hong Kong Lawyer*, August. Retrieved January 18, 2009, http://www.hk-lawyer.com/2000-8/Default.htm.

Lear, Jonathan. 1990. *Love and Its Place in Nature*. New York: Noonday Press.

Lee, Yuk Ming. 1994. "The Training of Court Interpreters in Hong Kong." Master's thesis, Department of Chinese, Translation, and Linguistics, City Polytechnic of Hong Kong, Hong Kong.

Lethbridge, Henry. 1978. *Hong Kong: Stability and Change*. Hong Kong: Hong Kong University Press.

Levenson, Joseph. 1968. *Confucian China and Its Modern Fate: A Trilogy*. Berkeley: University of California Press.

Levi, Edward. 1949. *An Introduction to Legal Reasoning*. Chicago: University of Chicago Press.

Lewis, D. J. 1983. "A Requiem for Chinese Customary Law in Hong Kong." *International and Comparative Law Quarterly* 32(2): 347–379.

Li, David C. S. 1999. "The Functions and Status of English in Hong Kong: A Post-1997 Update." *English World-Wide* 20(1): 67–110.

———. 2002. "Cantonese-English Code-Switching Research in Hong Kong: A Survey of Recent Research." In *Hong Kong English: Autonomy and Creativity*, Kingsley Bolton, ed. Hong Kong: Hong Kong University Press, 79–99.

Lin, Angel Mei Yi. 1996. "Bilingualism or Linguistic Segregation? Symbolic Domination, Resistance, and Code Switching in Hong Kong Schools." *Linguistics and Education* 8: 49–84.

———. 1997. "Bilingual Education in Hong Kong." In *Encyclopedia of Language and Education*, v. 5, *Bilingual Education*, Jim Cummins and David Corson, eds. London: Kluwer Academic, 281–289.

———. 2000. "Lively Children Trapped in an Island of Disadvantage: Verbal Play of Cantonese Working-Class Schoolboys in Hong Kong." *International Journal of the Sociology of Language* 143: 63–83.

Llewellyn, Karl. 1960a. *The Bramble Bush: On Our Law and Its Society*. New York: Oceana.

———. 1960b. *The Common Law Tradition: Deciding Appeals*. New York: Little, Brown.

Lo, Terence, and Colleen Wong. 1990. "Polyglossia in the 'Printed Cantonese' Mass Media in Hong Kong." *Journal of Asian Pacific Communication* 1(1): 27–43.

Lord, Robert. 1987. "Language Policy and Planning in Hong Kong: Past, Present, and (Especially) Future." In *Language Education in Hong Kong*, Robert Lord and Helen N. L. Cheng, eds. Hong Kong: Chinese University Press, 3–24.

Luk, Helen. 1999. "It's All a Matter of Interpretation." *South China Morning Post*, August 22, p. 8.

Luke, Kang-kwong, and Jack C. Richards. 1982. "English in Hong Kong: Status and Functions." *English World-Wide* 3(1): 47–64.

Lyczak, R., S. G. Fu, and A. Ho. 1976. "Attitudes of Hong Kong Bilinguals Toward English and Chinese Speakers." *Journal of Cross-Cultural Psychology* 7: 425–437.

Lyons, John. 1995. *Linguistic Semantics*. Cambridge, UK: Cambridge University Press.

Macauley, Melissa. 1998. *Social Power and Legal Culture: Litigation Masters in Late Imperial China*. Stanford, CA: Stanford University Press.

Mamdani, Mahmood. 1996. *Citizen and Subject: Contemporary Africa and the Legacy of Late Colonialism*. Princeton, NJ: Princeton University Press.

Martin, Robyn. 2002. Review of *Tort Law in Hong Kong*, by Rick Glofcheski. *Hong Kong Law Journal* 32(3): 727–729.

Mather, Lynn, and Barbara Yngvesson. 1980. "Language, Audience, and the Transformation of Disputes." *Law and Society Review* 15: 775–821.

Matoesian, Gregory M. 1993. *Reproducing Rape*. Chicago: University of Chicago Press.

———. 2001. *Law and the Language of Identity*. New York: Oxford University Press.

Matthews, Stephen, and Virginia Yip. 1994. *Cantonese: A Comprehensive Grammar*. London: Routledge.

Mauet, Thomas. 1996. *Trial Techniques*, 4th ed. Boston: Little, Brown.

Mellinkoff, David. 1963. *The Language of the Law*. Boston: Little, Brown.

Merry, Sally Engle. 1987. "Disputing Without Culture." *Harvard Law Review* 100: 2057–2073.

———. 1990. *Getting Justice and Getting Even*. Chicago: University of Chicago Press.

———. 1991. "Law and Colonialism." *Law and Society Review* 25: 889–922.

———. 1992. "Anthropology, Law, and Transnational Processes." *Annual Review of Anthropology* 21: 357–379.

Merryman, John Henry. 1985. *The Civil Law Tradition*, 2nd ed. Stanford, CA: Stanford University Press.

Mertz, Elizabeth. 1985. "Beyond Symbolic Anthropology: Introducing Semiotic Mediation." In *Semiotic Mediation*, Elizabeth Mertz and Richard Parmentier, eds. New York: Academic Press, 1–19.

————. 1992. "Language, Law, and Social Meaning: Linguistic/Anthropological Contributions to the Study of Law." *Law and Society Review* 26: 413–445.

————. 1994a. "Legal Language: Pragmatics, Poetics, and Social Power." *Annual Review of Anthropology* 23: 435–455.

————. 1994b. "A New Social Constructionism for Sociolegal Studies." *Law and Society Review* 28: 1243–1265.

————. 2007. *The Language of Law School: Learning to "Think Like a Lawyer."* New York: Oxford University Press.

Mills, C. Wright. 1956. *The Power Elite.* New York: Oxford University Press.

Milroy, James, and Lesley Milroy. 1999. *Authority in Language*, 3rd ed. London: Routledge.

Miners, Norman. 1975. *The Government and Politics of Hong Kong.* Hong Kong: Oxford University Press.

Mommsen, Wolfgang J. 1984. "On the Question of the Relationship Between the Formal Legality and the Rational Legitimacy of Rule in Max Weber's Works." In *Max Weber and German Politics, 1890–1920.* Chicago: University of Chicago Press, 448–453.

Morris, Ruth. 1999. "The Gum Syndrome: Predicaments in Court Interpreting." *Forensic Linguistics* 6(1): 6–29.

Murray, Peter. 1995. *Basic Trial Advocacy.* New York: Little, Brown.

Ng, Kwai Hang. 2009. "The Court Interpreters' Office." In *Introduction to Crime, Law, and Justice in Hong Kong*, Mark S. Gaylord and Harold Traver, eds. Hong Kong: Hong Kong University Press.

Ng, Tat Lun. 2000. "The Bilingual Legal System in Hong Kong: Its Past Development and the Way Forward." Master's thesis, Department of Chinese, Translation, and Linguistics, City University of Hong Kong, Hong Kong.

North, Roger. 1824. *A Discourse on the Study of the Laws.* London: Charles Baldwyn.

Norton-Kyshe, James William. 1971 [1898]. *The History of the Laws and Courts of Hong Kong*, 2 vols. Hong Kong: Vetch and Lee.

O'Barr, W. M. 1982. *Linguistic Evidence: Language, Power, and Strategy in the Courtroom.* New York: Academic Press.

Pannick, David. 1987. *Judges.* Oxford, UK: Oxford University Press.

————. 1992. *Advocates.* Oxford, UK: Oxford University Press.

Pegg, Leonard. 1975. "Chinese Marriage, Concubinage, and Divorce in Contemporary Hong Kong." *Hong Kong Law Journal* 5(1): 4–38.

Peirce, Charles Sanders. 1998. *The Essential Peirce*, v. 2, Peirce Edition Project, ed. Bloomington: Indiana University Press.

Pennington, Martha C., and Francis Yue. 1994. "English and Chinese in Hong Kong: Pre-1997 Language Attitudes." *World Englishes* 13(1): 1–20.

Pennycook, Alistair. 1998. *English and the Discourses of Colonialism.* London: Routledge.

Philips, Susan U. 1986. "Reported Speech as Evidence in an American Trial." In *Georgetown University Roundtable on Languages and Linguistics 1985*, Deborah Tannen and James E. Alatis, eds. Washington, DC: Georgetown University Press, 154–170.

————. 1992. "Evidentiary Standards for American Trials: Just the Facts." In *Responsibility and Evidence in Oral Discourse*, Jane H. Hill and Judith T. Irvine, eds. Cambridge, UK: Cambridge University Press, 248–305.

———. 1998. *Ideology in the Language of Judges: How Judges Practice Law, Politics, and Courtroom Control*. New York: Oxford University Press.

Pierson, Herbert D. 1998. "Social Accommodation to English and Putonghua in Cantonese-Speaking Hong Kong." In *Language in Hong Kong at Century's End*, Martha C. Pennington, ed. Hong Kong: Hong Kong University Press, 91–111.

Pierson, Herbert D., Gail S. Fu, and Sik-yum Lee. 1980. "An Analysis of the Relationship Between Language Attitudes and English Attainment of Secondary School Students in Hong Kong." *Language Learning* 30: 289–316.

Pildes, Richard H. 1999. "Forms of Formalism." *University of Chicago Law Review* 66: 607–621.

Pollner, Melvin. 1987. *Mundane Reason: Reality in Everyday and Sociological Discourse*. New York: Cambridge University Press.

Pomerantz, A. 1984. "Agreeing and Disagreeing with Assessment: Some Features of Preferred/Dispreferred Turn Shapes." In *Structures of Social Action: Studies in Conversation Analysis*, J. Maxwell Atkinson and John Heritage, eds. New York: Cambridge University Press, 57–101.

Postema, Gerald J. 1986. *Bentham and the Common Law Tradition*. Oxford, UK: Clarendon Press.

Putnam, Hilary. 1975. *Mind, Language, and Reality*. New York: Cambridge University Press.

Rapoport, Amos. 1982. *The Meaning of the Built Environment*. Beverly Hills, CA: Sage.

Regan, Mark. 2000. "Language 'Essential to Future of SAR' Hong Kong." *South China Morning Post*, February 29, p. 23.

Remedios, Corinne, and Mohan Bharwaney. 2000. "The Golden Age." In *Hong Kong Bar Association 50th Anniversary*. Hong Kong: Sweet & Maxwell Asia, 57–62.

Richland, Justin B. 2005. "'What Are You Going to Do with the Village's Knowledge?' Talking Tradition, Talking Law in Hopi Tribal Court." *Law and Society Review* 39(2): 235–271.

Roberts, Paul, and Adrian Zuckerman. 2004. *Criminal Evidence*. Oxford, UK: Oxford University Press.

Rock, Paul. 1993. *The Social World of an English Crown Court*. Oxford, UK: Clarendon Press.

Romaine, Suzanne. 1995. *Bilingualism*, 2nd ed. Oxford, UK: Basil Blackwell.

Rorty, Richard. 1989. *Contingency, Irony, and Solidarity*. Cambridge, UK: Cambridge University Press.

Rosen, Lawrence. 1989. *The Anthropology of Justice: Law as Culture in Islamic Society*. Cambridge, UK: Cambridge University Press.

Schauer, Frederick. 1989. "Is the Common Law Law?" *California Law Review* 77: 455–471.

Schegloff, Emanuel A. 1988. "Goffman and the Analysis of Conversation." In *Erving Goffman: Exploring the Interaction Order*, Paul Drew and Anthony Wootton, eds. Boston: Northeastern University Press, 89–135.

Scheppele, Kim Lane. 1991. "Facing Facts in Legal Interpretation." In *Law and the Order of Culture*, Robert Post, ed. Berkeley: University of California Press, 42–77.

Schiffrin, Deborah. 1990. "The Management of a Co-operative Self in Argument: The Role of Opinions and Stories." In *Conflict Talk: Sociolinguistic Investigations of*

Arguments in Conversations, Allen Grimshaw, ed. Cambridge, UK: Cambridge University Press, 241–259.

Schluchter, Wolfgang. 1981. *The Rise of Western Rationalism: Max Weber's Developmental History*. Berkeley: University of California Press.

Schneider, Edgar W. 2007. *Postcolonial English*. New York: Cambridge University Press.

Scott, James C. 1990. *Domination and the Arts of Resistance*. New Haven, CT: Yale University Press.

Scott, W. Richard. 1995. *Institutions and Organizations*. Thousand Oaks, CA: Sage.

Sebok, Anthony J. 1998. *Legal Positivism in American Jurisprudence*. New York: Cambridge University Press.

Shapiro, Barbara J. 1983. *Probability and Certainty in Seventeenth-Century England*. Princeton, NJ: Princeton University Press.

———. 2000. *A Culture of Fact*. Ithaca, NY: Cornell University Press.

Shapiro, Martin. 1990. "Lawyers, Corporations, and Knowledge." *American Journal of Comparative Law* 38(3): 683–716.

Silverstein, Michael. 1992. "The Indeterminacy of Contextualization: When Is Enough Enough?" In *The Contextualization of Language*, Peter Auer and Aldo Di Luzio, eds. Philadelphia: John Benjamins, 55–76.

———. 1993. "Metapragmatic Discourse and Metapragmatic Function." In *Reflexive Language: Reported Speech and Metapragmatics*, John A. Lucy, ed. Cambridge, UK: Cambridge University Press, 33–58.

———. 1998. "The Uses and Utility of Ideology: A Commentary." In *Language Ideologies*, Bambi B. Schieffelin, Kathryn A. Woolard, and Paul V. Kroskrity, eds. Oxford, UK: Oxford University Press, 123–145.

Sin, King-kui. 1992. "The Translatability of Law." In *Research in Chinese Linguistics in Hong Kong*, Thomas Hun-tak Lee, ed. Hong Kong: Linguistic Society of Hong Kong, 87–101.

Smith, Carl T. 1975. "English-Educated Chinese Elites in Nineteenth Century." In *Hong Kong: The Interaction of Traditions and Life in the Towns*, Marjorie Topley, ed. Hong Kong: Royal Asiatic Society, 65–96.

Steiner, George. 1998. *After Babel: Aspects of Language and Translation*, 3rd ed. Oxford, UK: Oxford University Press.

Stinchcombe, Arthur. 2001. *When Formality Works: Authority and Abstraction in Law and Organizations*. Chicago: University of Chicago Press.

Stockwell, Peter. 2002. *Sociolinguistics*. London: Blackwell.

Stone, Martin. 2002. "Formalism." In *The Oxford Handbook of Jurisprudence and Philosophy of Law*, Jules Coleman and Scott Shapiro, eds. New York: Oxford University Press, 166–205.

Tai, Benny Yiu-ting. 1999. "The Development of Constitutionalism in Hong Kong." In *The New Legal Order in Hong Kong*, Raymond Wacks, ed. Hong Kong: Hong Kong University Press, 39–93.

Taylor, Katherine Fischer. 1993. *In the Theater of Criminal Justice*. Princeton, NJ: Princeton University Press.

Teubner, Gunther. 1998. "Legal Irritants: Good Faith in British Law and How Unifying Law Ends Up in New Divergences." *Modern Law Review* 61(1): 11–32.

Tewksbury, William J. 1967. "The Ordeal as a Vehicle for Divine Intervention." In *Law and Warfare*, Paul Bohannon, ed. Garden City, NY: Natural History Press, 267–270.

Thayer, James Bradley. 1898. *A Preliminary Treatise on Evidence at the Common Law.* Boston: Little, Brown.

Thomas, Michael. 1988. "The Development of a Bilingual Legal System in Hong Kong." *Hong Kong Law Journal* 18: 15–24.

Trinch, Shonna. 2003. *Latinas' Narratives of Domestic Abuse.* Philadelphia: John Benjamins.

Trudgill, Peter, and Jean Hannah. 2002. *International English*, 4th ed. New York: Oxford University Press.

Tse, Alan Chung. 1996. "The Introduction of a Bilingual Legal System in Hong Kong: Cross-Cultural and Cross-Linguistic Views on Transferability and Translatability." Ph.D. dissertation, Department of Law, University of Hong Kong, Hong Kong.

Tse, Daniel. 1996. "Foreword." In *The English-Chinese Glossary of Legal Terms*, Editorial Board, Glossary Working Group, Legal Department, ed. Hong Kong: Legal Department, Hong Kong Government, 5–6.

Turner, Victor. 1974. *Dramas, Fields, and Metaphors: Symbolic Action in Human Society.* Ithaca, NY: Cornell University Press.

Twining, William. 1997. "Civilians Don't Try: A Comment on Mirjan Damaska's 'Rational and Irrational Proof Revisited.'" *Cardozo Journal of International and Comparative Law* 5:69–78.

Unger, Roberto Mangabeira. 1983. "The Critical Legal Studies Movement." *Harvard Law Review* 96(3): 561–675.

Urciuoli, Bonnie. 1998. *Exposing Prejudice: Puerto Rican Experiences of Language, Race, and Class.* Boulder, CO: Westview Press.

Vandevelde, Kenneth J. 1996. *Thinking Like a Lawyer.* Boulder, CO: Westview Press.

Vidmar, Neil. 2000. *World Jury Systems.* Oxford, UK: Oxford University Press.

Volosinov, V. N. 1986 [1929]. *Marxism and the Philosophy of Language.* Cambridge, MA: Harvard University Press.

Wade, E. C. S., and George Philips. 2001. *Constitutional and Administrative Law*, 13th ed. London: Longman.

Wadensjö, Cecilia. 1998. *Interpreting as Interaction.* New York: Longman.

Waluchow, W. J. 1994. *Inclusive Legal Positivism.* Oxford, UK: Clarendon Press.

Weber, Max. 1978 [1922]. *Economy and Society.* Berkeley: University of California Press.

Weinrib, Ernest J. 1988. "Legal Formalism: On the Immanent Rationality of Law." *Yale Law Journal* 97(6): 949–1016.

Wescott, K. 1977. "Survey of English in Hong Kong." British Council, Hong Kong. Unpublished.

Wesley-Smith, Peter. 1984. "Editorial: The Legal System, the Constitution, and the Future of Hong Kong." *Hong Kong Law Journal* 14(2): 137–141.

———. 1994. *The Sources of Hong Kong Law.* Hong Kong: Hong Kong University Press.

———. 1999. "Comment: The Geographical Sources of Hong Kong Law." *Hong Kong Law Journal* 29(1): 1.

Wigmore, John Henry. 1923. *A Treatise on the Anglo-American System of Evidence in Trials at Common Law.* Boston: Little, Brown.

Wilkins, D. A. 1972. *Linguistics in Language Teaching.* London: Edward Arnold.

Wilkinson, Michael, Vandana Rajwani, and Raymond Pierce. 2007. *Advocacy and the Litigation Process in Hong Kong*, 3rd ed. Hong Kong: Lexis Nexis.

Wittgenstein, Ludwig. 1953. *Philosophical Investigations*. New York: Macmillan.

Wong, Martin. 2000. "Cabbies Hit Out at Language Kits." *South China Morning Post*, November 18, p. 3.

Woodbury, Hanni. 1984. "The Strategic Use of Questions in Court." *Semiotica* 48(3/4): 197–228.

Woolard, Kathryn. 1998. "Introduction: Language Ideology as a Field of Inquiry." In *Language Ideologies*, Bambi B. Schieffelin, Kathryn Woolard, and Paul Kroskrity, eds. Oxford, UK: Oxford University Press, 3–47.

Woolard, Kathryn, and Bambi B. Schieffelin. 1994. "Language Ideology." *Annual Review of Anthropology* 23: 55–82.

Yablon, Charles M. 1995. "Judicial Drag: An Essay on Wigs, Robes, and Legal Change." *Wisconsin Law Review* 5: 1129–1153.

Yau, Frances Man Siu. 1997. "Code Switching and Language Choice in the Hong Kong Legislative Council." *Journal of Multilingual and Multicultural Development* 18(1): 40–53.

Yen, Tony. 1997. "Bilingual Legislation in a Chinese Community: The Hong Kong Experience." *Perspectivas do Direito* 2: 61–71.

———. 2001. "One on One." *Hong Kong Lawyer*, June. Retrieved January 16, 2009, http://www.hk-lawyer.com/2001-6/Default.htm.

Yip, Virginia, and Stephen Matthews. 2000. *Basic Cantonese: A Grammar and Workbook*. London: Routledge.

Yngvesson, Barbara. 1993. *Virtuous Citizens, Disruptive Subjects*. New York: Routledge.

Yu, Patrick Shuk-siu. 2002. *Tales from No. 9 Ice House Street*. Hong Kong: Hong Kong University Press.

Zhao, Yuhong. 1999. "Bilingual Legal System in Hong Kong: Explorations in the Languages of the Law." Ph.D. dissertation, School of Law, City University of Hong Kong, Hong Kong.

Zimmerman, Don H. 1974. "Facts as a Practical Accomplishment." In *Ethnomethodology*, Roy Turner, ed. Baltimore: Penguin Books, 128–143.

Zweigert, Konard, and Hein Kötz. 1998. *Introduction to Comparative Law*, 3rd ed. Oxford, UK: Clarendon Press.

Index

Abbott, Andrew, 39
adversarial trial: orality and, 116; as
    performative event, 79–83; role
    specificity in, 101–4, 104–15;
    unrepresented litigants and, 165–66,
    238
After Babel (Steiner), 92
American English, 68–69, 95
amicus curiae (*amici curiae*), 134,
    294n17
anachronism, in courtroom symbolism,
    79–93, 169–70
Anagnost, Ann, 181
Andrews/Adomako test (law), 43
Anscombe, Elizabeth, 97
Application of English Law Ordinance
    (1966), 284n20
Arendt, Hannah, 10
argument (Peirce), 298n12
"Arrangement Between the Sexes, The"
    (Goffman), 235, 297n1
Atiyah, P. S., xxi, 16, 31
Attorney-General v. Phung Van Toan,
    126
Au Kam Ming (pseudonym), 185
Au, Kenneth, 72–73
Austin, J. L., 100–101, 118, 197
Australia, 3, 5, 14–16, 87, 126–27, 161,
    229, 251, 264, 284nn12, 15, 290n24
Au Wai Tong (pseudonym), 185
Au Wan Man (pseudonym), 187
Au Yiu Tong (pseudonym), 185–90
authoritative formality, 16, 22, 251

baihua. See Standard Modern Chinese
Bakhtin, Mikhail, 6–7; carnivalesque, 5;
    dialogic, 294n19; double-oriented,
    139; on professional genres, 197–98
bar, of Hong Kong, 90, 208–9, 276

barristers, 23, 81–82, 250, 276, 291nn8,
    18, 19, 295n3; attire, 85–86, 87; on
    Chinese judgments, 247–49; cross-
    examination and, 105–6, 108–10,
    136, 171–72; on English as legal
    language, 250; examination-in-chief
    and, 102–4; expatriates, 206, 233,
    295n3; on legal bilingualism, 204;
    and mode of address in court, 90,
    169; re-examination and, 115. *See
    also* elitists; mavericks; strategists;
    white wigs
Basic Law (Hong Kong constitution),
    22–23, 231, 285n32, 286n43; Article
    8, 284n12; Article 9, 241, 283n3;
    Article 23, 24, 285n31; Hong Kong
    Bill of Rights Ordinance and, 22
bauhinia, as the emblem of Hong Kong,
    80–81, 291n3
benge ritual, 35–36
Bentham, Jeremy, 283n2. *See also*
    Utilitarianism
Berk-Seligson, Susan, 125, 142
Berlins, Marcel, 296n8
bilingual judges, 74, 124, 228–29, 231–
    32, 247, 249, 256, 261, 277, 297n15,
    299n15
bilingual legislation, 71–73. *See also*
    statutes
bilinguals, compound, 57; in Hong Kong,
    57
Bloom, Alfred, 31, 287n48
Bokhary, Kemal, 16
Bolton, Kingsley, 56, 63, 68, 289n6,
    290n18
bona fide, 94, 137–39, 141–43, 147,
    294n20
Bourdieu, Pierre, 8, 40, 50, 90, 197,
    284n13, 287n4

319

Langdell, Christopher, 33
Latour, Bruno, 43
Lau, Timothy (pseudonym), 232
law-fact distinction, 41–42; bilingual law
    and, 236–53
leading questions, 102, 104, 108, 109–
    10, 136
"learned friend," 88, 90; translating into
    Cantonese, 91, 169, 212
Lee, Martin, 69
Lee, P. F. (pseudonym), 216
legal bilingualism, 71–76, 204–5, 207–
    8, 215, 221–53; the postcolonial
    dilemma and, 254–69
legal dualism, 12–13, 166
legal facts, 41–42, 44, 48–49; evidential
    versus constitutive, 42–43
legal incomprehensiveness, 10–11
legal laissez-fairism, 12
legal rationalization, 34–36, 40, 235,
    287n3
legal segregation, 11. See also legal
    dualism
legal text: wider meaning of, 41, 96, 116–
    17. See also statutes
Legal Year, opening ceremony, 24, 86–
    87, 267
Legislative Council, 19–20, 54, 66–67,
    69, 80, 281, 285nn28, 36, 288n3,
    290n15
legislature. See Legislative Council
Leong, Alan: comparing Chinese and
    English, 215; on Chinese statutes,
    244, 290n22; on rule of law, 24.
Letters Patent, 20, 286n39
Leung, Keith (pseudonym), 218
Levi, Edward, 42
lex non scripta, 250, 265
Li, Andrew, 87, 262, 267, 295n1
Li Chi (The Book of Rites), 284n17
Li Chok Hung v. Li Pui Choi, 284n16
Li, Kit (pseudonym), 190–95
libel, 15, 83, 190, 273
liminality, 8–10, 123
Lin, Angel Mei Yi, 53–55, 58, 289nn8, 9
linguistic asymmetry, in legal system,
    236–38

linguistic determinism. See linguistic
    relativism
linguistic relativism, 6, 31, 46, 168, 214
linguistic repertoire, 61
litigants, 6–7, 217, 260, 263–64, 289n6,
    297n10; in Cantonese trials, 163–65,
    170–72, 195–99, 263–64 (see also
    "catching fleas in words;" "speaking
    bitterness"); court interpreters and,
    120–21, 123, 125, 293n3; in early
    colonial period, 12; in English trials,
    98–101; unrepresented, 237–38,
    249–50; vexatious, 26–27, 257
Llewellyn, Karl, 267
Llewellyn report, 289n8
localization, of common law in Hong
    Kong, 15–17, 80
Lochner v. New York, 288n8
Lyons, John, 96, 196, 292n24, 295n7

Ma, Kwai Chun, 26–7, 286n47
Ma, Rebecca (pseudonym), 129–35, 137–
    44, 146–59
Mak, Fanny (pseudonym), 217
magistracies. See magistrates' courts
magistrates, 236, 259; as parental judges,
    260; interacting with litigants, 7,
    260; mode of address in court, 89; on
    Chinese as legal language, 229. See
    also judges
magistrates' courts, 297nn2–3; expatriate
    recruitment in, 230; as unreported
    courts, 251; the use of Chinese
    and, 73, 75, 167, 229, 236–38, 259,
    284nn10–11, 291n25; the use of
    English in, 75, 236–37; Weber's
    criticism of, 287n4
Magistrate's Justice (Carlen), 118
Magistrates Ordinance, 298n4, 299n1
Malaysia, 14, 16
mama-san, 64
Mandarin. See Putonghua
Martin, Robyn, 15
Matoesian, Gregory, 45, 99, 105–6, 110
Matthew effect, 210
Matthews, Stephen, 289n12, 294n14
mavericks (barristers), 223–28

Merry, Sally Engle, 27, 296*n*14
Mertz, Elizabeth, 45–46, 101, 205, 292*nn*25, 27
metapragmatics, 99, 123, 134, 145
Mill, John Stuart, 19. *See also* Utilitarianism
Miller v. Fenton, 288*n*7
mixed-language trials, 121, 238–41, 251, 253, 267, 298*n*7, 299*n*4; white wigs and, 222–23
moral facts, 49, 184, 255, 262
moral judgments, 189–90, 259–60
morality: in colonial law, 15, 17; formalism and, 33, 37; in postcolonial law, 5, 22–23, 26, 28, 190, 260, 268, 283*n*2, 287*n*1, 287*n*3
Mortimer, John, 4
"Mr. Barrister" (*daai leot si*), 4, 173, 175
"My Lord," 88–91, 296*n*8; translating into Cantonese, 92, 169

National People Congress (China), 285*n*32, 286*n*43
natural law theory, 36, 283*n*2; formalism and, 33, 287*n*1; Weber's discussion of, 35, 287*n*2
neologism, 47, 73, 246
"network American" English, 68–69
New Zealand, 16, 229, 251, 264, 284*nn*12, 15
Ng Choy (Wu Tingfang), 54
nongovernmental organizations (NGOs), global, 263
North, Roger, 297*n*9

O'Barr, William, 45–46, 118
Occupier's Liability Ordinance, 293*n*11
Offences Against the Person Ordinance (1997), 288*n*9
Official Languages (Amendment) Ordinance (1995), 283*n*3
Official Languages Ordinance (1974, 1977): 59, 71–72, 75, 283*n*10, 291*n*25
orality: Chinese and, 257; literacy and, 63; in English courtrooms, 116
ordeal, trial by, 35

"parental judge" (fu mou gun), 259–61
parole, 226
Paul v. Constance, 39, 41
Philips, Susan U., 45
Peirce, Charles Sanders, 291*n*2. *See also* argument; iconic; indexical; symbolic
performative utterance, 116–18, 183–84, 195, 197, 198, 261
personal injury cases, 127–28, 273–74, 284*n*26, 293*n*2
Piggott, Sir Francis, 12
Pitt, Judge (pseudonym), 129, 138, 144–45, 147–51, 154, 157
poisonous oath, 183–84
Poon, Melissa (pseudonym), 185, 188–89
positive law. *See* positivism
positivism, 34; formalism and, 33, 287*n*1; Weber and, 34–35, 287*n*3
postcolonialism, ix; colonialism, and, 203; legal bilingualism and, 9–10; the rule of law and, x, 18, 22–23, 262, 264
presumption against retrospective legislation, 21
presumption of innocence, 21
Privy Council, 14–15, 251, 284*n*25
probate 30, 39, 273–74
procedural justice, 21
Putonghua, xxi, 59, 62, 70, 268, 283*n*4, 289*n*6; court trials and, 167, 292*n*1

QC. *See* Queen's Counsel
Queen's Counsel, Hong Kong 85; England, 82, 206, 233, 283*n*1. *See also* Senior Counsel

R. v. Attard, 126
R. v. Hayes, 292*n*16
R. v. Ip Chiu, 126
R. v. Li Kin Wai, 126
R. v. Tam Kwok Yeung, 126
R. v. Tam Yuk Ha, 245–47, 298*n*13
R. v. Thakoen Gwitsa Thaporn Thongjai, 126
Re Cheng Kai Nam, Gary, 296*n*1
Received Pronunciation (RP) English, 55, 68, 288*n*5, 290*n*18